Trapped in Key West

On the Back Side of a Tourist Island

Peter M. Bacle

Trapped in Key West

On the Back Side of a Tourist Island

Peter M. Bacle

Mangrove Publishing, LLC
Key West, Florida

Trapped in Key West: On the Back Side of a Tourist Island

By Peter M. Bacle

Published by Mangrove Publishing, LLC

Cover design by Lisa Hainline, Lionsgate Book Design
www.lionsgatebookdesign.com

Back cover photo by Alan G. Kennish III, Key West Fine Art
Photography http://www.keywestfineartprinting.com

To contact the author or to order additional copies of this book,
e-mail: bacle26@aol.com

Library of Congress Control Number: 2013940364
Publisher's Cataloging-in-Publication
(Provided by Quality Books, Inc.)

Bacle, Peter M.
  Trapped in Key West: On the Back Side of a Tourist Island / by
Peter M. Bacle
  pages cm.
  LCCN 2013940364
  ISBN 978-0-9855646-0-5
  1. Bacle, Peter M. (Peter Martin) 2. Key West (Fla.)
--Anecdotes. 3. Key West (Fla.)--Social life and
customs. 4. Restauranteurs--Florida--Key West--
Biography--Anecdotes. I. Title.

F319.K4B33 2013   975.9'41063'092
                         QBI13-600114

Key West
PUBLISHING, LLC

Printed in the
United States of America
CPSIA:1-1000-13-21747

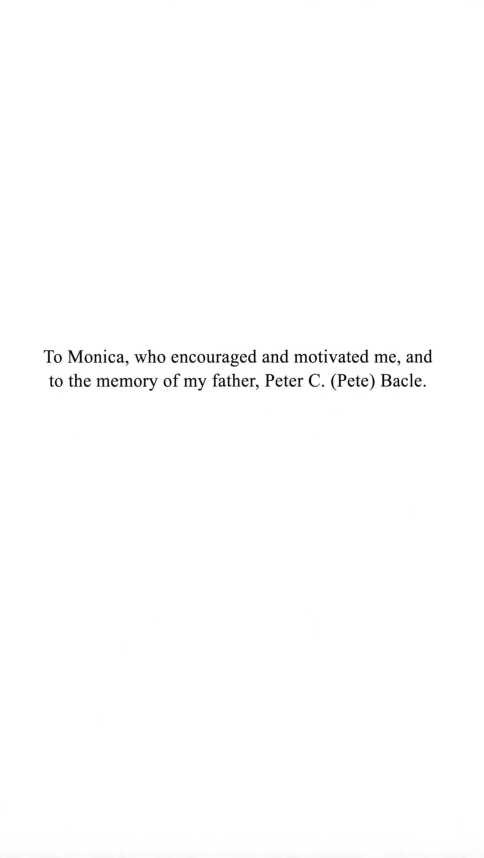

To Monica, who encouraged and motivated me, and to the memory of my father, Peter C. (Pete) Bacle.

Contents

Preface

Trapped in Key West is drawn from my memories of a lifetime spent living, working, and playing around my island home. It is not intended to be a historical account, or even biographical, but rather to offer a glimpse of island life that could not be experienced by visitors or latter-day residents.

The stories and recollections are meant to convey a picture of the non-tourist side of Key West, and reveal a family side to commercial fishing. It is also a story about my father (pictured on the cover) and the large presence he was in the life of our family.

With the exceptions of a few names that have been changed and some details that have been left out to save embarrassment, everything in the book is true to the way I remember it.

— Peter M. Bacle

Introduction

Key West has been famous several times in its two-hundred-year history. Throughout the nineteenth century, it was notorious for its wrecking industry, when the native Key Westers, known as "Conchs," were accused of luring ships onto the surrounding coral reef so their cargoes could be salvaged. At the turn of the twentieth century, it was the cigar manufacturing center of America during a time when most American men still treasured their daily smoke.

Fifty years later, it was on the nationwide movie screen newsreels as a retreat for Presidents Roosevelt, Truman, and Kennedy. Then, Cuba brought Key West worldwide attention with the Cuban Missile Crisis, Mariel Boatlift, and a million refugees from Castro's communism. Today, it is famous as America's laid-back, let-your-hair-down Caribbean island.

Fantasy Fest, Duval Street, Sloppy Joe's, and Ernest Hemingway make up the public image that the tourist industry so successfully sells. While the coral reef, beautiful waters, and spectacular fishing are a large part of the overall image, Key West is accurately portrayed as the ultimate party town and ranks as one of Florida's premier tourist destinations. Jimmy Buffet—who lived here before he became famous—personified Key West when he was inspired to write his wildly popular song, "Margaritaville."

In the shadow of its glitzy image, however, is the other Key West. It's the Key West of families who have been here for generations—families who have children in school, socialize at the ball fields, and party together on weekends and holidays at beaches known only to them and reached only by boat. Many of them were born in Key West, and will live out their lives here as eight generations of native Conchs have done before them.

They manage to raise children in a town where Duval Street rocks 365 days a year—where the laws on public drinking, obscene behavior, and nudity are suspended each year for Fantasy Fest, and the drug culture is quietly tolerated and frequently glorified in song. The values most parents try to instill in their children come into direct conflict with Key West's party town image.

Yet, all Key West residents recognize that tourism is the lifeblood of the island. Once supported by the wrecking industry, then cigar factories, sponging, the Navy, and commercial fishing, the high standard of living is now maintained by a year-round stream of tourists arriving by car, plane, and cruise ship. Properly recognizing that every good thing has a bad side and that any place is what you make of it, the local people are supportive of the tourist industry and quietly go about their lives as the party rocks around them.

The five children Monica and I have raised are seventh generation Conchs. My son Lucas works a lobster boat and daughter Jenny runs the office of Stock Island Lobster Company, our family business. The descendants of one hundred-twenty years of commercial fishing, they are the sixth generation in their lineage to make a living from the sea. Sixty years on the Bacle side and sixty years before that on the Barber-Weech side place them among a handful of native Conchs to carry on the long tradition.

While most people want to eat fresh seafood when in Key West, they only have the vaguest notion of a commercial industry. Charter and recreational fishing on the other hand, are very high profile and justly famous worldwide. The confluence of the Gulf Stream current, the nutrient runoff from the Everglades, and the fallout of the Mississippi River make Key West waters some of the richest in the world and support large commercial and recreational industries.

With Key West Harbor completely converted from commercial fishing in the last thirty years, most people are surprised to learn that in dollar value, Key West is still in the top ten commercial fishing ports in the United States. The warm Gulf of Mexico and Florida Bay waters spawn prodigious amounts of lobster, stone crab, shrimp, snapper, and grouper. In years past, there also existed large fisheries that processed turtles, sponges, and conchs.

Key West is ideally situated to be a commercial fishing port. The National Marine Fisheries declares the waters north of Key West to be the Gulf of Mexico, and south of the island to be the Atlantic Ocean. Key West and all of the Florida Keys are protected from heavy seas on the north side by the shallow waters of Florida Bay and on the south side by the one hundred-fifty-mile-long coral reef. It is so centrally located between Cuba, Mexico, and the tip of Florida, that the United States built three nineteenth-century brick forts on the island, and another massive one sixty miles to the west at Dry Tortugas.

Stock Island Lobster Company—the oldest operating fish house in the Florida Keys—was started by my father in 1953, and is still owned by our family. Dad was the classic man of the sea. He joined the Navy at fifteen, and served twenty years before 'retiring' to fifty-one years of operating a fish house and lobster boat in Key West.

Thirty years ago there were more than twenty fish houses in Key West, but today there are only two others. Mother, at the age of ninety-one, still comes to the office each day and pays fishermen as she has done for over fifty years. Jenny has worked at the fish house for seventeen years, and taken over the operation of the office as well as running the business when I am away. Lucas has run his grandfather's boat—*Big Crawl*—for the last nine years, and hopes he and Jenny can keep the fish house going for another generation.

The combining forces of regulation, booming tourism, intense environmentalism, soaring property values, changing work ethic, and the institution of the Florida Keys National Marine Sanctuary have all conspired to reduce the commercial fishing industry down to the three fish houses. The downsizing of the fleet is likely to continue until the remaining boats are eventually consolidated into one commercial fishing location.

Stock Island Lobster Company

While lobsters have been harvested for two centuries in Key West waters, the modern trap industry only started after World War II. Dad was among the early trap fishermen, and left Thompson Fish Company in 1953 to open the first fish house on Stock Island—just across the Cow Key Bridge from Key West. He was a consistent innovator in the industry and the first to work traps in the deep waters outside the reef and the Dry Tortugas area.

I came into the business in 1969—fishing for lobster, stone crab, snapper, and grouper, while Dad and I jointly ran the fish house. Though he started deferring the full operation to me in the 1980s and was fully retired from day-to-day decisions by the '90s, he still came to the fish house every day and worked his lobster boat until the age of eighty-six.

Commercial fishing from the 1950s through the 1970s was to the Key West economy what the tourist industry is today. Big seasons and big catches were front-page news, and the impact on production by hurricanes and poor seasons was felt by the entire community. Though fishermen themselves were generally at the low end of income-earners during that period, modern fishing methods, sophisticated electronics, and rising prices eventually moved them solidly into the middle class.

Key West may appear to be laid-back and even lethargic to many visitors, but upheaval and change have come frequently to commercial fishing. With Cuba being only ninety miles away, their people and culture have always played a large role in the life of the island. The Fidel Castro revolution of 1959 brought a million refugees to South Florida—including several thousand commercial fishermen. The Cuban Missile Crisis of 1962 gave us gunboats and jet fighters zooming around the ocean, and the Mariel Boatlift of 1980 saw every commercial boat either bought or chartered by resident refugees desperate to get their relatives out of Cuba.

The drug industry appeared suddenly and glamorously. Bales of marijuana littered the ocean. Freighters loaded with illicit cargoes anchored within sight of the island, and fishing boats boldly raced out to offload the 'square groupers.' The fishermen who became involved, strutted around with double handfuls of gold chains, medallions, and crosses hanging from their necks, and new boats and loaded pickup trucks appeared without any lobster or fish being caught to pay for them. For a couple of years, it seemed as if no one outside of Key West even noticed and the 'gold rush' would never end.

The 1980s brought in the present era of intense fishery regulation. Sophisticated electronics and modernized fishing methods had impacted certain fishery stocks, and new rules were required to deal with the problems. Some good and necessary updating of fishery regulation was instituted, while at the same time, other hasty and unnecessary restrictions were passed that would dramatically impact the commercial fishing industry.

Though our lives have been unavoidably dominated by the surrounding sea, we still treasure our schools, churches, and ball fields. We have raised our children to avoid the crowds and focus on their family and friends. We have fished and dived and cooked our catch for a lifetime, and still, at our frequent family gatherings, everyone wants to eat seafood.

With my friends, we set aside days and weeks for the boat like other people schedule haircuts and business meetings. We have cruised the waters of the Bahamas more times than we can count, and had encounters with sharks, cannons, and AK 47's. Though we use a windlass now to pull the anchor, we can still spear a fish, tickle a lobster out of a rock, and drink a little too much rum, while puffing on fine Cuban cigars.

Today at the fish house, life goes on much the same as it has for the last fifty-nine years. The men are still building traps and doing maintenance on their boats. Someone is still frying fish, with the smell floating to all corners of the property. Strings of brightly-colored buoys are still being painted, and men still measure the trap ropes by walking them out and coiling by hand. Loud talk and boisterous laughter come from the boats and sheds, and the slam of dominoes and shoosh of pop tops is still heard when work is done. Fishermen and their families still party at the fish house when the boats are unloading, and the Bacle family is still buying, selling, and catching lobster.

1

Seasick

Good grief, son! I've been on just about everything that floats on water—from battleships to outrigger canoes, on every ocean of the world, through typhoons, blizzards, and bombs, with thousands of men who had never even been off a farm before—**and I have never yet seen anyone die of seasickness!**"

Thus spoke Captain Pete—my Dad—when I asked him if we could take my seasick friends back to the dock. My three best buddies lay moaning in the cramped, diesel-fumed bunkroom of Dad's thirty-four-foot lobster boat *Freddie M.* For three hours, they had remained below, no longer bothering to rush out to vomit over the side, instead merely leaning from the cluttered bunks to throw up on the lower deck.

Dad and I were pulling fish as fast as the line reached the bottom, and I prayed for the first time in my nine-year-old life they would stop biting. The distressful sound of my retching friends had long before ruined the fishing trip for me, but except for an occasional chuckle, Dad seemed oblivious to their plight and methodically went about the business of filling the barrel with fish.

Merrell Sands, Kenny Mesa, and Titi Roque, had excitedly accepted my invitation to go red snapper fishing with Dad. All week, talk had been of nothing but the upcoming trip. Though it was their first trip on anything bigger than a skiff, each imagined they were an expert on deep-sea fishing and had complete confidence in their knowledge of the sea.

"I don't care what anyone says, the best bait for red snapper is squid."

"What are you talking about, Merrell? Everyone knows that mullet is the best."

"You guys can say whatever you want," piped in Titi. "But Papi says when he was building the Seven Mile Bridge, one of his friends caught a twenty-two-pound red snapper with a chicken leg for bait."

On Saturday morning, we were on the boat at 4:00 a.m., wide-awake and anxious to start pulling fish. After checking out the entire boat, the boys were sure Dad's fish barrel was too small and were worried we would have to come in early once it was filled. Before fiberglass and foam insulation, all fishermen used pickle barrels filled with ice and water to chill the fish and preserve the brilliant colors for marketing. The barrels were made of oak staves about one-inch-thick, and each one held six hundred pounds of fish.

The sea was fairly calm and Dad assured us we would all catch fish until our arms were too tired to pull. We scrambled to the bow, as the boat pulled away from the dock in the morning darkness, and sat atop the cabin with our legs hanging over the front windshields. Dad snaked his way through the unmarked channel without a spotlight, and we suddenly emerged from the mangrove islands bordering Boca Chica to face the intimidating blackness of the open ocean. As we headed east toward American Shoals, the barest hint of light from the rising sun glowed dimly in the distance.

Our excitement level was so high we could hardly contain it, and after half an hour, the boys were really getting anxious. Titi—the sparkplug of our adolescent crew—leaned forward with his head between his legs and shouted to Dad over the roar of the engine, "Are we almost there Mr. Bacle?"

"We'll be there before you know it."

"Sir, is that blinking light up ahead American Shoals?"

"Yes."

"How far away is it?"

"Not too far."

"Is it a mile?"

"Something like that."

"Is that where we're going Mr. Bacle? To American Shoals?"

"Right near there."

"Well, how much longer before we get there?"

Dad sat behind the wheel on a wooden fish box with a boat cushion for a seat, smoking a cigarette and drinking a cup of coffee. He never went in the boat without a thermos full of coffee, and the ride out in the morning was his favorite time of the day. Like some ancient mariner with the early morning watch, he didn't care to have his thoughts interrupted with conversation.

"All right now! You boys listen up! When you see that sun peek up over the horizon, we'll be there. So let's hold down the noise and keep an eye out for the sun. The first one to spot it gets to catch the first fish."

I knew Dad far too well to fall for the old sun-trick; but for the next hour, three sets of eyes never blinked. Like watching for a pot to boil, the sun never seemed to quite show itself, and as it got lighter and lighter, the boys—who had never actually experienced a sunrise on the ocean—called out a dozen false alarms.

"All right boys! Enough of that malarkey! The next one who gives me a false sighting is going to throw chum instead of fishing."

The three lookouts stood on the cabin to get higher for a better look, but that only aggravated Dad more. "Peter! Tell those boys to get their legs down where I can see them!"

Three screams suddenly rang out as one and three boys leaped from the cabin together, each trying to be the first one to point out the sun to Dad. The seriousness of my friends left me somewhat incredulous and not completely sure I wasn't missing something by thinking this was only Dad's trickery. The leading tip of the sun was shining like a spotlight, so when Dad said, with a hint of false excitement in his voice, "Where is it boys?" I was relieved I hadn't been fooled.

"Right there Mr. Bacle! Right in front of the boat! I saw it first!"

"You're lying Titi! I was the first one to see it!"

Kenny looked at me for support, "Peter! Tell your Dad it was me!"

"Okay boys! Okay. I see it now. So let's settle down a little! You boys did a yeoman's job. Since it sounds like you all saw it at the same time, I'll have to let all of you put your lines down together, and the first one to catch a fish will get credit for the sighting."

A few minutes later, Dad was circling an area in two hundred feet of water, searching for the right spot with his new Bendix depth recorder. Dad was one of the first Key West fishermen to buy a Fathometer, and even though it was a thirty-pound monster, it was state-of-the-art technology that allowed him to fish areas few other boats had ever tried.

The burn marks on the paper made by the circling stylus fascinated my buddies. It would disappear behind the carriage and then emerge on the small screen, and strike a tiny black scratch on the slowly advancing paper. The closest experience any of us ever had with electronic machines was with radios. Television had not yet made its way to Key West, and to view anything on a screen had a hypnotic effect on us all. Kenny was studying the technical marvel and wanted to know more.

"What is that machine, Mr. Bacle?"

"It's a Fathometer."

"Oh . . . What's a Fathometer?"

"It tells you how deep the water is."

"Oh . . . How does it tell you?"

"If it's marking where it says thirty, that means you're in thirty fathoms of water. Each line in between is one more fathom."

"Ohhh . . . I see now . . . What's a fathom?"

"Six feet."

"Oh . . . But how does it know?"

"There's a transducer on the bottom of the boat. It bounces a sound wave off the bottom, and that tells you how deep it is. Now let's finish up with all these questions and get down to business! I need some lookouts to help me line up the spot."

Seasick

Dad was alternating between watching the screen and looking toward shore. The Keys were visible five miles to the north, and with no navigational aids to put the boat in the right area, he had to rely on land markings. The markings were mysterious to my friends, but I had been with Dad many times and knew what he was looking for.

"You boys see those two humps over there that look like a saddle?"

"Yes sir!"

"Well that's the Saddlebunch Keys. When those two humps touch, we go straight south until those three radar domes on Boca Chica are lined up, and that will be the spot. Now you boys get on up to the top of the cabin and keep a sharp lookout!"

The three raced to the top of the cabin, though none of them really understood what they were looking for, while I stayed below to help Dad. Anchoring the boat precisely was critical to success, and I was certain Dad didn't need their help, but merely wanted the boys 'out of his hair' while he concentrated on placing the boat.

Within minutes, Dad pulled the two-foot-long shifting arm into reverse and raced to the bow to throw the anchor, leaving me to handle the steering wheel. Unlike the small, four-pronged grapnel used in the shallower waters, he had to use a huge shrimp boat anchor with four hundred feet of line to ensure the boat didn't drag off the small fishing spot.

Few fishermen would ever think of anchoring in two hundred feet of water because of the exertion required to pull the anchor. At just under six feet tall and one hundred eighty pounds, Dad was a muscular man who took quiet pride in his strength. Partly because of metabolism, but mostly because he was always a physically active man, Dad's body never had an ounce of fat, and he actually enjoyed extreme physical exercise like anchor pulling.

By the time the anchor was set and Dad got back to the main deck, my friends had each staked out a position behind one of the gunwale-mounted bicycle reels. The reels were constructed from the sprocket and pedals of a bicycle, with a sixteen-inch metal spool of wire welded next to the sprocket. The customized bike was mounted on a frame, with a long arm and pulley connected to a rubber tube that broke the fight of the fish. A fisherman would stand behind the reel and turn the pedals with his hands.

Each reel had a simple brake—a small steel flap that clicked along the sprocket and could be set to stop the reel from either going forward or backward. Having the brake properly set was crucial to the safe operation of the reel, as a large fish or shark could easily set the pedals spinning and break the hand or arm of the fisherman.

My buddies, ready for action behind the pedals, had no idea how to operate the reels and Dad chuckled at their enthusiasm. "Okay boys! Let's belay that fishing for the moment. First, we have to get everything ready, so when we start pulling fish we don't have to stop for anything. Peter knows how I want the bait cut, so he's going to do that while I get the lines ready. You boys will make the chum.

"Merrell! Grab three of those short two-by-fours over there. Kenny! Get that five-gallon bucket sitting next to the icebox and take it to the starboard side. Titi! Titi!! Son, you better listen up when I'm talking to you! You're holding up everyone by not paying attention. Now get each of you boys a pair of those gloves up there by the wheel."

Titi, who might be diagnosed with Attention Deficit Disorder in today's world, did not like the sound of the word chum, and wanted a more specific job. "Yes sir! But Mr. Bacle, I think I'll help Peter cut the bait."

"No you won't! You're going to get the gloves and help the boys with the chum."

"Well, how about if I tie the hooks with you?"

I was on guard as Titi bounced around the boat—first grabbing a knife to cut bait and then a handful of hooks to help Dad— oblivious to the seriousness of ignoring an order from the captain. Despite the severity of the offense, Titi's infectious enthusiasm was too much for Dad, who was forced to turn away and smile before bellowing out, *"Boy! When I give you an order, you'd better jump to it!"*

6

Seasick

Titi flew to the front of the boat, and then stood wide-eyed and at attention after handing out the gloves. I watched with amusement and a little dread, as Dad prepared the boys for their assignment by assembling them around the bucket. I could see the grin in Dad's eyes, as he set them up for the grim task of making chum. Their hands were too small to fill the blue cotton gloves, and the ends of the fingers flapped loosely as they held the two-by-fours. Like three little savages they stood poised around the covered bucket, ready to pound whatever might emerge.

"Kenny, get that screwdriver and pry the lid off the bucket!"

Dad had given no hint as to what was in the bucket and the boys had no idea what the two-by-fours were for, but they were ready for action as Kenny popped the lid off. He instantly recoiled, and Merrell and Titi leaped back instinctively.

"Whoaaa! Gees man! Wow, what's that smell?"

Dad suppressed a grin, but I knew he was pleased at the boy's reactions. "Smell? Why that's a sweet smell to the fish. Those lobster heads are going to bring every snapper within miles around to our boat. Now, you boys get around this bucket and smash up the heads with the end of those two-by-fours. We can't fish until we have chum in the water, so let's get a move on."

My friends jumped to their task with boisterous enthusiasm. The hard crustaceous heads crackled and snapped as the boys pounded. They laughed and joked as the thick shells were smashed. When the meaty parts of the heads became crushed along with the shells, it started turning into the mushy chum Dad wanted.

The laughing stopped when the splattering started. Each hit with a two-by-four sent more of the juicy concoction flying out of the bucket and onto the clothes and faces of my buddies. The stench from the bucket was bad enough, but when chum got on the face, the smell could not be wiped off and could sicken the strongest of stomachs. As the raunchy odor had its effect, the pounding turned to stirring and the boys breathed though their mouths, as they stared at the chum they had made.

"Mr. Bacle, I don't know if these lobster heads are very fresh."

"Fresh? Why sure they're fresh, Merrell. I just caught them last week."

"Last week, huh? . . . Boy they sure do stink for only being a week old."

"Listen here boys! Now you don't think those fish can see anything down there in two hundred feet of water do you? Of course not! It's black as night down there. They have to smell the chum, and those heads are just right for smelling. Now, are you boys finished with that bucket?"

Three "yes sirs" rang out at once, as the boys dropped their two-by-fours and raced to the fishing reels. "Good. Then take the lid off that icebox over there and get the rest of the heads out. As soon as you get them mashed up we can start fishing."

My three stunned friends looked at the icebox and then at Dad, hoping to see he was joking. Dad went back to his hook tying, purposely avoiding looking at the boys. Ever so reluctantly, they turned again to their grim task. The pounding was halfhearted, and they worked with mouths open and heads constantly turning into the wind to gulp down big mouthfuls of fresh air.

I knew they were all getting sick, but I was powerless to stop it. They had never been seasick before, and they all had a 'deer-in-the-headlights' look as they tried to ward off the devil that was after them. Each of them had taken on the pale look that comes right before the final nausea: "A little green around the gills," as Dad liked to call it.

Dad was fully aware of what was happening. Twenty years of active duty as a chief in the 'old Navy' had imbued him with many quirks and traits. The most disconcerting of them to a young son was the fact that he never seemed to miss anything. No matter that he wasn't looking, no matter that he couldn't hear it, and no matter that he was preoccupied with something else. After all the years of being in charge of "raw recruits" and "green seamen," Dad just seemed to have an instinct for knowing what was going on.

Seasick

Among his oddest quirks however, was the fact that he had no sympathy for anyone who was seasick. Even worse, he actually enjoyed seeing people get sick. Seasickness was a rite of passage into manhood in the old Navy. It was a weakness that had to be overcome before a man could walk with his head held high. As a chief, Dad had been a facilitator through that passage, and anything he could do to help a person get it over with was just part of his job.

Once the inevitable purging was near, Dad would usually help things along with innocent sounding comments like, "Hey son, how about opening up a can of sardines for us?" Or, "Jeepers, I'm sure glad no one's sick today. Last trip everyone got sick and upchucked all over the place." His favorite, he usually saved for last: "Boy, some good old buttery biscuits and salt pork gravy would sure go good about now."

No one but Dad and his Navy pals ever thought the comments were funny, but that never stopped him from getting the greatest amusement out of them. Our family made many excuses for his behavior, but as I watched my friends turn greener and greener, I was hoping against hope he would not say something to make matters worse.

Within minutes, my worst fears were realized. Without ever looking up or changing expressions, Dad deadpanned, "When you boys finish that chum, there's some pork chop sandwiches in that bag by the wheel. They're a little greasy, but you'd better get something in your stomach before we start fishing." If Dad had unexpectedly fired off a shotgun, it wouldn't have gotten a quicker reaction. Kenny spun around to the rail and hung his head over the side, as his stomach contents shot into the ocean. Dad gave a sideways look with a grin only I could detect, while Titi and Merrell watched in horror.

Seconds later, Titi lunged for the other side of the boat. Holding onto the rail with his fingertips and knees, his entire upper body was hanging over the side, and with each violent retch, I expected him to rocket into the water. I thought about grabbing him so he wouldn't fall overboard, but found myself immobilized by the terrible scene unfolding in front of me.

The old Navy chief was then in his full glory, and enjoying every minute of the disaster. Ever true to his nature, he waited for a little break in the action and let out his familiar "heh, heh, heh" chuckle. "Gosh boys, if I'd known you were going to chum for us, I could have saved those lobster heads for the next trip."

I watched Merrell as his eyes darted back and forth between Kenny and Titi. There was a look of sheer terror on his face, as if he knew the end was coming and had to do something to avoid it. In a panicked moment, he ran to the cabin, disappeared through the companionway, and sprawled across the tools and fishing gear covering the bunk—as if that action could spare him the grisly fate of his buddies.

Merrell quickly learned the bunkroom was no friend to a sick person. The heat from the engine combined with the smells of exhaust fumes, diesel fuel, and bilge water, could make even a well person feel sick. Moments later, Merrell came flying back up from down below, spewing his breakfast over the deck and engine box. As he raced for the side of the boat, he slipped down in the vomit and coated his pants and shirt with the odorous bile.

Crawling, slipping, and heaving, he made it to the rail, but most of his stomach contents were spread across the deck. I was mortified at the sight of Merrell's tribulation, but Dad was even more upset, and for him the fun was over. Obviously, the boys did not know how to play the game properly. With pure disgust in his voice he barked out, "All right you boys! Let's keep that stuff over the side! Kenny! You and Titi grab that bucket and scrubber and get this deck washed down. Merrell! Get some of that fresh water over there and clean yourself up . . . Now, you boys should be ready to fish, so let's get a move on with this cleaning so we can start working on filling that barrel."

Titi and Kenny were still breathing heavily from their ordeal and seemed confused by Dad's order, so I rushed into action. Grabbing the short piece of rope tied to the bucket handle, I quickly dipped up several pails of seawater and threw them across the deck. Within minutes, the deck was clean and the boys were composed and ready for a new assignment.

Seasick

Seasickness is a very strange malady. When people are sick, they feel as if they would rather die than continue on in that condition. Once they have purged the first time however, there is an immediate sense of relief and an adrenalin rush that has them excited about getting back into the action. Unfortunately, for most people the euphoria does not last for long and the second wave of seasickness is accompanied by the dread knowledge that the entire day is to be spent in that condition.

The boys were ready to fish, and Dad knew he had to turn them loose if he was going to get anything out of them that day. He retrieved a fifty-millimeter gun casing—about fourteen inches long by six inches in diameter with an eye welded to the firing end—and attached it to the wire on his reel. After packing the shell with chum, he let it down to the bottom and shook out the contents.

"All right boys! Now pay close attention to me because I'm only going to tell you once. This little lever here on the reel is a brake. It keeps your line from going out very fast. You leave that on all the time! I'm the only one here who can use one of these reels without the brake on. That's an eight-pound lead weight on there, and if a big fish grabs that line without the brake on, you'll end up with a broken arm. Everyone understand?

"Yes sir!"

To my relief, the fish started biting immediately. The boys were excited beyond words, and I hoped they would be among the few who recovered for the day after one round of sickness. My friends were not prepared for the strength of the fish. A twenty-five-pound red snapper fights so wildly that it could pull the arm of a nine-year-old out of its socket. With the brakes secured, the bicycle reels prevented the boys from injury, but gave them little help in gaining line on the thrashing fish.

I knew from experience—and my friends were advised by Dad—to allow the fish to fight themselves out by letting them pull against the tough rubber tube connecting the two arms of the reel. The boys immediately forgot the instructions, and quickly wore themselves out trying to hand-pedal the far stronger fish while they were still fresh and full of fight. As they lost fish after fish, Dad was far more patient with them than he would have been with me. "Come on now, boys! You've got to play those fish. Let them fight that rubber tube, not you. Watch how Peter and I are doing it. Once that rubber breaks their spirit, you'll be able to reel them in and we can make a dent in that barrel."

Author with red snappers 1953

Each of them managed to catch at least one fish before the bell rang for round two of their seasickness. One by one, they went to the side rail and continued where they had left off earlier. Dad knew it was coming and simply made the best of it. "Heh, heh, heh. If you boys could just upchuck inside that gun casing, we could send it right down to the bottom. That ought to get those fish really fired up."

Seasick

Round three followed very quickly, and despite Dad's warning to stay out in the fresh air, my whipped friends disappeared through the companionway and lay across the bunks. From then on - unable to gather the strength to run to the rail - they simply leaned their heads over and vomited on the below deck. With the barfing sound periodically echoing from the companionway, I hoped Dad would have mercy on them, and I made my futile appeal for him to take them back to the dock.

Dad was unmoved by their misery, and casually replied, "Well son, it looks like you and me will have to fill that barrel by ourselves. The boys will be fine once they get back on the dock."

It should have been the perfect day, but my mood was somber. The sea had calmed with only the deep water swells rocking the boat, and the fish were all large. Then, while Dad was pulling up a very big fish, the rubber stretched to its limit and suddenly went limp. He knew immediately a shark had taken his fish, and when the hook surfaced it held nothing but the head of a thirty-five-pound red snapper. Dad held it up and shook his head, "That skunk bit him off right behind the ears."

Knowing a monster shark was right under the boat should have been the most exciting event of the day for my friends, but even that could not roust them. I stood in the companionway holding the head and relating the story, but none of them gave more than a subdued "uh huh."

I worked as hard as I could to help fill the barrel. Many of the fish were too big for me to pull and Dad would have to help reel them in, but my setting the hook and keeping the fish on the line until Dad could help were important contributions. After Dad's refusal to take my friends in, I knew it was either fill the barrel or be out until 4:00 p.m.

I was well aware of Dad's reluctance to quit fishing unless it was the most compelling emergency. Though he was an extremely perceptive man, it was not unlike Dad to be indifferent or even oblivious to other people's suffering. Seasickness, anxiety, depression, and injuries were all problems that would take care of

13

themselves if you just kept on working. Real men didn't complain or "yak" about their problems, and even the most dramatic situations could be handled with his simple reasoning.

When Dad first discovered the red snapper bottom with his new Fathometer, he shared the find with a fellow fisherman who ended up being traumatized by the resulting experience and Dad's reluctance to quit fishing. At that time, Dad had a smaller and much slower boat named *Fan-tan*. Because of the distance to American Shoals and the limited fuel capacity, he would go for three days or until his icebox was full. He preferred to stay anchored where he fished, but after a couple of close calls at night with oil tankers and freighters, he started running back inside the reef to spend the night. If the seas were too rough, he would go all the way in to the shallow waters near Sugarloaf or Cudjoe Key.

To fish the deep water for such large fish, special fishing gear was needed, so Dad helped his friend Wilton Roberts construct one of the bicycle reels. Because of the strong current in that depth of water, it was also necessary to have large lead sinkers to get the hook down and keep it on the bottom. The sinkers were made by burying soda or beer bottles in sand and then pouring in molten lead, after an eye fashioned from a metal coat hanger was secured through the top. The resulting bottle-shaped sinkers weighed between five and ten pounds each, which meant the line was hard to pull even when it didn't have a fish.

Will had never ventured out to two hundred feet of water with his small boat, but he was having a poor year with yellowtail and Dad convinced him to tag along on the next trip. Like Dad, Will fished his old twenty-eight-foot boat alone. Many fishermen didn't want any part of being outside the reef after sunset, but Dad's years in the Navy had made him as comfortable on the sea at night as he was in the day.

They left well before daylight and arrived at the buoy marking the spot with light enough to see. They had spent the week getting Will rigged to fish, and anchored side by side, they started catching red snapper as soon as the lines were down. The fish were averaging over twenty pounds each and the poundage in the boats was adding up quickly.

Seasick

By mid-afternoon, they each had over five hundred pounds in the boat as the weather started to breeze up. With the sea conditions becoming sloppy and the weight of the fish stressing the hull, Will's old boat started leaking far more than usual. Concerned that his bilge pump might not be able to handle the increased leakage, Will wanted to go in.

It was then too late to make it back to Key West before dark, so Dad pointed out a place near Sugarloaf Key—about five miles distant—where Will should anchor for the night. The fish were still biting, so Dad told Will he would meet him at the anchorage around sunset and they would transfer some of the fish to get the weight out of his boat.

The fish continued to bite and Dad started for shore later than expected. It was after dark when he arrived at the anchorage, and looked in vain for the light of Will's boat. Figuring he had decided to go back to Key West, Dad turned on his spotlight for one last look around.

He didn't see Will's boat, but something caught his eye about two hundred feet away. As he got closer, he saw a large red snapper floating in the water. Thinking he had dropped one overboard while gutting the fish, he knew Will must be in the area with his lights out. While searching further, he ran across another snapper, and near it, an icebox lid and a half-full jug of drinking water. He realized then that Will had sunk, and followed the trail of floating items until he came to the boat.

The boat had gone down in about eight feet of water, with only the very tip of the cabin sticking out, and sitting on top was Will. According to Dad when he told me the story some years later, "I called out to him, but he didn't answer. He just sat there staring into the dark. At first I couldn't figure out what was going on. He looked like he was all burnt up, and I figured his engine must have blown.

"When I got a little closer though, I realized what it was. The poor devil was covered with roaches! Hell, there must have been a thousand of them crawling all over his head and face. As the boat was sinking, they just kept crawling higher until Will was the only thing left sticking out of the water.

"I kept yelling at him to jump in the water and get all those damn roaches off so I could take him aboard, but he just kept sitting there staring. I knew then that he was shell-shocked, and I was going to have to get him aboard myself. Luckily, the breeze had died down and I was able to get my boat right alongside.

"I wasn't about to take him in the boat like that, so I threw a couple of buckets of water on him to rinse the roaches off. Then, I lassoed him with a trap rope and dragged him away from the boat and the roaches. He was nothing but dead weight, and that little man liked to have killed me getting him aboard, but I finally had him dry and warm. I assured him we would get his boat up and have him fishing again in no time, but he never did say anything.

"I spent the next hour picking up fish and whatever else was floating that could be salvaged. I made sure to anchor far up-tide from those damn roaches, and cooked us a warm plate of eggs and hash. Will didn't eat, so I rigged him up a bunk on top the icebox and he finally went to sleep.

"The next morning we got back on the fish, and they were biting as well as the day before. I figured with Will's fish in the box and both of us fishing, we could finish up that day and get back to the dock. I told him the sooner we got the trip finished the sooner we could get his boat raised, but he pretty much just sat there like he was in a trance and wasted the whole day."

"Well Dad, didn't you ever think you should have taken him right in after that experience?"

"Take him in! Good grief son, the man couldn't even talk! How was I to know if he wanted to go in or not?"

"Well, what did he say about it when he finally spoke?"

"He never did say too much. Just that the water kept rising as he was heading to shore. He tried bailing by hand, but still couldn't stay ahead of the leaking. He was going to beach the boat, but when the water rose above the engine and it conked out, he knew he was going down.

Seasick

"Poor guy never did learn to swim, and when he dug out his life jacket it just fell apart in his hands. Roaches ate it up I guess . . . Hell, he didn't even remember the roaches.

"Anyway, a bunch of us went out a few days later—Will didn't go—and raised the boat. In a week it was ready to fish with a new bilge pump, a Navy life jacket, and no damn roaches. But the funny thing is; after we did all that, he just sold the boat and went to work in the Navy yard. You know he never did go fishing again . . . It's just hard to figure out some people."

My hope of filling the barrel quickly and taking my friends in early was not to be. We caught several warsaw groupers of over one hundred pounds each, which would have filled the barrel, but Dad released them. The warsaws were only bringing ten cents a pound if Freckles Higgs could use them in his fish market, and only four cents a pound if they were sold in Miami. Though I wanted to keep them, Dad thought we might have a last minute bite, and he would not have thrown over a dead fish—even to make room for the higher priced red snapper.

At 4:00 p.m., despite the barrel being not quite full, Dad mercifully announced it was time to quit. "Well son, it looks like it's time to call that barrel full and put this old girl to bed."

Dad always referred to his boat in familiar feminine terms. He thought it very strange that someone had named his boat *Freddie M.* after a man, but would not change the name. "Only warships should ever be named after a man. Boats should properly be named after a woman, but whatever you name them, it should never be after a man."

"Well Dad, couldn't you just change the name?"

"I guess we could, but they say its bad luck to do that."

"Do you believe that, Dad?"

"No son. That's just an old wives' tale. Superstition is all it is."

"So we can go ahead and change the name?"

"Sure son. Someday when we think of a good one, we might just go ahead and do that."

17

I was very relieved that Dad did not decide to stay later and hurriedly put away the gear. Neither the engine starting and the anchor being pulled, nor the roll of the boat as we got under way, rousted my friends from their deathbeds. I steered while Dad gutted the fish and cleaned the boat. To my consternation, he was constantly looking up to see that I was steering the right course.

"Peter, you see the hole don't you?"

"Yes Dad. I see it."

The "hole" was the cut between Stock Island and Boca Chica that was the entrance of the channel into the fish house. I had been steering his boat since I was old enough to turn the chain driven wheel, and was always annoyed when he checked on my course. It was the lifelong habit of a Navy chief, and even when I was forty years old with my own boat, he was constantly ordering small course corrections.

I felt a profound sense of relief when we tied up to the dock. I had seen enough seasickness to know it was instantly cured once a person stepped on shore. One by one my friends stumbled up from down below.

Merrell stepped out first, "Man oh man, I thought I was going to die out there."

"Geesum!" was all Kenny could say, as he stood blinking at the bright light of day.

Titi pushed his way past both of them, "Man! This is the worst day of my whole life! I ain't never gettin on this boat again."

As my friends climbed onto the dock, Dad walked to the companionway. He leaned over to look down below, and when his head snapped back I knew there was more trouble coming.

"Hold on there boys! That's quite a mess you made down there. Now, who do you think is going to clean that up? Merrell! You think I'm going to clean up your mess?"

"Uh, no sir."

"You bet your life I'm not going to clean it up! Now you boys get that bunkroom squared away while Peter and I weigh up these fish."

18

Seasick

Again, I was mortified, but not about to offer help with that job. The boys gagged their way through the cleanup and then stood quietly by the car, hoping Dad wouldn't find another job for them. None of the three ever went in the boat with Dad again, and we confined our future fishing to the docks and old railroad trestles.

2

Early Years

After World War II, Dad was discharged from the Navy in Charleston, South Carolina, and immediately settled in Key West. While previously stationed at the Key West Naval Base in 1937, he decided to leave the Navy and make his life fishing in the waters around the island city. By that time, he had already spent thirteen years traveling the oceans of the world with the Navy, and having become a dedicated man of the sea, knew he would never return to dry land. But his dream of becoming a commercial fisherman in Key West would be delayed a long seven years by World War II.

Dad was born in 1911 in a Louisiana backwoods log cabin, near the town of Manghum. His father James Bacle, was the grandson of Pierre Bacle, a French immigrant who sailed to New Orleans in 1842. Their cabin was without electricity or running water, and they lived in the twentieth century essentially as people had a hundred years before. James scratched out a living for his wife Ida Mae Bell and eight children, through subsistence farming and taking whatever work he could find. Dad realized at a very young age that it was not a life for him, and was determined to get out as soon as possible.

At the age of fifteen with a sixth-grade education, Dad and his older brother Jim left home and joined the U.S. Navy. His parents signed a paper claiming he was eighteen, but born at home and without a recorded birth certificate, there would be confusion for the rest of his life between his Navy age and his actual age.

After a brief training period, Dad and several other recruits assigned to the Pacific Fleet were put aboard an ocean liner bound for China. The men were quartered in the bowels of the ship and only allowed on deck late at night when the paying passengers were in bed. In Shanghai, he was placed on the cruiser *USS Pittsburgh*, a coal-burning relic of the Great White Fleet.

As the newest and youngest crewman, he was given the worst job on the ship—shoveling coal. He described it as long hours and days of being burning hot and chronically black with coal dust. There was no relief from the job and no mercy from the officers. It was a rite of passage in the old Navy, and helped develop in Dad a mental and muscular strength that he would maintain for his entire life.

Though the work was physically hard, Dad was used to long hours on the farm, and he truly loved his new life at sea. Through the '20s and '30s, his ships visited most every major port in the world, exposing Dad to sights and cultures he had never even imagined. With little for entertainment on the ships, he became a voracious reader during the long days and nights at sea, and read everything he could get his hands on—including protocol and instruction manuals. Despite little formal education, he had a sharp mind and was able to pass all the Navy exams for advancement, and at a very young age, worked his way up to chief boatswain's mate, which is equivalent to a sergeant in the army.

Fighting and even brawling—though not officially condoned— were accepted as a crucial part of developing tough men and also as a form of entertainment. Though Dad never talked about his fighting, others did, and they made it clear that a man was never promoted to chief unless he had the fear and respect of his men in physical confrontations.

By the time Dad first saw Key West in 1937, he was a tough veteran Navy chief who was not yet thirty years old. With almost half of his young life spent at sea, he was ready for a change. The old slogan, 'join the Navy and see the world,' had been real for Dad, and as a single man who loved the shipboard life, he had been on sea duty virtually all the time. While he was never one to sit and tell of all the places he had been, a lifetime of storytelling revealed the extent of his travels. When he was relaxed and comfortable, all it took was, "Hey Dad, have you ever been to Singapore?"

"Singapore? Good grief, yes!"

If the mood and time were right, a story about Singapore would follow. The question could be asked of practically every ocean and seaport in the world. "Hey Dad, have you ever been to Africa? . . . Australia . . . Egypt . . . the Arctic . . . around Cape Horn . . . Tahiti?" The answer always seemed to be "Yes," and the stories intriguing. Yet after all the exotic places he had visited, when he was stationed in Key West in the 1930's, he knew it was the place he wanted to live. However, with World War II looming and his hitch not up, he was transferred to the U.S. naval base at Guantanamo Bay, Cuba.

At Guantanamo, Dad was assigned to the net depot. The detail was set up on the small island of Hospital Cay, and charged with installing a submarine net across the entrance to the bay. With German subs known to be in the Caribbean, it was necessary for the security of the naval station to have the entrance blocked. Each time an American ship entered or left the base, the net had to be opened and then quickly closed.

Though he wasn't thrilled with being stuck on land in Cuba, it would prove to be a life-changing move. At the naval base, he struck up a friendship with Jose Solomon, a Cuban civil service electrician who lived with his parents and sisters on Hospital Cay. Because his father Felipe was the crane operator in charge of loading coal on the ships and on call twenty-four hours a day, Jose and his two sisters were allowed to attend the base school for military dependents and learned to speak excellent English. Dad immediately began calling him Joe, and they started hanging out together when they were both off duty.

Felipe and his wife Jesusa lived on the island in the middle of Guantanamo Bay with their three children—Rosa, Jose, and Maria.

Because of his important job, Felipe was supplied with a house on Hospital Cay and given free use of all the base facilities.

According to Dad's version of first meeting the family, "The moment I saw Maria, I said to myself that she was the girl I was going to marry. I thought she was the most beautiful woman I had ever seen and I wasn't leaving Guantanamo without her."

"How did you convince her to marry you so quickly?"

"Good grief, son! How do you think I did it? I just swept her off her feet with the old Bacle charm," he said with a sly grin. "Why hell, back then no woman could resist the chief."

Maria Solomon: Mother with snook - Cuba 1937

Though he was obviously joking, there was probably something of the truth in his story. Mother however, had a very different version of their whirlwind romance, claiming all the women of her family detested Dad before they even met him. They all maintained that he had been a bad influence on Jose by teaching him to drink and gamble.

"In those days your father was a carouser and a gambler, and he had this huge ego because he thought all the women were crazy about him. He practically ruined Jose's life with the gambling. They would have a poker game every night, and my brother—who had always saved his money for the future—lost everything he had. They even got my father to play for a while, but he had the sense to quit when he saw how much they were losing.

"For some reason, my father liked Pete, and he was the one who first brought him to the house. We were very cold toward him because of the gambling, but my father required us to be respectful of anyone he brought home. Even though I didn't like Pete and he knew it, he kept coming around. Because of my anger, I wouldn't admit that I was attracted to him, but he was always a gentleman and very good-looking.

"I guess looking back, you could say he was charming, and I finally agreed to go to a movie with him. A small launch came each morning and evening like a bus service, and the twenty-minute boat ride to the base was the first time we were alone together. I was nineteen and he was twenty-nine. My mother warned me about him, but I was headstrong and went out with him anyway.

"It was true he was a carouser, a gambler, and a fighter, but as I got to know him, I saw there was a whole other side to him that nobody knew about. He always treated me respectfully, and in fifty-five years of marriage, he always made sure everyone else did—including you kids. He was also very smart. I had thought he was a typical Navy dope, but I found out he read every book he could find and he seemed to know about everything.

"I had never been farther from home than Caimenera and Guantanamo City, so his stories about the world had me fascinated. I found it hard to believe that one man had seen and done so much in such a short life, but even though I knew he was cleaning up the stories for me, I also knew everything was true. Your father wasn't much for small talk, but he had a real sense of humor and he could sure tell a good story.

Early Years

"The other thing about him was that he was so good to me and my family, and I knew he really meant it. He had a very soft heart and truly loved children. With his reputation as a tough guy, I had not expected to find him like that. Would you believe that after we were married and he was in the Pacific, I found poetry in his belongings? He claimed it was somebody else's mixed up with his things, but I know it was his.

"I guess today they would say your father was a romantic, and I think that's the reason I married him. He loved adventures, and was always dreaming about things like treasure hunting and wandering the mountains looking for gold. Lord knows he caused me enough problems with his trips to the Bahamas and the Yucatan and God-knows-where-else, but your father was his own man and nothing was going to change him . . . Well, I guess I shouldn't say that. For the most part, he did give up gambling and fighting for me—at least recreational fighting, as he called it."

Pete and Mary (Maria) Bacle – Mother and Dad wedding day - Cuba

Trapped in Key West

Shortly after their first date, the Japanese attacked Pearl Harbor and life became hectic. When a German Submarine blew up an ammunition ship just outside the harbor, Guantanamo went on full alert. War preparations went into high gear, and Dad knew he would soon be transferred to a war zone.

Maria agreed to marry him, and he was given a one-week leave before he was to be transferred to a minesweeper off North Africa. They were married in Guantanamo City and spent a five-day honeymoon in Santiago de Cuba. As a Navy dependent, Mother was sent to the United States, and for the next four years saw Dad only when he was on leave. Basically alone in a strange country, her salvation was being perfectly fluent in English. Mother simply maintains, "It was hard for me, but at that time everyone was making quick decisions, and I never regretted mine."

Dad was to see action in both the war in Europe and the Pacific. His assignment in the Mediterranean was aboard a minesweeper preparing for the invasion of Italy. He served aboard a number of warships in the Pacific campaign, but never cared to talk about it. The only mention he ever made about his role in the fighting were the incidental stories that started with a related subject, such as the time a member of the Rockefeller family was supposedly eaten by cannibals in New Guinea.

That got Dad remembering the time the Navy wanted to set up a base in New Guinea and needed to secure the site. Several shore parties were sent out to flush the Japanese from the jungle around the landing site, and Dad was in charge of one. "Son, I've been in some rough places in my life, but New Guinea was the worst hellhole that I've ever seen. I believe it has more snakes and spiders and mosquitoes than any place in the world. And leeches? My God, the leeches! They got in places that you never thought possible, and you had to burn the damn things off with a cigarette.

"Now those Japs were some mean fighters, and you never knew where they were going to come from in that jungle, but the thing that really scared the hell out of us was those damn cannibals. You would never hear them or see them until they wanted you to,

26

and then you'd turn around and there were these little guys with rings and bones stuck all in them, just staring at you.

"I guess they never actually did anything to us, but there was something about the way they looked at you, that made you think they were wondering how you would taste . . . Heh, heh, heh. Yeah son, it sounds crazy, but we were more worried about getting cooked than we were about getting shot. We could just picture ourselves turning on a spit over their fire, or sitting in a big pot waiting to be boiled. It seems stupid now, but it sure had us spooked."

When the war ended and Dad joined Mother after returning from the Pacific, he had to remain on active duty for an extra year in order to receive his pension benefit. At the end of his twentieth year in the Navy, he was sent to Charleston, South Carolina to be discharged. Shortly after I was born in 1946, they purchased an old car and headed for Key West to start their new life.

His intention upon arriving was to get a job as a deck hand on a shrimp boat, and then buy his own boat once he learned the business. Several trips of extremely hard work and very low pay convinced him his future was not in shrimping, and he decided on fishing as his career on the water. Not long after, the discovery of the 'pink gold' shrimp beds around Key West and Dry Tortugas would cause Dad to question his decision, but his love of being a small boat captain was by then already well-determined.

With the long ago demise of wreck salvaging and the turn of the century move of the cigar industry to Tampa, commercial fishing became the major source of income for Key West. Fishing alone however, was not enough to sustain the local economy and Key West became the poorest city in the state in the 1930s. The buildup of the Key West Naval Base leading to World War II provided the cash infusion the island needed, and Key West quickly recovered from being just another impoverished city of the Depression era.

The U.S. Naval Station Key West—with its permanent fleet of submarines and other medium-sized warships—along with the Boca Chica Naval Air Station, not only fueled the local economy, but also put Key West on the world map. Its only recent claim to fame had been as the home of Ernest Hemingway, but then President Roosevelt visited, as did President Truman, and the provincial little island was on its way toward becoming a recognized name.

Tourism had yet to become a major force in the local economy. The few hotel rooms available were only booked for a couple of months during the winter, and the impact on island life was minimal. There were few cars in Key West, and the 'traffic jam' the native Conchs worried endlessly about when the Navy Base let out at 4:00 p.m., would be barely noticeable on today's busy island.

Key West was fully in the military rhythm in the late '40s. The Navy yard had a full crew of civilian Conchs who operated machine shops, administrative offices, and a major dry dock facility. Every family had someone working on the base, and therefore had a connection to obtain the surplus lumber, metal, and paint that always seemed to be available. Life was good on the island, and except for every other Friday—payday for the military—the pace was slow and easy.

Thompson Fish Company controlled commercial fishing in Key West. The fish house was a weathered concrete building perched in the middle of Key West Harbor, and it stands today as a tourist-oriented canvas shop. The large rectangular building was at the end of a stout wood dock that extended from the shore about two hundred feet. The fish house sat about six feet above the water, and all blood, guts, and carcasses were washed directly into the harbor. Even before the buildup of the shrimp fleet, the fish house was a beehive of activity, and boats were usually docked three and four abreast.

The owner, Jack Thompson, was a nice man, but he maintained a tight control over all aspects of commercial fishing. In addition to the fish house, he also owned Thompson Enterprises—the proverbial company store—as well as the ice plant and turtle kraals. Maitland Adams was the manager, and the man who encouraged Dad to try fishing instead of shrimping.

The fish house and docks were a never-ending source of entertainment for young boys. I accompanied Dad every time

Early Years

I wasn't in school, and kept myself occupied for days on end. Between boats constantly being unloaded, and fishermen working on their traps and nets, there was always something to watch. But nothing else quite matched the excitement of the turtle fishery.

The turtle kraals were located on the side of the same pier that led to the fish house, and consistently attracted a crowd of onlookers. The boats arrived with the turtles turned onto their backs to keep them immobilized. The turtles were dragged off the boats and across the dock, and then pushed down a wooden slide into the kraal—a fenced-off part of the harbor—where they awaited butchering.

By the time I was old enough to catch them, green turtles were protected, but it was still legal to take loggerheads. Though they are similar in appearance, many of the old Conchs would not eat the loggerhead, claiming the meat was too strong. However, after slicing the steaks thin and layering them in ice for a day or two, I never found anyone who could tell the difference.

Into the 1970's, butchering a turtle seemed nothing more to us than cleaning a fish. Ben Lowe, my close friend and an investigator today with the Sheriff's Department, worked on the boat with me in the early 1970s, and together we kept our families supplied. Turtles will frequently float on the surface, and it's possible to approach from behind without them being aware of your presence. We carried a trolling lead with a large embedded treble hook, attached to a length of strong cord. Ben was extremely good at throwing it over the top of a turtle and snagging him as the lead was pulled back across the body. He would occasionally hook one from forty or fifty feet away, though the farther away they were, the harder it was to keep their head up. A two hundred-pound turtle is a very powerful swimmer, and if it is allowed to get its head pointed down, landing the turtle could be a very tiring job.

The job of butchering the turtle was mine, and we usually took one or two a month, which was enough to keep our families and friends supplied. It was a regular part of our family diet, and my first-born daughter Lauren, when asked what she would like for dinner, unfailingly answered, "Daddy, I want tuttle."

Trapped in Key West

After his abortive attempt at shrimping, Dad put all his efforts into hook and line fishing. Snapper, grouper, and king mackerel were the primary commercial species. Though the native Conchs were very protective of their fishing industry, many of them befriended Dad and taught him the fundamentals of Key West fishing. Like most fishermen of the era, he managed to eke out a living, but without ever really getting ahead.

In the late 1940's, catching lobster with traps was relatively new to Key West, and the fact that only a few people were doing it attracted him to the fishery. The first fishermen to try trapping used Maine lobster pots, but they soon evolved into a basic wooden trap that is still in use today. Dad experimented with many trap designs, but just when he became established in the lobster fishery, the Korean War intervened.

Though Dad had twenty years of active duty in the Navy, he remained in the Reserve to get in thirty years for his full retirement pension. When the Korean War started, he was recalled into the active military and shipped off to the Great Lakes Naval Station in Michigan in 1951. That time he took his family with him, and after two years of training recruits in Great Lakes and Newport, Rhode Island, he returned to Key West to resume his fishing career.

While away, he made up his mind that he would no longer fish for Thompson's on his return. Though Jack Thompson and Maitland Adams had always treated Dad well, fishing for someone else felt too much like still being in the Navy. Circumstances—like growing up poor, living during the Great Depression, and serving during World War II and the Korean War—had dictated the direction of Dad's life, and he was determined to live the rest of it as his own boss.

He decided to move his fishing operation to Stock Island, which was just across the Cow Key Bridge from Key West, but considered by the Conchs to be 'up the Keys.' It was a hardscrabble island that had been used primarily as a place for livestock and not for people. Mangrove, buttonwood, and other native plants were all that could survive on the sparse pockets of soil which accumulated between the exposed cap rock and the swampy wetlands. Key West had its fair share of mosquitoes, but Stock Island was home to the black cloud swarms that could drive a person insane during the rainy season.

Since World War II, Key West had been sprayed regularly to control the mosquito population. As children, we watched as the mosquito truck came through the streets of Key West each day during the summer rainy season, with a cloudy fog of DDT billowing out from the sprayer in the back. Block by block, as the distinctive spraying sound was heard, children would appear from houses and play areas and chase the truck down the street. As new kids disappeared into the fog, others would drop out laughing and gasping for air. It was impossible to see while in the fog, and if the truck stopped unexpectedly, kids would run into the back of the sprayer and receive a soaking with the insecticide.

Then in the 1950s, the Mosquito Control Board purchased a couple of Army surplus DC-3 airplanes and started aerial spraying. It was a very effective way to combat the hated bloodsuckers, and allowed for direct attack on the wooded mangrove areas that were the source of the plague.

The DC-3's flew regularly over the schools, and it was a thrill to be at recess when the big plane lumbered in twenty feet above our heads. As the airplane laid its billowing cloud of DDT, we would cheer and wave as the pilot tipped his wings and waved back. We were bathed in the foggy dampness—intoxicated by the smell we all loved, and secure in the knowledge that the mosquitoes would not be sucking our blood that day.

Stock Island on the other hand, was sprayed only as a control to keep the insects out of Key West. After World War II, it was increasingly populated with trailer parks, but the residents were not considered influential enough to warrant regular spraying. Much of Stock Island was wet during the May through October rainy season, and besides the shallow swampland, it was littered with abandoned cars and other junk that made natural catch basins for water. As the water stagnated, it bred billions of mosquitoes each day, and a couple of days without spraying after a rain were enough to make life unbearable.

Trapped in Key West

As Stock Island became more inhabited, the shallow ponds were filled in, the shorelines bulkheaded, and the junk removed. Residents were then able to receive regular mosquito control which dramatically improved life on the island. The spraying encouraged some public places to open like the stock car racetrack, two drive-in movie theaters, and several disreputable places frequented by sailors and gamblers.

When Dad moved his fishing operation to Stock Island, he set up his boat dock and trap building area on Stock Island Bay, just off Maloney Avenue. Within sight were the two most notorious of the red-light establishments—Wylk's Bar and Mom's Tea Room—located where Boyd's Campground is today. Wylk's was a drinking and gambling establishment so rowdy the Navy put it off limits to sailors.

Mom's was a house of prostitution that had been moved to Stock Island after being run out of Key West. Located next to Wylk's, but several hundred feet off the road, it was a pretty white Conch house with a big porch that always had women sitting on it. Due to pressure from the Navy brass, the local authorities—who were reputedly receiving cash or in-kind services from Mom—forced her to move the house along with the girls. As an eight-year-old boy, I was fascinated by the prettiest home on Stock Island and questioned Dad as we rode by.

"Who lives in that house, Dad?"

"That's not a house, son. That's Mom's Tea Room."

"What do you do there, drink tea?"

"I guess so."

"Is that what the ladies on the porch are doing—drinking tea?"

"Probably."

"Well Dad, our Mom likes to drink tea. Can we all go there some time?"

"You're not old enough yet for that kind of tea."

"Ohhh. You mean like the kind they serve in bars, right Dad?"

"Heh, heh, heh. That's right son."

Early Years

With a rented dock space, Dad started Stock Island Lobster Company. When he began buying a few fish from other boats, he caught the attention of Jack Thompson and quickly found that Jack was no man to lie back while competitors became established. As the major supplier of Miami wholesalers, Thompson informed the buyers that he would no longer sell to them if they bought from Dad.

Shortly after leaving Thompson's, Dad contacted National Fisheries—the largest fish dealer in Miami—and they agreed to buy Dad's catch as long as it could be kept quiet. It wasn't long however, before Dad realized he was working too hard and too long for too little profit. He either had to expand his business to include a fish house and truck on his own piece of property, or simplify his life by returning to Thompson's Fish House. National Fisheries never liked being dependent on Thompson's for supplying all of their Key West fish, so agreed to back Dad in setting up his own fish house.

Dad found a piece of property near the end of Maloney Avenue that was primarily bay bottom, but included a three-hundred-foot section of the abandoned old U.S. Highway 1. The original Overseas Highway roadbed made up the small land portion of the property, and two hundred yards down the road, the highway once crossed a wooden bridge from Stock Island to Boca Chica. When the new U.S. Highway 1 was built at its present site, the old bridge—except for the abutment and a small section at the end of Maloney Avenue—was removed.

Ever since Dad had moved to Stock Island, Mother would take us to the dilapidated section of bridge each evening to watch for Dad returning from trap pulling. Across the channel was the beautiful Boca Chica Beach. Today it is overgrown with mangroves, a result of the Navy taking over control in the 1960s and putting it off-limits to the public. But in the 1950s, it was considered the finest beach in the Florida Keys, and Saturday and Sunday would find it populated with local people. Though just several hundred yards from Stock Island, without the bridge, it necessitated a circuitous ten-mile ride by car. Most Conchs considered the drive a major journey, so it was never too crowded and was completely unknown to the relatively few tourists who came each year.

Trapped in Key West

The new fish house site was not readily accessible by boat, but the $10,000 price was fair, and Dad immediately made plans to have the bay bottom filled with material from the new channels to be dredged into the property. Charley Toppino and Sons—heavy equipment contractors—had recently moved to Key West from Marathon, and were working to become established in the Lower Keys. Needing any work they could get, the Toppino's agreed to dredge Dad a T-shaped basin and fill one hundred thousand square feet of bay bottom on a pay-me-when-you-get-the-money basis. There was only a handshake for a contract and both parties fulfilled their obligations. Twenty-five years later, after they established a statewide reputation as road and bridge builders, the Toppino family worked the same sort of handshake deal with Dad and I when the fish house property was expanded to its present size.

Shortly after the dredging and filling was completed, Dad made an arrangement with the Navy that supplied him with all the wood he would need for years to come. The Navy's Trumbo Annex contained a huge wooden hangar for the seaplane fleet. The planes would land in the water next to Fleming Key and then taxi up a ramp to the field and hangar. When the Navy built a new hangar, Dad allowed them to use a portion of his newly-filled property as the dump site for all the wood from the building.

Dad and John Nero – lumber from seaplane base hangar 1953

Early Years

With an almost limitless supply of wood, Dad quickly built docks for unloading and a large open shed with an office and storeroom at one end. Additionally, he allowed other fishermen to use whatever wood they needed to construct their own dock on the property and even started building traps from the salvaged lumber.

Despite the innumerable nail punctures, splinters, and scorpion stings, the mountain of wood was a magnet for kids. During summer vacations and on weekends, we scampered over the pile like carpenter ants, and built our own docks and forts with the weathered wood. We started fires every day, telling ourselves we were helping out by burning the scrap when in truth it was just children's fascination with flaming wood. Dad's only concern was that we not accidentally set the whole pile ablaze. Several years later, when the pile was little more than a huge scrap heap, Dad set it afire, and people came from all over Stock Island to watch it burn.

Aunt Rose and truck that served as original fish house 1961

Unable to afford a cold storage building for the fish and lobster, Dad purchased an old truck and built an insulated storage body on the back. The truck was supposed to be a temporary solution, but ended up serving as his holding room for a number of years. When the truck was full, he would drive it to Miami in the wee hours of the morning and then rush back to have it available when the boats arrived in the afternoon. With an unloading dock and a truck for a holding room, he was officially a fish house, and the life of our family would permanently revolve around it.

Mother had her hands full raising three small children, but spent any available free time helping Dad get the traps ready. Building traps with hammer and nails was a continuous, yearlong operation. Today, with precut wood and staple guns, a man can build one hundred traps in two days, but with hammer and nails, it took a full month of everyday work. In the early years when Dad was becoming established, Mother and us children were primarily "go-fers" for Dad, stacking the wood and picking up dropped nails.

Each trap had a rope with a float attached and was pulled from the ocean bottom by hand. Foam-type plastics were not yet in use, so the float was a one-gallon glass jug. Soda fountain soft drinks then came in syrup-form and were mixed with water when ready to serve. Coca Cola syrup was the primary source for gallon jugs, but most all other liquids came that way also. Mother had a regular route to pick up jugs that had been saved for her, and then take them to the fish house for cleaning. Each fisherman had his own color for float identification, and Mother would pour the paint in the clean jug, swirl it around for complete coverage, and put a cork in the top.

With the business expanding, Mother was forced to start doing office work when Dad was in the boat. Her office was a six-by-eight-foot corner of the shed. It did have a real door, but the windows were both made of plywood salvaged from the hangar and propped open to allow a breeze while working. The small desk was military surplus and painted battleship gray with the U.S. Navy logo still on it. The office equipment consisted of a telephone and a huge hand-cranked adding machine that did not multiply or divide. There was no file cabinet, so all paperwork was stored in shoeboxes and all transactions were handwritten into a ledger book.

Early Years

Before long, Mother was performing all the tasks at the fish house, including the dispensing of bait and even the weighing and grading of fish. We children helped out to the degree that young children can be helpful, but Mother was often running the fish house by herself. Later, when Dad was gone for weeks at a time trapping in the Bahamas and all of us children were in school, she ran the fish house on a full-time basis.

Through the '50s and '60s, operating a fish house was a constant struggle. Profit margins were low, competition was fierce, and financing was unavailable. Combined with hurricanes, cyclically poor seasons, and modern fishing gear too expensive for most fishermen, the fish house was kept open on a subsistence level. The only money for the family was what Dad actually made in his own boat, and even that often disappeared into the operation of the business. Fortunately, Dad's pension for thirty years of Navy service paid our monthly rent at Poinciana Apartments on Flagler Avenue.

As a retired chief, Dad was allowed base privileges, including shopping at the Commissary and Ship's Store and full medical treatment for the entire family. Mother and Dad never discussed money around the kids, and without television to elevate our expectations, we never understood that money was a problem in our family. It seemed I could always make money for candy and drinks by hunting up discarded soda bottles and turning them in for the two-cent deposit or by checking out a hand push lawn mower from the apartment office and cutting someone's grass for a quarter.

While we never went on a vacation and rarely ate at a restaurant, we did spend a weekend each month in Miami. Mother's sister Rose married Gerritt deGraaff, a Dutchman from Curacao. Because they owned a small house in Coral Gables and owned a television, they were considered to be our wealthy relatives. After a near-fatal car accident left her unable to have children, Rose and Gerry devoted their spare time to collecting seashells. Both worked for KLM Airlines, so they were able to travel the world diving for specimens, and eventually accumulated a well-known collection.

Trapped in Key West

Despite the demands of the fish house and chronic money problems, Dad maintained an adventurous spirit. He was constantly involved in projects that would divert his attention from the fish house—a business he was increasingly finding to be too demanding on his time. Usually his diversions had something to do with making more money from the ocean, but they might just as well have been serendipitous escapes from a business for which he had little enthusiasm.

One month he might be constructing a shell dredge to find unknown specimens outside the reef, and then spend the off-season working a longline to prove swordfish existed in commercial quantities around Key West. He built dozens of experimental lobster traps, and was constantly searching out new areas to place them. With his new Fathometer, he charted the deep waters of the Gulf Stream, and found rock piles and wrecks far out in the Gulf of Mexico.

However, nothing fired Dad's imagination like hunting for sunken treasure. He read everything he could find about the Spanish pillaging of the Mayan empire in Mexico, and many years before Mel Fisher arrived on the scene, Dad was convinced the waters around Key West contained untold amounts of treasure. He also became friends with Art McKee, a real treasure hunter from Matecumbe, and became even more convinced that treasure was waiting to be found.

Dad had little trouble firing the imagination of an eight-year-old boy. "Son, this water you're swimming in is lousy with Spanish treasure. Why, there's enough doubloons and pieces of eight out there to fill old Uncle Scrooge's vault two or three times, and one of these days we might just go out there and find some of them."

Shortly after opening, and before the fish house became a fully functioning business, Dad's treasure hunting dream became a reality after he became friends with an officer at the Navy's Underwater Swimmers School. Soon after meeting, they organized a trip, and with the boat loaded down with dive gear, they headed in the direction of Dry Tortugas for their first hunt. Scuba tanks were a relatively new invention in the 1950s, but the Navy had a huge inventory that certain officers were able to check out for personal use.

By towing dive sleds, they were able to cover vast areas of ocean that had never been dived on before. They dove on dozens of piles of ballast, and found scores of anchors and cannons. Expecting to find coins, silver bars, and jewelry lying on the bottom, they paid little attention to other things that may have been of historic value, though they did salvage several boxes of the most interesting artifacts.

Most of the cannons were too heavy to get in the boat, but they did raise at least two, as well as all of the anchors which they sold to pay for the expeditions. When I later asked Dad about the cannons he said, "They were just in the way, so I gave them to a couple of different people who wanted to put them in their front yards for decoration. Same thing with the anchors and other stuff we brought up. I guess they're still lying around town somewhere. What was I going to do with them anyway?"

3

Dry Tortugas

The treasure hunting expeditions in the mid-1950s seemed to bring out the wanderlust in Dad, and spurred him toward finding a new area for his traps. Like the old American homesteaders who became anxious to move on if anyone settled within five miles of them, Dad was ready to find new ocean bottom that no one else had ever worked.

By the standards of today, the ocean around Key West in the 1950s was virtually deserted. There were less than one hundred full-time commercial fishermen on the island, and only half of them worked lobster traps. The shrimp fleet was rapidly expanding, but most of the boats were in Key West for only three or four winter months and were unobtrusive to the local fishermen because they dragged their nets during the night and far out in the Gulf of Mexico.

While Dad was undoubtedly concerned with overcrowding, his experience with trap robbers is probably what pushed him to leave local waters. Other fishermen were often tormented by the prospect of someone taking lobster from their traps, but Dad usually preferred to brush it off with humor; "The banditos have got to eat too." However, when it became a systematic and consistent robbing of his income, he knew he had to take action. He felt certain he knew who the culprits were, but despite being a man who never backed down from a fight, he had a great respect for the written law, and was reluctant to take it into his own hands.

Dry Tortugas

The prime suspects were two fishermen whom he had recently told to leave the fish house after discovering they were responsible for putting undersized lobsters on his truck. Dad had physically wrung the confession out of them, and they were both carrying a grudge over him forcing them to publicly confess their duplicity in court. Working out of another fish house, they were apparently exacting their revenge by working over Dad's traps.

"Hell! I should have run them off, and given them a good ass kickin' to boot. Lord knows they both needed one, and that might have been just the thing to straighten the boys out."

Dad came up with a plan to catch them robbing his traps, and enlisted Florida Conservation officer Boyd Dowling to help. With a can of fluorescent paint, they marked one hundred lobsters with a dab of paint on their underside, and left them in the traps. Two days later, the suspects were out trap pulling, and Dowling was waiting for them when they returned to their dock. The setup had worked perfectly, and they were found to have all one hundred lobsters in their boat.

Dad was overjoyed that he was going to get real justice, and the culprits were going to be publicly exposed for the thieves they were. Dad and officer Dowling walked confidently into court, and found they were the ones being "set up." The judge ruled—with virtually no testimony as to the facts, and a perfectly straight face—that he was dismissing the case because the lobsters could have crawled out of Dad's traps and into theirs.

It was his first experience in a civilian court, and Dad had expected justice to be sure and harsh like the military courts. That a judge would allow personal or family connections to influence his decision left Dad in shock, and realizing he would have to take care of the problem himself.

Dad's partner on the boat and long-time Navy shipmate John Nero thought it was time for him and Dad to come out of 'retirement' and return to their brawling days for one "good ole navy ass whippin'." It was a very tempting way to deal with the thieves, but Dad and John both had a past that would not look good in court—especially in front of the same judge.

John was a huge man, with gnarled features and cauliflower ears. He became a boxer in the Navy, and was reputed to have been the heavyweight champion of the Pacific Fleet. He was a kind and gentle man with me, but even at my young age, I could see that men were careful around him. What he could do to the two scrawny thieves was almost unthinkable.

Dad with Navy pal and fishing partner John Nero aboard Freddie M.

Dad's fighting history was a little more obscure. I once heard a man ask him, "Well Pete, what do you think was your greatest accomplishment in the Navy?"

He answered without hesitation, "Making chief." And then with a grin, "Three times."

His response was good for a laugh, but he had indeed been 'busted' twice, and once, he was actually thrown out of the Navy. In the most notorious incident, Dad was a member of a crew that escorted President Roosevelt on boat rides and fishing trips aboard a navy crash boat. The crew was on shore leave in Norfolk, Virginia, and got into a major barroom brawl. "President Roosevelt's Fighting Crew" read the newspaper headline, and what would normally have been a minor infraction in the old Navy became cause for dismissal because of the publicity.

Dry Tortugas

Shortly after, he was allowed to re-enlist, but apparently had not learned his lesson. In another brawl, a pool cue was launched and struck him in the eye. Miraculously, he did not lose vision in the eye, though the injury would affect him severely later in life.

Dad never talked about his fighting ways as a young man, but it seemed to be the first thing old shipmates wanted to talk about. As a young boy, the men would tell me coyly about how "tough the old man was," "Your Dad didn't take no guff," and "Nobody messed with the Chief." It seemed such a contradiction to my young mind that the man who read me Donald Duck comic books at night could be the same person they were talking about.

As I became older, the stories became more detailed, but it still was a side of Dad I had never seen. His close friend and long-time shipmate, Tom Ratcliff—another friendly guy whom no one 'messed with'—said that pound for pound, Dad was the toughest man he had ever known. When I asked Dad about the fighting, his only response was, "Son, if you wanted to stay in the Navy and keep your self-respect, you had to fight. But now remember what I'm telling you. Don't ever start a fight, but don't ever back down from one. It's better to get your butt kicked than lose your self-respect."

With the trap robbers, Dad had a different kind of fight. A physical one would almost surely land him in front of the same judge, and would not end favorably. He decided retaliation was the only way left, so after a couple of weeks passed, he and John cut away half of the thieves' two hundred traps. The message was clearly and quietly received, and not only did Dad not have any more trouble with them, but in one of those ironies of life, they actually became friendly in later years. When I asked how he could be friendly after what they had done, he shrugged, "What the hell. They were just kids, and I guess that was their way of getting back at me for embarrassing them in front of everyone."

Not long after the trap-robbing incident, John Nero was forced into retirement by arthritis, and Dad started making plans to move on to bluer waters. Dry Tortugas was a pristine coral reef containing four small islands, sixty miles west of Key West. On one of the islands sat Fort Jefferson—a massive, Civil War-era brick fort that was then the lonely and forgotten guardian of the Gulf of Mexico.

The forlorn beauty of Dry Tortugas captured Dad's imagination in 1939, when his crew accompanied President Roosevelt on a fishing trip to the deserted fort. Set in the middle of the most brilliant and vibrant reef tract in America, the crumbling ramparts presented a haunting allure for Dad, and he vowed he would one day return.

A few boats occasionally made their way to Tortugas to fish for snapper and grouper, but transporting lobster from such a distance was a far greater problem than bringing fish because they had to be brought in alive. The logistical problem of getting the lobster back alive had prevented other fishermen from taking traps to Tortugas, but Dad would not be deterred. He would simply build wire cages, and keep them penned up alive until he was ready to go home.

Dad was certain Tortugas held more lobster than anywhere in the world. Though his treasure hunting trips had barely touched Dry Tortugas, and they never reached the more distant Tortugas Bank, his divers saw enough to convince Dad the entire area was "lousy with crawdads." Even more than the lobster, the thought of hundreds of square miles of virgin bottom all to himself made Tortugas irresistible. Tortugas had not yet been designated a National Park, and all the reefs and banks that are now preserved were open to him.

Fort Jefferson also provided the perfect port during a storm. No matter which way the wind blew, Dad could always anchor on the lee side of the fort, or run his boat up onto the sandy beaches that dropped off sharply—leaving the stern in deep water. Behind the fort was a reef-enclosed area that proved perfect for storing his lobster cages, and in August of 1956 he started the new season at Tortugas.

Dad cruised the crystalline waters like a man in a dream. Crisscrossing the bank, he often rode around just to see what was there. Without the tidal flows from Florida Bay that affected Key

Dry Tortugas

West, the waters at Tortugas were as clear as any in the Caribbean, and on a calm day—even in forty feet of water—it was like a private viewing of a spectacular aquarium.

Dad was a fine storyteller, and to an eleven-year-old boy, his descriptions of Tortugas made it sound like a fantasyland. Having no television, no Disney World, and no experience of a real vacation, my imagination was fired. The deserted old fort "right smack in the middle of the ocean" became a fairy tale castle I had to see.

Though Dad did not really think women and children belonged on a commercial trip, he frequently took me to pull traps, and often allowed my sister Suzy on board because of her love of the ocean. A trip to Dry Tortugas however, was a very different story. Dad was willing to take me, but deferred to Mother on the final decision. She was reluctant to let me go, wondering out loud what I would do all day and worrying that Dad would be too busy to properly watch me. But with four children to care for, including three-month-old Jimmy and three-year-old Nancy, Mother was no match for my pleading and finally agreed to let me go. We left the day after Christmas, and Dad promised to have me home for the start of school one week later.

Dad was taking Jack Miller as his mate, a man who was on leave from the Navy. His son John—a schoolmate of mine—was also going with us, and we were more excited about the trip than we were about Christmas. John's family lived in the old Ernest Hemingway home on Whitehead Street, and on a visit just before Christmas, we raced up and down the stairs and round and round the yard, giddy with wild thoughts of the adventure ahead.

The fort could be seen from many miles away, and John and I watched for two hours from the bow as it slowly appeared in all its grandeur. It was more massive than we had ever imagined, and the entire back half of the fort rose straight up out of the water, while the front half was encompassed by a beautiful island several hundred yards around. We were amazed to see that the fort was surrounded by a moat, which only made the strange scene a little more fantastical.

Trapped in Key West

We pulled up to the island by going through a channel on the south side leading to a white sand beach lined with coconut trees. I expected Dad to anchor close like we always did when visiting an island, but instead he yelled out, "Hold on boys!" and ran the bow of the boat onto the beach. Dad was never one to explain to children what he was about to do, so the unexpected high-speed race straight onto the shore had our adrenalin flowing.

When the boat came to its sudden stop, we raced to the bow and leaped onto the soft sand, as Dad dropped over the anchor for John and me to drag to the top of the beach. The water depth dropped quickly from the edge of the beach, and the back half of the boat was in no danger of touching the bottom. Though the boat was firmly grounded on the beach, by hauling in the anchor and revving up the engine in reverse, the boat would easily slide back into the water.

After eight hours of monotonous riding from Key West, we were like a pair of puppies that had been untied. We ran up and down the beach, tripping in the soft sand and pushing each other into the water. We foraged among the coconut trees and brought back prizes of exotic-looking driftwood and strange but beautiful glass bottles. We surveyed the island while our dads secured the boat, and found we had it all to ourselves.

"Can we go in the fort now?" I asked.

"Not yet son. We have to do something first."

The men dropped from the bow onto the sand with Dad carrying a paper bag. "What's in the bag, Dad?"

"Just a little something for Old Bill."

"Old Bill? Who is Old Bill?"

"He's the one who is going to be in charge of you boys while we pull traps. He's the caretaker of this island, so you boys have to do whatever he says."

"You mean we get to stay here all day by ourselves?"

"That's right. Unless you would rather spend the day pulling traps with us."

"No sir. We'll be fine here."

Dry Tortugas

It was another unexpected but exciting development. Dad would not have mentioned it sooner, knowing if Mother found out, she would not have let me go. Dad gave little thought to what might happen to two eleven-year-old boys without adult supervision, but only knew we would be happier running around the fort all day, and 'out of his hair' while he pulled traps.

A hundred yards from the front gate of the fort, Old Bill's cottage sat on a precarious loading dock. With missing planks and leaning sections, it immediately reminded us of the dilapidated Mallory Docks at the end of Key West. "Old Bill" was the perfect name for the man who would "watch out" for us the next week. He was well into his eighties and looked as if he could not walk the distance to the front gate, much less be of any use in handling two rambunctious boys.

He was happy to see Dad, and when he peeked into the bag, seemed very pleased with his present. "Why sure I'll keep an eye on them. They look like good boys. Anyway, they'll be so busy exploring that old fort, they won't have time to get in trouble. Why hell, I've been here more years than I can count and I still haven't seen it all."

Fort Jefferson, Dry Tortugas. Our beach center,
Old Bill's cottage at right.

Trapped in Key West

It was getting late, but Dad said we could get in a quick look at the fort before the sand flies came out. About one hundred yards from the caretaker's house, the front of the fort appeared as a medieval castle with a wooden footbridge crossing the imposing moat. John and I ran headlong through the front gate and then stopped quickly. Outside, the sun was still shining and the world was bright, but suddenly the corridors under the ramparts appeared dark and mysterious. Feigning bravery in front of each other, we walked confidently down one side, but quickly became fearful of entering too far alone into the unknown depths of the cool, echoing corridors. We walked noiselessly on the balls of our feet back to the front gate and waited sheepishly for our fathers to accompany us.

The center of the fort held the officers' quarters and a large barrack for the troops. However, the impressive sight for us boys was the huge parade ground. We never imagined the center of the fort would be so spacious, and wished we had brought our football and baseball gear. That evening, we fell asleep while talking of nothing else but the fort. It was grander than anything we could have ever imagined, and it would be all ours for a week.

Shortly after daybreak, we leaped to the beach with our supplies for the day. With peanut butter sandwiches, vanilla wafer cookies, and a jug of water, we set off to explore the island. The feeling of exhilaration was so intense that as soon as Dad backed off the beach, we waved and took off running.

We had been ordered to check in with Old Bill first. He acted glad to see us, but after a few minutes told us to "run along"— and better yet, he didn't tell us a single thing we couldn't do. The docks that held Old Bill's cottage—like the Mallory Docks— were in major disrepair, but still solid enough to be functional. Like playing hopscotch, we danced across broken and missing timbers, each hoping the other would be the first to fall in the water.

Attracted by the noise we were making, large schools of fish congregated around the deep water by the dock. They were apparently used to being fed, and our dropping rocks in the water immediately excited them into a feeding frenzy. Hanging over the edge of the dock on our stomachs, we were both startled when a three-hundred-pound jewfish slowly rose to the surface directly under us. With much bravado, we vowed to bring a fishing line the next day and "catch that sucker."

Without our dads, we were a little intimidated by the strange island, and decided to scout around before we checked out the fort. Like good Indians, we proceeded as if there was a bear behind every tree and a rattlesnake under every bush.

The far side of the island, like our landing spot, was a sandy beach. Instead of coconut trees though, the higher ground was covered by a large tract of cactus. The plants were loaded with red and green fruit. Neither of us had ever tasted a cactus apple, but we knew from the cowboy movies that they were good to eat.

We saw the apples were covered with small clumps of hair-like needles. They appeared harmless and we tried rubbing them off, but found that the fine hairs stuck to our fingers and had to be pulled out one by one. With a small pocketknife, we cleaned one as best we could and tried it.

Unfortunately for us, we found the fruit to be delicious. The needles however, proved impossible to avoid, and we learned why the Conchs called them 'prickly pears.' Like trying to paint without spilling a drop, the needles ended up everywhere. Our fingers, lips, and tongues took the worst of it, but our feet, legs, and bodies also accumulated their share. The needles were too fine to be painful, but having them stuck in the tongue and lips was a source of constant annoyance. Others would have stopped eating, but we were always sure that with the next one we would avoid the stickers.

When we could delay it no longer, we approached the front of the fort and stood in wonder before the front gate. There were three ancient brick forts in Key West, but none of them looked like Fort Jefferson. To the two little boys standing alone on the drawbridge, the fort seemed massive, and the darkened entrance foreboding. We both knew there was no 'punking out,' and with a courage only slightly greater than the fear of being called 'yellow,' we walked through the gate.

Trapped in Key West

In the brighter light of midmorning, the corridors were not quite as intimidating as they'd been the previous evening. Cautiously, we walked the halls and inspected each cool, damp room. Slowly at first, but then with suddenness, our fears subsided. We scurried through the corridors and cells with the reckless abandon of boys gone wild; climbing every staircase, opening every door, and slithering through every crawl space. Standing on the cannons and shouting from the ramparts, we ran ourselves into a sweat-soaked state of exhaustion.

We staggered out to the parade ground and flopped down on the low-lying weeds. Having spent hours exploring the fort, we still had only seen a small part of it. We surveyed our kingdom with pride and knew it was good. Covering our eyes with the backs of our hands, we lay on the ground as the midday sun beat down on us. The walls of the fort stopped any breeze, and we sweltered contentedly in the broiling heat.

By late afternoon we had been through every room, and stood on the western rampart waiting for our fathers to return. The boat was visible many miles away, and we watched with curiosity as they pulled up to the back of the fort instead of our beach on the front side. When they dropped the anchor, it became apparent the cages of lobster would be stored in the shallow water near the wall of the fort until it was time to go home. Dad had long before spotted us watching, and as the boat pulled away, we took off running to beat them to the beach after he pointed in that direction.

We stood in the sand like two daredevils, directly in front of the boat as it raced to the beach. As the boat hit the beach we leaped aside, even though we knew the boat would stop about ten feet from us. We were babbling on about our exciting day even as Dad was dropping us the anchor to drag up the beach and bury in the sand. While we told him about the fort as if he had never been in it, he reached down from the bow, grabbed our hands, and lifted us onto the boat as easily as he would pick up a lobster by its antennae.

Bathing as usual on the back deck with dishwashing detergent in a bucket of salt water, we all scrubbed down and then washed the soap off with more seawater. Then everyone was allotted a small pan of fresh water to wash off the salt. By bathing in that way, the trash can of fresh water easily lasted the entire trip, and we felt as clean as if we had washed in the shower at home.

For some reason, our fathers got a good laugh out of our story about the cactus apples, but trying to eat dinner with fine needles sticking in our lips and tongues was no fun. Dad made an attempt to pull the stickers out, but was unable to get hold of them with his bulky fingers.

Dad's hands were always a source of wonder to me. Like all fishermen, his hands were thick and hard, and so calloused he was barely able to make a fist. It was no surprise he was unable to extract the tiny, hair-like needles; yet, he was able to tie a fishhook on a pitch-black night and light a match in thirty-mile-per-hour winds. Like sprouting whiskers when I got older, I always assumed my hands would be like Dad's once I was a man.

Though we scarcely paid attention, Dad was almost as excited as we were. He pulled some traps in a new area, and the lobsters were larger than any he had ever seen. Some of them were weighing as much as eight pounds, and he was already making plans to build bigger traps with larger funnels.

Our lunch bags for the next day had us far more prepared for survival. Dad made up two fishing lines, which he wrapped around two short pieces of trap lath. With a knife, matches, a piece of folded tinfoil, and a full gallon of drinking water, we felt completely self-sufficient. Instead of simply foraging for cactus apples, coconuts, and sea grapes, we could actively catch and cook our own food.

We went immediately to the dock, and within minutes caught two snappers, and had a fire started to cook them. The island was littered with driftwood, and for the rest of the trip we started a fire whenever and wherever the mood struck. In the days to follow, we would even carry wood into the fort and cook our catch inside the cells. We rarely saw another person, and did exactly as we pleased with no fear of being reprimanded.

The first day we simply wrapped our fish in tinfoil and cooked over the open fire, but we soon were expanding our cooking skills. We spent hours trying to maneuver our baited hook into the mouth of a giant lobster under the dock and finally managed to land him. After rejecting many that were too rusty, we found a one-gallon-can to use as a cook pot and feasted on the huge tail we boiled in seawater.

Each day we found something to cook in our pot. One day, Dad approached a shrimp boat while pulling traps and traded beer for shrimp. We ate them for dinner, but still boiled some in our can the next day for lunch. A pair of frisky land crabs became another meal for us, even though we had a hard time getting them cooked. Each time they hit the boiling water, they would leap from the can and we would have to catch them again. A piece of wood slapped on as a lid as soon as they were dropped in, finally solved the problem.

There were many conchs on one side of the island, but we had no experience with cleaning them. In order to get the meat out, we smashed the shell to pieces. We had both eaten conch, but never skinned them or pounded them to make them tender. The whole animal went into our cook pot, and we declared the rubbery meat to be delicious, but ended up using most of it for bait. The fish soup with cactus apple and sea grape was discarded immediately, even though we labored over it for some time.

Occasionally, a boat would pull up to the dock and visitors would tour the fort. We had inspected the visitor's book in Old Bill's office and saw that the people came from all over the United States, but on most days no one signed in. We shadowed the visitors as they made their way through the fort, but never let them see us. The fort had become as familiar to us as our backyards, and no one would have been able to find us unless we let them.

Dad stayed in one day, and it was a thrill for us to have our fathers' company. Mother often joked that Dad was just an overgrown kid, and in many ways, he was. We gave him a guided tour of the island, including all our foraging secrets. He loved to 'mess around' the island as much as we did and was genuinely interested in everything we had done. He was most impressed however, with the moray eel we caught.

During the Civil War era, Fort Jefferson served as a prison, most famously holding Doctor Samuel Mudd, the physician who treated Abraham Lincoln's assassin John Wilkes Boothe. Some of the cells—including the one with a small sign identifying it as Dr. Mudd's—had a grate in the floor that overlooked water from the moat. It was apparently a simple latrine system at one time, but we looked through and saw fish swimming under the cell floor. We spotted a large moray eel under one of them and managed to pull the slithering, serpentine creature through the grate, after catching it with our hand line. John and I did not think much of the catch, but Dad was amazed we had managed to get the fat green eel through the grate, and he retold the story for years after.

That evening, we made a fire on the beach. It was my first campfire at night, and I was spellbound by a brilliant sky full of stars I had never before noticed. We wandered bravely into the dark night—but never too far from the fire—and played incessantly with the sparkling embers. Dad and Jack drank beer and talked long after John and I became silent. We fell asleep as their voices became murmurs and the crackling fire hypnotized our tired little minds.

The next morning, I asked Dad if we could have another fire on the beach that evening. "Another fire? Good grief, no! You boys like to have killed us last night. We couldn't wake you up, and we had a devil of a time getting your dead weight up onto the bow. Then, we couldn't walk around the rail with you, so we had to pass you through the front window into the cabin. No boys, tonight I think we'll just relax on the boat."

Even as eleven-year-olds, we knew it was a special trip. We were ecstatic to have our fathers all to ourselves, and the island seemed the greatest playground that any boys ever had. We never saw Old Bill except on the dock, and by the end of the week we were thinking of the fort as our very own. We did not want to think about going home, but Dad would not be talked into staying.

Trapped in Key West

The day before we were to go home was another perfect day. Something about it though, made Dad suspicious, and he said, "If the wind comes around to the west this afternoon, we're going to get a northwester tonight. We should probably go back today . . . but what the heck. Even if it's rough tomorrow, the wind will still be at our backs while we head home."

Without a radio, we couldn't receive an official weather report. Old Bill was in occasional radio contact with Key West, but the reports were usually sketchy, and since most of the winter cold fronts lost their punch by the time they reached South Florida, Dad was not overly concerned.

When I awoke in the middle of the night, the wind was howling and the boat was being pelted by rain. The engine was started and we were bouncing and rolling—obviously, not still beached. Dad was searching through the rain with the spotlight, trying to find the beach we had been blown from. When he spotted it, he yelled out, "Hang on boys, we're going in!"

He revved up the engine and hit the beach at full-speed. We boys and everything else on the boat went flying. Dad raced to the bow before we were blown off again, jumped to the beach, and wrapped the anchor around a coconut tree. With the boat secure once again, we all went back to our bunks, though I doubt Dad slept very much with gale winds blowing.

The weather was no different in the morning. I was used to sudden squalls that blew furiously for a short time and then calmed back down, but the weather seemed more like a hurricane than a cold front. Dad was saying it was the strongest northwester he had ever seen in Key West, and was berating himself for not going in the day before. "We sure can't go out in this weather, but if I don't get you home by tomorrow, your mother is going to be furious."

All that day, the wind blew as the temperature dropped. We wrapped ourselves in blankets and huddled around the single butane burner we used to cook with. Fifty degrees does not sound very cold, but it becomes bitter when fanned by a forty-mile-per-hour wind. Dad was disgusted that he could neither pull traps nor get us home, but it was another part of the adventure for us boys, and we knew we were going to miss at least one day of school.

The wind blew just as strong the next day, and according to Old Bill, it might stay like that for a week. Dad was anxious to get us boys home, but he was more concerned about the two thousand pounds of lobster penned up behind the fort. We walked through the fort and could see from the back rampart the lobsters were still there, but Dad knew that even under normal conditions, some would die each day. He was concerned the cold temperature and winds buffeting the crates in the shallow water would kill most of them. Nevertheless, Dad approached the problem with his usual aplomb. "Well, we'll just have to let the Big Man upstairs take care of this problem. There's sure nothing we can do."

The following day, the wind was still whipping when Dad said, "We're going for a ride, boys." The ride was just around the corner to the windier, but still protected anchorage in front of the docks. We approached an ancient-looking sailboat with a single short mast. We had seen the ragged-looking vessel since the wind started blowing, and Dad identified it as a Cuban fishing boat that was allowed to take refuge in bad weather, but not go ashore.

The boat was what Dad called a Cuban "smack." It was an old, forty-foot sailing vessel that had been converted to commercial fishing. There was a small squared-off cabin in the stern, and the boat was painted in the once brilliant, but then faded, red, blue, green, and yellow that was typical of the Caribbean. The single shortened mast was still functional, but the small auxiliary motor was its primary source of power.

What had originally caught my attention with the exotic-looking vessel was its peg leg of a bowsprit. From the dock the day before, I watched as three scantily-clad men gathered by it. One by one, they took turns walking out on the protruding stem with arms outstretched like tightrope walkers. One had fallen, but held on, and climbed back in the boat with only his feet getting wet. The others appeared to be laughing, but I was mystified by their actions.

Trapped in Key West

Dad explained to me that like us, the men were bored with the bad weather and were merely playing a game. I thought it wonderful that grown men were playing children's games, and asked Dad if he could put a bowsprit on the *Freddie M.*

The Cubans' boat was one that primarily fished for snapper and grouper with hand lines, but also had a couple of large fish traps on deck. As we drew near and Dad hailed the captain, I could see the traps were about six feet long and made entirely of mangrove branches. There were also strings of sponges scattered on the deck and tied to the roof of the cabin.

Four men appeared on the stern of the boat, and one of them threw us a line. Each of them had on a tattered coat, but two of them were in shorts, and all were barefooted. Dad handed us across the bow, and they set us aboard as easily as a bag of dry sponges.

They chatted at us in Spanish, little of which I understood, though I had been exposed to it for all of my life. Mother's parents came from Cuba when Grandpa Solomon retired, and were living in Miami with Rose and Gerry. Besides English and Spanish, Grandpa was fluent in French, Hebrew, Arabic, and Greek and had a passable use of the Caribbean Creole dialect. Grandma, who was born in Bilbao, Spain, spoke broken English and preferred to communicate in Spanish.

Despite having a mother whose first language was Spanish and having heard it spoken to me frequently by my grandmother, I could speak but little, though I could understand enough to get the drift of a conversation. I learned much later that the Spanish spoken in our house was mixed with the more regional language of my grandmother's Basque upbringing, and had significant differences in both pronunciation and cadence from the Spanish spoken by the Cubans.

The Spanish I heard in Key West was a Cuban-Conch lingo that combined English and Spanish with the local island dialect derived from the Bahamian heritage. The fishermen at Tortugas used only Spanish words, but spoke with extreme rapidity and in a dialect roughly equivalent to Appalachian English. Only an occasional word sounded familiar to me, yet Dad—who never mastered any foreign words—seemed somehow to understand everything they were saying.

When I gestured questioningly and said the word *"pescado,"* they showed me where they kept the fish. There were no iceboxes for fish storage. In fact, there was no ice on the entire vessel. They opened a huge hatch in the center of the boat revealing a live well. The live well was once a large cargo hold that spanned the entire midsection. The bottom of the hull had been cut out and replaced with heavy metal grates, which allowed a free flow of ocean water.

John and I were astonished at what we saw. In the water were fish of every kind and size. Smaller yellowtail and lane snapper mixed with sixty-pound black grouper and giant amberjacks. Huge cobias prowled the surface, while mutton snapper, hogfish, and red grouper covered the bottom. There were even a few lobster and stone crab, which had apparently been caught in the mangrove traps.

Several years later, as Cubans fled the repression of Fidel Castro's communist regime in the early 1960s, we would see many boats with live wells unload at Dad's fish house. Emptying the live well was a show that always attracted a crowd. With a large dip net, they would take out all the smaller fish and dump them in a tub. Unlike in Cuba, all fish had to be gutted—which was a near impossibility with the wildly flopping snappers, but was a popular part of the show. Dad eventually made them dump the live fish into a slurry of ice and water, which not only killed them quickly, but also preserved the beautiful colors that helped make the Keys' fish so marketable.

The real show, however, was in extricating the larger fish. Black grouper—some as big as seventy pounds—are very powerful fish, and the ones in the well were every bit as strong and live as they were in the ocean. If the crew were performing for a crowd, they would try to gaff the free-swimming fish from the deck, and two or three men would attempt to lift it out in one clean motion. It was a fun but inefficient method, and always resulted in the crazed fish flopping itself free in a maelstrom of splashing and spraying water. To the raucous sound of Spanish curses and laughter, the men would mercifully finish off the fish with a short club carved from rock hard ironwood. The victorious fisherman would then straddle the dead fish like a modern day jock, and with a fierce look on his face, 'talk trash' to his vanquished foe.

But on that day at Tortugas, we had not yet seen a live well, and the men did not give us long to look, as a cold rain was added to the chill temperature and gale force winds. The Cubans opened another hatch in front of the small cabin, and we all climbed down a short ladder into the living quarters. The space was about eight-by-ten feet and high enough for John and I and the Cubans to stand up, but Dad and Jack had to stoop to keep from hitting their heads.

The room was warm and smoky, and to our delight, lit only by a fire in the middle of the floor. The fire was in a round metal pan, which appeared to be the cut out bottom of a fifty-five-gallon oil drum. On each side of the room there was a blanket and a small pile of clothes—the crewmen's bunks and personal space. The crew pushed aside their belongings, and the men squatted around the fire, while John and I stood behind our fathers, leaning over their shoulders to get a good look at the low flames.

The captain looked like a typical crewman, except for the fact he was older, and when he spoke, they jumped. His authoritative voice croaked out orders: *"Coje las cupas! Traime la caña!"* I noticed there was no *por favor* or *gracias* with the orders, and the crew quickly brought out cups and an unlabeled bottle of rum.

Each of us were given metal drinking cups which, judging by their banged up appearance, had hit the deck many times over many years. The Cuban crewmen used soup cans for cups and the captain very formally poured rum for everyone. Our fathers and the captain received cupfuls, but the three mates each got only a shot. The captain looked at me for a second as if he was going to pour some in my cup, and then barked out in exasperation at one of the crewmen, *"Con yo cabron! Trai la malta por los ninos!"*

Dry Tortugas

The smallest of the crew, a young man with longer hair who looked more like a girl than a tough fisherman, hurriedly fetched a small bottle of *malta*. He carefully poured John and me each a cup of the dark thick liquid, which I later found was a Cuban soft drink made from molasses. The syrupy sweet drink was apparently an acquired taste I could not stomach. I whispered, "Dad, this is the worst thing I've ever tasted. I can't drink it."

He turned his head, looked me straight in the eye and said softly but emphatically, "Yes you can!"

I was too young and too inexperienced to understand the social significance of our get-together. By today's standards, our family would have been classified with the nation's poor. I knew our Poinciana apartment was in the 'projects,' but the word meant nothing to us children.

Except for a radio and a rusted-out car, we had none of the luxuries that are today considered essential for a comfortable life; yet we never felt like anything was missing. Key West was not then a playground for the wealthy, but a workingman's town, and as far as we children knew, everyone ate lobster, spam, fish, and baloney for their nightly meals. In any event, Mother and Dad had too much pride to ever complain about things we didn't have or to express envy of what other people had.

Dad however, fully understood that to the Cuban fishermen we were wealthy Americans, and they were far poorer than anything we boys had ever seen. Having always been in charge of scouting unfamiliar territory with naval shore parties, Dad had eaten with Mexican Indians in the Yucatan jungles, headhunters in New Guinea, and indigent natives in backwater Pacific Islands. He was well aware that being poor did not mean they didn't have pride. Everywhere he traveled, the people shared their meager food supplies with him, and would have felt slighted if he had not graciously accepted.

The rum and *malta* were among the Cubans' few luxury items, and they took great pleasure in sharing them with us. Dad acted surprised and pleased at everything they offered, while I merely observed the strange scene. With Dad speaking in English and the Cubans speaking Spanish at the same time, I was certain they couldn't understand each other; yet they were laughing, vigorously shaking their heads, and throwing out hand signals as if they were communicating in sign language.

As the party heated up, so did the room. Between the fire and the amount of bodies in the small room, we were starting to sweat. When the smoke from the fire and cigarettes was added, we were also barely able to breathe. With a single *"oye"* from the captain and a quick nod toward the ceiling, one of the crewmen mercifully cracked open the hatch, and a slice of fresh air swirled through the smoky room.

"Oye! Muchacho! Trai la carne!" Once again, the captain spoke harshly to the youngest crewman as if he had neglected his duties. I was uncomfortable with the captain's brusqueness, but the man scampered through the hatch and returned a moment later with an empty pot and a bowl full of meat. He handed them both to the captain, who showed the meat to Dad, as they all heartily voiced their approval.

The captain reached behind himself for a shirt lying on the deck, and wiped something out of the empty pot before placing it over the fire. He added a little oil to the pot, and when it was hot, threw in some of the meat. I was ravenous, and the delicious smell of the sizzling meat filled the air despite the heavy cigarette smoke. I thought the meat was beef, but then realized it must be bite-sized chunks of turtle.

Turtle was not part of our family's regular diet, and I was not too anxious to be eating it then. I thought back to the times at the turtle kraals when I watched the butchering process. There was little concern over observers—even little boys—as long as they watched from the doors and didn't get in the way. While I didn't actually like the butchering scene, it held a fascination that made it hard for a young boy to turn away.

"What kind of meat is that, Dad?"

"Don't worry about that son. You're going to like it."

Dry Tortugas

As the guest of honor, the first bite went to Dad. He chewed on the meat, while everyone watched expectantly for his response. As he swallowed, he broke into a big smile, shook his head in approval, and said it was the best thing he had ever put in his mouth. I had never seen Dad so demonstrative over food, and knew that part of his reaction was just a show for the Cubans' sake.

The captain then tried a bite and quickly nodded to Dad that he agreed with the assessment. When finally given a bite, I had to agree it was delicious. "It's not turtle, is it Dad?"

"No son, it's not turtle."

"Well, what is it then?"

"First tell me if you liked it."

"Yeah! It's really good."

"I'm glad you liked it son. It's goat"

"Goat? . . . People eat goats?"

"Eat goats? Good grief son, except for us, the whole world eats goats. Why, I've probably eaten as much goat in my life as I have beef."

Somehow, the captain picked up on our conversation and had a very satisfied laugh with his crew. He kept urging me to eat more, which I really wanted to do, but could see there wasn't that much. When the goat was finished, the young man climbed through the hatch and returned with a bowl of rice and some chopped fish and lobster. The captain threw the fish and lobster in the same pot he had cooked the goat, and then a few minutes later, stirred in the rice. Once again, it was not nearly enough for all of us, but was the end of eating.

The rum pouring continued after dinner, and the noise level kept getting higher. The captain yelled out to the young crewman, *"Se te olvido algo?"* I wondered what he had forgotten, when he leaped to his feet and quickly retrieved a small bag from the corner. To Dad's obvious delight, the captain handed him and Jack each a cigar and took one for himself. With much formality, he stuck a small stick in the fire and lit all three cigars.

With the cigars burning, the smoke became even worse, but I still liked the smell of the cigars better than the cigarettes. The men continued to talk and the rum continued to flow. Even with burning eyes and a slight dizziness, the once spooky room felt warm and comfortable, and I drifted into sleep on the back of Dad's shoulder.

In the morning when I awoke, we were back at our anchorage—high up on our beach with the wind still howling. Dad was sitting quietly on the rail and looking very subdued with a cup of coffee and a cigarette. When I asked about breakfast, he said, "Get yourself some cereal."

I was still excited about the live well, but Dad was not interested. "We'll talk about that later, son. Just go on over there and finish your breakfast."

"Well Dad, do you think we can go back to the Cuban boat today?"

"Go back? Great God Almighty, no! You boys falling asleep is going to be the death of me! It took all six of us to get you guys back on this boat last night. Every time I had you standing, your legs would just collapse from under you. Jeepers, with those boats bouncing in this gale, we almost dropped you in the water a couple of times! But besides that, your mother is going to kill me if I don't find a way to get you back to school."

"Well Dad, you didn't have any way of knowing this was going to happen, did you?"

"Son . . . now let's keep what I'm going to tell you just between us men, okay? . . . No need to discuss this with your mother . . . When that wind starts shifting around to the west, you know a cold front is coming. Of course, if I had known it was going to be this strong, we would have gone back before it hit. I mean, good grief! Who would have figured on this? This is the strongest cold front I've ever seen this far south . . . Then, to top it all off, Old Bill can't get hold of anyone on the radio to relay word to your mother . . . Good Lord! Your poor mother. Not only you to worry about, but little John, too."

Dry Tortugas

Later that morning, we made our way over to the main dock. Dad talked to Old Bill while John and I looked in vain for fish in the murky water. We huddled out of the wind and then ran to the fort and back to warm up. Dad came out and announced, "All right boys, you're going home."

"We're going home? What about you?"

"We have to wait until the wind drops off enough to put the lobster in the boat and get the *Freddie M.* home. You boys will be riding back in the morning with the Coast Guard."

The news was greeted with mixed emotions. On the one hand, we were thrilled to be missing school and living on the boat, but on the other hand, a ride on a Coast Guard cutter would also be a big thrill.

Mother was not usually one to fret about the weather. After four years of Dad being off to war and returning safely, she had complete confidence in his ability to deal with the ocean. However, after three days of roaring wind and no word of her boys, she had become a bit frantic. She finally called the Coast Guard to report us overdue, and a cutter was dispatched. When it was close enough to Tortugas, they were able to contact Old Bill by radio and tell us to be ready to go.

The cutter was even more impressive than we had imagined. I had been on submarines and even a cruiser during an open house at the Navy base, but never on anything at sea larger than Dad's lobster boat. Dad had to go out of protected waters to get us aboard, and once again, because of the heaving seas, I almost ended up in the water.

The ride home was more boring than glamorous. The huge ship pitched and rolled with a new motion that made us lethargic if not quite seasick. The captain allowed us in the wheelhouse, which was fun, but we could not go on deck because of the spray. Mother had been notified by the Coast Guard of our arrival, and we were greeted like returning heroes when we reached the dock.

4

The Fish House

Dad's second year at Tortugas was his last. Though he consistently caught large amounts of lobster, he could not overcome the logistical problems. He didn't mind the extra work, but the increasing demands of the fish house on Mother, was something he couldn't allow to continue. More and more fishermen were leaving downtown and moving to Stock Island. While that was good for business and the fish house was bustling with activity, Mother was struggling with raising four children and running the business alone.

By the time his Tortugas venture ended, Dad's business had grown to the point where he needed to give up working the boat, but that was something he was unwilling to do. He immediately went back to working his traps around Key West, which took much of the pressure off Mother, and allowed him the personal contact with fishermen, which is so important to operating a successful fish house.

By the late 1950s, Dad accumulated a mix of fishermen, which included Conchs, old Navy pals, and several fishermen of Bahamian origin. All the fishermen were independent types who for one reason or another did not like fishing for Thompson's. Though Stock Island Lobster Company was in many ways just another fish house, there was something about Dad's casual—"Listen mister, if you don't like it here, go somewhere you can be happy"—approach, that appealed to them. Though hundred's of fishermen came and went over the years, Onelio Lopez, Solomon (Sol) Bowe, and Tom Ratcliff became Dad's closest friends for life.

Onelio was a Cuban Conch whose family originally came to Key West in the late 1800s with the cigar industry. According to his own assessment, Onelio knew as much about fishing as anyone in Key West, and favored Dad by sharing his most secret fishing methods. He took full credit for Dad's success, but was a fishing purist and disdained trapping lobster. Eventually, Onelio changed his mind when he saw how well the lobster boats were doing, and Dad returned the favor by teaching him how to work traps.

Onelio and Dad butted heads often because they were both obstinate in their beliefs, but seemed to like each other more for it. Unlike Dad, whose temper was slow to rise, Onelio had a fiery one and tended to go off half-cocked. Dad saved a man, or maybe saved Onelio from jail, when he tackled him as he was about to shoot someone. Onelio was convinced the man had robbed his traps, and had him pinned against the fish house wall with his rifle. Dad grabbed Onelio just as the gun fired, and the victim took off running with nothing more than a hole through the fleshy part of his thumb.

To Onelio's disgust, Dad held him down until the man got away. "Dammit, Pete! Why did you do that? I wasn't going to kill him! I just wanted to put a little hole in him for a reminder the next time he thinks about pulling my traps. Hell, it's only a single shot 22."

Besides being an accomplished fisherman, Onelio also fancied himself to be a master boat builder. Dad had a couple of loose planks on the *Freddie M.*, and was preparing to haul the boat at the marine railway next to the A and B Fish Company. Willy Wickers ran the boatyard, and the railway consisted of old railroad tracks running into the water, with the boats being slid up on them with the pull of a gasoline motor. Onelio convinced Dad to forego the railway, and let him repair the boat at the fish house.

With a crane from Charley Toppino, they lifted the thirty-six-foot boat out of the water, and set it conveniently next to the dock.

Trapped in Key West

Without the pressure of the water holding them in place, the two planks immediately sprung loose from the bottom, showing how close the boat had come to sinking. A closer look revealed that other planks in danger of popping loose, and would also have to be refastened. Onelio reassured Dad he would have the boat shipshape in no time at all, and warned him in advance he could not do a quality job if he was rushed.

Almost from the beginning, Dad felt he had made a mistake. With a cup of coffee in his hand, Onelio studied the boat endlessly, as if it were a work of art rather than a repair job. To Dad's frustration, he made numerous suggestions for improvements on the boat "while they were at it," and made little progress with the repair, other than the occasional prying off of another plank. After a week of studying the problem, and another week's worth of personal matters that had to be taken care of, Onelio informed Dad that the problem with the boat was not necessarily the fasteners.

The reason the planks had pulled loose, he surmised, was the rotten rib they were attached to. Unfortunately, there was no way to fix the rib without taking off a section of the deck. Dad was disgusted, but agreed to the removal of the deck if it was going to get his boat back in "short order." Onelio assured him he could just attach a sister rib to the side of the old one, and it would be as good as new.

Once the section of deck was off, and Onelio was able to do a real inspection of the boats' condition, there was more bad news. Several other ribs were bad, and the best way to fix the problem was to take off the entire deck and put in new ribs, rather than bracing up the old ones. Also, in order for him to have easy access and therefore get the job done more quickly, he needed to remove the deck beams. That was not perceived by Onelio as a big deal, since several of them were bad anyway, and it would be a simple matter of putting them back in once the hull was sound again.

True to his word, Onelio was not to be rushed. He once worked in the navy yard, and liked the relaxed work schedule that eventually forced the closure of the facility. He showed up precisely at the same time each morning with a thermos of coffee, and spent the first hour or so 'shooting the breeze' with the men who had fished the previous night, while arguing with others about the best way to proceed with the rebuilding of Dad's boat. No detail was too insignificant for dispute, and contention over the use of bronze fasteners, compared to monel, could take up an entire morning.

Last days of Freddie M.

Each fisherman it seemed, knew a better way to repair the boat, and Onelio spent endless hours defending his decisions. At 10:00 a.m., he took his half-hour morning coffee break, and precisely at noon, the whistle blew for his two-hour lunch. On the few days he didn't have to attend to personal matters after lunch, he took a coffee break at 3:00 p.m., and "knocked off" precisely at 4:00 p.m.—just like the navy yard.

Dad's frustration turned to anger, and then to sarcastic resignation. As Dad became more upset, Onelio seemed to work even more slowly. He stood by his original warning that he was not to be rushed, and made the point each time Dad pleaded for his boat back. When Onelio informed him that he would need to remove all of the planks in order to do the job properly, Dad rolled his eyes, and barked out, "Well then, by all means, pull them the hell off! Just get the damn thing done, so I can get back to work!"

Shortly after, Onelio came to Dad with one last request. Without planks and deck beams, the boat would not be strong enough to hold the cabin, and he would need to temporarily remove it while he completed the hull. In truth, however, the cabin was not in great shape either, and Onelio told Dad he could build a new one as easily as repairing the old one. Dad was by then like the calm eye of a hurricane. "Why sure, old pal. Go ahead and take it off. No point in leaving the cabin, when the whole rest of my boat is over at the city dump. Now, I don't know if you can actually build a boat, but you're damn sure an expert at tearing them up! So, sure, go ahead and finish it off!"

Onelio was stung by Dad's grumbling and retaliated with petulance. Reasoning that since he was originally only supposed to refasten a couple of planks, he was doing Dad a huge favor by rebuilding the entire boat for him, and Dad was unappreciative. It seemed impossible to Dad, but Onelio actually slowed down on the job, and then started communicating through third parties. Each day brought new excuses, and it was a big week if a single new rib was put in place. Between tending to his sick wife and taking care of his "bad back," he would go days at a time without showing his face.

Dad was convinced Onelio had torn apart a perfectly good boat, and it was becoming increasingly obvious it would never be put back together again. Forced to do something to survive, he purchased a much newer forty-foot boat, named the *Ocean Motion*. As soon as Dad had the new boat, Onelio abandoned his effort to rebuild the *Freddie M*. Though he assured Dad the work would get done as soon as his back was better, he only appeared once or twice a month.

The following summer, Dad stood staring at the skeleton of his once proud vessel. The keel was dried and split, and the few new ribs in place were bleached from exposure. Dad calmly walked over to the shed, and took out his twelve-pound sledgehammer.

The Fish House

With cool release, he beat the remains of his boat to pieces. The next day, there was no sign of the *Freddie M*, and Dad made no mention of it. Onelio—once again his jovial self—immediately returned to the fish house, and he and Dad went back to their friendship as if the *Freddie M* had never existed.

Sol was a Bahamian by heritage, and probably the first black man Dad ever called his friend. When Dad started fishing, Key West was a relatively isolated island in which most Conch fishermen were suspicious of all outsiders. Fortunately, some of them were very helpful to Dad, but it must have come as a major cultural shock to a boy from rural Louisiana to find a black man among the first to befriend him.

Solomon "Sol" Bowe

Like all other children in Key West, I was fully aware of racial differences, and took separate bathrooms, water fountains, and schools for granted. Possibly because race was another 'adult' subject never discussed in front of us kids, or maybe because of Dad's friendship with Sol, I was not raised to believe there was anything bad about blacks, only that they "had their own" of everything.

Trapped in Key West

Racial separation became real to me when I moved up to the sixth grade and rode a city bus to school. I had never ridden alone before, and my friend Skipper and I were silly with excitement as we waited at the bus stop across from Chappel's Variety Store on Duck Avenue. We saw the black smoke belching out of the exhaust far down the road, and waited anxiously as the bus made two other stops before it reached us. We put our dimes in the meter and walked slowly toward seats near the middle of the spacious bus. The bus suddenly lurched forward, and we were thrown headlong to the bench seat running across the back of the bus.

With the tension of successfully boarding our first bus over, we laughed and punched each other in the arms, as we wrestled in the huge back seat. When we had gone little more than a block, the bus came to a sudden stop in the middle of the street. There were no cars or side streets, and we wondered what was happening, since we knew there was no bus stop. The other passengers turned and looked back at us, as the huge driver slowly got out of his seat and started walking toward the back of the bus. We both thought we were in trouble for the horseplay and froze in our seats.

The driver walked ever so slowly down the aisle, never looking directly at us, but out the side windows, as he casually rolled his tongue around in his mouth and sucked his teeth. When he reached the side door, he leaned against a hand pole and stared directly at us. After pursing his lips for a few seconds, as if thinking about what to say, he took in a deep, tired-looking breath, and asked flatly, "You boys know how to read?"

"Yes sir," we squeaked..

"You know what that sign right there says?"

"Yes sir."

"Well! What does it say?"

"Colored."

"Colored, huh? . . . You boys know what colored means?"

"Yes sir."

"Are you boys colored?"

"No sir."

The Fish House

"You see this pole right here with the word colored written on it?"

"Yes sir."

"Now that means that everything back of that pole is for colored folks. So, you boys are sitting in their seats, and I don't think they're going to be too happy about that. Now, get your little boongies up to the front of the bus, and don't ever let me see you back here again!"

We hustled past the driver to the front of the bus, more embarrassed than we had ever been. We looked out the window the rest of the way to school, avoiding the stares of the other passengers, and not daring to speak or move. The lesson of racial prejudice was lost on us, and we worried only that our parents would find out, or worse, that word would get back to the coloreds we had been sitting in their seats.

Sol was one of the first fishermen to move to Dad's new fish house, but it was easily apparent that Sol did little fishing. Well into his sixties, his most productive days as a fisherman were behind him by the time he moved to Stock Island Lobster Company. Whereas the other boats were required to produce in return for their free dock space, Sol's boat often remained at the dock for weeks at a time without any complaints from Dad. Even as a young boy, I could see —probably because of their friendship—Sol had special privileges other fishermen didn't have.

Sol was my favorite fisherman, and he always seemed glad to see me. Unlike most of the others, he devoted his full attention to me when we were speaking and patiently answered my never-ending questions. When he spoke, I was spellbound. His voice was a blend of the soft-spoken Bahamian dialect and African American. It came out in the most expressive tones, and when he laughed—which was often—it emanated from deep down and burst out in a soundless rumble that shook his whole body.

In all likelihood, he had never been to school, and I was never sure whether he could do much more than sign his name.

Trapped in Key West

As with many of the fishermen, education had little to do with brains, and Sol was very wise about most things—other than women. He obviously had an ear for language, since his Bahamian roots allowed him to speak very proper English or Ebonic with an island twist—depending on the company and his state of excitement. He was a genuinely kind man who didn't speak badly of anyone and never used profanity.

Aside from his reputation as a fisherman, Sol was famous for reputedly having had seven wives. "Mr. Sol," I asked him. "Have you really been married seven times?" He looked at me in surprise, and then let out his slow rumble of a laugh. As usual there was barely any sound associated with it, but his whole body slowly bobbed and shook, and his smile was so big it closed his eyes.

"Married seven times? Lord, Junior! Who told you something like that?"

"I don't know. I just heard it. Is it true?"

"Well now, I'm not sure I know myself. Let me see." He then held out his hands and started counting fingers. With the first couple, he said a name as he touched the fingertip to count. With the others, he just mouthed a name. He shook his head and started over several times as I watched with rapt attention. When he used up all ten fingers, he stared for a moment, and then looked at me and said, "I don't know Petah, I must have done something wrong here. If you marry the same woman twice, does that count as one or two marriages?"

Sol's true weakness seemed to be with women, and the fact he had been married so many times only added to the exotic allure of his being black and speaking in a very different way. When he moved to the fish house, I became intrigued with his current wife. She was a very large woman and drove a huge pink Cadillac. Sol said only that she was from Goulds, and that's where his home was.

Goulds was a small town between Homestead and Miami. In the 1950s, it was a farming community, isolated on U.S. Highway 1 by woods and farmland. Today, it is indistinguishable in the dense development running solidly north from Homestead. His wife was a wealthy property owner and a very important person in Goulds. She made frequent and apparently unexpected trips to Key West. I was with Sol several times when she pulled into the fish house, and he always let out a quiet "Uh oh," and would hustle over to her with a parting, "Gotta go, Petah. See you in a few days."

Occasionally, other women would come to the fish house looking for Sol, and more than once he would hide if he hadn't been spotted. When a determined-looking lady on foot walked onto the property, he told me as he ducked behind a car, "If she asks for me, tell her I'm not here."

After she left, I asked Dad, "Who was that lady looking for Mr. Sol?"

"His wife, I guess."

"His wife! I thought the lady in the pink Cadillac was his wife?"

Thinking better of his first answer, he replied, "Well, maybe this one used to be his wife."

"Well, didn't you know his other wives?"

"No son. Sol's wives are his own business."

"Is that why he didn't want to see her? Because she used to be his wife?"

"I don't know son. Maybe."

I vaguely knew what divorce was, but Sol was the only person I knew who had actually been divorced. I also knew there was something very odd about Sol's relationships with women, but with an upbringing protected from adult matters, I couldn't quite figure out things like his pink Cadillac wife.

One summer day, we heard a horn honking and looked up to see Sol coming onto the property driving a brand new fish truck. It was as big as Dad's, and Sol was sitting at the wheel grinning from ear to ear. When all the men had finished admiring it, I stood staring at the name on the side.

SALMON BOWE—GOULDS FISH COMPANY

I knew his real name was Solomon, because he once told me it was just like the king in the Bible. When I questioned Dad about the name Salmon, he just said that Sol must have changed his name.

Trapped in Key West

I assumed anyone could change their name whenever they wished, and only thought it strange a man that old would want to do it.

Stranger to me was what Sol did with the truck. I understood Dad bought the fish from the fishermen and made the money for our family by selling them at a higher price. I also knew all the boats docked there were required to sell all their catch to Dad. Sol however, would come in from his infrequent fishing trips and load all or part of his catch on his own truck and take it to Goulds. When I questioned Dad about the arrangement, he just shrugged and said, "Sol's just got himself into another woman mess. This deal won't last very long."

Later in life, I came to understand the consummate sense of loyalty Dad felt for people he considered to be his friends. He could be cold and hard to those who wronged him, but as long as a friend did not commit some purposeful offense against him, Dad's tolerance was almost unlimited. Sol's initial kindness toward Dad was never forgotten, and Sol basically had free run of the fish house.

Sol had always seemed old to me, but like Dad and other men of the sea from their generation, the thought of retirement never seemed to enter his mind. When he was presumed to be in his late eighties—no one, including Sol himself, knew how old he was—he had been working part time in the fish house for a couple of years, when he told Dad he didn't know how many more good years he had and needed to get back on the ocean.

A year before - at the age of seventy-nine - Dad bought Willy Wickers' old boat, the *Sandy Bill*, and got back to working traps himself. Understanding fully Sol's feeling, Dad rigged the boat for bottom fishing and let Sol use it whenever he wasn't pulling traps. On Sol's first fishing trip, he ran the boat aground, and I realized it was because his vision was so poor.

A trip to the eye doctor confirmed my suspicion, and Sol walked out of Dr. Oppenheimer's office with his first pair of glasses and twenty-twenty vision. The doctor said Sol's vision was extremely poor without the glasses and had surely been that way for many years.

"Well Sol, how does the world look now," I asked as we walked to the truck.

"Uh huh."

"Uh huh? What do you mean by uh huh?"

"Looks okay, Petah."

"Okay! It looks okay? The doctor said you couldn't see across the room, and you say it looks okay!"

"Uh huh. Looks okay," he said as he removed the glasses, folded them very carefully, and put them in his shirt pocket.

"What are you doing Sol? You're supposed to wear them all the time."

"Uh huh. Don't worry Petah. I'll wear them when I need them."

I doubt that Sol ever again put on the glasses. He never took the *Sandy Bill* out again, and when I visited him at his house on Galveston Lane, he was unable to locate the glasses. He didn't give up on fishing however, and convinced me to take him as mate whenever I went fishing during the off-season summer months.

Though it meant extra work for me—such as pulling the anchor and doing all the heavy lifting a mate would normally do—each trip with Sol was an education. Both with his fishing routine and his personal hygiene, he was the most meticulous man I had ever seen. He always brought all of his personal items aboard in a paper bag, including his own food.

On the way to the fishing spot, he would lay out his own fishing lines, and then rest until we were anchored. Once anchored, he would take his fishing clothes out of the bag and change in a corner—discreetly hidden by the iceboxes. Each item of removed clothing he carefully folded and put in the bag. After removing his shoes, he'd tie the laces very precisely and position the pair perfectly in their usual corner. He always fished barefooted, and convinced me to do the same, so I could better feel when the limp line was under my feet.

When he finished dressing, he would prepare his fishing area and cut whatever bait he might need for the next couple of hours.

Trapped in Key West

It didn't matter whether I was pulling fish hand over fist the whole time he was preparing, he would not be rushed. Like a superstitious ballplayer, his routine never varied, and no amount of cajoling could get him to start fishing any sooner.

He would not eat out of a plate he hadn't washed himself. Likewise, each piece of silverware was cleaned and minutely inspected to make sure there was no residue from previous meals. He usually brought his own food and preferred to do the cooking when we prepared meals on the boat. I never thought he had a phobia about dirt and germs, but the extremes he went to for cleanliness were amusing to watch, and all the fishermen joked with him about his fastidiousness.

He fished the same way he prepared—methodically. No matter how heavy the bite of fish, he worked at the same easy pace. Though he seemed to work slowly, he always ended up with more fish because he rarely took a break and had his bait and hooks ready at all times. Unlike the rest of us, he rarely got excited and carried on a nonstop conversation with the fish. In his comfortable, mixed-up dialect, which he always resorted to when fishing, he talked softly to them as if they were little children.

"Uh huh. Uh huh. Das right. I know you lookin'. Now you smellin'. Uh huh. Uh huh. Now! Now you be tastin'. Uh huh. Das right, little bit mo. Go on. Take it all baby. Ah hah! Now you done it. Now you really done it. No, no. Don't fight me too hard now. Old Sol gon put you to bed in that nice cool barrel."

When he pulled a fish, it was hard to tell how big it was. He pulled all sizes with the same motion and at the same speed. He often told me to get the gaff when I thought he had a small fish, and it would turn out to be a twenty-pound mutton snapper or a forty-pound grouper. "You see, Petah. You just got to let him know who is boss."

Sol's easy manner served him well for the nighttime yellowtail fishing. When others were pooped out in the wee hours of the morning, Sol would still be plugging away at his same easy pace. When there was a lull in the action, we would rest by sitting on the rail. He frequently lapsed into stories about Dad and how green he was when Sol started teaching him about fishing. He was a master storyteller, and I listened through the calm nights as he related a lifetime of experiences.

In his world, there was a reason for everything that happened, and each incident provided a clue for what would follow. It was difficult to discern which of Sol's stories were factual and which were just old fishermen's tales. He never confessed when he was putting me on, but he always averted his gaze when teasing—he could hide the smile, but not the gleam in his eyes.

On a slick calm night, we were both half-dozing on the back rail. The fish had quit biting, and we were thinking about going in. It was a cloudless, moonless night, and from the stern of the darkened boat, it appeared as if the entire sky was a solid mass of twinkling stars. As I stared up, a brilliant shooting star flashed across the sky. "Wow! Did you see that Sol?"

"See what?" he answered from his half-sleep.

"That shooting star. Man, it was a beauty!"

Sol immediately leaped to his feet and scanned the night sky. "Shootin' star! Where is it?"

"It was right up there Sol," I said, pointing to the northern sky. "But it's gone now."

"Which way was it going?" Sol was immediately energized and reverted to speed talking.

"Which way was it going? What do you mean, which way was it going?"

"Which way was it going?!" He impatiently repeated the words, more insistent and excited than I had ever seen him.

"Well, if I had to say a direction, I would say it was going south."

"South! You say it was going south? You sure now?"

"Well, it started over there and went that way, so I guess it was south. Yeah Sol. It was definitely going south."

"Okay," he said softly, and then calmly sat back on the rail.

Trapped in Key West

I waited patiently, expecting an explanation, but he went quietly back to his fishing.

"All right Sol. I'll bite. What if it had been going north?"

"North? Petah, if it was going north, that means a norwester's coming."

"A northwester? You mean a cold front?"

"That's right."

"But Sol, this is July. We don't get northwesters in the middle of the summer."

Sol stared at me for a moment, and then slowly shook his head as if educating me was the most frustrating of burdens. Ever so slowly, he spoke with a professorial weariness in his voice, "That's right. Thaaats right. Why do think it's going south?"

I couldn't think of a response to Sol's piercing logic, so I shut my mouth and went back to fishing. Throughout the night, Sol replayed the lesson he had taught me. By the light of the stars, I could see his lips move and his head shake. Occasionally, a muted "south" or "uh huh" would unconsciously escape from his mouth, and I could lipread the "no, no, no's" far into the night.

Certainly, the lesson has remained with me. Now, I always look to see what direction the shooting star is traveling, and I'm waiting for the July night when I see one traveling north—and Key West has its first cold front in the middle of summer.

Tom was a big, friendly man with an easy laugh. A navy chief like Dad, he settled in Key West after the war, and worked as a civilian machinist with the Navy. When Dad opened the fish house, Tom decided to give commercial fishing a try, but never gave up his civil service job. Also, like Dad's partner John Nero, he had a reputation as a friendly, easy going man, whom you didn't want to cross. As a boy of ten, I watched wide-eyed as a man Tom was arguing with pulled a knife on him. Though he was also a big man, Tom took the knife away, and beat him so soundly that the man scrambled on his hands and knees to the end of the dock and flopped into the water.

The Fish House

Yelling curses and threats, he swam toward the open bay. I was shocked, but transfixed by the violence of the whole scene. A moment later, Dad called out, "Damn Tom! You keep running off all my fishermen, and I'll have to close the doors." Then inexplicably, Tom started to laugh, as if the whole fight had been nothing more than a friendly boxing match.

I was even more confused when I realized Dad had just been feigning indignation. When Tom walked back to the shed, they both started laughing about the confrontation. It was the first time I realized that for the old Navy men, fighting was some strange form of entertainment and didn't necessarily involve anger and hard feelings.

For young boys, the fish house was a magnet. There were always people around, there was always something to watch, and there was always something to do. Swarms of kids often overran the property, but the only girl I ever saw there—maybe the only

Sister Suzanne holding dolphins (mahi mahi)

one who was ever allowed—was my sister Suzanne, who usually stayed by Dad while the boys ran wild. Most of the kids were required to help their fathers, but much of the work was too physically demanding for young boys, and a good deal of the time we were free to entertain ourselves in whatever way we liked.

The boat basin was like a large swimming pool and practically every day started or ended with a herd of boys in the water. Some fishermen were annoyed by our presence, and those we shied away from. Most however, were amused by the crowd of admiring kids who watched as they gutted fish or cleaned a turtle. Though Dad and the other men were concerned about us getting into mischief, they weren't often worried about our safety. We swam unwatched, started fires, shot BB guns at everything—including each other ("Let's keep those shots below the waist, boys!")—and threw knives with reckless abandon.

My neighborhood and school friends—Kenny Mesa, Titi Roque, Merrell Sands, Billy Pearson, Benny Volpian, Bo Anderson, Bill Trout, and John Hilke—were regulars at the fish house on Saturdays and during summer vacations. The Edwards brothers—Joe, Richard, and Robert—slept in their trailer home across the street, but otherwise were always at the fish house. Tom Ratcliff brought his three sons—David, Frank, and Paul—over, whenever they weren't in school. And Henry Pierce was a young but productive fisherman, who would drive his dilapidated pickup truck to the fish house with his younger brothers—Phillip, Mike, and Jimmy—piled into the back.

Even with mischievous young boys running all over the place, Dad always knew what was going on around the fish house. Though he never seemed to be paying attention, he almost instinctively knew what boy was responsible for what trouble and 'squared it away in short order.' When the Pierces arrived however, Dad went on full alert. Before the truck came to a complete stop, the young brothers were leaping from the tailgate and scouting out the best spots for mischief.

While they weren't above sticking something interesting into the back of the truck (if it was lying around, they figured no one wanted it), they had a particular fondness for throwing things in the water. Whatever wasn't tied down was liable to end up at the bottom of the channel, and if it was something too heavy to pick up and throw, like an old engine, all the boys would get around and roll it to the water. Dad alternately chuckled and raged at their actions. "Uh oh, here comes the Pierce Tribe! Peter! Keep an eye on those propellers and shafts behind the shed and let me know if they get near the boat!"

The Fish House

Henry, as the oldest boy in a very large family, was forced to work at an early age. He loved the water and was an accomplished fisherman at an age when most kids were still in school. Despite his seemingly hard life, he was a happy-go-lucky person whom Dad liked, and because of Henry's sunny disposition and youth, Dad tolerated things from him he wouldn't have from others. In a time when all older men were referred to as "Mister," Henry called Dad, "Pete," and joked with him as casually as if they were old buddies.

Henry fished from an eighteen-foot homemade plywood boat with a thirty-five-horsepower outboard motor. There were no fiberglass boats at the time, and though his skiff was always in deplorable condition, it was typical of many small fishing boats. His outboard motor was in even worse shape than the boat. He scavenged parts from many engines to keep it running, and it smoked and misfired even when it was running well.

Like most of the older fishermen, he called me "Junior" and occasionally took me with him to catch bait. Dad would not let me go with Henry without knowing exactly where we would be, and threatened Henry's life if he ever had to come tow us in and we weren't in the designated area. When Henry found out I had a small cast net my grandfather had woven for me mesh by mesh, it became his mission to make me a proficient bait catcher.

Other fishermen teased that I should have a man teach me to throw the net, and not a boy who wasn't yet shaving. I knew, however, that Henry could already throw a net better than any of them. They did it out of necessity, while Henry actually enjoyed doing it. He was as concerned about making a perfect circle each time as he was with the amount of bait he caught. The challenge of catching a handful of mahoa by making a tricky throw under a low-hanging mangrove branch was far more appealing to him than a huge school in open water.

Henry's attention was constantly diverted from bait catching. One minute he was wasting half a dozen throws in a futile attempt to catch a single snook, and the next minute he was cranking the engine and taking off after an unimportant school of mullet. Like a rodeo cowboy with his lariat, Henry made the net go where he wanted. Whether casting under a branch, between two limbs, around a rock, or "tickling" it away from sea fans, he always put on a show for his admiring fan.

Mixed in with his own fun, Henry did manage to teach me to cast a net. He first told me my five-foot net was too small, and made me learn with his eight-footer. The net was twice as long as I was and too heavy for me to ever get a full spread, but the lessons of proper throwing I never forgot. After making me what he called a "master caster," he had me give a demonstration off the fish house dock while Dad and several other fishermen watched. A terrible cast brought a round of laughter from everyone, but Henry only smiled and said, "Don't worry Junior. They laughed at me too, until I brought in my first skiff-full of bait."

The fish house also seemed to attract certain people who were not connected to commercial fishing, and at any given time, there might be several living on the property. Captain Bill was the first of many unusual people to take up residence. Whether he was really a captain or just bestowed the nickname is unknown, but he was a quiet, dark person, who was missing his left hand. He always dressed in black and struck fear in the hearts of us kids. Most of the time, he wore a wooden prosthesis covered by a black leather glove. The petrified hand looked as if it came from some nightmarish horror movie, and whenever he was using it, we watched closely—half expecting it to lunge out and seize our throats in a death grip. Sometimes, when both hands were needed, he took it off and clipped on a pincers. On other occasions, he wore a hook like the Peter Pan character, and was always known to us kids as "Captain Hook."

After Dad hired him to drive the fish truck back and forth to Miami, Captain Bill was allowed to move a trailer onto the property. The trailer became a permanent fixture and housed a number of different people through the years, but as long as Captain Bill was living there, all kids stayed well clear of it. After he ran the truck into the empty dining room of Bauman's Chinese Restaurant on Southwest 8th Street in Miami, he disappeared and

The Fish House

Dad inherited the trailer. A month later, Dad gave up running his own truck after he caught the two fishermen taking advantage of his honor system by placing 'short' lobster on the truck.

No sooner had Captain Bill left than another castaway appeared on the scene. Pop Harris seemed to materialize from nowhere, and my questions were met with the usual explanation from Dad: "He's just an old fisherman." We noticed very quickly that Pop was a fisherman without a boat, and except for an occasional day pulling traps with Dad, he rarely left his trailer. Unlike Captain Bill, Pop was usually friendly to us boys, but sometimes snapped and ran us off in the harshest manner. One of the older boys explained that Pop was a "lush" and not responsible for what he said.

Along with John Hilke and Benny Volpian, I built a fort on the point across the channel from Pop's trailer. Inexplicably, Dad put Pop in charge of 'keeping an eye on us' when we spent the night in our fort. Though the front door of Pop's trailer was only one hundred feet across the water, it was a quarter of a mile around the docks, and we never once caught him checking on us.

There may have been some quiet reason why Dad tolerated Pop, but as I got older, I could see clearly that Pop really was a lush and couldn't understand why Dad kept him around. Dad was not usually tolerant of men who showed any signs of weakness. He frequently ran off those who couldn't "hold their beer," and would quickly say, "Well, that's enough bellyaching for now," when someone started whining about their problems. Stress and anxiety were something to be taken care of with a couple of "brews", and crying about financial problems to someone who never cared about money was a waste of time.

Yet, Dad had a soft spot for certain bedraggled humans who washed up on shore with some enigmatic story of origin. He seemed to take a liking to anyone who was "down on their luck" and didn't "beef about it." But if a man could tell a good hard-luck story in a humorous way, Dad would listen all day. He was far too proud to ever complain about his own problems and Dad expected everyone else to be that way also. But when it came to the way other people led their lives, Dad was non-judgmental, and extremely tolerant of all lifestyles that didn't bother other people.

Until Tennessee Williams' death in 1983, he was a regular at the fish house whenever he was in Key West. He loved his seafood fresh off the boat, and through many years, he and Dad remained friendly, and carried on many fish house conversations. On a slow day in the late 1970s, one of the Conch fishermen recognized Tennessee while he was talking to Dad. As Tennessee left in his car, the fisherman sidled over to Dad with a smirk on his face.

"Hey Pete. You know who that guy is?"

"Yeah Thurston. His name is Williams."

"Williams, eh? Well, what do you know about him?"

"Not too much. He seems like a nice guy, and his checks are good."

"Nice guy, huh? You know what they say about him, don't you?"

"No Thurston. What do they say about him?"

"Yeah, they say he's punk."

"Hmmm. Punk you say? Well I don't know about that. He's never tried anything with me."

"Yeah, you see that pretty boy in the car with him?"

"Yes, I've seen him several times."

"They say that's his *friend*. Hee, hee, hee."

"Well Thurston, thanks for the heads up. From now on I'll keep a sharp eye on him, and I'll get back to you in short order if he tries any funny stuff."

His tolerant attitude notwithstanding, a night watchman who passed out by sunset seemed of little use, yet Dad let Pop stay on without complaint. He finally got some use out of Pop when he started trapping in the Bahamas. In 1968, the year after I left for college, Dad was desperate for another man and took Pop to run one of the boats. I made a trip with Pop the following summer and found him to be a very poor captain. I learned he had come to Key West from Alaska, but was very evasive about his commercial fishing background.

The Fish House

Dad had a very strict prohibition on drinking during working hours. To my knowledge, he never had so much as a single beer while on the job and would not tolerate anyone who did. When I reluctantly reported to him that Pop was drinking during the day and because of it we were only able to pull half the number of traps we should, I expected him to rip into the old man. Instead, he pointed out, "Pop's an old man, son. He's not much use to anyone but me. Let him have his medicine."

My brother Jimmy, who was only ten years old, made several trips with Pop, and confirmed that he would sneak sips of alcohol throughout the day. But Pop worked with Dad until he decided to give up on the Bahamas. Shortly after the Bahamas venture ended, Pop became sick and disappeared. While Dad expressed sympathy, Mother just said, "He went back to the family he abandoned in Alaska, so they could take care of him."

Until the local government made us remove the trailers because of zoning restrictions, they provided residence for a continuous mixed bag of people, including a dentist, several Cuban refugees, and even a murderer who was tracked to the fish house by the FBI. All the while, the fish house carried on its real mission of processing millions of pounds of lobster, fish, and stone crab.

5

Cubans Arrive

When the Fidel Castro revolution rocked Cuba in 1959, we had little hint of how dramatically it would affect Key West. The initial euphoria at the ouster of military dictator Fulgencio Batista soon gave way to the realization that Castro was a communist, and the Cuban people were exchanging one form of repression for another that was even worse. Understanding what they were looking forward to with Castro, tens of thousands of Cubans fled from the island. Fishermen with a ready escape method in their boats, were among the first to make the ninety-mile trip to freedom.

The first wave of refugees in the early 1960s brought Jose "Pipo" Acosta. Dad hired him to help Mother with the fish house while he was out in the boat working traps. Pipo was bright and congenial and Dad took an instant liking to him. He quickly proved himself to be a dynamo with both work and women. Within a couple of months, Pipo could speak English and handle all of the work at the fish house, including the weighing in of product and writing out fish tickets.

A second trailer was moved next to Pop's, and Pipo became a full-time fixture at the fish house. As a fifteen-year-old, I was drawn to his nonstop energy, and especially his success with women. No matter how hard he worked, in the evening he was showered and shaved and ready to seek out a new *señorita*—or *señora* as the opportunity presented itself. He was several years older than me, but his directness with girls, both impressed me and made me cringe. He was always polite and smiling, but his advances were so blunt that I could only attribute his unabashed directness to the cultural and linguistic differences.

I soon realized his method with women had little to do with culture and everything to do with his unshakable self-confidence. No rejection could be harsh enough or persistent enough to ruin his mood. It didn't seem to matter whether the woman was older, larger, or of a different race—he truly seemed to be attracted to all women.

When I drove him to Porter's Grocery, he approached a woman with one of his no frills pick-up lines. "Hey, you like to go drive-in movie with me tonight?"

"What?"

"Drive-in movie tonight. I pay."

The woman was taken aback by his directness, and obviously did not like being targeted as an easy pickup. "No, I'm not going to a drive-in movie with you! And leave me alone!"

I was mortified to even be seen with him, but he just turned to me with a grin and shrugged his shoulders. Moments later, as we waited to pay, another woman came up behind us and Pipo went into action again. "Hey, you like to go drive-in movie with me?"

"No!"

"I nice guy. I pay"

"Look, you asshole! Shut up before I call a cop!"

I wanted to hide under the counter, and didn't even turn my face to glance at them. Mr. Porter, who was running the register and knew me, stopped what he was doing and appraised the situation. I knew Porter was no man to mess around with. He was a quiet, hard-nosed southerner who reputedly kept a pistol and baseball bat under the counter.

Like most all merchants of the segregation era, he would sell to black people, but unlike the others, he would not allow them inside his store to make the purchases. The top half of his sturdy back door was hinged, and he would serve them through it as they stood outside. Even for the times, it seemed extreme, but I was just a silent observer. Dad got in the habit of buying his evening beer there, and he referred to Porter—admiringly, I thought—as a "no-nonsense" kind of guy.

Porter had a beautiful daughter my age named Carole. I was intimidated by her good looks and too shy to ever do anything except talk to her in the most casual manner. Pipo tried to assure me that all women liked macho men who came on strong, and urged me to ask her out on a double date to the drive-in. At fifteen years old however, the fear of rejection was too strong, and while Porter was friendly enough and appeared to be a good father and provider for his family, I feared to ask his daughter out anywhere, much less to a drive-in movie.

Some time after my Pipo experience, a single incident caused Dad to stop patronizing Porter. Dad walked in the front door with a reluctant Sol, and Porter ordered him out and around to the back door. Dad was embarrassed and outraged that Porter had done such a thing. He knew full well about the back-door policy for blacks, but assumed if Sol came in with him, it would be all right. Dad never went in Porter's again and only said when I asked him why, "That man carries some of his policies a little too far." The rest of the story I had to get from Tom Ratcliff a couple of years later.

So when Pipo bothered the woman in line, Porter was not one to ignore it. He had not yet made up his mind whether Cuban refugees were to be front-door or back-door patrons, and the fact that one of them was bothering his lady customers got his immediate attention. "What are you doing to that lady, boy!"

"Nothing, sir."

"Nothing? Is that true, ma'am?"

"No, it's not true! I only wish my husband was here to kick his butt!"

"I'm really sorry ma'am. Now you get the hell out of this store, boy, and don't ever come back!"

As Pipo slunk out the front door, Porter turned to me. "Is he with you?"

"Uh. No sir, not really. He's just one of the fishermen who gave me a ride."

"Yeah, well tell your daddy he needs to teach that boy some manners before he gets his sorry ass shot."

"Yes sir."

I rushed from the store, cringing at the thought of his brazen behavior. Pipo was waiting in the truck with a big grin on his face. "I think she likes me."

"Likes you? She called you an asshole in front of the whole store! I never even heard a woman say that word before! Do you even know what it means?"

"Don't worry Petey. Next time she go with me."

Despite the rejections, his indomitable persistence provided him with many successes. In truth, his winning way with women soon became a problem for Dad, as Pipo became increasingly preoccupied with trying to maintain so many different girls at the same time. When one of his ladies—apparently assuming she was the only love of his life—waved a butcher knife at the fish house and threatened to remove a vital part of his anatomy with it, Dad had enough.

Pipo was told in no uncertain terms to keep his women and work separate or he would be fired. He loved his job at the fish house and dutifully kept the women away from his actual workplace. He also tried mightily to stay away from the girls during working hours, but many times on the way to the ice plant or to pick up fish from a shrimp boat, we stopped off in front of a trailer for fifteen minutes while Pipo talked to one of his lady friends.

His success with women was amazing, but there were other things about the young man that interested me. While sitting behind the shed cutting barnacles off the trap floats, a large rat ran past us and stopped about ten feet away. Before I realized anything was happening, Pipo threw his knife and stuck the rat squarely in the side. The huge rat flailed around for a couple of seconds and then died.

Pipo was pleased at my astonishment, and casually picked up his knife and wiped the blade on the ground. Once I fully comprehended that the perfect hit by the point of the knife was no accident, I asked Pipo to teach me. Like all the boys around the fish house, I had thrown knives at trees and boards, but any time it stuck was by pure chance. As often as not, the knife ended up broken after hitting on the handle or the side of the blade.

One of our favorite pastimes was a game of 'chicken,' played by throwing the knife at the ground. Two boys faced each other with legs spread wide apart. Each in turn threw the knife between the legs of his opponent. Wherever the knife stuck in the ground, the boy had to move one foot to the spot. As the distance between the feet shortened, the danger of having a knife stuck in the foot became greater, and the first one to 'chicken out' on receiving a throw was the loser.

Pipo's throwing was a different thing altogether. He was a true professional, like the Indians we watched in the cowboy movies. He could throw a knife one hundred times and not only make it stick, but come within inches of his target every time. He was proud of his skill and enthusiastically took me on as his student. Once the basic grip was learned and the throwing technique established, the rest became sheer repetition. Over and over, the knife had to be thrown to get the perfect flick of the wrist and a comfortable arm motion.

No one had to encourage me to practice. Pipo presented me with an official throwing knife, which I later learned came from the Army-Navy Surplus Store and was the common sheath knife all soldiers were issued. I practiced at every opportunity, and fortunately, the knife was virtually unbreakable for I bounced and clanged it off every surface at the fish house. Within weeks, most of the fish house's coconut trees were nearly sheered in two, but I learned to throw a knife. I was not as good as Pipo, but proficient enough to impress all my friends.

Encouraged by my skill with the knife, Pipo decided to take me under his wing and make a real commando out of me.

Slitting someone's throat looked simple and clean in the movies, but when Pipo showed me how to grab someone from behind by the forehead and run the knife across the jugular vein and the windpipe, it became a little too real for me and I lost interest in becoming a jungle warrior.

Unbeknownst to me, Pipo was actually preparing for real battle. A Cuban underground had organized and was accumulating weapons and men for an invasion of their homeland and the overthrow of Fidel Castro. Pipo and many of the others in the clandestinely formed Brigade 2506 had fought with Castro for a free Cuba, and then been betrayed when Fidel turned out to be nothing more than another communist despot looking to rule his own kingdom.

Pipo disappeared one day, and the mystery was explained a few weeks later when the ill-fated Bay of Pigs invasion hit the news. Along with several hundred others, Pipo was captured by the Castro military three days after landing at the *Bahía de Cochinos* on the south shore of Cuba. When the expected help from American fighter planes did not come and their main supply ship was sunk, the landing force was virtually helpless and had no choice but to surrender.

Pipo remained in the Cuban prison for twenty months, and saw a number of his comrades executed for their part in the invasion. America eventually negotiated the release of the prisoners in return for food and medical supplies, and they were brought into Key West by the U.S. Navy. Pipo was a genuine hero in my eyes, but as a seventeen-year-old with a '58 Ford convertible, I had a busy social life, and was not so interested in hanging out with him anymore. He worked at the fish house again for a short time, but then moved to Miami where he melded into American life and became a successful business owner.

Throughout the '60s, the massive arrival of refugees in Key West threatened to ruin the stable structure of island life. Commercial fishing was probably impacted more than any other industry. The Cuban fishermen with their boats had the easiest way out of the island nation, and a stream of bizarre-looking vessels arrived on a daily basis loaded with refugees. The ninety-mile run to Key West was a relatively short one for experienced fishermen, and they came in every type of craft that would float. Since the fishermen brought their boats and fishing gear with them, they—unlike the other refugees—didn't even have to find a job.

The Key West fishermen tried to exclude them from fishing local waters and expected the fish houses to refuse their catch, but Dad knew from his time in Guantanamo what skillful fishermen the Cubans were. He saw them not as a threat, but as an asset, and—partly because he was told he couldn't—immediately started buying their fish. The fish house soon took on the look of a foreign port, as it filled up with a throng of exotic-looking vessels. Most were converted sailing boats and generally ranged in size from twenty to forty feet. None of them had provision on board for icing the fish, but instead, they converted storage holds and below deck living quarters into large live wells.

Compared to the Key West boats, the Cuban vessels were a riot of color. The Conch fishermen, who were also excellent boat builders, prided themselves on a fleet of uniform-appearing homemade crafts. Many were in the modern style of a flared bow and a flatter bottom built for speed. Most had a white hull, and either surplus battleship gray cabin paint from the Navy yard or a very pale blue or green.

In startling contrast, the Cuban boats were painted from stem to stern in the most brilliant Caribbean colors. Red, green, blue, and yellow predominated, and they were of the brightest hues possible. The Conch fishermen at first dismissed the garish flotilla manned by crewmen who didn't even speak English, as unprofessional and unlikely to be much of a threat. They quickly found however, that the look of the boats had nothing to do with their ability to catch fish, and the Cuban production soon had a major impact on the snapper and grouper markets.

Most of the Cuban boats had engines, but they were of a very modest type. Diesel motors in the primitive fishing fleet were nonexistent until the Russians became established in the mid-'60s.

Cubans Arrive

The more modern vessels had car engines, while most of the smaller boats had Briggs and Stratton-type gasoline motors without transmissions, which meant the boats went forward as soon as the engines were started—or as one fisherman explained about having no reverse, after running headlong into the dock, "She go, but she no come back."

The Russian diesels were a source of curiosity for all Conch fishermen, who frequently came from downtown just to look at the unusual motors. Mostly one and two-cylinder engines, they were massive in size and caused many of the old Cuban boats to sink from the weight. They featured a compression release and were hand-cranked from the front like an old Model T Ford. The engine turned so slowly it was often difficult to tell when it actually started. At full throttle, the engines still fired so deliberately it was possible to count the strokes, and each boat could be identified by the distinctive chug of its motor.

The new Cubans—compared to the Cuban Conchs who arrived with the cigar industry in the late 1800s, and had long ago become Americanized—seemed as if they originated from a completely different culture. Whereas the Conchs were reserved and proper, the Cuban refugees were vivacious and emotional. Even the personable ones and jokesters among the Conchs seemed quiet next to the loud and laughing Cuban *pescadores*. I was fascinated with the garrulous joy they took in their work and how they could make the most menial task seem as if it was fun.

None of them could speak a word of English when they arrived, yet with little formal education in their lives—some with none—they quickly learned to function with a hybrid language that came to be known as Spanglish. The Cubans would throw two or three words of mispronounced English into a sentence, and Americans would respond with a couple of butchered Spanish words. Initially, the conversations brought laughter from both sides, but soon, the Conchs started saying English words with a Spanish accent when talking to a Cuban, and the Cubans purposely mispronounced many of their own words so the *Yanquis* could understand them better.

Trapped in Key West

Within a few years, most all the Cubans had a working use of English, and most Conch fishermen managed to pick up some Spanish.

However, no American I ever observed learned to speak the Cuban language properly because they always left out a very distinctive cultural trait; Cubans spoke with their hands as well as their mouths. Like piano players using both hands, the Cubans accompanied all of their conversation with corresponding hand motions. It was an endless source of amusement to the Conchs to see Cubans' hands move rapidly with the talking and watch the gyrations get wilder as the conversation intensified.

Regardless of the situation, when a conversation reached a certain level, work would cease so the exchange could be carried on properly with both hands. Even while on the boat, a Cuban fisherman would often put down his line so he could make his point more effectively with his hands. In order to respond effectively, the other man would put his line down also, and fishing would stop until the most serious issues were settled.

The Conchs, consistent with their reserved English heritage, observed unobtrusively, but missed none of the nuances of the amusing idiosyncrasy. Later, they laughed together at such things as the thought of a Cuban talking on a telephone: *If he wasn't making all the hand motions, would the person on the other end still be able to understand him?... Would he be able to speak if you tied his hands to his side and held the phone to his ear?*

The Cubans fully understood the Americans were fascinated with their mannerisms. Despite their lowly status in Cuba and having to start at the bottom in America, the fishermen maintained an indomitable sense of humor. The ability to laugh at themselves as well as others buoyed them through the tough years of adjustment to a new culture. The Americans were rarely aware that the Cubans were equally amused by the Conchs' own odd mannerisms. Though the Conchs had a very refined and often merciless sense of humor, it was far different from that of the Cubans. The proper stiffness and subtle wit of the Conchs contrasted sharply with the open and emotional spirit that gushed from the Cuban mind.

Cubans Arrive

There was a constant playfulness to the Cuban humor. Whereas the Conchs were notorious for practical jokes and were willing to wait days or even weeks for a satisfying laugh, the Cubans wanted instant gratification, and were at their best with a teasing banter. When I was still getting to know the Cuban manner, I often thought two men were arguing when they were actually playing. They would verbally attack each other with such vehemence and violent hand motions that they appeared ready to fight. Just as they got inches from each other's faces and I expected the first punch to be thrown, the potential combatants would break out in uproarious laughter.

The Conch humor was of a far more subtle variety. While they did engage in milder face-to-face teasing, they were true masters at exploiting a weak spot. Any man who let on he was annoyed or angry over something, was liable to find himself bedeviled by it for life. The Conchs had a lifelong memory for such peculiar humor, and derived the greatest satisfaction out of tweaking someone thirty years later over a long past embarrassment. With a virtuosic sense of timing, they would bide the years until exactly the right group was gathered, and then nip the shocked victim with a seemingly innocent reminder of a discomfiting incident he had hoped was finally forgotten.

In one area of humor however, the Conchs and Cubans were much the same: They both liked to hang nicknames on people. The Cubans tended toward group labels, such as all skinny people being called *flaco*, fat ones *gordo*, and most blacks simply *negro*. With many *flacos* and *gordos*, there was often confusion over the identity of a particular one. Whereas—except in the case of nicknames that were handed down from father to son—the Conchs rarely gave two people the same one.

Both the Cubans and the Conchs however, had also refined nicknaming to a more highly developed art form. Some were simple and some were obvious to everyone, but the originality that went into many of them left most people either smiling or puzzled. Captain Grass did not have a fine-looking yard, Wimpy was not a sissy, and Big Dilly did not eat chocolate covered ice cream bars from Dairy Queen. With the Cubans, the young boy *Nino* was sixty years old, Toro was short and thin unlike a bull, and *Chorrisito* was 'little sausage' only because his father was *Chorriso.*

With fifty Cuban fishermen added to the fish house by the mid 1960s, Dad's production of snapper and grouper increased dramatically. Their basic fishing methods were the same as the Americans, but the Cubans did it with an intensity missing from the Conch fishermen. Each day at 4:00 p.m., the boats took on ice and bait and headed for the nighttime fishing grounds outside the reef. Whereas the Conchs anchored as far away from each other as possible and maintained a quiet throughout the night lest they scare the fish, the Cubans were gregarious and piled into the smallest possible spaces—even tying up to each other on calm nights.

I loved yellowtail fishing with Dad, and especially enjoyed the serene sounds of the ocean at night. The whispers of other fishermen were carried to us on the evening breeze, and even Dad spoke softly, so as to not spook the fish. The solitude of a night was broken only by the distant flapping of a fish followed by the thump of a club "calming him down" or the sudden shock of a profanity bursting across the quiet waters. Dad always smiled at the expletives and always speculated on their origin. When I was younger, he would have been upset that I heard the cussing, but by the time the Cubans arrived, he was no longer treating me like a child and the "good griefs" and "jeepers" were occasionally replaced with a "damn" or "hell."

A night with the Cubans was exactly the opposite experience. A party atmosphere prevailed and the tranquil fishing nights of the Conchs became a thing of the past. Nonstop talking and laughing churned across the fishing grounds. Streams of Spanish profanities— which I had learned quickly—were a natural part of conversation, and they never seemed as shocking as the English versions. Eventually, I even became accustomed to the harsh-sounding banter between the Cuban fishermen, and learned to distinguish the serious argument from the one that would end in laughter.

Cubans Arrive

With so many boats in such close proximity, the smell of cooking food was always in the air. Fish crackling in grease seasoned by a hundred fryings, floated a hungering smell over the sea that started fires under a dozen other skillets. The aromatic scent of highly-seasoned *picadillo*, fish and fried rice, and chunks of Cuban pork sizzling in a pan, mixed sweetly with the smell of bait, chum, and the fresh sea air. Forty years later, I am still reminded of those pungent nights every time a boat pulls up to the dock with fish frying.

Shortly after daylight, all boats returned to the dock to gut and weigh-in their catch. The morning scene at the dock appeared like mass confusion. The small Cuban smacks would pile in at all angles, while thousands of one-pound yellowtail snapper were gutted. Hundreds of screeching seagulls filled the air and dove at every fish gut thrown in the water. Droves of pelicans and cormorants patrolled the water and even flew into the boats—attempting to pilfer a whole fish whenever the fisherman's attention was diverted. The Cubans, who often spoke loudly to begin with, raised their voices several decibels to be heard over the din of the screaming birds. Baskets of fish were carried across boats to the scales and the perpetual smell of frying fish permeated the morning air.

Adding to the bedlam were the family members who arrived to check out the nights catch, and others who were just hoping to bum a few fish. Those who came looking for fish, Dad disdainfully referred to as "land pelicans hoping to mooch a free meal." To Dad's consternation, the generous fishermen rarely failed to supply them, and often offered free fish even to total strangers.

Dad and the Conchs were also generous with their catch, but looked upon giving away their main catch as just handing out money. Grunts, porgys, jacks, and other low-priced fish were the ones they offered, not the money fish like yellowtail and grouper. Though Dad never sold an undersized lobster, he brought in the dozen 'shorts' each day that the Florida Conservation agent allowed, and always gave them away. He frequently took friends on fishing trips, and if he reasoned they had worked hard enough, he would give them enough of the money fish for a meal.

The Cubans on the other hand, were disdainful of the cheapness of the Conchs. They viewed giving away anything but the best as almost insulting, and no matter how desperate their finances, never took money for the fish. The Conchs frequently operated on a tit-for-tat basis when it came to trading, but the Cubans were used to a more extensive bartering system and often received back more in trade or service than the value of the fish. Many of the people who lined up for free fish were either too old to provide for themselves, or friends who would later return the favor in some way.

Dad eventually changed his opinion of the "mooching," and admitted the Cubans were probably right. He was a great observer of people, and after studying the situation for a few years, had to admit, that not only did it seem to genuinely please the fishermen to give fish to others, but they usually did receive as much in return.

Though I loved the carnival atmosphere at the fish house and saw the Cubans as continuously carefree and fun loving, it was only a teenage boy's shallow view of life in the adult world. As Cubans continued to arrive, the local fishermen felt more and more threatened. The Conchs as a group were easygoing, but protective of their livelihoods. They understood the Cubans had to work for a living, but it was the general opinion that with unlimited stocks of fish and perpetually low prices, they should only be allowed to work in the hook and line fisheries.

Lobster trapping however, was a different matter. All the Conchs, including Dad, were adamant that trapping lobster was the domain of the American fishermen. No local man would help the Cubans get started, and those Cubans who tried on their own immediately received retaliation from the other fishermen. While Dad seemed uncomfortable with the situation, he willingly agreed lobster trapping should remain reserved for American citizens only.

Dad was once an outsider himself and understood the prejudice the Cubans were feeling. However, he also understood that once you were accepted, it was without reservation, and he reasoned if the Cubans stayed and became American citizens, they would be fully accepted as lobster fishermen. It had taken Dad time to become accepted, but less than ten years after settling in Key West, he was elected Vice President of the Lower Keys Spiny Lobster Association in 1955. Berlin Felton of A&B Fish Company was the president of the fishermen's association, and Jim Ayers and Mervin Albury were secretary and treasurer.

By the time the new wave of Cubans arrived, Dad served as president several times and was a prominent member of the Key West fishing community. Though the Conchs were a fiercely independent bunch who rarely agreed on a course of action without heated debate, the association gave a sense of brotherhood to the local fishermen. Among other accomplishments, the organization worked for permit numbers as a "valuable check against poaching," strong enforcement on the taking of undersized lobster, and the institution of a voluntary individual trap limit.

The association also worked toward environmental goals, including the preservation of the reef. There were no laws restricting the harvesting of coral, and several people made a living by selling to tourists and aquariums. The preferred method of harvest was to blow up a stand of coral with dynamite and load all the pieces on a homemade barge. With few recreational divers around, the commercial fishermen were the primary observers of the practice and they were determined to get it stopped. The association lobbied for support from politicians, and when the state representative for Monroe County introduced a bill in the legislature, the first law protecting the coral reef was passed.

Dad and the association remained firm in their opposition to the Cuban refugees trapping, but the resilient Cubans were not to be denied. Bully netting was a method of harvest used occasionally by many of the Conchs, but because it had never been a primary method of harvest, there were no restrictions placed on the Cuban's participation. On calm dark nights when the lobsters came out to feed, the fishermen would pole around in skiffs with a light in the water—spotting the lobsters by the red gleam of their eyes. An eighteen-inch hoop net secured perpendicular to the end of a twelve-foot wooden pole would be lowered over the top of the lobster, which was then lifted and dropped into the back of the skiff.

Bully netting was often a family affair for the Conchs, as it was more of a diversion than a profession. Because there were so few favorable nights, it was a difficult way to make money consistently, and very few fishermen thought anyone could actually make a living with bully netting alone. For that reason, they placed no restriction on the Cubans selling bully net lobsters. The Conchs however, were unaware the Cubans had taken bully netting to an entirely different level.

Not only did the Cubans work the good nights, but using twenty-foot and thirty-foot poles, they also bully netted the lobsters during the daytime. They got the lobster out of the hole with the use of a tickle stick, which consisted of a thin metal rod attached to the end of a pole as long as the net stick. Leaning over the side of the skiff with his face in a floating glass bottom bucket, the fisherman would tickle the lobster out into the open with one hand and drop the net over it with the other. They were so proficient at the strenuous method of harvest that the best of them caught as many lobsters as the trappers did.

Onelio Lopez, Dad's closest friend and advisor on all things Cuban and Conch, warned him about having too much to do with the new gang of refugees. They would never be real Americans, Onelio argued, because they didn't come to the United States willingly, and as soon as Castro was gone, they would all be back in Cuba. Though Onelio himself was descended from the cigar-making Cubans of the late nineteenth century, he saw no similarity. The tobacco-rolling families had come from Cuba in the 1880s and turned Key West into the cigar-making capital of the hemisphere. After initially being shunned as carpet-bagging foreigners who would never wish to become Americans, they were fully absorbed into the Key West culture by mid-century, and the island was almost as much Cuban as it was Conch.

Contrary to Onelio's warning, some of the refugees applied for citizenship, and once they became full-fledged Americans, were freely allowed to trap. Within a couple of years, the stubborn but practical Conchs realized that adjustment to Cuban competition was inevitable and made no more attempts to stop anyone from trapping. Like every other group of immigrants, the Cubans were soon fully integrated into the American scene and today work with the Conchs as if there had never been a conflict.

If anything, Dad's Tortugas trapping only heightened his desire to find a new area to work, and about the same time the Cubans started arriving in 1960, he started working an area no one had tried before. He had long speculated that lobster covered a far greater depth range than anyone had imagined, and started experimenting with traps in deeper water. According to the Conch fishermen, lobsters were a shallow water species and did not exist in any number outside the reef. Dad—referring to their hard crustaceous shells—maintained with tongue in cheek (I think), "Those old crawdads aren't armor-plated for nothing, son. That's so they don't get squashed by the pressure in that deep water."

In his initial attempt, he experimented with a few traps in depths up to one hundred-fifty feet. For the first two months of the season, he caught nothing and was beginning to think the old timers were right. However, when the first northwester came through in October, he found his traps loaded with lobster. The traps were so full that no more could get in, and the lobsters were even covering the outside of the trap as it came to the surface.

About the time Dad was finding lobster in the deep water, several other fishermen, including Philip Niles and William (Big Dilly) Gibson, tried the offshore waters in Florida Bay. Thought to contain no lobster because of the flatness of the bottom, they discovered the lobsters there in great abundance until the first cold front came through in October. With faster boats, trappers also started moving farther west and finding productive areas during the late autumn and winter months when they were normally forced to resort to the highly unprofitable and work-intensive hook and line fisheries.

Trapped in Key West

Fishermen were at last realizing lobsters were spread over a greater area than they had thought, and there were far more in the ocean than they had ever imagined. It also became clear the lobsters crawled *en masse* when the cold north winds blew, and were to some degree at least, migratory creatures. Even more enlightening was the realization that one area could be completely dead, while another was extremely productive.

It was then obvious, that by limiting themselves to two hundred traps, they were precluding the possibility of covering multiple areas. Fishermen started gearing up with more traps, and by having two hundred traps on the reef, two hundred more in the bay, and two hundred west of Marquesas, yearlong production increased dramatically. With rising prices in the '60s and the expanded trap numbers and fishing areas, fishermen at last moved out of the subsistence category and into the middle class of wage earners.

Soon enough, others realized the deep water was a fairly reliable source for lobster and moved traps near Dad. The water depth drops off quickly outside the reef, and though Dad experimented as far out as three hundred feet, he found the lobsters generally staying in a range of water less than two hundred feet deep. That made a very limited area for traps, and once again, Dad was being crowded by other fishermen.

6

School Days

Throughout the 1950s and '60s, Key West was a tight island community, and though we never really understood at the time, was essentially insulated from the rest of America. The narrow highway from the mainland crossed several dozen even narrower bridges, and stretched for a distance of one hundred-fifty miles. Television had only recently come to the island, and in 1960, it was still a novelty in most homes. Key West was run firmly and exclusively by the local Conchs, and laws were administered and enforced in a very loose process known as the 'bubba system.'

Under the bubba system, family, friends, and political supporters were always given priority by those who held elected power and positions of authority. In any dispute with outsiders, Conchs were always given preference, and any favor done for anyone was considered an IOU to be repaid at a later date. Receiving special treatment in any given circumstance was the basis of the bubba system, and failure to recognize and return a favor led to many long-simmering resentments.

Island politics were always taken very seriously. Key West was completely dominated by the Democratic Party and there were less than two hundred registered Republicans in a population of twenty-five thousand. Even by 1967, when I went to the elections office to register to vote, Key West was a one-party town. When I said I wanted to register as a Republican, the Supervisor of Elections was called from his office.

"Mr. Freeman, you might want to talk to this gentleman. He wants to register as a Republican."

Mr. Freeman looked me over for a long second, "How are you, young man?"

"Fine, sir."

"So you want to register Republican?"

"Yes sir."

"Can you tell me why you want to register Republican?"

"Well, uh, I guess because my parents are Republicans and I don't really care much for President Johnson."

"Well son, it's certainly your right to register any way you want, but I think you should be aware of something. There are hardly any Republicans in Key West, so there's never one running for any office. What that means is that all the elections are decided in the Democratic primary. As a Republican you wouldn't get to vote in that election, so you wouldn't have any say in who your elected officials are. In other words, as a Democrat, you would get to vote in the local elections and you could still vote against Johnson for president. Do you understand what I'm telling you?"

"Yes sir."

"So, do you want to register Democrat?"

"No sir. I still want to register Republican."

"Okay. If that's what you want . . . Miss Knowles, so there's no confusion, have him write in Republican himself before he signs it."

As in most small towns, sports played a large role in the life of the community. Key West was, and still is, a baseball town. Key West High has won more state championships than any other high school in Florida, and young boys are groomed for the baseball team from t-ball on up. Football in the '50s and '60s was a close second and drew thousands of people to the stadium on Friday nights.

Though never a star in any sport, I was a good enough athlete to play as a starter in the organized boys' leagues for baseball, football, and basketball. Baseball was my favorite, and I played catch and bounced balls off the wall year-round. In Cuba, baseball was the only sport, and because of Key West's proximity to the island nation and Key West's large Cuban population, a strong rivalry existed between the two.

Each year, the all-star teams from the rival islands played each other in exhibition games, and every young Key West boy dreamed of one day playing in Cuba. The lurid stories from the older boys, told of an exotic place that few of us could imagine. Beautiful girls were everywhere, the music and dancing were wild and went on all night, gambling was legal, and best of all, there was no age limit for anything—including alcohol. It all sounded too good to be true, and in a less insulated community, we might have been skeptical. However, as twelve-year-old boys, we swallowed the stories completely, and only learned years later about the coaches and chaperones who prevented the boys from being led astray.

With Havana only ninety miles away, there was a constant flow of people between the islands. Q Airways ran a number of flights to Havana each day, and the cost was a modest $8 a ticket. A car ferry provided the most popular way for Key West people to travel, and sailed daily to Havana. Many Conchs owned property in Cuba, and it was a vacation destination for generations of local people. With convenient travel available, there was an ongoing exchange of social and cultural ties between the islands, and Cuba played an important role in the life of Key West.

For boys my age, 1959 was the target year. We would be thirteen years old and the Junior Major League All-Star team would be traveling to Cuba. The team I played for was coached by Ralph "Bow Wow" Roberts. He was fun to play for and an excellent coach, but didn't like crybabies and wanted his players to be tough.

Before our regular season started, we played a practice game against a team from what is now known as Bahama Village. The scruffy field was next to the community pool and was little more than several empty lots lined-off as a baseball diamond. The fifty-foot-high left field fence – where a high pop-up could become a

105

ground-rule double—was less than one hundred-fifty feet away, and an Aqueduct Authority pumping station sat squarely in the middle of right field.

I played second base that night, and our center fielder was my good friend Benny Volpian, who possessed the strongest arm in the league. From the farthest reaches of any field, he was able to reach home plate without the ball bouncing, and no runner ever tried to take an extra base when the ball was in Benny's hand. Unfortunately, Benny possessed a scatter arm, and when he was attempting to throw out a runner, the ball was liable to go anywhere. Players scrambled out of dugouts and fans dove for their lives as the errant missiles headed their way. He was every bit as likely to hit a passing car or a neighboring home as he was the catcher.

Bow Wow tried to make Benny a pitcher, but the reaction from the opposing players and coaches was loud and strong. Terrified boys ducked during Benny's windup and swung the bats when the ball sailed fifteen feet over their heads. The coaches asked for league action, and parents threatened to pull their kids from play if Benny pitched. Bow Wow thought they were a bunch of "pantywaists," but gave up on his attempt to turn Benny into Don Drysdale.

The night of our practice game, the second baseman didn't show and Bow Wow placed me there. During pre-game warm-ups, when the ball was hit to Benny and he was told to "come home with it," every player knew to keep their eyes on him while he was throwing a ball. As a third baseman, I was normally out of the line of fire for a throw from center field to home—even one of Benny's throws. As a second baseman however, I unthinkingly looked toward the shortstop just as Benny threw to home plate, and felt myself suddenly floating through the air.

I tried to think of what was wrong with me, and in my altered state could only imagine I was being abducted by aliens. When my senses partially returned, I heard "Bacle! Bacle! Come on! Wake up! Wake up!" while I was being lightly slapped on the cheeks. The vision was blurry out of my left eye, but I couldn't see at all with my right one.

I heard them say I had been hit by the ball, and when I reached up to feel my aching head, I realized the ball was still there. "Why is the ball stuck to my head?"

"That's not the ball stuck to you," Bow Wow said reassuringly. "You've just got a little knot on your head where the ball hit you."

As my blurry vision cleared a little, I saw a black man with a clerical collar leaning over me, and thought for a moment I might be dying. "Don't worry son, you're going to be all right. Now, let's get you on your feet and get you home."

Bow Wow and the pastor lifted me to my feet and held my arms to keep me from falling back over. "Bow Wow. I can't see out of my eye."

"You'll be all right Bacle. The swelling will go down in a few days and you'll be good as new. Right now you need to get home and go straight to bed . . . Benny! Go bring his bike. Damaso, get his glove and help us hold up the bike while we get him going."

They helped me to the seat of my bike, and held me up for about one hundred feet to make sure I could stay upright with a good running start. With only one blurry eye and no light on the bike, it was a long four miles to the house. Mother was horrified when she saw me, and the "little knot" on my temple was—as I had originally thought—much closer to the size of a baseball.

Though I was still selected as the third baseman for the all-star team, the dream of playing in Cuba was not to be fulfilled. Fidel Castro's takeover in 1959 had Cuba in turmoil, and the baseball exhibitions became a casualty of the revolution. As Cuba's political relations with the U.S. disintegrated, the ties between Cuba and Key West dissolved along with them. Social and cultural exchanges became very limited, and all property held by Americans was confiscated by the communists. Within a couple of years, there was virtually no contact between the islands, and a century-old familial relationship was unceremoniously ended.

The Cuban Missile Crisis of 1962 was not the event that ended Key West's connection with Cuba, but it was the final notice that things would be different for a long time. While President Kennedy and the U.S. Navy confronted the missile-carrying Russian ships, we teenagers watched with curiosity as the Army moved into Key West. Daily convoys of trucks and jeeps poured into the city, loaded with troops, guns, and missiles. They set up a command post at the Casa Marina Hotel and took over the beaches. Boca Chica Naval Air Station was a beehive of activity, and jets flew night and day while a missile base was erected behind the Key West International Airport.

The nation was apparently transfixed by the crisis and fearful that a nuclear war could start over the confrontation. Unfazed by the worldwide implications of the showdown, we high school kids were merely fascinated with the activity, and went about our lives as if everything was normal. Ball games were still played, and dances were held on Friday nights. There was little discussion of the issue in school, and if the adults were preoccupied with the crisis, they did an excellent job of hiding it from the kids.

Our curiosity often turned to amusement as we rode back and forth by the beaches, and watched the Army prepare for an imminent invasion. We thought it hilarious that barbed-wire bunkers and machine guns were clustered on our favorite beaches to repel an attack. We joked endlessly about the possibility of Fidel's ragtag army launching an Iwo Jima-style invasion of Key West, while the girls giggled and waved to the busy soldiers from my turquoise Ford convertible.

Key West had long been a 'Navy town,' and it was only a small adjustment to see Army uniforms everywhere. Fortunately for us boys, the Army personnel either did not get as much leave time as the Navy or were kept under stricter orders concerning interaction with the local people. There had always been conflict between the Navy men and the Key West boys. The hated 'swabbies' usually congregated in groups on Duval Street, and whistled and commented on every girl who walked by. Taking a girl to the movies was a major source of anxiety for a Key West boy, and we all went to great lengths to avoid the men in white.

Early Years

Most of the sailors were barely out of high school, and highly interested in the local girls. Compared to the local boys—most of whom had been no farther away than Miami—the sailors in uniform were irresistibly exotic. Many of the girls, enjoying the attention, flirted with them and teased the local boys about the manliness of the sailors. In retaliation, girls who went out with sailors were labeled as 'swabbie bait,' and shunned by boys who didn't want to be teased unmercifully by their friends.

The Army troops by contrast were rarely seen on the streets in uniform, and while some girls did have whirlwind romances with the soldiers, the Army presence never did have the impact of the Navy. We expected the troops would move out as quickly as they had entered once the Russians backed down, but a year later it appeared as if the Army presence would be permanent. Nevertheless, the Army finally turned the beaches back over to the tourists and abandoned the Casa Marina Hotel—which sat empty for years afterwards. The missile base however, outlasted the U.S. naval base which closed in 1969, and Army green eventually became a more familiar sight than Navy white.

Before the missile crisis, President Kennedy was a popular man in Key West. In 1961, Kennedy visited Key West along with British Prime Minister Harold MacMillan. Like Roosevelt, Truman, and Eisenhower before him, Kennedy continued a tradition of presidents visiting Key West and reinforced the Conchs' strong support for the Democratic Party.

In the summer of 1962, the movie PT 109 was filmed in Key West. The movie documented and dramatized the wartime heroics of the young John F. Kennedy as a PT boat captain in the South Pacific during World War II. Munson Island—now Little Palm Island—was the main site for the filming, but the movie stars stayed in Key West and most of the local families were touched in some way by the filming. Though he never made an appearance, several months of filming gave Kennedy a very high profile in Key West and added to his already high public esteem.

Trapped in Key West

Kennedy's appearance in Key West one month after the Cuban Missile Crisis made him about as popular as a man could be with the laid-back Conchs. With the entire Joint Chiefs of Staff joining him, he came to congratulate the military for their fine showing during the crisis. Accompanied by Sheriff John Spottswood—the owner of Munson Island—Kennedy received a rousing welcome from the people of Key West during a motorcade through the city.

The Conchs were rightly known for their reserve, and their typical disdain for hero-worship made the reception for Kennedy all the more unusual. Well-known people, such as Ernest Hemingway and Tennessee Williams were drawn to the island because the local populace left them alone. While celebrities were certainly noticed, they were rarely approached, and very few Conchs would ever bother someone for an autograph.

However, despite his hero status with most people, everyone did not love Kennedy. Many in the Cuban exile community blamed him for the failure of the Bay of Pigs Invasion. Maintaining he had promised air support for the invasion and then withdrew it during the battle when they needed it the most, many remain bitter toward Kennedy even to this day. A close friend, who is a naturalized citizen and a fiercely patriotic American, typifies the resentment every time he spits out the name: "John 'efffa' Kennedy!"

On November 22, 1963, my senior year, our high school football team was in Miami to play Palmetto High School. When we stopped at the Holsum Bakery café on U.S. Highway 1 for our pre-game meal, we were informed the president had been shot. It was not immediately apparent whether the president had been killed, and the decision was made to play the game. We learned shortly before the game that Kennedy had died, and we went through the motions of playing football on a lined-off tomato field in South Miami.

The very subdued bus ride home, had nothing to do with us losing the game. The nation was shocked by the tragedy, but the people of Key West took it even more personally. Most felt Kennedy was more of a native son than a distant president, and his memory is warmly and indelibly inscribed on those who lived through the era—even some Republicans.

Throughout our high school, the dream of every student was to get out of Key West. Like small town kids everywhere, we wanted to see the world—even if it was only as far away as Gainesville or Tallahassee. As we matured, the feeling of living 'fenced in' grew greater as we rode round and round the same little island, day after day. It seemed everyone knew our business and our parents found out about every little indiscretion.

My good friend John Hilke and I daydreamed constantly about heading out for parts unknown. The day after Christmas in 1962, we left on our first trip. We convinced our parents that at sixteen, we were old enough to be out on our own, and left on a five-day camping trip to the Everglades. The headquarters for the new Everglades National Park was at Flamingo, and consisted of a ranger station and a cleared area for campers.

There was little to do in the park, but we were thrilled at the feeling of freedom that came with being away from Key West and our parents. In a rented canoe, with two peanut butter sandwiches and a gallon of water, we paddled into the mysterious swamp. Within a couple of hours we were hopelessly lost, with every channel through every mangrove island looking the same.

The first alligator sighting had us paddling carefully and methodically, fearful at the thought of capsizing. The canoe felt extremely unstable as we imagined the grisly fate awaiting us should it tip over, but we soon became used to the sight of the small gators and our fear turned to complacency. Not yet concerned about being lost, we continued enjoying the sights, and then made the mistake of both leaning the same way at the same time to look at a fish in the water.

We instantly rolled over, and the metal canoe sunk before our shocked eyes. We were one hundred feet from shore, and without a word, both of us started thrashing toward a small island that would save our lives. No thought was given to the ranger's advice to stay calm and swim smoothly if we fell in. We both knew the gators were at our feet—about to roll us underwater at any second—and nothing was going to stop us from getting to land as quickly as we could.

The side of the island was a hard mud bank about three feet high, and we clawed desperately at the slippery slope. Finally out of the water and still in one piece, we caught our breath and assessed the dark situation. We had little hope of rescue before nightfall, since we didn't even know where we were ourselves. The ranger's dire warning about being caught in the swamp after dark was foremost in our minds, and we both knew we would have to rescue ourselves by raising the canoe.

I rejected John's contention that I was the better swimmer, and having no coin to toss, decided we would have the best chance of quickly floating the canoe if we tried together. With hearts pounding, we got hold of the bowline and dragged it to shore. Purely by the grace of God, we found our way back to Flamingo and received a good lecture, and then a horselaugh, from the rangers.

The Everglades trip only whetted our appetite for travel, and we made plans for a trip to California the following summer. John obtained a dilapidated two-wheel tow trailer, and we started constructing a crude camper for the long trip. By the time summer arrived, and our project unfinished, we decided to head for Smoky Mountain National Park in North Carolina, and sleep in my car.

With minimal objections from parents, we left with only enough money for gas, sodas, and baloney sandwiches. We did little except ride and see the country. In Georgia, we were shot at (or at least, a shot was fired) while we sat in a field eating someone's watermelon, and in Tennessee, we coasted for several miles down the mountain into Gatlinburg after running out of gas. It was an enjoyable, but unexciting cruise through the South.

The uneventful trip became memorable when we ran into a torrential rainstorm in Alabama while making our way home. Driving at night and unable to see the road, I pulled off the highway until the rain let up. We both fell asleep and were rudely awakened by a pounding on the side window as a half-dozen cops ordered us out of the car. The one at my door had his gun pointed at me, and the moment I opened the door, he grabbed my arm and threw me against the side of the car.

With legs spread and my hands across the hood, he roughly patted me down. John was out on the other side, and two officers started searching the car. "What are you boys doing here?"

"Nothing sir! Just sleeping."

"Just sleeping, huh? That where you boys like to sleep—in somebody's front yard?"

I looked for the first time, and saw that not only were we squarely on someone's lawn, but I had stopped less than ten feet from the front window of the house. "No sir! We don't like to sleep in people's yards. It was raining so hard last night, sir, I couldn't see where we were, sir, and I pulled off the road and we fell asleep. Honest, sir, I didn't know we were in anybody's yard."

"Yeah? Well, just what the hell business have you boys got in Selma?"

"Nothing sir. I didn't even know we were in Selma. We were just on our way home."

"Home, huh? Yeah, well where exactly is this Key West, Florida, place you got here on your driver's license?"

"It's an island one hundred-fifty miles south of Miami, sir."

"An island down at the end of Florida? Well now! You boys are a long ways from home, aren't you?"

"Yes sir."

"So, maybe you've been watching your TV set down there on your island and decided to come to Selma and get in on a few of these racial shenanigans, huh?"

"No sir! We don't know anything about any shenanigans, sir. I swear we were just passing through on the way home!"

"You boys go to school?"

"Yes sir. We both go to Key West High School."

"So, you boys are in high school and you never heard anything about these so-called civil rights demonstrations. Is that right?"

"No sir! I mean we've heard about them, but we didn't know there was any here. We were just on a trip to see the Smoky Mountains, sir. We hadn't ever been out of Florida, sir, and we just wanted to see the country."

"Okay now, let me get this straight. You just happen to be here in Selma with all this hullabaloo going on. You got $16 between the two of you. You're parked on this lady's lawn, right under her bedroom window. You're from some island down in Florida, and you got a momma and daddy who let you run all over the place at sixteen years old. Is that about right?"

"No sir. My Mom and Dad don't just let me run all over the place. They just thought I was old enough to do something like this."

"Well, it looks like they were wrong now, weren't they boy?"

After the deputies conferred for a minute, he turned me around and tapped his police club lightly against my arm. "Now, I'm going to give you boys some advice, and if you're smart, you'll take it . . . Go on over there and apologize to that lady for scaring the living hell out of her. Then, get in your car and head south, and don't ever let me see you in Selma again. I assure you that you won't get off so easily next time."

"Yes sir."

In September of 1964, along with a dozen of my classmates, I enrolled at the University of Florida in Gainesville. Most of us had never lived anywhere but Key West and had little experience with traveling. Freshmen were not allowed to have cars at state universities, but four of us piled our luggage in my recently purchased 1959 Ford and wound our way up U.S. Route 27 to Gainesville. All freshmen were a little lost, but for us the mainland university was a strange new world, and we had a lot to learn.

We vaguely understood that in college no one would be checking on class attendance, but were caught off guard by a classroom of three hundred students and a television monitor for a professor. Maintaining the self-discipline to attend the boring lectures was difficult, but adapting to the impersonal nature of university life was downright dispiriting. After a life of familiarity with teachers and administrators in our small Key West world, suddenly becoming little more than a social security number amongst thousands of other unfamiliar faces was a tough transition.

Like the classic small town boy who went to the big city, I was helpless with all the temptations. The girls, the parties, and the freedom to not attend classes took their toll. Even my roommate Allen McCrae, who was the son of a Federal District Court judge in Jacksonville, contributed to the problem since he liked to party as much as I did. My poor grade point average placed me on academic probation, and also not eligible for initiation into the brotherhood of the Alpha Tau Omega fraternity I had pledged.

Meanwhile back home, Key West High School had been integrated. For the first time, black and white students were in class together, and the all-black Douglas High School was being converted into Monroe County Junior College (MCJC). Along with Ben Lowe, Danny Roberts, Art Sheppard, Ed Swift, and several dozen other high school classmates, I enrolled for the school's first semester in the fall of 1965.

With so many familiar faces, it felt like a return to the comfortable days at Key West High School—minus the discipline. The faculty was a grab bag of unconventional characters. Some were escapees from the real world, hoping to find themselves at the end of the road. Others would not have been qualified to teach at a grade school, much less an established college, so they took what work they could get at a brand new school desperate for teachers. Some came for the love of the ocean or the party town reputation, and a few simply flew in on the days of their class and flew home when finished. Rounding out the faculty were several highly qualified professors—who were either tired of the stilted world of high-level academia or looking to wind down their careers in a more relaxed environment—and a number of true oddballs, who were rumored to have been kicked out of their former positions for being too loony.

Trapped in Key West

On the first day of class, we found the old cafeteria set up as the student union, and it became the social center of the school. It soon resembled a casino however, with money-stacked tables featuring bridge and poker games. Expecting to be stopped, everyone went easy at first, but the union soon turned into a raucous affair with jukebox blasting and cigarette smoke filling the air. The serious students avoided the clamorous union, and for a while it seemed nothing would be forbidden. The limit was reached however, when a cooler full of beer appeared and a professor was found to have joined our poker game. Alcohol was then formally banned, and professors were forbidden from gambling with students on school property.

Academic life at the new school was the polar opposite of the University of Florida. Informality ruled, and failing a class was harder than passing. Students and professors became friends and even socialized outside the classroom. Classes were sometimes held at a professor's apartment, featuring wine and cheese and far-out subject matters. One particular class even marched across the street each week to the bar of the black American Legion for their break.

Unexpectedly, the school decided to have a basketball team. Probably because the former Douglas High School had a fine gymnasium and the administration thought it would promote school spirit, tryouts were held and uniforms were purchased. On a whim, I decided to try out for the team. I loved to play basketball and was on the high school junior varsity team in the ninth and tenth grades. As my junior year approached however, Harold Allen, the head football coach, called me in for a heart-to-heart talk.

"Listen son. You've got a good future with my football team. You're probably going to be running back punts and kickoffs and starting at defensive back. Next year, you'll probably be a starting halfback as well. Now, I know you like to play basketball and baseball too, but the simple truth is that you're just not good enough to play all three sports. You need to concentrate on just one, and in my opinion it should be football. Now, you can be a solid performer for this team, or ride the bench if you want to keep up this three-sport business. So, what's it going to be?"

Football was the glory sport, and due to Coach Allen's harsh assessment of my athletic ability, I quit basketball and baseball, but never gave up my love of the sports. I was excited just to be trying out for a college team, and thrilled when I actually made the squad. Though there were some excellent ball players at the school, there were not that many willing to dedicate the time to the sport, and I made the team as a reserve player.

The stars of the team were three former Douglas High School players—Griff Thurston, Cedric Allen, and Raymond Navarro. Griff could shoot three pointers and drive like an NBA star. Cedric could leap to the top of the backboard, and Raymond could direct the team at point guard like the most accomplished college players. It was easy to see that without the segregated schools, they would have been stars at Key West High School, and possibly led the school to a state title.

Cedric died tragically young, but Raymond went on to a fine career in the military. Griff was by far the most talented, and had he attended Key West High School, would surely have received a major college scholarship and possibly had a shot at the NBA. However, he remained in Key West, and through the years we played together in several different basketball leagues.

As soon as I decided to attend MCJC, Aunt Rose, who worked for KLM Airlines in Miami, arranged a job for me with Southeast Airlines. It was a small carrier servicing the Key West to Miami run with a forty-passenger prop jet and two World War II vintage DC-3's. My position at Key West International Airport was called 'ticket agent,' but included everything from getting coffee for the manager to loading baggage on the planes. Though only making $1.10 per hour, I was thrilled to have my first indoor job. I quickly learned the simple tasks of writing tickets, stacking suitcases, and waving the plane in and out of its parking place.

Trapped in Key West

Paul Galagher, the stationmaster, was an irascible Yankee and another of those characters who seemed to have drifted south until he ran out of road in Key West. He was not a big man, but had the prickly manner and feisty temperament of a true New Yorker. Though he and I got along just fine, others were not always so lucky. Twice in two years, I pulled him off customers after he leaped over the baggage scale and physically assaulted them. With his fists flailing and spittle flying, extracting him from the traumatized passenger was like grabbing hold of a wildcat.

Paul cared little for the day-to-day operation of the airline, but quickly assessed my potential and put me in charge of the first flight of the day. Flight 530 was so named because it took off at 5:30 in the morning. It arrived from Miami at 5:00 a.m., and I had to be on the job at 4:30 a.m. to start ticketing passengers. Paul worked every flight with me at first, but soon started leaving me on my own for the ones with few passengers. Before long, I was working every flight by myself and thought little of writing the tickets, loading the baggage for forty passengers, checking them through the gate, and flagging the plane off.

For a nineteen-year-old college boy, arriving on the job at 4:30 each morning bordered on the incredulous. In high school, there had been few places to have a real blowout party, but by the time MCJC opened, several of my old friends—including Mike Wilson and Ed Swift—had places of their own, and many of our new northern friends lived in apartments. The parties were frequent and lively, and the out-of-town students gave us our first exposure to the folk music culture by playing their guitars and singing.

Though marijuana use was starting to catch on and we had recently heard of LSD and speed, drug use was minimal and discreet. The Key West Police Department was small and primarily staffed by local people known to us all. A number of the officers had been schoolmates, and there was a general tolerance of the parties as long as they only involved alcohol and not drugs.

Occasionally, the complaints of neighbors would require the police to tone down or end the party, and periodically, a show would be made by loading a paddy wagon with revelers and putting them in the 'drunk tank' for a few hours. The busts were usually good-natured, and there was a lot of pleading and laughing, as the officers filled the wagon with random partiers.

On my only trip in the wagon, I was not even a participant in the raided party. An apartment on White Street rented by a group of out-of-town students, was the source of the revelry. With a carload of friends, I arrived late from another party, and as we stepped from my car, a paddy wagon and two police cars suddenly appeared. Unbeknownst to me, Paul Sawyer stashed a flask of bourbon under the front seat of my car when the police appeared. When a search of the car revealed the liquor, we were all herded into the paddy wagon for 'possession,' and Paul, as the only one at the legal age of twenty-one, was blusteringly threatened with the charge of 'contributing to the delinquency of minors.'

We had little concern over the arrests and even less for the threatened charge against Paul. His father was the attorney for Monroe County, and while he would be angry with Paul, we knew there was no chance Paul would have any legal problems or that we would actually be charged with anything.

When the wagon was stuffed with merrymakers, Officers Robert "Cuban" Santana and George Lastres drove the overloaded wagon to the jail. One of the soused revelers had the brilliant idea that everyone should pile to one side of the wagon, so we could travel down the street with a starboard list. As everyone lurched to one side, Officer Santana turned the corner and the wagon teetered on two wheels, nearly turning over. We prisoners convulsed with laughter, until someone noticed a furious Officer Lastres pointing his 38-caliber 'police special' through the viewing window at us.

The 'drunk tank' cell contained only one other person when we arrived. He was a mountain of a man whom none of us had ever seen before. As we approached the barred enclosure, he stood at the door cursing and threatening the guard with both fists sticking through the steel bars. The cage-like cell sat in the middle of the room, and the officer in charge managed to get us into the cell as the wild man raged. The raving monster turned on us and we huddled together on one side of the cell, instantly sobered.

"All right, punks! Which one of you sissy boys wants his ass kicked first? I'm gonna beat the hell out of every one of you, so you might as well step forward and get it over with!"

He was a full head taller and one hundred pounds heavier than the biggest of us. My high school friend and teammate Mike Blatt, however, was not a man to be threatened by anyone. Though less than two hundred pounds and shorter than six feet, he played inside linebacker for the Florida State Seminoles, and made up for his lack of size with a ferocious toughness. "You wouldn't be including me in that threat, would you, asshole?"

"What? Why you punk! I'm gonna tear you up!"

Shockingly quick for his size and inebriated condition, the man charged forward and threw a wild punch at Mike's head. Faster than any of us could react, Mike ducked his head and charged forward. As if he were meeting a fullback at the one-yard line, he buried his shoulder in the man's chest and knocked the stunned attacker on his back with a perfect tackle.

Mike was immediately astride the dazed man, pounding him relentlessly. The guard, who had been so verbally abused by the belligerent man, stood at the cell door with a grin on his face and whispered, "Stop. Stop."

When Mike had battered the man into total submission, the guard opened the cell door, while the humiliated blowhard crawled to a corner. Tapping his left hand with his nightstick, the guard looked scornfully at the man for a minute and then chuckled, "Are you all right, mister tough guy?"

The guard then turned to us with a scowl on his face. "All right, everyone! Now you listen to me and listen good, because I'm only going to tell you this once! I will not have this fighting when I'm on duty! Now, you boys get the hell out of my jail cell, and don't ever come back!"

Early Years

With so many social diversions, making it to work in the morning was a major challenge. I got in the habit of keeping a black pair of pants and a white shirt in my car, so I could go directly to work after weekend parties. If I arrived too early, I occasionally caught a short nap under the front counter, and several of the regulars would look for me there if the front desk was not opened.

My supervisor, Paul, was a personal friend of the owner of Southeast Airlines and ran the Key West Terminal as if he were his partner. He was scrupulously honest with the company's money, and he showed up often enough and randomly enough to make certain the operation ran smoothly and efficiently. However, where they concerned him, he had little use for rules. When he assigned me to work the first flight alone five days a week, it was a clear violation of the rule requiring two people to work every flight. I never questioned his orders, and his saying, "If you can't handle it by yourself, give me a call," ensured I would never ask for help.

The major perk associated with my employment was being allowed to fly for free. Not only was I allowed to fly, but I could also let any of my family or friends fly for free as long as there was space available. I was reluctant at first to issue too many free tickets, but it became apparent that no one minded, and the forty-passenger plane sometimes had more free riders than it did paying customers.

With the Navy base still operating and the holdover Army personnel from the Cuban Missile Crisis, the flight often resembled a military plane. The service men received a 33 percent discount on a space available basis, but every duffle bag we weighed was over the forty-pound limit and the ticket discount was made up in overweight payments. Paul seemed to enjoy collecting the overweight charges, and expressed little sympathy for the homesick young soldiers—some on leave for the first time. However, Paul's sometimes callous attitude, combined with his zeal for helping friends, almost led to his downfall.

The last flight of the day was leaving and I filled the plane with standby military personnel. The doors were closed, the engines running, and the plane moving when Paul came running out on the tarmac with his arms crossed in an X—the signal for the plane to stop immediately. "I've got one more passenger to put on!"

"Sorry Paul. The plane is full."

"I don't care how full the damn plane is! Jimmy Yaccarino's daughter needs to get back to college, and I'm putting her on that plane!"

The pilots were frantically waving to us through the window, wondering what emergency had caused Paul to stop their taxiing. Paul's highly agitated state had them troubled, and when he signaled them to shut down the engines, everyone on the plane was concerned.

"But Paul, there's no place for her to sit!"

"Put her in the jump seat!"

"There's a pilot from National Airlines already in it."

"Look! This man never charges me for dinner in his restaurant, so take one of those military guys off! I need that seat!"

"Paul, I can't do that! Their baggage is already loaded and all of it is checked on to northern cities."

"Damn it! Where's the passenger manifest?"

"Over by the gate."

"Get me the name of the last soldier to get on the plane!"

As I raced to the gate, Paul signaled the stewardess to open the door. When I returned with the name, he was standing in the doorway of the plane. "James Watkins is the man's name."

Paul turned toward the aisle and made an announcement that shocked me to the core. "James Watkins! Please report to the terminal. You have an emergency phone call!"

I stood transfixed as the bewildered soldier leaped down the stairs and raced toward the terminal. As he disappeared, Paul signaled for Jimmy and his daughter to come out, and she hurriedly boarded the plane. Paul ignored me and had the plane pulling away faster than I thought possible.

I stood watching the plane leave, while my mind reeled at the consequences of Paul's actions. I was brought back to reality by the screaming of the soldier.

"Hey, wait! What are you doing? I have to be on that plane!"

The soldier ran out on the taxiway and raced after the plane at full speed with arms flailing. "Stop! Stop! Please stop! I have to be on that plane! It's an emergency!"

I hesitated for a moment, and seeing that Paul had disappeared, took off running after the soldier. As we ran down the runway chasing the huge propjet, I imagined us both in jail and the poor soldier being court-martialed for such a bizarre offense.

Blessedly, the teenaged soldier stopped running and turned to me—almost in tears, as I raced up to him. "I have to get home. My grandfather died, and my mother needs me. She's not taking it well and I think that phone call was about her."

We walked back to the terminal with me feeling as badly as he did. Pitifully he whispered, "What time is the next flight?

"I'm sorry. There are no more flights until tomorrow."

"You don't understand. This is a real emergency. My grandpa's dead, and my mother's not well. I have to get home right away!"

"I'm really, really sorry. Maybe you can rent a car, and get to the Miami Airport. There will be flights out all night."

"They won't let me rent a car. I'm not old enough."

"Well, our first flight is booked tomorrow, but I'll be here and I'll get you on it somehow."

"What about my bag? I don't even have a toothbrush."

"Your bag will be waiting for you when you arrive at home."

"Can I use your phone? That call for me got disconnected. I'm sure it was about my mother and I need to see what's happened."

"Sure."

Paul was nowhere to be found and the boy soldier was immensely relieved to find that his mother was all right. I could say nothing, but he speculated the mysterious emergency call was either work-related or a mistaken identity—incapable of even imagining the real reason. Several days later—probably at the behest of wiser family members—the soldier reported the incident to his superior officer. Paul was summoned to the Miami office and barely managed to talk his way out. I was forced to plead ignorance of the emergency phone call, consoling myself with the fact it was over and Paul had learned a lesson by almost losing his job.

When Paul returned from his dressing-down by the owner, he was chagrined, but in a New York sort of way. "Jesus, Joseph, and Mary! The story of my life. A thousand G.I. Joes going home on leave to get drunk with their buddies, and I got to pick the one poor bastard who's going to a freakin' funeral! How's that for luck?"

Because I was a part-time employee for the airline and worked almost exclusively the early morning shift, my afternoons and weekends were usually free. Bill Wickers had a sixteen-foot boat with a forty-horsepower outboard motor, and we derived a very substantial income by diving and fishing. Lobster was our primary target, and we supplemented the catch by spearing whatever large fish we saw during the day, and occasionally fishing for yellowtail and mutton snapper at night.

The ocean was practically devoid of recreational boats, and there were no others diving for lobster commercially. Once the lobster season started on August 1, we systematically covered every rock pile from Washerwoman Shoal to the Marquesas, and back up the north side to Snipe Point. While every rock pile was not loaded with lobster, none of them were ever dived on by others, and Bill and I consistently caught two to four hundred pounds per day—usually receiving about forty cents per pound.

In addition to the lobster, we normally speared about one hundred pounds of grouper and snapper each day, but would occasionally run across a rock pile covered with bait fish—in which case, we might spear four or five hundred pounds. We saw many jewfish up to three hundred pounds apiece, but usually left them because of the low price and the difficulty of handling such large fish in a small boat. Jewfish had to be sold to Freckles Higgs at his fish market, and he rarely paid more than ten to fifteen cents per pound. When he was desperate for fish, he would let me know he would pay as much as twenty-five cents per pound, and we would then actively search for the fish.

Early Years

Jewfish and grunts had long been the favorite fish of the native Conchs, and are as different as any two species in the ocean. The jewfish grows to over four hundred pounds, but is best eaten when weighing between seventy-five and one hundred-fifty pounds. The grunt, by contrast, is a bony little fish that rarely weighs a pound.

The one thing both fish have in common, is very little demand for the species outside of Key West. The names of the fish themselves are not conducive to successful marketing, and when you add in the facts that the jewfish is huge and exceptionally slimy, and the grunt is small and exceptionally bony, you end up with two low-priced fish as the staple foods of depression-era Key West.

The name of the jewfish was recently changed to goliath grouper by federal fishery managers. Some years ago, the name of the dolphin fish was changed to mahi-mahi to prevent confusion with Flipper the bottlenose dolphin and to promote easier marketing of the fish. The jewfish name was ostensibly changed for similar practical reasons, but the Conchs—suspecting more duplicitous motivations—have resisted the change. Doris Rolle, a black lady with a long Bahamian heritage, was suspiciously amused when she heard the new name and laughingly said, "Honey, as long as they call it *black* grouper, I'll be calling it jewfish!"

Freckle's Fish market was the place to sell jewfish in Key West, and since his price was usually about ten cents per pound while Miami gave 4 or five cents, Dad sold most of the large ones to Freckles. Freckles also paid cash for everything he bought and had little use for checks or receipts.

Through high school and college, whenever available, I was Dad's delivery boy. It was not unusual for me to haul four or five large jewfish to Freckles one day and then have him call for more the next day. His market was little more than a six-foot-wide hole in the wall at Thompson's Ice Plant on Caroline Street, but he was known to every person in Key West, and sold thousands of pounds of seafood each week

Trapped in Key West

Having grown up around the docks and fishermen, I was exposed to many different types of abrasive personalities. Some fishermen were just loud and obnoxious, while others were always spoiling for an argument. Still others were constantly looking to stir up trouble, and a few thought kids were nothing but headaches and should never be around a fish house. All of them, however, were tough men, and they all worked long, hard hours in a backbreaking profession.

Freckles Higgs though, was about as crusty and irritable as any man I had ever met. To him, I was just a delivery boy, which was only a small step up from a flunky. My usual greeting was, "Put them over here" or "I needed that fish an hour ago. What took so long?" When he was in a good mood, it was, "Bubba, you just in time. Gimme a lift with these boxes over here" or "Thanks, now get out of here, so I can get some work done."

Yet, for some inexplicable reason I liked Freckles and looked forward to delivering to him. Each trip produced an endless stream of invective against all those who made his life miserable. Ida Kennedy was a "pain in the ass" who always wanted a different or fresher cut. Joe Rolle always "bitched about the price being too high," so Freckles "fixed him good" by telling him he was out of turtle steak when he actually had a cooler full. Then, that Mrs. Waite—who was, not just a pain in the ass, but also a "royal pain in the ass"—was always holding her nose when she bought her fish, and making comments like, "Have you ever thought about cleaning this place once in a while, Mr. Freckles?"

His number one nemesis however, was Sea Farms Inc., the company that bought out Thompson's and became his landlord. Sea Farms Inc. had a grand agenda for the fishing business in Key West, and Freckle's little hole-in-the-wall operation did not fit into their plans. Each day, there was a new outrage from the "Northerners who don't know a damn thing about Key West or how to run a business." They did get Freckles out eventually, and we lost contact after I left for college and his market closed.

Early Years

Some years later, when Freckles was long out of business and I had opened a fish market of my own on Duval Street, I heard he had been felled by a stroke. I was surprised shortly after to be contacted by his daughter who said Freckles wanted to see me.

Upstairs in bed in a house on Elgin Lane, I found him partially paralyzed and very feeble. I quickly found that though he was physically incapacitated, the old fire was still there. He immediately lit into me for stabbing him in the back, claiming he had treated me like a son and taught me everything he knew about the fish market business and then I went out and opened one of my own. He concluded with a dire warning: "When I get out of this bed, I'm going to open back up and put you right out of business! And you can count on that!"

Though he was still feisty, there was little doubt in my mind that Freckles would never get out of bed again. After many years of delivering and selling to Freckles, he was a familiar person to me and had become even cordial toward me at times, but I never felt like he treated me as a son. As I listened to him rant, I was nevertheless surprised I felt a certain affection for the old man and wanted to put his mind at ease.

I calmed him by explaining that I thought he was retired, and would never have opened a fish market if he had still been in business. Furthermore, feeling certain he was near the end, I assured him when he was ready to open a new market, I would close mine.

My conciliatory words relaxed him, and he actually started to make some friendly small talk. "How's your daddy? . . . Is Willy Wickers still alive? . . . How many jewfish are you selling?"

I had not known Freckles outside of his market, and never heard him ask conversational questions. His cordial manner caused me to realize that with his family and friends, he was probably a very different person than I had known. His final words were kind and made me glad I had gone to see him one last time. "You not gonna hold it against me when I open back up . . . eh bubba?"

"No, Freckles. Of course not."

Trapped in Key West

Danny Roberts and I were friends in high school, but began hanging out together more often at MCJC. After our first year at the college, we decided to do something different, and with the help of Aunt Rose—who was then a travel agent—planned a European trip. American college kids were traipsing all over Europe at the time, and Danny and I wanted to get in on the action. Neither of us were backpacking types and we definitely didn't want to travel as the hippies did—crashing for the night anywhere they could find shelter. With our extremely limited funds, Rose went to work and found us incredibly cheap airfare and accommodations for the entire trip. We weren't thrilled with her meticulously-planned itinerary that put us on a strict travel schedule, but we couldn't possibly have arranged a trip on our own.

With $5-a-night hotel rooms prepaid and $200 each in our pockets, we flew to New York for the first leg of our trip. The eight-hour layover in New York did not bother us because we wanted to see the 'Big Apple,' and had become friends with a boy at the college who made us promise to look up his father at the family bar in Manhattan. No sooner had we given the address to the taxi driver, than we noticed he kept looking at us through the rearview mirror.

With him constantly watching us, it was an uncomfortable ride, but we attributed it to the reputed strangeness of New Yorkers. When we arrived in front of the bar, the driver turned full around and looked us in the face. "You boys sure this is where you want to go?"

"Yes sir. This is the address and that's the name of the bar. A friend of ours owns it."

"Really? Well, you want me to wait here for you."

"No thanks, we'll be here a while."

"Oh well. To each his own."

As the taxi pulled away, we were left with an uneasy feeling. "What the heck gives with that guy?"

"I'm telling you Peter, that's just the way New Yorkers are."

The room was large and dark, and when our eyes adjusted

we sat on stools at the far end of the bar. There were only eight or ten people in the place, but it took a while for the bartender to approach us. "What can I do for you boys?"

"Is Mr. Magelli here?"

"Mr. Magelli? You want to talk to the owner?"

"Yes, please."

He stared at each of us trying to figure out what two boys wanted with the old man. Apparently reasoning we were looking for the younger Magelli, he asked, "Which one? The father or the son?"

"Oh, I didn't know Tony would be here. The son, please."

"Sorry, he's not here."

"Oh well, then the father."

"Sorry, he's not here either."

"Do you know when he'll be back?"

"Soon maybe. Now you boys want something to drink, or not?"

"I guess we'll have a couple of draft beers while we wait."

Two men came in and sat shoulder to shoulder at the long, empty bar—a little too close for comfort we both thought as we moved slightly farther apart. After he served them, the bartender came straight over to us and said, "So, what are you boys up to?"

"We go to junior college with Tony in Key West, and he told us to be sure and look up his Dad when we got to New York."

"Key West, huh? . . . What did he tell you about the bar?"

"Nothing really. He just gave us the name and address."

"So, he didn't tell you it was a homosexual bar?"

"What? Homosexual bar! This is a bar for homosexuals?"

"What are you blind, kid? You think those two there are snuggling up to tell business secrets? Look around, what do you see?"

"Whoaaa! You're right! Now I see what you mean."

"Ahh. The light goes on. Now, are you boys queer?"

"What? No way we're queer, man! I mean, not that there's anything wrong with it, you know—but we both like girls."

Trapped in Key West

"That's what I thought. Now you boys get on out of here before you end up in trouble. Go see the Empire State Building or something. I'll tell Tony you came by to see the old man."

The New York incident proved to be the fitting start of a European trip that opened the eyes of two island boys to the ways of the outside world. Our flight from New York arrived in Lisbon on time, but our suitcases were not so lucky. Iberia Airlines assured us they would find our bags and we should go ahead to the hotel and wait. An hour and a half and $37 later, the taxi arrived at our $5 hotel room. We were warned by Rose to always take the bus or shuttle from the airports, and the shocking taxi fare had seriously depleted our cash supply.

Our room was also a problem. Though we had not expected the Ritz, a double bed that took up the entire room and a bathroom down the hall was far from what we had imagined. Since we put our traveler's checks in our carry-on bags and then checked them through in New York, we were not only without our suitcases, but without money as well. Aunt Rose made us carry a toothbrush and change of clothes in our carry-on bags, but we hadn't wanted to be burdened with carrying them around in New York, so we had nothing but our wallets, passports, and the clothes on our back.

We waited anxiously at the hotel, fearful of missing the call from Iberia, and tried to imagine what to do if our luggage was never found. The room was so small, it was necessary to climb over the bed in order to open the tiny window allowing in a bit of fresh air. We tried waiting in the room, but with the New York experience fresh in our minds, we moved down to the small lobby after perching on our respective edges of the bed for a few minutes.

Suffering from jet lag, we waited all day and into the evening for our luggage. The airline didn't call until 11:00 that night, and then refused to deliver the bags to the hotel. When we rousted the hotel owner from his sleep, he explained there were no buses or airport shuttles until the morning and we would have to take a taxi to the airport.

Early Years

In our unreasonable state of exhaustion and misery, we decided to get our luggage before it was stolen, and flagged a taxi. We stared at each other in bewilderment when we arrived at the airport ten minutes later and the driver said, "That will be $3." After spending $37 to get from the airport to our hotel, we felt like first-class chumps. The driver made us feel even worse when he said he would wait and take us back to the hotel for $2, since $5 was the standard round trip fare to the airport.

Mercifully relieved, we slept straight through until the next evening. By then, we had spent two days in Lisbon without seeing anything but the inside of a taxi. We nevertheless woke up invigorated and ready to make up for lost time by sampling the nightlife of the cosmopolitan city. Not having learned our lesson with taxi drivers, we asked ours to take us to the hottest nightspot in Lisbon.

We noticed immediately upon entering that there was no band, and as our eyes adjusted, we saw we were the only customers in the place. We turned to leave when a pretty young hostess took us by the arm and led us to a booth. No sooner had we sat down than two very sexy ladies sat next to us and a bottle of champagne arrived. "Wait a minute," Danny said to the waitress in Spanish. "We didn't order champagne! How much does it cost?"

The waitress did not hesitate or answer, and proceeded to unscrew the cap on our bottle of champagne, while the ladies cuddled close and assured us the cost was a pittance. We sat dumbly as the ladies told us, in a confusing mix of English, Spanish, and Portuguese, how handsome and exciting we were. When Danny asked the girls what they did for a living, they both laughed and the lights in our simple brains went on once again.

Realizing we were being solicited by prostitutes, and abashed that we had once again naively fallen into an embarrassing situation, Danny became angry and said we were leaving. The girls refused to let us out of the booth and one started cursing him when he nudged her, while the other tried to mollify the situation. A huge, mean-looking bouncer appeared from nowhere, and demanded to know what the problem was. Danny tried explaining in Spanish that we wished to leave, but the ladies wouldn't let us out of the booth.

The man became very angry and wanted to know what the ladies had done to offend us. The women started loudly defending themselves and calling us names in Portuguese that even I could understand. Fearful for our lives, Danny broke in, "Wait, wait, wait! The only reason we want to leave is because my friend is sick. He ate something at the restaurant that didn't agree with him and he's about to throw up all over the table."

Both ladies immediately moved away, and the bouncer, after looking me over with suspicion said, "Okay, pay for the champagne and get out of here!"

"All right, how much is it?"

"Forty dollars."

Danny could not believe what he was hearing. "Forty dollars! You've got to be kidding me! It had a screw top! I never even saw champagne with a screw top!"

"Forty dollars!"

"But we didn't even drink any of it!"

"Forty dollars!!"

"Come on, man. Give us a break. We didn't even order it. They just brought it over to the table without asking us."

"Okay *cabrones*. Let's go into my office and discuss this."

We both stared at him for a minute, and reached for our wallets at the same time. With our tails between our legs and having been embarrassingly naive two times in a row, we escaped to the dingy streets. In our newly enlightened state, we easily recognized the red-light district as we searched for a cab. Enthusiasm for our European vacation had been seriously damaged, but we left for Madrid the next day, hopeful it would finally fulfill our European expectations.

My grandmother was born in Bilbao and left Spain to live with an uncle in Cuba at the age of twenty. Though I had never met a single relative from Spain, I was very conscious of a familial connection to the country, and felt far more comfortable with a language that sounded familiar to me and one Danny could converse in fluently. Though we wanted to sightsee like every other tourist, we were most excited about the cultural favorites of bullfighting and flamenco dancing.

Once again, we turned to the trusty taxi driver for advice, and asked him to take us to a flamenco establishment the local people would patronize. On a dark street, he dropped us off in front of a building that looked to be a thousand years old, and told us to go through the unmarked door. With our newly developed street smarts kicking in, we shrewdly deduced that we had once again been delivered to a house of ill repute, and shaking our heads at our continuing stupidity, turned to leave.

But on an impulse, I opened the heavy old door and saw steps leading down to a dark basement. To our delight, emanating up from the smoky darkness were the spirited sounds of Spanish guitars, castanets, and clicking heels. We walked tentatively down the stairs to a large dark room with a well-lit stage in the middle and tables all around. On the stage were gorgeous, whirling flamenco dancers. The room seemed on fire with the frenzied strumming of the guitars and the wild dancing of the sensuous *señoritas*.

A matronly woman motioned us to a table and immediately delivered a large pitcher of fruit punch. The entire room was devoid of decoration, and the tables—which were almost all occupied—had nothing on them except the punch. I had never been a fan of dancing, but the flamenco I was seeing for the first time had me hypnotized. The rest of the patrons seemed as enthralled as we were. There were no conversations going on, and everyone applauded enthusiastically after each dance.

We drank down the pitcher of tangy fruit punch, and another one appeared at the table. We were both feeling on top of the world and wanted something to drink with alcohol in it. Danny asked if we could order a beer or liquor, and was told they only served the punch. Halfway through the second pitcher, we were ready to get on the stage ourselves, and realized the punch must have more in it than the sliced oranges and lemons. "What did you say she called it, Danny?"

"Sangria."

"Sangria? You mean like blood?"

"Yep. That's right, just like blood."

We remember the lady bringing the third pitcher, and vaguely recall standing outside the building waiting for a taxi. We awoke in the morning with the hostile glare of the Spanish sun in our eyes. People were walking by and staring at us in disgust as we sat on the sidewalk, leaning against the building. After the flamenco, we sat down to rest while waiting for a taxi and fell asleep. Our heads pounded, our stomachs were sick, and we were shading our eyes from the sun, as we made our way back to the hotel room and crashed out for the day.

We had then spent four days in Europe without seeing a thing, and vowed from then on, we would be the perfect tourists. With a sobering four-day education under our belts, we were first in line the following morning at the Prado Museum. Aunt Rose had assured us the paintings would take our breath away. We dutifully paid our respects to Goya, Velázquez, and Aunt Rose— grinning at each other, as we proclaimed each somber painting to be magnificent.

We were most impressed by *El Greco*, the adopted Spanish artist who was born in Greece. The next day, after a neat trip to *El Greco's* walled city of Toledo, we returned in time for the afternoon bullfight. Aunt Rose was thrilled she'd been able to obtain the tickets. The *matador, El Cordobes*, was the rock star idol of Spanish bullfighting. According to Aunt Rose, his fights were sold out for years in advance and tickets were scalped for ungodly amounts of money. She was sure we would see "the most fantastic *matador* in the history of bullfighting," and the experience would stay emblazoned in our memories for the rest of our lives.

With several beers under our belts—the first alcohol since the *sangria*—we entered the *Plaza de Toros*. The impressive ring, the pageantry, and the air of excitement were everything Aunt Rose had predicted. Our seats were down low and next to the celebrity section where the famous actress Rita Hayworth was the honored guest. The *matadors, banderilleos*, and mounted *picadors* paraded through the ring, and *El Cordobes* brought the crowd to a frenzy of cheers and piercing whistles.

The whirling cape of the warm-up *matadors* brought infectious cries of *"Ole!"* from the excited crowd. We were caught up in the action, and bellowed like natives with each pass of the bull. When the *banderilleos* came out to further anger the fearsome bull by piercing his hide with their bright paper-tasseled darts, the stadium again rocked with whistles and applause. When the mounted *picadors* gored the bull with their long lances and the blood started flowing, the crowd cheered, but Danny and I were abruptly sobered. The reality of bullfighting was suddenly right before us, and our fine seats were way too close.

Several passes later, the bull stopped charging and stood confused and fatigued. With the brightly-colored *banderilla* darts hanging from his neck and blood running to the ground, he looked more pathetic than fearsome, but still the people cheered. When the *picadors* made another charge with their lances, the bull made one last run around the ring, slinging blood into the stands—barely missing us, but splattering Miss Hayworth. The crowd was at a fever pitch when the *matador* applied the *estocada* with his curved sword, and the bull wobbled around drunkenly before finally dropping to the ground.

Though both my mother and Danny's were of Spanish blood, we had little stomach for the favored sport of our ancestors. It wasn't that we objected to bullfighting, or even that the bull was killed in the end. It was just that we didn't enjoy watching it happen. For Aunt Rose's sake, we waited for *El Cordobes* and watched as the crowd went insane with every pass, but left before the bull was killed. We both agreed with Aunt Rose however, that the one bullfight would stay with us for the rest of our lives.

Trapped in Key West

Back for our second year at MCJC, the administration had the school more firmly under control. There was no gambling allowed and poker was banned—even if just for fun. Fraternization between teachers and students was cut to a minimum and the atmosphere in class actually resembled an institution of higher learning. After graduation, it was one uneventful semester back at UF and then on to Florida Atlantic University in Boca Raton.

Florida Atlantic University had only recently opened its doors, and was limited to being an upper division school. Its few buildings were set in the middle of an obsolete Air Force base, and students parked their cars on the deserted runways while attending class. Ben Lowe, Tommy Roberts, David Sellers, George Parks, Art Sheppard, and I rented a four-bedroom place at a student apartment building near the school called Boca Hall. Our apartment was essentially in the woods, as the city of Boca Raton had not yet expanded that far west toward the Everglades.

FAU was a far different world than hometown MCJC. With only upper division students working on their majors, classes were serious and intense. All students had their freshman and sophomore years behind them and the mature students were now thinking toward graduation and careers. Outside of the classroom though, little had changed.

Boca Hall was for all practical purposes an unsupervised college dorm. There was a party somewhere every night and the weekends were a two-day binge. Surprisingly however, drug use was low, and even the biggest drinkers frowned on those who puffed or popped. Serious study was difficult at Boca Hall, so the large new library at FAU was the place of choice to cram for an exam.

The woods surrounding the apartments were lousy with wildlife. With the first paycheck from my part-time job at the IBM warehouse, I purchased an old shotgun, and we added dove, quail, and rabbit to our menu. Soon enough, someone complained about the shooting, and we were forced to give up hunting outside our front door. George brought five dove traps from Key West, which were very successful until the armadillos discovered them and routinely destroyed the traps while dining on our catch.

On the west side of the university, the runways ended in woods, so we moved our hunting to the new location. None of us actually knew anything about hunting, but we found nothing difficult about shooting small creatures with a shotgun. The palmetto scrub woods were perfect for quail, and we traipsed through the rattlesnake-infested brush in our tennis shoes, taking turns with firing the gun and flushing the birds. We knew nothing of licenses, bag limits, private property, or seasons, and innocently hunted where and when we felt like it.

Southern Manor Golf Course opened on the west side of the turnpike, which was then completely within the Everglades. Because there were few customers, they allowed college students to play for fifty cents after 3:00 p.m. In the late afternoon, the fairways were alive with birds and animals, including deer, turkeys, and bobcats.

Our attention was particularly drawn to a small lake full of ducks. Real northern ducks were rarely seen in Key West, and since the entire county is a bird sanctuary, it was illegal to shoot them. None of us had ever tasted duck, but we knew it was supposed to be a gourmet's delight, and made a plan to take a few of them. Just before dark, we hid in the woods with the shotgun, waiting for the last golfer to finish. The pond was on the other side of the fairway directly in front of us, and there were several dozen ducks slowly paddling around.

I had the gun, and was to run directly at the huddled ducks, while David ran to my left and Ben to the right. Barefoot and in shorts, they were to dive in the lake and retrieve whatever birds I managed to shoot. As we tore across the fairway, I noticed a man fishing on the opposite side of the narrow lake—directly behind the ducks. Since we were looking for food and not sport, I intended to fire while the birds were clustered in the water, but I hesitated as we got close, realizing the man fishing would be directly in the line of fire.

Trapped in Key West

When we were almost to the lake, the birds flew, and I was able to get off two shots, downing three birds. Ben and David quickly retrieved them and we crashed through the woods to my car as if the entire Palm Beach County SWAT Team was after us. Crazed with the thrill of the lightning strike, we congratulated each other on the successful raid and replayed the action a dozen times on the way back to the apartment.

David said that once he noticed the old black man fishing on the opposite bank, he could not take his eyes off him, fearing the man might be accidentally hit by the birdshot. As we ran toward the lake, the man was sitting on his haunches with his knees drawn up comfortably and holding a very long cane pole. When he first noticed us, he sat up straight, craning his neck to see what was going on. When he spied the shotgun, he stood up and stared wide-eyed at us as we ran directly toward him. When he saw the gun pointed in his direction, he threw his fishing pole high into the air and took off running. The moment I fired, he dove to the ground and covered the back of his head with his hands.

We later learned the man was an employee of the club and frequently fished after work. Like true mindless college kids, we laughed ourselves sick at the frenetic scene that could have been from an old Keystone Kops movie. It was days later before we started feeling guilty over the terror the old man must have felt during a time of extreme racial tension throughout America. To our relief, we learned the old man told the story to anyone who would listen, feeling the joke was on him once he realized we were just after the ducks.

Like triumphant warriors, we related our daring exploit to our roommates, as we cleaned our prizes over a cooler full of Budweisers. That evening, we prepared our gourmet meal and raved about how good the awful-tasting ducks were. Several hours later, we were all up with severe stomach cramps, and spent the night commiserating with each other and wondering why the ducks had made us all so sick. The next day, we found out from a friend that we had dined on coots, which was roughly the equivalent of eating seagulls at home.

Early Years

Fraternities at FAU were only as old as the school, but like the University of Florida, being a member of one conferred an acceptable social status. All other students were known at best as independents and at worst as geeks. None of us were actually geeks in the modern picture of the word, but we all disdained fraternity life, feeling we were members of a more elite group—the Key West boys.

Many of our new friends were fascinated with the thought of growing up in Key West, imagining it as some sort of cloistered island with an inbred population of feuding families who hung together against all outsiders. The strange things people thought about Key West were disconcerting at first, and we tried to fit in by making it sound as normal a place to grow up as any other. It wasn't long however, before we started having fun with the misconception and played up to the flawed thinking.

We liberally sprinkled our sentences with exaggerated Conch dialect and embellished the stories of intermarriage and suspicion of all outsiders. Everyone was our "bubba" and all the girls had nice "boongies." When we were surprised at something said, we countered with the traditional, "Go on boy!" or the Conchs' common response of astonishment, "godahell." We amused and puzzled everyone—including ourselves—with pithy Conch sayings we made up or used completely out of context like; *time is longer than rope—check your baggage down at the bus station—*and, *that same street goes uptown and downtown.* Soon, we were greeted all over campus with a lively "go on boy!" and even "your mumma" was finally accepted as a benign substitute for damn, rather than a personal insult.

We introduced the game of corkball and it became the rage at Boca Hall. The boys flailed away with their broom handles at the spinning cork, as we made it curve, drop, jump, and flutter. The most athletic boys soon picked up the skill needed and we had a very competitive league going at the apartment building.

139

Trapped in Key West

When we saw the notice for the school championship in flag football, we decided to enter. Though it was open to everyone, it was essentially a fraternity championship since no one else seemed able to field a team at the predominately commuter university. As the first and only independent team entered, we were looked upon with derision by the cooler fraternity teams. Without team uniforms, we played in white skivvy shirts, which only added to our uncultured image.

Along with our six Key West boys, we added Bob Madge and Stu Weinstein to round out a team. Stu had become our close friend at Boca Hall and was a star football player at Norland High School in Miami. He was a large man who was both nimble and tough, and went on to become Director of Security for the Miami Dolphins. With Stu, Tommy, and David on the line, we had three really big men who were deceptively fast and agile in a game that required speed and finesse.

Without a practice or a single preset play, we took the field for our first game. We were fully expected to be a joke team and everyone anticipated an easy victory against us in the double elimination tournament. Making up plays in the huddle, we unexpectedly won game after game. The fraternity teams were frustrated and angered at the athleticism of our ragtag team, but stopped short of fighting—unsure of what other skills we might exhibit. When we won the school championship, there was little sportsmanship exhibited by the losers, and none of them accepted our invitation to the blowout victory party back at Boca Hall.

By the summer of 1969, our crew at FAU had all dispersed, and I had one semester left before graduation. Art fell in love and got married, while Ben decided he'd had enough fun and went home to work. David's wife Cindy knew he was having too much fun and aborted his college career. George gave up his avocation as a pool hustler when he became serious about his education and moved into the new on-campus dorm. Tommy finished over two years of commuting from Key West and graduated with a master's degree in education.

Early Years

Tommy graduated from Key West High School the year before me, but we became good friends when we both worked at Southeast Airlines. At FAU, we called him Dr. Jekyll because the serious student became such a different person when he was partying. However, when it came to his calling as an educator, he was all business. After graduation, he returned to teach at Key West High and went on to become one of the youngest principals in the school's history.

Tommy often spoke of his ambition to be in charge at Key West High School, and by the time he was appointed, my oldest daughter Lauren was in the eleventh grade. In his first year, he was already talked about by parents and students as the finest principal the school had ever had. It was also assumed he would move on to become Superintendent of Public Instruction, and the future of Tommy and our children looked very bright.

It seemed the best of times and Tommy was sublimely happy. Then shockingly, he was tragically struck down by a heart attack after his first year as principal. Tommy made such an impression in such a short time that the entire island was devastated, and the community's most hallowed sports site—Key West High School Stadium—was renamed after him.

7

Different Families

I met Monica in the summer of 1965. Having finished my first year at the University of Florida, I was home for the summer and about to start classes at the new Monroe County Junior College. For many years, the Elks Club sponsored a teen dance every Friday night of the summer at their hall on Duval Street. As an eighteen-year-old college student, I was feeling a little too old for the teen dances, but with the closing of Pizios Drive-In, it was the best place to see everyone I knew and maybe even find a date for Saturday night.

About halfway through a late summer dance, I caught up on talking with all my friends and started checking out the girls. I noticed a table on one side with four girls having a good time laughing and talking. I didn't know any of them, but couldn't take my eyes off one of the girls.

Unable to stop staring, I kept looking at her from different angles to see if she was really as beautiful as I first thought. Even while talking to others, I kept glancing over at her. I finally told myself she was too young for me and that's why I had never seen her before.

Try as I might to ignore her, I still found myself looking her way. I studied her movements and her laugh, looking for some fault to would ease my momentary obsession. When she stood up, I saw she had a beautiful figure to go with her beautiful face, and was convinced I had to meet her.

Different Families

My friends noticed my inattention with them and kept asking me what I was looking at. I repeatedly said, "Nothing," but sooner or later, I had to ask someone if I was to find out who she was. I knew that asking my friends could be embarrassing, but despite all of their exaggerated pointing, gesticulating, and extra loud, "Which one? The blonde or the brunette? You mean those really young girls over there?" the girls never seemed to notice us, and I found out what I wanted to know.

"Mary Immaculate girls," said Bill. So they attended the Catholic high school, which explained why I had never seen them before.

"I think the one you're talking about is Greg Barber's little sister," said Ben. I knew Greg casually as he was a year ahead of me in high school and had been the catcher for the high school baseball team.

"Man, she's only about thirteen years old," laughed Bill. My heart sank.

"No she's not," said Herbie. "She's at least fifteen, and maybe even sixteen." I was instantly relieved—realizing she was young, but still possible.

I put my friends off by agreeing she was just too young, but found I could not stop looking over at her. My mind was flustered, thinking "Ask her to dance" one minute, and "Forget it, she's too young" the next. It was finally settled for me when someone else asked her to dance. Fearful of losing her before I ever even met her, I made up my mind to dance with her on the next song.

A little unsure of myself, I nevertheless walked over and asked her to dance. She stared at me for the longest time with one of those "Who are you?" looks, and for a moment, I thought she was going to say "No." I pictured all my friends watching intently and then hooting and laughing if she turned me down. Then mercifully, she gave a big smile and said, "Sure."

We stayed on the dance floor for three or four songs. The last dance was a slow one, and I felt as if we were the only ones on the floor. Half an hour before, I had been thinking of five or six girls

Trapped in Key West

I wanted to take out. The last thing I wanted was just one girl, but after five minutes of holding her close, I was already imagining her as my girlfriend. Abandoning all of my how-to-get-the-chick rules, I impetuously asked afterwards if I could sit with her, and we both ignored our friends for the rest of the night.

We wanted to go out the following night, but Hurricane Betsy took an unexpected turn from the Bahamas, and with it bearing down on us, we knew that would be impossible. Though hurricane hunter planes supplied us with some notice of hurricanes, life on the island went on as usual until the winds actually started picking up, and I can't recall that any thought was given to calling off the dance the previous evening.

The night of the hurricane, Monica and I talked on the phone for hours as the wind howled. What we talked about I can't recall, but neither of us wanted to hang up and the conversation was as comfortable as if we were the same age and had known each other for years. We made plans to meet at the dance the following Friday, and only the phone lines going down got us to stop talking.

After a lifetime of living in tiny run-down apartments, my parents had moved into their first home on Raccoon Key during my freshman year at the University of Florida. Hurricane Betsy, which went on to slam the Gulf Coast, was memorable in Key West primarily for the storm surge which followed. Raccoon Key, a small island next to Key West proper, was renamed Key Haven when homes started being built. When Betsy came through, Key Haven was inundated, and the rising water came up to floor level in the new house. Dad's lobster traps, which were usually the first victims of a hurricane, were spared by being in the deep water, and our only real loss was a yard full of fresh sod that floated away.

With electricity restored, the dance came off as planned the following Friday. Monica and I danced every slow dance and most of the fast ones, while my friends teased me unmercifully about "robbing the cradle." I didn't care what they said, I was in love and didn't care who knew. I drove her home after the dance, and we made a movie date for the following night.

Different Families

As a hotshot young college boy, I expected to slide in on Saturday night and really impress her parents. Donald and Ann Barber were both beauticians and lived above Donald's Beauty Shop, which they owned. Unlike my parents, who were uncomfortable with people they didn't know, Donald and Ann dealt with the public every day, and were sizing me up as soon as I walked into the room.

Donald and Ann Barber, Monica's parents

Unbeknownst to me, I was to be Monica's first date alone with a boy in the car. Though she'd had a number of boyfriends and been on double dates, sixteen was considered the age for dating and she was not quite there. She also neglected to tell them I was a college student who looked even older than my eighteen years. I could see they were none too thrilled with me, but after a whispered meeting in the other room, they allowed us to go out with an 11:00 p.m. curfew.

The next day when I called, Monica was in tears and said her parents would not allow us to go out again. I was caught off guard, but felt if I could just talk to them, I would convince them my intentions toward their daughter were honorable.

Trapped in Key West

Donald was very nice, but firm: "Peter, you're probably a very nice young man, but you are too old for my daughter and this will never work out. You just need to find someone else until Monica is out of high school."

Monica and I were devastated, but too much in love to allow it to end there. While I would have been willing to sneak out with her, Monica would not go against her parents' order. Instead, she did what every teenager does—wear them down little by little. *Is it all right if I talk to him at the dance? Can I dance with him? Well, what about just one dance a night? Can he sit with me? What if there are other people at the table? Can we talk on the phone? Please! Just once a week for five minutes? I'm almost sixteen, and you're still treating me like a baby. Besides, he's a really nice boy. If you would just get to know him, I know you would like him. Can't he just go with us to the wedding next week? You'll both be there, what harm can there be in that? Please? Please! Pretty please?"*

The same scene was played out for Monica and me years later with our own four daughters. We made a rule that the girls could not go out with a boy more than one year ahead of them in school, yet each managed to find an unacceptable older boy. Though we were very familiar with the method of breaking down a parent's resistance, we had to face a whole different set of arguments. *"Daaad! This is the '90s, not the '60s! Kids are much more mature today . . . I'm the only girl at Key West High School who's not allowed to go out with a senior!"* And then the one that always caused the biggest battle: *"But you and mom were three years apart when you started going out! Why was it okay for you, but not for me? I can't even believe that you guys are being soooo hypocritical!"*

Monica finally wore down her father, and Donald agreed to allow me to attend a wedding with the family. Monica and I were thrilled to be out together with the approval of her parents—even if they were right there at the table with us. Though she had been warned that it did not mean we could date, we knew it was the breakthrough we needed. I was already imagining it was Monica and I at the altar and wondering what our children would look like.

Different Families

Even then, I knew I had 'lost my cool' over her, but was unable to help myself.

Donald and Ann tried to stick to the no-dating rule, but like typical teenagers, we broke them down over a period of time with incrementalism. First, I would stop by after school just to say hi and play a little catch with her eight-year-old brother Stuart, while Monica watched with six-month-old Adam. Next I graduated to running errands, washing the family car, and doing odd jobs around the beauty shop. Eventually, I was invited in to watch TV with the boys, followed by a ride to Juan Maygs' Grocery for a soda and chips.

Facing the inevitable, Donald and Ann finally agreed to let us go out, but with one stipulation—we had to take Adam with us wherever we went. We were already treating her baby brother as if he were our son, so it was a small price to pay. We enjoyed the fact that people who didn't know us thought he was our child. His fair complexion and red hair next to our dark hair and tanned skin often had people asking, "Who has the red hair in your family?"

Peter and Monica with chaperone baby Adam

Trapped in Key West

We often speculated that Monica's mother was just looking to have a babysitter for Adam, but in reality, she probably thought I would get discouraged and move on once the infatuation was over. I started at the junior college in September and by Christmas— with Monica then sixteen years old and her parents becoming used to me—we were allowed to go to an occasional movie or dance together. Donald and Ann still didn't like the idea of us 'going steady,' but after they invited me to dinner for the first time, I was forever after treated as one of the family.

From the beginning I was aware that our families were different. Mother and Dad were not socially active people. Except for Aunt Rose and Gerry, we rarely had company for dinner at the Bacle house—partly because Mom and Dad were so uncomfortable around people, and partly because the cramped Poinciana Apartments I grew up in were not conducive to entertaining. When they did have company, we kids were expected to go in the other room or outside while the adults talked.

Dinner table conversation at the Bacle house was guided by an unspoken set of rules and taboos. Sex was not only never mentioned, but with kids not allowed in the room while adults were talking—and without having television—we were barely aware of its existence until we were much older. Though we might get teased about a cute boy or girl, any talk of relationships between adults was strictly forbidden. Women never even got 'pregnant' in the Bacle world, but as we children got older, we did finally learn what it was that women were always 'expecting.'

Profanity—even an accidental hell or damn—was never tolerated in the Bacle household. Dad, the old Navy chief, could let fly with the best of them at the fish house, but never uttered a single expletive at home. His rule was firm: Never curse around women and children. He was so good at controlling his language, I believe Mother was unaware of the fact that he ever used profanity. When she overheard me telling my sister Suzy, "Dad cusses at the fish house," Mother immediately chastised me. "Don't you tell your sister stories! Your Father does not use bad words!"

148

Different Families

Mentioning minor illnesses and accidents such as, "Billy has the measles," or "Titi fell off his bike and scraped his knee," was okay, but cancer, polio, and fatal accidents were not. Talk of operations or bodily functions was unthinkable, and any hint of the conversation heading in that direction brought an instant reprimand. Despite the limits, dinner conversation was light and casual and there were no restrictions on laughing, joking, and teasing.

When a small Mexican restaurant opened on Duval Street, Dad said he wanted a *tortilla* like he had eaten in Mexico. Afterwards, he swore he had been poisoned, and except for an occasional ice cream cone at Howard Johnson's, it was the only time I remember our family eating at a restaurant. Weekends at Rose and Gerry's in Coral Gables were the only trips the family took together, and the big excitement each week was getting dressed up in our good clothes to attend church. Monica jokingly referred to my family as "funky," but her family was equally unusual to me, and in truth we were more average for the times than they were.

Because Mom and Dad treated rich and poor in the same manner, it never even occurred to me that in addition to being too old to suit Monica's parents, I was also the son of a commercial fisherman. For socially conscious people like the Barbers, I was far from being a good catch for their only daughter. They were however, far too polite and sensitive to ever mention the fact, and by the time it occurred to me, it didn't really seem to matter.

Donald and Ann were the social opposites of my parents. They talked with hundreds of different people each week in the beauty shop, and Friday and Saturday were the nights to go out for dinner and dancing. They went on a couple of vacations each year, and they frequently visited other peoples' homes and entertained in their own. They even threw parties with dozens of people attending and had a regular card group that included Rose and Herman Moore, Gilmore and Louisa Parks, and Meima and Evelio Cabot.

Dinner with the Barbers gave me my first real look at just how different our families really were. Unlike the Bacle household, there were no rules for dinner table conversation at the Barber's, and it seemed no subject was off-limits. I sat awestruck as words like divorce, cheating, affair, sleeping together, and pregnant were casually sprinkled in the conversation and often accentuated with a hell, damn, or bitch.

Other peoples' lives were threshed out in beauty shop detail. Love children, sexual perverts, mistresses, quickie marriages, premature babies, and closet queens were all discussed as casually as fishing, school, and sports were at the Bacle house. I had nothing to contribute to any of the conversations and remained dumbstruck as the exotic stories swirled around me. I felt as if I was eavesdropping on a private world I never even knew existed, and became known to Donald and Ann as a "very quiet young man."

Adam was just a baby, but eight-year-old Stuart never batted an eye at the adult conversations. Monica however, left me stunned. Not only did she listen with no apparent discomfort, but she was also an enthusiastic participant and contributed to the conversation as if she were an adult.

My first meal with the Barbers was a preview of the new world I was entering, and my teenage jitters were only intensified by the first night's menu. Spaghetti at the Bacle house meant a heaping plate of the classic vermicelli with melted butter and salt and pepper. Traditional sauce with tomatoes and ground meat was unheard of at our house. Dad detested tomato sauce and ground meat was only served in the form of hamburger or meatloaf.

As soon as the food was served, I saw that spaghetti at the Barbers was not even really spaghetti. They called rigatoni, 'spaghetti,' and it was served with a huge portion of red sauce chocked full of ground meat. Except for liver, they could not have placed a more distasteful-looking meal in front of me. As everyone else was oohing and ahhing over Donald's specialty, I stared at the chunky red sauce and wondered how I was ever going to get it down.

As I forced the first bite into my mouth, Ann started the conversation with an innocent sounding question. "Donald, one of my customers was asking about Millie. Did you hear anything?"

"Yes I did. Well, you know they diagnosed her with cancer and Doctor Moore sent her to Miami for surgery. Yesterday, she went for the operation and the doctors opened her up, took one look, and sewed her right back up."

I was horrified. The most vivid picture of what the doctor had seen came into my head, and it looked exactly like what was sitting on my plate. I looked helplessly toward Monica for understanding, but not only was she was hanging on every word, but also managed to make things even worse. "Why did they sew her right back up? What did they see?"

Donald, as the ever-patient teacher, explained. "Well honey, she was so eaten up inside that the doctors knew there was nothing they could do for her. They told her she should just go on home and get her affairs in order because she only has about thirty days left."

The mere mention of the word cancer would have brought a reprimand in the Bacle house, and any mention of the details would have been unthinkable. Dad would have stared across the table at the offender and shaken his head in disgust, as he crossed his knife and fork over his plate before leaving the table.

At that moment, I desperately wanted to do what Dad would have done, but knew there was no way out. After forcing down a couple of bites, I lamely explained how I couldn't finish because I had been feeling badly all day, but hadn't wanted to pass up my first meal with the family. With total incomprehension of what I might be going through, they accepted my explanation without question.

Afterwards, I explained to Monica how unusual the conversations seemed to me, but it was not until she met my parents and started eating at my house that she could fully appreciate the radical difference in the ways we had been raised. Once she understood, she became more sensitive to the direction of the conversation at her household, though she never really understood why sick stomachs, operations, and bodily functions were considered distasteful subjects at the Bacle dinner table. "I could understand if you were trying to eat in the operating room, but just to talk about it? Boy, you sure need to get over that if you're going to be around my family."

I also found that embarrassing Monica and I was something of a playful game for Ann. Donald would never think of doing it, but Ann would occasionally pop out with a question or statement that would leave Monica and I red-faced and keep us constantly on our guard whenever she was speaking. Though we tried to prepare ourselves for anything, we were too young to anticipate her thinking.

Shortly after my first meal, when Ann was still getting to know me, she blurted out in the middle of a quiet meal, "Stuart, have you ever seen Peter and Monica kiss?"

Donald immediately sputtered out an indignant, "Ann!"

Monica expelled a horrified, "Mother!" and I was too shocked to say or do anything except hold my breath.

Ann, in her typical manner, would not be deterred and asked again, "Well Stuart, have you?"

Stuart looked at her with the earnest surprise that only an eight-year-old can exhibit and said, "Oh no Mumma! Peter says you can get germs from kissing."

Ann stared in stunned silence for a moment, while trying to comprehend what had just been said. She slowly turned toward me, and then leaning away as if I had a communicable disease, gave me a "what kind of weirdo has my daughter taken up with" look.

No one else said a word as the wildest of thoughts were racing through Ann's mind. Finally, realizing his wife had been set up, Donald mercifully broke the silence and burst out laughing. Monica and I laughed with relief while Stuart, oblivious to it all, calmly kept eating. Realizing the joke was supposed to be on her, Ann finally gave out with a halfhearted chuckle of her own, but it was a long time before she stopped eyeing me suspiciously every time I spoke.

For Monica, the Bacle family was equally and oppositely as strange. The innocence with which she approached her first meal with my parents both amused me, and filled me with dread. Dad, who was the undisputed king of his household, often came across as a gruff person because he was not a smiley man and was not much given to small talk. In reality though, he was as gentle as a kitten with all females, and his sense of humor was always ready just below the surface.

Monica, who had a very outgoing personality, seemed oblivious to any intimidation others may have felt in Dad's presence and sat comfortably down at the table. The blessing—which was never said at her house—was no sooner finished than she seemed completely at home.

Whenever Dad was not in the boat, our big meal was lunch. I imagined Monica had never sat down to a meal of pinto beans with ham hocks, rice, and cornbread, but I soon learned that her mother—despite her sophistication—was a farm girl from Arkansas who had grown up eating country food, and routinely served it to her family.

Monica was the first girl I had ever brought home to meet the family, and though she was calm and cool, I was as nervous as I had ever been. Neither Dad nor Mom felt comfortable with strangers, but they were unfailingly polite and gracious when in those situations. I knew, however, that sooner or later, the Bacle quirks (as Monica came to call them) would show themselves.

Everything was fine until Monica reached for the cornbread and mother quickly told her, "Oh no Monica, that's Mr. Bacle's cornbread. Here, take some from this pan—it's for everyone else. Mr. Bacle likes his southern-style without any sugar in it, so I make a special pan for him."

Dad immediately said, "Well, good grief Mary! She's a Southern girl. Maybe she likes real cornbread."

"That's okay, I'll try the sweet cornbread." Monica was puzzled by the double serving and asked Mother, "You mean every time you cook cornbread, you make another special pan just for Mr. Bacle?"

"Why sure Monica, I've always done that."

For the first time, I was getting a little nervous at the direction of the conversation. I saw Dad give her a suspicious look and hoped that was the end of the discussion. Monica sat quietly for a minute buttering her bread, but it was obvious she was mulling over the strange situation. Finally, she looked down the table at Dad and said, "Boy, you would sure be in trouble at my house."

If she had thrown a ham hock at him, she couldn't have shocked Dad more. No one in my eighteen years had ever dared to express that kind of impertinence to the master of the Bacle household. Dad just stared at Monica for a moment in disbelief, but she went back to casually buttering her cornbread, oblivious to the unspoken crisis she had caused.

Dad's scorned look turned on me. His eyes narrowed, and his "what kind of a girl did you bring into this house" look, mirrored Ann's thought about me.

Mother, who was mortified and speechless, finally found her voice and did a credible job of soothing Dad's feelings by explaining to Monica that Dad's way was the right way and she actually made the sweet cornbread especially for everyone else. Monica still thought the whole situation was humorous and gave Dad a conspiratorial grin and a knowing nod.

Dad was wary of Monica for the rest of the meal, and Mother and I were anxiously wishing the lunch would be over. Monica however, seemed completely at ease and engaged us all in a steady stream of conversation for the rest of the meal.

The occasional comments Dad made—which Mother and I knew to be commands—went completely over Monica's head. When she asked Dad if he would like more rice, he responded with, "No thank you Monica. With all this talking going on, I haven't had a chance to eat what I've got."

Mother and I, knowing that meant for everyone to shut up, exchanged 'uh oh' looks, but Monica just laughed and said, "Oh, nothing stops me from eating." Dad, looking out from under raised eyebrows, gave Monica a bewildered grin and shook his head in resignation.

By the end of the meal, I could tell Mother and Dad both liked her and everyone was fairly comfortable. Monica ended the meal in fine fashion by asking Dad to pass his empty plate and silverware. Again, Dad stared at her as if he could not believe what she was asking. Mother immediately leaped up from the table. "I'll get these dishes Monica. Just leave them."

Different Families

Monica watched silently as Mother scurried around the table, picking up everyone's dishes, including mine. It suddenly occurred to her that the Bacle men don't do dirty dishes, and she eyed me with a disbelieving look. At Monica's house, everyone took their own plate to the sink, and only the person who cooked didn't help with washing the dishes. I knew if she and I stayed together, there would be big changes coming to the Bacle household.

For the next thirty-four years, Dad genuinely adored Monica despite her outspokenness—or maybe because of it. The conversations in our house were dramatically changed, and over the years, most every subject was discussed. Dad would still quietly shake his head at many of the conversations, but as the family rapidly expanded, we had many 'table monitors' who steered the conversations away from particularly offensive talk like operations and bodily functions. But even those subjects would occasionally slip into the conversation, and we always knew it had gone too far when Dad crossed his knife and fork over his plate and silently left the table.

Monica accepted Dad's 'peculiar' behavior, but never quite understood it. One day, she confronted him with, "Now Mr. Bacle, I want you to explain something to me. When you were in the Navy, you saw thousands of new recruits vomit all over your ship. In the war, you ate during battle when men were being killed around you. You ate in the jungles of New Guinea when you had to burn leeches off with cigarettes, and you eat everyday out in your lobster boat with rotten fish heads, cowhides, pig's feet, and spurting sardine cans. Yet, when I merely mention at the dinner table that someone got sick to his stomach, you're so offended you get up and leave. Now, will you please tell me what sense that makes?"

Dad listened carefully with his elbows on the table, hands folded under his chin, and his head cocked slightly to the side. When he thought she was finished, he slowly shook his head in frustration, and as the patient father explained, "Monica, there's a time and place for everything, and the dinner table is not the place to talk about upchucking."

Mimicking Dad, Monica shook her own head in frustration and grinned. "Boy, you Bacle's are a real trip."

Through the years, Monica changed many things at our house, but she never did succeed in getting Dad to clean off the table or wash dishes. When the next generation of males came along and would—apparently without thinking—start picking up their dish, Dad inevitably barked out in disgust, "Boys! Leave those dishes alone. The girls will take care of that."

Monica would throw her eyes heavenward and ask for strength, but as long as Dad lived, the girls always took care of the dishes. Monica finally realized she had a better chance of changing him than she did with changing Mother. None of Monica's exhortations could get Mother to stop waiting on Dad hand and foot. Without fail, Mother would end each discussion by saying, "Oh Monica, I'm too old to change now."

Monica would then playfully scold Dad. "You should get down on your hands and knees every day and thank the Good Lord that he gave you this woman. Then, thank him again that you weren't married to me, because you would be in for a very rude awakening."

In 1970, Monica and I moved next door to my parents, so she saw Dad almost every day. The banter between them was always in good humor, and Monica's affection for Dad was sincere and unchanging. In twenty-eight years of living next door to each other, a harsh word never passed between them, and Monica truly became like a daughter to him.

8

Trapping in the Bahamas

I n 1966, during my first year at Monroe County Junior College, Dad was once again a very restless man. Despite its modest success, Dad increasingly disliked the demands of his fish house business and the constant struggle to keep it operating. Trapping in the deep water outside the reef had been very profitable, but word spread quickly, and many other fishermen dropped their traps around his. He was still catching well, but never lost his strong distaste for working next to other fishermen and was keeping his eyes open for somewhere new.

Several of his friends had recently started working traps in the Bahamas and were bringing back some very large catches. While Dad was impressed by the amount of lobster, the real hook for him was the sheer adventure of it all. Only a small part of the thousands of square miles of bottom had ever been worked, and the thought of trapping in virgin waters only three hundred miles from Key West was all too enticing.

Had he been born one hundred years before, Dad would probably have been one of the forty-niners who rushed off across the continent to get rich in the great California Gold Rush. He had always wanted to hunt for gold, and in his later years, he once told me, "What the hell son, I've done just about everything I ever wanted to do except pan for gold in the Black Hills. I guess that's not too bad."

Trapped in Key West

The only song I ever heard him sing was "There's a Gold Mine in the Sky," which he sung throughout his life. In 1966, his romantic fantasy of hunting for gold was manifesting itself in the form of the distant Grand Bahama Bank—where he could search for the golden lobster.

The Bahamas were a British possession in 1966 and Bahamian fishing laws were virtually nonexistent. The entire fishing business in the Bahamas was a small boat, near shore fishery, that supported little more than a subsistence industry. The vast rich outer banks were virtually untapped, and there was no enforcement agency to prevent American fishermen from harvesting the immense resource.

What Bahamian fishing laws there were, no one seemed interested in enforcing. The British periodically sent a destroyer to patrol the islands, but it was primarily to establish sovereignty and not to enforce fishing laws. As for their part, the American fishermen simply fished the waters as if they were their own, since there was no one to stop them.

The first time Dad mentioned it to Mother, she knew he was going. He said he couldn't make up his mind, and poured out all the reasons why he couldn't or shouldn't go. She listened quietly for weeks and when she could stand it no longer, said, "We both know you're going, so why don't you stop talking and get it over with."

Dad was truly excited at the chance to go, but reluctant to leave Mother alone for two weeks at a time. Unlike the week-long Tortugas trips when he mistakenly thought the fish house would run without him, he then knew the full burden would fall on Mother. Mom and Dad surely had some serious talks about the Bahama venture, but even though I was nineteen years old, they would still never have discussed such an important subject in front of one of the children. With Jimmy and Nancy in school and her past experience with the fish house, she apparently convinced Dad she could deal with the role of 'boss lady.'

Mother was the classic model for a traditional American mom. Her role as wife and mother took precedence over everything else in her life, and Dad was the undisputed head of the house.

Trapping in the Bahamas

Because he was the provider, every important decision had to be approved by Dad, and from the day they were married, she always signed her name Mrs. Peter C. Bacle. For his part, Dad always treated her with respect and gentleness, and there was never an argument between them in front of the kids—though in lighter moments she would make comments like, "You heard the master," the subtle message of which, was over the heads of her children.

With children still in school and a fish house to run, her life was going to be very difficult for a long time. Like a true pioneer woman, Mother accepted whatever came her way without complaint. If it meant functioning as the acting head of the house and becoming boss of the business while Dad was away, then that was what she would do.

Once the decision was made, Dad immediately started making preparations. He would take two boats—his own, the forty-foot *Ocean Motion*, along with the thirty-six-foot *Mary Jeanine* that belonged to Onelio Lopez. Though they were relatively close in age, Onelio was tiring of the fishing life and gladly gave up his boat in return for a share of the catch.

Next, he needed a crew. Very few fishermen were willing to go so far with nothing more than the hope of a great catch. It would take at least two months of trap building and preparation before there was the possibility of a paycheck, and Dad was in no financial position to pay people to work.

Roberto Gonzalez was a young Cuban immigrant who brought his family to America in an old fishing boat in 1962. From the beginning, he fished for Dad and worked part time in the fish house when needed. Roberto was hardworking and ambitious and was one of the first to leave Cuba when he realized Fidel Castro was a communist. As an independent young man who wanted to run his own life, the prospect of living under socialism was unthinkable.

Roberto quickly learned English and Dad took an instant liking to him. Despite the age and cultural differences, they were very much alike and Dad especially admired the fact that "Roberto doesn't take guff" from anyone. They remained friends for life and

Roberto is still fishing at Stock Island Lobster Company with his son, Robert Jr.

Roberto was the first one Dad wanted to line up for his crew. Though he was nervous about being in the southern Bahamas and working so close to Cuba, Roberto was assured by Dad that they would stay well clear of Cuban waters and Castro would never risk confrontation with the United States by entering our waters. Roberto was not really convinced, but being young and adventuresome and probably feeling an obligation to Dad, he agreed to go.

Dad intended to take three hundred traps, and building them with hammer and nails would take about two months. Using today's methods, the traps could be built in three days by two men using air compressors and staple guns, but in 1966, it was a tedious and time-consuming job. Each trap was constructed of sixty-two separate pieces of cypress wood and required over three hundred nails for assembly.

Dad still needed some cheap labor for the rest of the crew, and he found it in the form of Bill Wickers and me. As my diving partner for the past two years, Bill and I made a very productive team. Dad was highly impressed with the amount of lobster we dove up, and the hundreds of pounds of fish we could spear in a day.

We were perfect candidates since we both lived at home and were at an age where the pot of gold in the ocean still seemed possible. Bill loved the ocean, and even after a college degree and a try at teaching, he ended up following in his father's footsteps and becoming one of the most successful charter captains in Key West.

Bill accepted the opportunity to work in the Bahamas after convincing his parents he would make a large amount of money to contribute to his college funds. We were both about to graduate from the junior college and would be heading off for different universities in the fall. That gave us two months to get the traps built and two months to make a small fortune working them. We started with high hopes and an enthusiasm that matched Dad's.

Starting early and finishing late each day, we soon realized what we were getting into. Helping Dad was something I had done all my life, but Bill had never built a trap, and even I was finding it far different work as a real job rather than a son helping his father. Like an old Navy chief, Dad kept us going by alternating a kick in the seat of the pants with a pat on the back. The nailing seemed endless, and we discovered it took over two thousand swings of the hammer to get one trap built. By the end of the trap building, we resembled stone crabs, with normal-sized left arms and large muscular right arms that had been swinging the hammer every day for two months.

Until we started loading the boats with traps, Bill and I were unaware of the fact that it would take two trips to get all of the traps in the water. That meant our first trip would take three days and we would have no income resulting from it. The *Ocean Motion* could hold 125 traps and *Mary Jeanine* seventy-five. The other one hundred we would try to load on the second trip when the boats were outfitted with large iceboxes, fuel drums, bait, and all the supplies necessary for two weeks of trap pulling.

As we loaded for the first trip, Bill began to get an idea of what trapping in the Bahamas would really be like. Each trap had to be baited with a fish head that had a wire through the eyes and then hung from a nail in the trap. Each trap also had a can of sardines wired through an ice pick hole and hung on the opposite side of the funnel.

The sardine cans were from cases marked, *seconds—not for human consumption.* We wondered who was to eat them if they weren't intended for humans, but Dad just casually said, "Cats, I guess." Some of the cans were puffed-up and spurted a foul-smelling liquid when punctured with the ice pick. Bill was repulsed, but would soon find to his dismay that the little spurts were only his first 'taste' of cat food.

Dad loaded as many traps as possible on the boats. Bill kept asking, "Mr. Bacle, where are we going to be? There's only a three-foot space in front of the traps."

Dad would just grin and say, "Don't worry, Bill, we'll squeeze you in somewhere."

Trapped in Key West

When the boats were loaded and ready to go, it was necessary to crawl into the cabin through the front window. The three-by-six-foot space next to the steering wheel on the *Mary Jeanine* would be Dad and Bill's home for the following forty-six hours. It was made slightly less confining by the fact that it allowed access to the down below area where there was supposed to be a v-berth for sleeping.

The v-berth was piled up on one side with supplies, while the other side was covered with rusty tools, spare engine parts, and assorted junk that had accumulated over the years. The bilge was covered by loose pieces of plywood which bounced off with each wave or misstep, and a trip down below often ended with a foot being ankle-deep in the bilge water. Bill asked Dad if he could nail them down, but Dad's reply stopped Bill from ever again asking such a question. "Good grief, Bill! You want to waste time tearing up bilge boards, while the boat's sinking out from under you?"

"The boat sinking! . . . Why would the boat sink?"

"Why would the boat sink? Because that's what boats do if they fill up with water!"

"Well sir, why would the boat fill up with water?"

"We don't really expect it to happen Bill, but we want to be ready in case it starts leaking too much."

"Gees, Mr. Bacle, have you looked at those life jackets? The cloth is all rusty and ripped and it looks like the cork inside is disintegrating. I don't know whether they'll hold us up if the boat sinks."

Dad loved to see people become anxious over the possibility of the boat foundering, and got a lot of mileage out of his sock solution. "Look Bill, don't worry about the boat sinking. You just keep your eye on that bilge while we're running, and if you see water squirting up, let me know immediately, so I can stick a sock or something in the hole."

As Bill said later, "My God! Here I am about to leave on my first trip across the ocean and your Dad's talking about sticking a sock in the hole if the boat starts leaking! . . . Stick a sock in the hole? . . . I wondered where he was going to get the sock, so I brought every old pair I had and kept them handy just in case.

Trapping in the Bahamas

"On that first trip over, I must have removed those boards a thousand times. Twice I called your Dad to look, but he finally told me, 'Unless it's spurting above your knee, don't call me.' Jesus! Even in my dreams I see that hellhole of a v-berth with the smell of oil, exhaust, bilge water, engine heat, and those damn cases of sardines with *seconds* stamped all over them."

With the boats so loaded down we had to plug the scuppers, we took off at 2:00 a.m. Hoping to arrive shortly after sunup the following day, we anticipated a trip of thirty hours. Our destination was a speck of sand and mosquitoes on the southern tip of the Bahama Bank known as Guinchos Cay.

With only a compass and a chart for navigation, I was put in charge of getting us there by the time-honored process of dead reckoning. That involved figuring out what degree of heading would get us there and then steering while never taking the eyes off the compass.

On a lake or a short run, the method works reasonably well. However, on a three hundred-mile ocean run with the wind blowing, overloaded boats, and a three-knot Gulf Stream current pushing the boats off course, it became very difficult. With the added facts that there was to be only one reference point of land along the way and an inexperienced ocean navigator, a direct run was almost impossible.

On our first leg of the trip, which was to take us to Cay Sal some one hundred miles from Key West, we missed the island by over twenty miles. Though I had taken the Gulf Stream into account, I substantially underestimated its force. Described as a river running in the ocean between Key West and Cuba, it carried us much farther east than I expected.

Cay Sal Island is on the southwest corner of the Cay Sal Bank, approximately twenty miles from Cuba, and we were expecting to pass five miles south of it on our way to Guinchos Cay. Instead, we first spotted a small abandoned lighthouse on Elbow Cay on the north side of the Bank. Until we were close enough to positively identify it as a lighthouse, we assumed it was a ship and continued along our errant course.

Trapped in Key West

After reluctantly accepting how far off course we were, we adjusted and finally spotted Cay Sal just before dark—some four hours later than expected. We forged ahead into the black night with confidence shaken and little realization that the worst was still ahead.

On the eastern end of the Bank, sixty miles from Cay Sal Island are the Anguilla Cays. They are a twenty-mile string of unlighted rocky islands, running from north to south. We were extremely wary of getting too close to those shipwreckers at night, and set a course down the center of the twenty-mile-wide Bahama Channel between Cay Sal and Cuba.

By midnight, we were all staring wide-eyed into the dark, hoping to pick up a glimpse of Anguilla to the north, and praying we wouldn't find it the hard way. Roberto and I, in the *Ocean Motion*, were communicating with Dad and Bill by CB radio, and after our first errant route, were anxious to have Anguilla behind us.

Roberto however, had even more reason for anxiety. As a Cuban citizen who fled the repression of Castro, he had reason to worry about being either too far north or too far south. It was only then occurring to him just how close we would be to Cuba.

As a young, healthy male, Roberto was in a group forbidden to ever leave Cuba. Abandoning Cuba for the United States was an offense so serious that he would immediately be tortured and jailed if he was returned. Roberto was far more concerned about being captured than hitting the darkened islands of Anguilla.

By 2:00 a.m., we felt we were past the islands and finally started to relax. Once again however, our course was off, and by erring on the side of safety, I had carried us too close to Cuba. We started seeing the lights of fishing boats to the south and knew they could only be Cuban.

We made radio contact with Dad, and he also saw the Cuban lights, but did not see us. A quick look showed we had become separated in the night, and we slowed to let them catch up. When we didn't see them after ten minutes, I called and said I would turn on the spotlight so they could find us.

Trapping in the Bahamas

Roberto pleaded with me not to turn on the spotlight, and his extreme anxiety suddenly made his situation very real to me. As an American boy, I had not given much thought to what would happen if we were detained by Castro, but vaguely assumed we would be released after questioning and resume our trip. I then understood it would not happen that way for Roberto, and his fears became mine.

With widened eyes, we both scanned the horizon. We searched vainly for Dad and Bill and then searched even harder for the dreaded gunboats. We stared without blinking at the tiny fishing boat lights, and then averted our gaze slightly as you must at night in order to see things most clearly. Roberto scampered to the bow and then to the roof of the cabin, shouting and pointing to imaginary gunboats in the night.

The radio crackled again and Dad said, "I still don't see you, but Bill says those aren't fishing boat lights—they're headlights on cars." Roberto and I both stared out the window and realized immediately Bill was right. Not only were we very close to the coast of Cuba, but also the coastline was unknown to us except for the chart indicating it was strewn with small rocky islands and jagged coral reefs.

We were then as fearful of sinking as we were of being captured, and immediately turned due north and away from Cuba. I called Dad and told him we would run north for an hour to be sure we were out of Cuban waters and then find each other at daybreak. A moment later, Dad called back and said, "Okay son, I see your spotlight. We're just to the southeast of you."

Roberto and I stared at each other in shock—both realizing immediately our spotlight was not on. "Dad, our spotlight is not on. Repeat, our spotlight is not on! . . . Come back Dad, come back . . . Did you read me, Dad? Our spotlight is not on."

"Peter, don't talk on the radio again. We'll meet at the island."

Roberto was softly murmuring pleas for deliverance, and my mind was racing with the new problem of finding each other again in the vast ocean, while at the same time wondering what would happen to Dad and Bill if they were captured. Roberto knew the

Cuban fishing boats were not allowed to have spotlights and there was no doubt a gunboat was searching the waters.

The *Ocean Motion* never seemed slower than it did then. We could actually see the patrol boats, and heading north at six miles per hour on a pitch-black night, we felt as if the boat was not moving at all. Each light seemed to be coming right at us and gaining each minute. We could hear muted voices the way you can on the ocean at night, and half a dozen times we felt certain we could make out uniformed men on the partially-lighted patrol boats. Roberto's feeling of despair was overwhelming him. At one point, he suggested we just stop and let them take him.

Through it all, we could never be certain of what we were actually seeing, and as the minutes passed, we began to think we might possibly escape. Within an hour, the individual lights had disappeared and we could only see the dim glow of lights on shore.

Roberto was then breathing more easily, and feeling we were safely out of Cuban waters, turned our attention to the problem of Dad and Bill. We had no way of knowing whether they had been captured or not. Dad said to meet at the island, but it was still about fifteen hours away and neither of us was feeling very confident about making it without Dad.

We finally stopped in the middle of the straights and idled for a couple of hours to see if they would show. We reasoned by then that they should have either reached our latitude or been captured. In either case, we didn't think it would matter if we turned on our lights, so they could see us. After a short time, we also turned on the spotlight and then tried the radio. We got no response for our efforts, and after another hour, reluctantly started toward Guinchos Cay.

For the next twelve hours, we tried the radio without success. We didn't think we had been separated long enough to lose radio contact, so as time passed we felt ever more certain they had been captured. At 2:00 the next afternoon we dropped anchor at Guinchos and prayed the *Mary Jeanine* would soon appear.

We both imagined Dad and Bill being grilled by the Cuban secret police. Roberto told me stories of how merciless they were and how easily people disappear without a trace in the communist world. The horror of communism never seemed more real to me than it did then, and I half-abandoned hope that they would be found.

By that evening, I was wondering how I was going to break the news to everyone. Mother had lived through four years of Dad fighting in World War II, so I assumed she would handle it somehow. Bill's parents were another story. I felt personally responsible for talking Bill into the venture—not just that he was the only son, but he was the only Wickers left to carry on the family name. It was not going to be pretty.

We debated over whether to notify the Coast Guard. Dad had always said to never call the Coast Guard unless you're actually sinking. Of course we weren't sinking, but even at my age, I realized it might be some kind of international incident and we could be in serious trouble. There was also the possibility their lives might be in danger, but in the end, we decided to wait until the next morning to make a decision.

We stared ceaselessly at the western horizon and had two or three sightings which turned out to be freighters plying the shipping lanes. We watched a spectacular sunset, and then saw a speck on the horizon in the exact place the sun had disappeared. We stared anxiously, but the sky darkened before we could be certain we had actually seen something.

There was no answer on the radio, but we still held out hope it could be them. When it was completely dark, we expected to see running lights, but it wasn't until I flashed the spotlight at them that we finally got a response. Seeing a spotlight shine back at us was the most blessed relief I had ever felt, and when we reached them on the radio a few minutes later, we both had a beer to celebrate.

It was midnight before they arrived and we secured the boats for the night. Roberto and I were anxious to find out everything that had happened, but Dad said the story would have to wait until morning. None of us had slept for forty-six hours, and neither the cramped quarters nor the smell of the ripening bait could stop us from crashing out in any available nook.

In the morning, the smell of the bait was so strong and the quarters so cramped, we decided to run the traps off first and then stop to clean the boats and have a bite to eat. By noon, the traps were in the water and we finally heard the story.

We had gotten separated because the leading *Ocean Motion* was faster than the *Mary Jeanine*. Usually, they would call and tell us to slow down, but we had agreed that while we were near Cuba, we would maintain radio silence unless it was really necessary.

Shortly after he lost sight of us, Dad spotted a light and headed for it, thinking it was us. Bill said later, "You know, your Dad doesn't see that well at night, and he kept insisting the lights were you. I finally convinced him it wasn't you when I said I had never seen a boat with headlights before. Then, a boat starts shining his spotlight around us and we both thought it was you. When you told us it wasn't your spotlight, we knew it had to be a gunboat. Apparently, they had seen our running lights, but their spotlight wasn't powerful enough to locate us after we turned our lights off."

After Dad told us to turn the radio off and head for Guinchos, they played a cat and mouse game with the gunboat. According to Dad, "Hell, we could see them perfectly—they had every light on the boat turned on. Whatever way they turned, we went the other way. They knew we were there, but with all those lights on, they couldn't see us and I guess they didn't have radar. They were so close, we could hear them talking, but they still never spotted us.

"They finally gave up after a couple of hours and we beat it out of there. We had a hell of a time finding this place without even a chart. I had to run up on the bank and then follow the drop-off the whole way. I had no idea how much farther we had to go, so we were about to anchor for the night when we saw your spotlight."

The trip home was long but uneventful. Bill had already been on the wildest ride of his life and we hadn't even pulled a trap. I had grave doubts over whether or not Bill would be ready to make the next trip. He eventually decided he had too much time and effort already expended to give up, and we started preparing for the first two-week moneymaking trip.

The boats had to be outfitted far differently for the second trip. Iceboxes would take up the greatest part of our deck space. The iceboxes were plywood over Styrofoam, and years of use left them permanently waterlogged. When filled with ice, they added more weight to the boats than the traps.

Neither boat had enough fuel capacity for a two-week trip, so it was necessary to carry six fifty-five-gallon drums of diesel fuel on each boat. Each one had to be lashed securely lest they slide in a heavy sea and smash through the side of the boat. The rusty old drums were Navy rejects and we were to wish many times in the weeks ahead that we had rejected them too.

Bait was another major problem. The fish heads were best when kept fresh on ice. However, with a two week-trip facing us, we couldn't take up valuable icebox space with fish heads. Tops were cut out of oil drums and the heads were packed in them and salted. Though we were concerned about the smell as they aged, we assumed the canvas covering would keep it to a minimum.

Dad took care of buying the groceries. His idea of what was necessary for survival was something along the line of the C rations the military ate during the war. Ten loaves of bread, a couple of cases of beanie-wienies, sixty cans of sardines, a half-dozen large jars of peanut butter, twenty pounds of rice, and two dozen cans of Spam were the staples for the trip. Two packages of ground meat, a smoked ham, and a package of chicken filled in the fresh meat requirement. "Good grief boys! With all that crawfish and fish out there, no one's going to go hungry."

Just before we were to leave the dock, and when everything else had been loaded on, it was time to put on more traps. We stacked them on top of the iceboxes, fuel drums, bait cans, and in every other space big enough to hold a trap. Once we plugged the scuppers, which were a full six inches under the waterline, the boats looked as if they might sink before we ever left the dock.

Trapped in Key West

Bill and I stood staring at the pitiful amount of freeboard as Dad cranked the engine. The exhaust was so far under the water we only heard a muffled rumble come to the surface. Bill moaned like a man resigned to his fate, "Jesus, I almost brought the life jacket from my small boat. I wish now I would have."

Once again, we left in the middle of the night, expecting to arrive on the morning of the second day. Though our navigation was considerably better after the first experience, the overloaded boats made very poor time. On the first trip, we baited the traps just before we left with fish heads that were still frozen. On our second load, we baited the traps with thawed fish heads, and then had a one-day delay in our departure because of the weather.

By the time we left the dock, the bait had a very strong smell and was covered with thousands of fat, buzzing green flies. Bill was repulsed by the scene, and anxious to leave so the wind would blow back the flies and the smell. "Good Lord! We haven't even left the dock yet and I'm already nauseous." While we did eventually lose most of the flies, the overloaded stern created a back draft that kept the smell of rotting fish heads strongly in the cabin for the entire trip.

Fortunately for our overloaded condition, the seas were very calm for the trip over. However, it created stifling heat in the cabin, and not only made the fish heads stink terribly, but also heated up the *not-for-human-consumption* sardine cans hanging in the traps, and started them spurting. We also found the canvas covers on the drums of salted fish heads did little to contain the sickening smell, and the overall condition was one of virtually unbreathable air.

Bill, who had never been seasick, found the smell so offensive that he rode for thirty hours with his head sticking out the side window. He also refused to eat, saying it was impossible to think about food under such conditions. "For crying out loud! Here I am with my head stuck out the window because I couldn't take a breath inside the cabin, and there's your old man sitting there calmly reading a book! Now mind you, I can't even breathe, and he's reading a book!

Trapping in the Bahamas

"Now, that's not bad enough! I turn around and look, and there he is opening a can of sardines! Sardines, for God's sake! We've got sixty cans of rotten sardines—excuse me . . . *seconds*—spurting all over the boat, and he's sitting there eating sardines as if everything is just fine. Then, just to top it all off, he looks over at me with that little grin of his and asks, "Want some Bill?"

When we finally sighted Guinchos, Bill was almost jubilant. For the first time, he talked on the radio and half-joked about how the trip had been the longest thirty-eight hours of his life. In the lee of the island, we anchored the big boat, tied off the *Mary Jeanine* to the stern, and congregated on the *Ocean Motion*. In his excitement, it took a minute before Bill realized we had anchored without first dropping the traps. "Hey, Mr. Bacle? Why did we anchor before dropping the traps? . . . We are going to drop them today, aren't we? I mean surely, you're not thinking about waiting until tomorrow? Are you?"

"Bill, it's a little late to drop them today. I'd rather wait until tomorrow when we can see real well and take our time getting them in the right spot."

"But, Mr. Bacle, I'll do the looking for you! There's plenty of light and I've got really good vision. Really sir, this smell is just unbearable. We'll never be able to eat or sleep if we don't get these traps off this boat today."

"Smell! Good grief, Bill! That bait's just getting right. By the time we get them in the water tomorrow, those old crawdads will be coming from miles around to find these traps."

Bill was devastated and found no humor in the situation. Roberto and I also thought the smell was awful, but since we had both been around it all our lives, found it at least bearable. Without the back draft from the running boat, it was possible to stand behind the open front window and let the fresh air blow in your face. Bill took up his position there for the next several hours and seemed better, though he still couldn't eat.

When it was time to sleep, Bill took a long look down below. The v-berth Dad had promised Bill was about a foot and a half too short for his six-foot-three-inch frame. One side had our supplies stacked on it, including both the edible sardines and the *seconds—not-for-human-consumption* cases. The other bunk was piled with rusty tools, hoses, belts, spare pumps, and engine parts, and was a general catchall for everything that didn't have a place.

The v-berth was always a collection point for every foul smell on a boat. The bilge was particularly rank, as the drippings from the rotting fish heads and spurting sardine cans had seeped through the deck into the overheated bilge water. To bring the mix to its most putrid state, there was no hatch for a flow of fresh air and the two six-inch portholes had been rusted shut for years.

We all watched in silence as Bill leaned his head down and surveyed his 'stateroom' from the top of the companionway. To our surprise, he took one last deep breath and slowly went down to his berth. The three of us looked at each other and grinned, but moments later, he emerged with a life jacket under his arm and a look of exhausted disgust on his face. Without a word, he threw his life jacket through the front window onto the bow of the boat, and then climbed out the window himself and laid on the bow with his life jacket for a pillow.

Roberto and I were watching Dad, who was quietly smoking a cigar and sipping a beer. After a long and thoughtful inspection of his cigar, he checked out Bill through the corner of his eye. A few moments later, when he was sure Bill was comfortable and almost passed out from exhaustion, Dad called out, "Bill, old boy, . . . if one of those squalls hits tonight, you're going to be in big trouble up there." Bill just gave a feeble wave of his hand and fell asleep. Dad looked at me with a grin and shrugged his shoulders.

Shortly after midnight, Bill found out very clearly what Dad meant by "big trouble." A clap of thunder brought us all up like so many jack-in-the-boxes. With a suddenness that is characteristic of summer squalls in the Caribbean, the rain started pouring and the wind was suddenly howling at fifty miles per hour. Bill, in a state of confused exhaustion, was desperately trying to hold onto his life jacket and get back into the cabin.

Trapping in the Bahamas

Dad was instantly in action. "Peter! Our anchor broke loose! You and Roberto get the *Mary Jeanine* under way and stay near us! And hurry! We're drifting back toward the rocks!"

Roberto and I were also confused. With the roaring wind and driving rain, we couldn't even tell the anchor was broken loose, much less know which way we were drifting. We were so disoriented we didn't even know where the island was. With each lightning flash, we tried to find it, but the rain was so heavy that visibility was limited to about fifty feet.

Fortunately, Dad knew exactly where Guinchos lay, and he wasn't about to let us founder on it. He yelled at me, "Peter! Get a move on!" and then screamed above the roar of the wind and rain . . . "Bill! Stay up there! You're going to have to pull the anchor!"

As I crawled out the side window to the *Mary Jeanine*, I saw Bill scratching for a handhold on the closed front windows as he slid across the bow. Dad's command to stay on the bow brought a look of disbelieving horror to his face. "Pull the anchor? Mr. Bacle, I can't even stand up!"

Dad bellowed above the roaring wind. "Then, pull the damn thing sitting down! And make it pronto, before we smash to pieces on the rocks!"

A few minutes later, Roberto and I were "standing by" with the *Mary Jeanine* as Dad and Bill tried to get the dragging anchor pulled. Without the load of traps eliminating all deck space, it would have been a fairly simple matter to run up on the anchor, gaff the line, and then pull it from the back deck. However, running the boat forward with the anchor still in the water to get away from the rocks would almost certainly end with the anchor wrapped in the propeller and the loss of all ability to maneuver the boat.

We shined our spotlight on the bow of the *Ocean Motion* to help Bill see. In the fifty-mile-per-hour wind, the rain was coming vertically and virtually blinding him. He was crouched low on his hands and knees, trying to make his way to the Samson post where the anchor was tied.

Trapped in Key West

As the boat heaved and pitched, Bill would slide from one side of the rain-slicked bow to the other, dropping down to his belly as he teetered on the edge. With each slide, we held our breath, believing he was certain to fall into the raging sea. Saved each time by an inch-high lip around the edge of the bow, he miraculously made it all the way forward and got his hands on the anchor rope.

We watched helplessly as he struggled to pull the anchor. Dad was running forward on the line, so there was not much resistance, but each pitch of the boat caused Bill to lose back some hard-won progress. After a few frustrating minutes, Dad stuck his head out of the window and yelled something at Bill we couldn't hear. Bill tied off the anchor and belly-crawled back to the cabin as Dad cracked open the front window and held a knife out to him.

Then, as suddenly as the storm started, it stopped. Within a minute, the wind went from fifty miles per hour to a dead calm. The driving downpour became a pleasant shower and Bill sprawled on his stomach in blessed relief.

We could then see that Dad was right, and in another five minutes, we would have been driven up on the rocks in front of the island. He sensed we were that close and was handing Bill the knife to cut the anchor line—leaving it to dive up in the morning. It made a lasting impression on all of us, that without Dad, we would probably have been snug in the cabin as the boats crashed onto the rocks.

After moving offshore and tying up together at a safer anchorage, Dad climbed aboard the *Mary Jeanine* to sleep and Bill gave me his version of the crisis. "Jesus! I thought I was going to die out there. I couldn't do anything but slide! If it weren't for that lip around the bow, I would've been in the water. Man, I've never been so scared in my whole life.

"And your old man! Boy is your old man brutal! He wouldn't let me come back in the cabin until I had the anchor pulled. Here I am being slung from one side of the boat to the other, blinded by the rain, and knowing that if I fall in I'm probably going to die, and he tells me, 'Just get the anchor pulled and you can come in.'

Trapping in the Bahamas

"And then! After the storm passes and I get the anchor pulled, he tells me, 'Bill, you might as well stay up there until we get it dropped again.' So, he leaves me up there soaked and freezing for another half-hour while he finds the perfect anchoring spot.

"I gotta tell you something, bubba. I never thought it was going to be like this. My God, we haven't even caught a lobster yet, and I've almost died in a storm, been asphyxiated with rotten fish heads, and thrown into a Cuban prison. What the hell is next?"

After the storm passed, Bill made his way down below. Dad was on the *Mary Jeanine* and Roberto was sleeping on top of the large icebox, but I still had my eye on another storm that kept flashing in the distance. When my curiosity got the best of me, I went to check on Bill and found him sleeping peacefully on top of the tools and pumps in the v-berth.

The next day, we got a late start as we dropped all the traps we had on board. We were all anxious to pull some of the traps we brought over on the first trip, but Dad refused to check even one. "We're going to anchor up and get these boats squared away for trap pulling. We all need a hot dinner and a good night's sleep. Tomorrow you boys are going to need all the strength you've got for those traps full of crawfish."

That evening for the first time, we felt as if we actually had room to move on the boats. With the traps in the water, the smell was much improved, though the fifty-five-gallon drums with salted fish heads had their own noxious odor. We also noticed for the first time a smell that would be our constant companion for the next two weeks—diesel fumes.

Of the twelve drums of fuel on the two boats, at least ten of them were leaking diesel onto the deck. Most of them had pinholes in the top, where sitting water had rusted the metal drums. We also found that a tightly sealed drum of diesel sitting in the hot sun all day would build up pressure and allow fuel to seep through the threads in the caps.

Diesel fuel has its own distinctive smell, and while it is not particularly offensive in occasional sniffs, it becomes loathsome when emanating from one's dinner plate or sleeping pillow. It is also very slick. We were forced to scrub the deck six or eight times a day for safety reasons, and realized for the first time why Dad had brought ten large bottles of Joy dishwashing detergent. The diesel fuel, which sticks to rubber boots extremely well, was soon tracked over the entire boat and made its way into every item we had, including our food and clothing.

However, on that first night without the traps on board, the smell of bait and fuel seemed a minor annoyance. Roberto cooked us a Cuban specialty of ground meat and rice, and we all sacked out on the *Ocean Motion* with full stomachs and dreams of what the next day would bring.

Dad and Roberto stretched out on the deck and were instantly asleep, while Bill and I lay restlessly on the iceboxes trying to doze off. There were only a few mosquitoes that first night, but enough to keep Bill and I half-consciously awake. As we lay there in exhausted misery, Bill whispered to me in a pitiful voice, "My God! Does your Dad always snore like that?"

I laughed in spite of our condition, and realized for the first time that Dad was indeed snoring. Dad's snoring was no more to me than the wind blowing, or the waves lapping the side of the boat. In the tiny Poinciana apartment I had grown up in, no sound went unheard. Dad's snoring was as much a part of sleep time as turning off the lights and turning on the fans.

As a child, I often awoke at night with a stomach growling for food. Mother would not allow us to eat at night, so I would have to sneak into the kitchen to raid the cookie jar. Tiptoeing next to the walls so the creaky old wooden floors wouldn't squeak so much, I would make my way to the jar and slowly unscrew the lid. It seemed each time I had the lid off and was reaching for a cookie, Mother's hushed voice would come suddenly and clearly through the house. "Peter! Put that jar down and get back in bed!"

I finally learned to time my thieving with Dad's snoring. When he was really cranked up, I would move toward the jar each time he inhaled, and then hold perfectly still on the quieter exhale. I never

176

got caught again, though Mother always seemed to know each time I pilfered from the jar. I assumed she was counting the cookies before she went to bed at night, but learned from her years later how an Oreo cookie leaves very telltale clues on a white bed sheet.

I tried explaining to Bill that there was absolutely no way to stop Dad from snoring, and he would eventually get used to it just like we had. Bill was not the slightest bit amused and saw the new deterrent to his sleep as one more insufferable misery that had purposely been kept from him. We solved the problem a few nights later by using all three hundred feet of anchor rope to tether Dad and the *Mary Jeanine* far behind the *Ocean Motion*.

With Dad so far behind, his snoring was just a muffled roar and the rest of us slept peacefully. That method to blunt Dad's snoring, we used even the following summer when Bill was no longer a part of the crew. It seemed a perfect solution until the next year when we awakened one morning to find the *Mary Jeanine* gone. The line had frayed during a rough night and we didn't find Dad until two days later. The Bahama Bank looks small on a chart, but with only a range of ten miles on our Citizens' Band radio, finding a small boat in a thousand square miles of ocean can be a very daunting task.

Unfortunately for Bill, there was no relief that first night. By morning, he was haggard, with bloodshot eyes and complaining, "I wish to God I'd never heard the word Bahamas!"

I also slept very fitfully, but Dad and Roberto were up long before the sun and fixing breakfast. After a cup of Dad's "Navy" coffee and a plate of corned beef hash and eggs, Bill and I perked up and were anxious to start filling the boats with lobsters. We all joked about what we were going to do with all the money, while we prepared the boats to hold a thousand pounds each.

As the sun came up, we were sitting by the traps ready to pull. It took only a couple of hours for our dreams of new cars and color TVs to be shattered. For some inexplicable reason, the virgin bottom and the crystal clear water that had never seen a trap, were practically devoid of lobster. By noon, we had checked all of the areas we expected to be good and only had a handful. Dad decided to call it quits for the day since it was obvious to him the traps needed a few more nights to start catching.

It was a glum crew anchored up behind the cay that day. When Bill came aboard the *Ocean Motion* he continued with his tale of woe. "Boy! Your old man is hell to work for! He knows I've never pulled a trap before, so I expected him to go easy on me until I got the hang of it. But all he does is hand me this gaff and says to hook the float when it comes by.

"That sounded easy enough until he comes roaring up on the trap at half-throttle. I managed to get the gaff on the first one, but it flipped off when I went to grab it. I could tell he wasn't happy, but he came around on it slower the second time, and when I missed it again, he was able to back down to it. He seemed all right as we pulled the trap, but when it came up empty, his mood changed and he said kind of sarcastically, 'We'll come up on the next one real slow and see if we can get it the first try.'

"Sure enough, he practically drifted up to the next float and broke out in a big smile when I hooked it, like you would with a little kid who did something right. That one came up empty, too, and I guess I made a mistake when I said, 'Mr. Bacle, where's all the crawfish?'

"He scowled at me and said, 'Don't worry about the crawfish, Bill! You just worry about gaffing those traps.'

"I could tell he was upset about no crawfish, and he came up on the next trap at half-throttle again. I yelled for him to back down, but when he realized I had missed it, he roared around on it again and this time wide open. I could barely stand up, and my knees were slamming against the rail when the wake of the boat pushed the float too far away and I missed it again. Man, I almost went overboard trying to hook that float, and I thought your old man was going to kill me.

"Instead, he stopped the boat and just stood there looking at me. Then, he started grinning and shaking his head while he walked back to me. I didn't know what to expect, but he came right up to me and said, 'You know Bill, when I was in Borneo during the war, there was an orangutan who sat up on a tree branch over the sidewalk, and with a long bamboo stick, he'd flip the hats off of sailors who walked by. Now surely, if an orangutan can do that, you can hook that big old float with that big old gaff, can't you?'

"Brother, I practically killed myself getting those floats after that. I almost fell overboard a dozen times and my knees looked like water balloons from banging against the rail, but that didn't matter to your dad. Every time I missed a float, he'd just look at me and grin, and I knew he was thinking about that orangutan."

Dad came aboard, and we found he was not discouraged and wouldn't let us be either. After passing around beers and lighting his cigar, he started pumping us back up. "Good grief boys! Those traps have only been in the water for a week. They just need a few more nights to get the newness out of them, and then they'll start producing.

"Why, hell! I was once looking in the water over at the seaplane base, and I noticed whips sticking out from under the ramp. The closer I looked, the more I saw, until I finally realized there must be a thousand crawfish under it. Since they weren't using the ramp anymore for seaplanes, I put ten traps right alongside it that same day. The next day, I went back expecting the traps to be full, and there wasn't one damn crawfish in any of them.

"I could still see all the crawfish, so I checked them each day. By the end of a week, I still hadn't caught more than a handful. Then, one night they decided to move and the traps came up stuffed. For the next five or six days, those traps filled up every night. So remember boys, you can put traps there and fill them to the top with any bait you can think of, but those old crawdads will move when they're ready, not when you are.

"Now, that's probably the same thing that's happening here. That bottom is lousy with crawfish and they just haven't decided to light off yet. We'll give them a few more nights and they'll be crawling like worms. And if they don't, we'll just move the traps to a different spot. Why hell, there's a thousand square miles of ocean out here and we've got it all to ourselves. You've got to have a little patience, boys—there's millions of pounds of crawfish all around you.

"So let's just take a couple of days off and relax. Peter, you and Bill can get your diving in, and maybe we'll run across one of those old Spanish galleons filled with treasure. The reef on the other side of the key looks like the perfect place to start. Even if it doesn't have any doubloons, it's bound to have crawfish. So boys, let's don't get discouraged here before we even get started."

Dad's pep talk made Bill and I feel a lot better. We recognized we weren't going to get rich quick, so we turned our full attention to the diving. Dad fired us up with stories of treasure ships traveling from Mexico to Spain and loaded down with Mayan gold. According to him, we were sitting in the exact spot every ship passed by on their way back to Spain. Dad assured us that hundreds of galleons had sunk in hurricanes and some of them had undoubtedly foundered on these very reefs in the dark of night.

Today, every island schoolchild knows of Mel Fisher finding the fabulous treasure of the Spanish treasure ship *Nuestra de Senora Atocha* near Key West in 1985. But before those discoveries and without television, we had only a vague knowledge of the Spanish plundering of the new world from our history classes in school. Dad's fascination with lost treasure however, led him to read everything he could find about the Spanish ships, and his stories had us fascinated far into the night. By the time we sacked out, visions of golden idols and boxes of Spanish doubloons filled our heads, while the empty traps were far from our minds.

The morning came clear and calm. The glassy ocean shimmered in the morning light and we anxiously motored around to the eastern side of the island where the coral reef was just below the surface. The water was so clear and calm we could see every detail on the bottom, even in thirty feet of water. On the northern side, we saw clearly the outline of a wrecked ship, and anchored above it.

Excited to finally be getting in the water, Bill and I put on our dive gear and grabbing our spear guns, raced to be the first one to get wet. After looking for a few moments, we both raised our heads at the same time and marveled—not at the wreck, but at the amazing clarity of the water. We were both excellent swimmers, and Key West was noted for its spectacular diving, but the water was unlike anything we had ever seen.

The brilliance and sharpness of the colors was like looking at high definition television for the first time. Every detail on the bottom was visible to us. Angelfish, triggerfish, parrotfish, and dozens of other spectacularly-colored species sparkled in the refracted sunlight. Snapper and grouper of all sizes seemed to be coming out of every rock and crevice. The snapper went about their business as if we weren't there, but the Black and Nassau grouper were all looking up at us as if they had never seen a human before. Neither of us dove down to get a closer look at the ship, but instead drifted on the surface, spellbound by the wondrous sights.

Normally, our instincts would have led us to start shooting as many fish as we could, but even at our impulsive age, we felt it would be a sacrilege to ruin the idyllic scene. We drifted with the current for a long time, barely moving our flippers for fear of disrupting the brilliant picture before us. The shipwreck, as we would have expected, was a magnet for every type of fish in the ocean, but even as we got farther and farther away, the sights on the bottom remained as entertaining.

When we looked off into the distance, it seemed the visibility was practically unlimited. It was then that we had our first dose of reality. Circling us in the far distance was a shark, and we both pointed to it at the same time. Then, we saw another and another, until we were spinning in the water, realizing they were all around us. We looked up and saw we were at least one hundred yards from the boat, and started inching our way back with spear guns armed and pointed out at the silent threat.

Neither of us considered ourselves to be afraid of sharks. Though the most common shark in Key West waters was the harmless nurse shark, we frequently saw other more unpredictable ones, like hammerheads, lemons, bulls, and whitetips. We were both wary of those species, and if we didn't always get out of the water, at least refrained from spearing fish until they left the area.

I had recently experienced an unnerving incident that was still fresh in my mind. While spearfishing with my college classmate David Duval in shallow water near Boca Grande, I shot a ten-pound mutton snapper. As I pulled back my line and got one hand on the spear, a huge shape came over my right shoulder. A fourteen-foot hammerhead shark barely missed me, and grabbed the fish on the end of my spear. Too stunned to understand immediately what was happening, I instinctively held the spear tightly as he ripped off the fish.

I had lost a few fish to sharks before, but never so unexpectedly and never to such a giant. Close to panic, I forgot everything about staying calm and moving smoothly in the water with a shark around. As fast as I could swim, I thrashed my way halfway to the boat before thinking of David.

With pounding heart, I vainly searched for his snorkel, hoping he had dived down to look at something. I re-cocked my spear gun as if the flimsy weapon would help against that monster, when David blasted up from under the water so near that I almost shot him. "Get in the boat - quick! A giant hammerhead just took my grouper!"

The recent hammerhead experience had me constantly looking over my shoulder, but we quickly identified the circling sharks as relatively harmless whitetips. They were small ones that would ordinarily be no cause for alarm, but we had never seen more than one in the water at a time, much less one hundred. It was also very clear they were circling us, and being the unmistakable center of their attention is what really had us spooked.

Whereas we had always imagined a shark attack by a monstrous great white or mako, the possibility now loomed that we could be devoured bite by bite as if by a school of piranhas. Our confidence returned as we made our way back to the boat and the sharks remained distant and calm. We would find that virtually every dive in the Bahamas was with the company of sharks, and not all as harmless as the small whitetips.

Trapping in the Bahamas

The Bahama reef shark was the most threatening, and had the classic look of a predator. We had never seen this type of shark in Key West and they exhibited no fear of us. We later learned they are the most erratic sharks in the Bahamas and are responsible for most of the recorded attacks. We never felt comfortable with them or any other large shark around and usually got out of the water when one appeared, but the only time I was ever actually attacked was years later by a bull shark on the Cay Sal Bank.

Crossing the bank from Anguilla to the island of Cay Sal on the last day of a two-week trip with Ed Swift, Tony Willis, and Chris Belland, we were expecting to arrive about 3:00 p.m. and shoot a Nassau grouper for dinner. Plagued by minor mechanical problems, it was nearly 6:00 p.m. when we ran across a shoal known as the Lavenderas Rocks. We had tried to find them a number of times in the past, but our loran was never accurate enough to pinpoint the several acres of rocks and coral, and we never wanted to spend the time to look.

The ocean was slick calm, and though it was getting late for diving, we knew it would be our only chance to spear a fish. Cay Sal was still an hour away, but the rocks looked so inviting that we expected it wouldn't take long to find our dinner. Since we had sunk our skiff a couple of days before and were unable to get the engine running again, we anchored our forty-three-foot *Big Crawl* over the top of some very large coral heads.

Immediately upon entering the water, we realized we would eat well that night. A large grouper was directly beside the boat, and we all circled it, trying to decide who was going to take the shot. Everyone was carrying a pole spear except me. Because of the late hour, and having nothing else for dinner, I dug out the arbalete (spear gun with a trigger) from under the forward v-berth.

Possession of an arbalete is not permitted in the Bahamas, but until we had them confiscated on a subsequent trip, we unwittingly carried them for use in American waters and protection against sharks. A pole spear is held in one hand with a rubber stretched from the back of the shaft to the front, and held tightly in the crook between thumb and forefinger. To effectively shoot a fish, it's necessary to have the spear tip within inches of the target and then hold onto the spear after the fish is shot. The three-pronged tip on the pole spear will easily pull out if a solid hit is not made, and in any circumstance, getting a fish with a pole spear was no sure thing for free diving weekend warriors.

As we hovered over the prize, I glanced around and spotted a large hogfish. Leaving the grouper to the others, I took off in pursuit and quickly got a nice shot. Just as I pulled the trigger, however, the fish turned slightly and I hit him with a glancing shot. Wounded and trailing blood, the fish took off with me in full pursuit. The hogfish was in panic flight and only the extreme clarity of the water allowed me to keep the distant fish in sight.

Each time I was about to give up, the fish would slow a little, and then take off again before I could get near enough for another shot. I chased the fish until I was exhausted, and decided if it slowed again, I would take one last shot and then get back to the boat. Soon enough, the wounded fish slowed again and I took a final long shot that missed.

Unbeknownst to me, Chris had shot the fifteen-pound grouper next to the boat, and after struggling and thrashing for a minute, the fish pulled off the spear and went under a rock. The thumping of the grouper and the blood in the water attracted the attention of a very large bull shark. It was our sixth dive trip in the Bahamas, and none of us was usually panicked at the sight of a shark. However, an excited bull shark is a particularly fearsome-looking creature in the water and my crewmen were not going to tempt him. Rationalizing that if they did manage to extricate the fish, the shark would undoubtedly take it anyway, they decided to wait in the nearby boat until the shark left.

Meanwhile, I floated on the surface, catching my breath before starting back for the boat. I had not yet looked for the *Big Crawl*, but knew I had a long swim back. Normally, the skiff would have been ready to pick me up, but because its engine was down, I had no choice but to swim back against the same tide that had helped speed me after the streaking hogfish. I retrieved my spear by pulling it to the surface with the string attached to it. I had just clicked the spear into the trigger mechanism when I caught a glimpse of something near me.

I assumed one of my buddies had swum out to accompany me, as we had long ago agreed to never swim alone. Thinking I might spot a fish on the way back to the boat, I had just started to cock the rubbers when I glanced to the side and my body froze. The bull shark was not six feet away from me, and it was the largest I had ever seen.

Unlike the sharks we normally saw, he was not calmly eyeing me, but exuded a look of extreme agitation. In my suddenly chilled state, it appeared as if his back was raised and he was ready to spring forward like a released coil. As his cold eye stared at me, I had the fearful impression he was trembling in anticipation of an attack. When I instinctively turned to face him, he moved away slightly, and with what seemed to be erratic motions, he turned to face me and then paused for a fraction of a second.

At that exact moment, I knew he was coming after me. With nothing else to defend myself, I raised my un-cocked spear gun and pointed it at his face. Holding the gun with both hands, it almost touched the shark's nose. No sooner did I have my gun pointed, and faster than I could ever have imagined, the shark charged.

How it happened remains a little unclear, but apparently the tip of my spear stuck in the shark's snout or around his mouth, and his charge bowled me over backwards. The stock of the gun smashed my face and knocked down my mask, but my tight hold on the gun pushed me back enough—and fended off the shark just enough—so that he missed me. Stunned—with my mask around my neck and gulping seawater—I expected to quickly feel the savage bite of the monster. As I struggled for composure, I had to have air and I had to see. As quickly as I had ever done anything in my life, I stuck my head out of the water and got my mask back on my face with one hand, while instinctively holding onto the spear gun with the other.

With my heart pounding so hard I could barely breathe, I immediately saw the shark circling closely, and ominously preparing for another charge. From a little farther away than the first time, he turned and faced me, and I knew he was coming again. As I prepared to receive his second charge, he shot toward me, but then broke off to the side before reaching the tip of my spear. It was a false charge, but even more fearful because I knew for certain it was coming.

The first charge happened so quickly that I had no time to think about it. But despite my shaken state, by the second charge, wild thoughts of being torn apart raced through my mind. After the false charge, the shark pulsed swiftly around, preparing for another pass. As he moved into position, my brain did an hour's worth of thinking in five seconds. I knew for certain I was going to die. I wondered how painful it was going to be. I wondered if I would pass out from the shock, or would I be conscious for the whole grisly deed? Would the shark leave anything for my crew to find, and how would they react? Of all the ways I could have thought of to die, I never once imagined it would be by a shark attack.

Strangely, once I had resigned myself to dying, I was able to think a little more clearly. As the shark stalked me, I cocked the rubbers on my gun and felt better protected for a moment. Then, it occurred to me how foolish I had been all my life to think a flimsy little spear would be any protection against such a powerful creature. I still pointed the gun at the shark, but made up my mind I would not pull the trigger if he charged. While sizing me up, he passed so close that I had a perfect shot at his brain, but feared what would happen if it didn't kill him instantly.

Wondering if all the commotion had attracted other sharks, I took a quick look from side to side and saw we had drawn the company of at least fifty large barracudas. I rarely swam in the Bahamas without a barracuda around, but had never seen more than two or three at a time. Though they were fearsome-looking predators, we primarily disliked them because they were so aggressive at going after speared fish, and not because we feared being attacked.

Trapping in the Bahamas

Now, the barracudas took on a more sinister look. The only prey in the water was me. My crazed mind filled with thoughts of the barracudas joining in the attack. *"My God! Is that the way it works? The barracudas know that when the shark attacks, there will be leftovers for them? Will the shark tear off my arm or leg, and then the barracudas rip chunk after chunk out of my body in their own feeding frenzy? Or does it work the other way? A barracuda takes the first bite from the back of my leg or body and sends the shark into a frenzy?"*

Since the first charge, I had been waving one arm above the water at every opportunity, hoping my friends would see me and recognize it as a call for help. Unconsciously clued by the current and roll of the sea, I knew the rough direction of the *Big Crawl*. I was being carried farther away from the boat each minute by the current, and realized I had to start moving toward the boat. I was floating immobile in the water, fearful that even the kick of my flippers would signal the shark that its prey was in trouble.

As the shark moved away from me, I popped my head out of the water and took a quick look for the *Big Crawl*. With my head instantly back in the water and watching the shark's every move, a new panic set in. *"Where the hell is the boat? It has to be toward the west! There's no way they would have left without me! Maybe they're searching for me—but then, why can't I hear the engine? Okay . . . Okay . . . The anchor must have broken loose, and they've drifted to the north of me. That must be it. They're probably close, and I just didn't look in the right direction. I've got to stick my head up again and look the other way."*

A look to the north and a quick spin of the head revealed the boat was nowhere to be seen. As I stuck my head back in the water, the shark made another fast move toward me and then broke off again. My mind still raced with thoughts of being eaten, but I knew the boat had to be there and I would have to chance a higher and longer look. When the shark moved off again, I flippered up until my shoulders were out of the water.

I didn't spot the boat at first, but finally saw it in the direction I had always thought it should be. My thrill at seeing it was immediately tempered by the fact that it was at least a quarter of a mile away and the forty-three-foot boat looked like a small skiff from my surface view. Even without a shark dogging me, it would have been a long, hard swim against the current. Attempting to reach the distant boat, while watching my stalker every second and trying to swim calmly and methodically so as to not incite him further, seemed impossible. Yet, I knew there was nothing else to do but start moving in that direction.

When I put my head back in the water after the long look, my mind and body froze. I was surrounded by huge sharks—so close I could reach out and touch them. In a panic-stricken reaction, I jabbed the one in front of my mask with the spear gun and he barely flinched. *"Oh my God! This cannot be! Where did they all come from? There are hundreds of them! Jesus! It's going to be quick. I won't last five seconds after the first one hits! . . . Wait a minute! That one doesn't look like a shark! . . . It's not. It's an amberjack! They're all giant amberjacks! . . . What are they doing swimming around me? Are they going to attack me, too? My God, what kind of a nightmare is this? . . . The shark! Where's the damn shark?"*

Desperately, I searched for the shark through the mass of huge fish, fully expecting him to use the amberjacks for cover, so he could hit me by surprise. I spotted him at last, and he was cruising just outside the school of amberjacks. He was about twenty feet away, and though he was still circling his prey, appeared calmer at that distance. I surveyed the scene, and even then it seemed surreal. A monstrous bull shark was stalking me, a school of one hundred-pound amberjacks encircled me, and a gang of barracudas was hanging out below me like scaly hyenas patiently waiting for a meal.

The situation still seemed hopeless, but I started flippering slowly backwards toward the *Big Crawl*. I never took my eyes off the shark, but kept one arm out of the water, constantly waving toward my friends—hoping one of them would respond by bringing the big boat over to pick me up. After several minutes, I realized I wasn't making much headway against the strong current, and at the risk of further inciting the shark, I picked up the pace.

Trapping in the Bahamas

The amberjacks left as quickly as they had come, and the barracudas drifted away until there was only a couple left to keep up the vigil. The shark was maintaining a fifteen-to-twenty-foot circle, and alternated quick streaking movements with slow gliding moments while sizing me up. I imagined he was trying to figure out the best plan of attack, and as he circled me, I spun in the water to always face him.

I was reluctant at first to swim forward when he was between the boat and me, but found that even when I moved toward him, he kept the same distance between us. *"What is this shark doing? He's not attacking, and he's not leaving. Is he trying to figure out whether I'm something good to eat, or just looking for the right opening to catch me off guard? . . . What's he thinking? . . . Thinking? . . . Wait a minute. Sharks have tiny little brains. Or do they have no brains at all? Is it sharks that only have a central nervous system? Okay, he's just reacting, not thinking. Keep all motions methodical and uniform—no appearance of thrashing."*

With each passing minute, I began to think I had a chance to survive. The shark still appeared excited, but was keeping his distance and made no more motions toward me. Since the moment I started swimming, I had been waving my left arm above the water until it was almost out of the socket. I was positive someone had to see me, and frequently looked toward the boat, expecting to see someone on the bridge or bow looking for me.

Either they had all three been eaten by sharks—which even in my altered state I thought unlikely—or they were being totally irresponsible in not coming for me after such a long period of time. *"What the hell are they doing? They had to see me or else they just can't find me—either way they should crank up the boat and come for me . . . Wait a minute. Crap! The engine trouble! The boat won't start. Of course, that's what it is. They must be working frantically to get the engine started, but none of them really knows what to do."*

The shark relentlessly followed me the entire long way back to the boat. Even when I reached the boat, he was so close I feared after making it all the way back, he would nail me as I turned to climb the ladder. I took off my flippers and threw them and my spear gun into the boat, and hurdled up the ladder in one swift motion.

As I dropped exhausted to the deck, I saw my three faithful buddies relaxed in their lawn chairs—each with a beer in his hand. "*Con yo* Captain! Where's the fish?"

Bill and I turned our attention back to the shipwreck. It was definitely not the Spanish galleon we had hoped for, and appeared to be some type of small island-hopping freighter. Except for a few jagged remnants of the superstructure, there was little left but the outline and a curious, long round tank sitting in the middle of the disintegrated ship. We assumed it was a fuel tank, but Dad identified it as the boiler from an old coal-burning steamer.

The rounded sides were intact, but one end had been completely blown out. The boiler was about fifteen feet long and we went down for a look inside. Peering into the darkness, I had a fleeting impression the boiler was alive. As our eyes adjusted to the dark, we got our first exciting moment of the trip. The huge drum was full of lobster. They were hanging from the top and sides and stacked on top of each other, and it appeared our trip would be made from the one spot.

We raced to the surface to tell Dad, and he seemed even more excited than we were. "Well jeepers, boys! What are you doing yakkin about it? Go get them!"

To capture the lobster, we wired a number eight fishhook to the shaft of a spear and flattened the barb. Then reaching between their antennae and hooking them in the mouth, we'd pull them toward us and grab the lobsters with our gloved left hands in one swift motion. We towed an inflated car inner tube with a gunnysack tied in the middle, and dropped the lobster in as we caught them.

Intimidated by the darkness of the metal cave, we reached in and hooked as many as we could without actually entering the boiler. Absorbed in our work, we gradually worked our way into the boiler, overcoming the claustrophobic feeling, and the fear that some kind of monster lurked in the gloom waiting to devour us.

Trapping in the Bahamas

The sides were grown over with barnacles and sharp corals, which required us to back carefully out of the boiler to keep from shredding our arms and legs. The last of the lobsters we speared with our guns, as they were all the way to the backside and we were increasingly exhausted.

While so completely absorbed in our work, we failed to notice that we had attracted an audience. It was as if we were the performers in a giant tank at Sea World. The commotion caused by hooking the lobsters, sent signals throughout the area, and the boiler was completely surrounded by a menagerie of sea creatures. They all appeared to be watching us with a genuine curiosity.

The small sharks were still there, but closer, and joined by a couple of larger reef sharks—the first we had ever seen. Nearer the boiler were numerous familiar nurse sharks, which even in Key West were always attracted to the sound of lobsters in distress. However, the sight that really startled us, was the number of 'money' fish calmly waiting to be taken.

There were numerous large black groupers and fifty or more Nassau grouper. The blacks calmly drifted as they inspected us, while the Nassaus rested on the bottom with their heads tilted slightly to the side as they stared at us with one green eye. Dozens of hogfish gracefully moved across the bottom while others stayed motionless, blending with the sea fans and coral. Schools of mangrove snapper moved in synchronization and large muttonfish moved back and forth in the distance, excited at the thought of a lobster dinner.

Mixed with the money fish—and far outnumbering them— were vast numbers of tropical species. Triggerfish and angelfish added color in every direction, while multicolored parrotfish crunched on coral as if they weren't the slightest bit interested in the ruckus on the old wreck. Every rock and piece of ship wreckage was a kaleidoscope of neon gobies, sergeant majors, French angels, cardinal fish, and dozens of other brilliantly-colored fish.

Typically, the skittery snapper kept their distance, but the grouper and hogfish exhibited no fear of us. We swam down and pointed our spears at them until they almost touched, and still they just stared with curiosity. Dad had asked us to get a grouper for dinner, but Bill and I looked at each other and shook our heads. Later, we would shoot a grouper in a different spot.

Repeatedly diving twenty feet into a strong current and taking the lobster one by one had left us completely exhausted. Dad and Roberto were tailing the lobsters as we caught them, and our first catch was quickly packed away in the ice. Dad was excited and ready to resume the hunt, but Bill and I found the strong current adding a new challenge to our diving.

We initially thought we were dealing with tides that would ebb and flow, allowing us slack periods when we could dive the deeper waters. Though we often dove every day for weeks at a time at home, it was usually in water of eight to eighteen feet. Some of our friends were excellent deep divers, often going down sixty feet to spear a fish, but our limit was thirty to thirty-five feet—and that was for spearfishing, not the extended time needed to get a lobster from under a rock.

We would find the strong water flow a constant near the edge of the bank, caused by the heavy current flowing through the relatively narrow Bahama Channel between Cuba and Guinchos. Farther up on the Bank, toward Andros Island, the current would subside and tidal flows dominated.

Dad was interested in the ship beneath us and was particularly intrigued by the boiler, but could not be enticed to enter the water. Though his curiosity had been aroused by the wreck, he was anxious to find more lobster. Bill and I were ready also, but needed to find shallower water. On the east side of the island, we clearly saw the entire outline of the shallow reef. The gently undulating seas were breaking on coral just under the surface. We realized that on a rougher day, it would be a very dangerous area and the waves would be breaking high into the air.

We anchored on the outside of the reef, barely twenty feet from giant coral formations rising twenty-five feet from the ocean bottom. The main reef appeared from the boat to be about four hundred yards long and one hundred yards wide. We pictured thousands of antennae bristling from every coral head and imagined we would make our entire trip with the lobsters from this one spot.

The bottom dropped very quickly on the outside of the reef, and looking over the starboard side of the boat, we saw only dark blue water. As we dropped into the water, we could see very clearly the sheer drop from eighty feet to a black nothingness. We found the sudden drop to two thousand feet very unnerving, and I never got over the irrational feeling that when I was near the edge, a suction was pulling me out into the abyss.

The reef itself was truly spectacular, and once again, we found ourselves fascinated by the sight. We drifted slowly over the reef, weaving our way in and out of giant staghorn and elkhorn corals, rising almost to the surface as far as we could see—their brilliant gold colors contrasting with the crystalline blue of the water. Blue and red sea fans waved on the bottom, and long, feathery gorgonians hula danced with the current.

Except for some unexpected tarpon, there were few large fish, but the amount of tropicals was more than we could have ever imagined. The blue neon gobies, golden wrasses, and rainbow angels flitted across the corals like blinking Christmas tree lights, and around every stand of coral, we were dazzled by the beauty and abundance of brilliantly-colored fish.

As we returned to the business at hand and started diving down to look for lobsters, we came across another surprise. The bottom was littered with debris. Broken glass and porcelain covered the sandy seafloor. We found enough large pieces to recognize the shards as broken dinnerware and green, hand-blown bottles.

With our imaginations fired by Dad's stories, we started fanning the bottom, hoping to expose something of value. We started turning up other items that were mostly unrecognizable, being in an advanced state of corrosion or covered with coral growth. After finding no coins, we threw some of the more interesting items into our sack and continued the search for lobsters.

At first look, it seemed the reef was devoid of lobsters. With closer inspection, we found some lobsters, but they were gathered far up in the elaborate coral formations and very difficult to hook. Often, we would have to stick our heads completely inside a hollow opening to find the lobster hanging from the top. We soon understood how we would have to work hard for the lobsters, and started a systematic covering of the reef.

Working about twenty-five feet apart, we slowly accumulated sacks full of lobster. With each dive, I never failed to check the bottom for treasure. Many dives came up empty as I spotted something interesting and spent the dive fanning the bottom— sometimes retrieving another item for later inspection. Each time we dumped the sack, Dad's contagious enthusiasm kept our adrenalin flowing, and we repeatedly jumped back in and continued the search. "Keep looking, boys! The treasure is here somewhere. These are handmade bronze spikes. They're what the old ships were fastened with. All this stuff you're finding is definitely from a galleon.

"Now, I don't want to rush you boys—go ahead and get the lobsters first if you want to—but the treasure is probably right here under the boat on the outside of the reef. The ship would have broken out the bottom on this first set of coral heads, and dropped the ballast and treasure first. Then, the top part would have scattered over the inner reef where you're diving. You'll probably find some good stuff in there, too, but wherever you find the ballast pile is where we'll find the mother lode."

Bill and I were fired-up by Dad's exuberance and half-thought about saving the lobsters for another day and looking for the treasure first. However, we were both still intimidated by the eerie blackness on the other side of the boat. The coral formations ended abruptly, and the rubble-strewn bottom dropped very quickly to the sheer wall.

My first swim away from the boat along the outside edge didn't help to ease my anxiety. I had the uneasy feeling I was being watched, and looking over my shoulder, was startled to see a large shark not ten feet away. It was my first look at a blue shark. It was long, sleek, and beautiful, but had the unnerving habit of coming casually closer than any shark I had ever encountered.

Trapping in the Bahamas

We were unfamiliar with the sharks of the deep ocean, but saw how the blue would frequently show when we dove near the drop-off. Filled with the first day's uncertainty, the exotic shark appearing out of the eerie blackness sent me scurrying back to the boat. Later in the trip, our fears would seem silly, but on that first day, we wanted the security of the reef around us.

Back to the business of getting lobster within the safety of the reef, I surfaced to the sound of Bill screaming out my name. I looked over at him, and he was out of the water up to his chest, apparently standing on the reef. "Peter! Come over here! There's something here you're not going to believe!"

Sticking my head back under, I could see in the clear water that Bill was definitely not standing on the reef. Under him was a very large cannon. We were both breathless with excitement as we inspected the find. It was about ten feet long and so clean it looked as if it had just been placed there. Except for being tarnished and having patches of light coral growth, it seemed to be in perfect condition. We speculated how it must have been buried in the sand for hundreds of years and then recently exposed by a hurricane.

It was only four feet under the surface and looked as if it was mounted for firing. We had never seen a cannon in the water, but there were many of them at the old forts in Key West and Dry Tortugas. However, unlike the others which were fat on the firing end and tapering to a narrow muzzle, this cannon was long and sleek like the fine barrel of a huge hunting rifle. With barely contained exhilaration, we swam back to the boat to give Dad the good news.

"Damn, boys! I knew it! I knew there was a treasure ship here! What you have found is a bronze cannon. They only had those on ships of the line, which were the only ones that carried the gold. Somewhere out here there's gold and silver, and maybe even emeralds and jewelry. Hell, even if it were salvaged back then, they would have missed a lot. Get me a mask, boys! I've got to see this thing."

It shocked me that Dad was going to enter the water. I had never seen him—or any other commercial fisherman for that matter—in the water in my entire life. I felt sure Dad and the others really could swim, but though we lived on an island and the men were on the water every day, the ones I knew never actually went in the water.

Even during Dad's treasure hunting trips with the Navy divers, he never tried one of the new scuba tanks. Though they never found actual treasure, it seemed some of the finds should have intrigued him enough to go in for a look. In addition to several cannons and ancient anchors, they retrieved piles of coral-encrusted artifacts. In his storytelling, the grown-over pieces were swords and muskets and other romantic-sounding period items.

But Dad's sense of adventure did not include him being in the water, and it almost worried me when he wanted to see the cannon. He refused to use either flippers or a snorkel and dismissed our warnings about the strength of the current. The cannon was only about fifty yards away, but what looks close from the boat can seem much farther when in the water.

As I watched Dad dog paddle against the strong current, I thought of Mother's favorite story of Dad *almost* going in the water. Mom and Dad had pulled up to Key West's Monroe County Beach, and watched me as a three-year-old run headlong into the water and disappear. With Mother screaming, Dad ran to save me, but then stopped at the water's edge to take off his shoes and socks and roll up his pants legs before wading in and retrieving me.

To Mother's hysterical admonitions, Dad calmly replied, "Good grief Mary. I've seen guys under water for five minutes and live to tell about it."

Dad could not make it to the cannon. Forty years of smoking left him breathless when less than fifty feet from the boat. He still would not use the flippers and snorkel which would have made it an easier swim, but was determined to see the cannon nevertheless, and agreed to let us get the inner tube and tow him over.

Standing on the cannon, Dad's face gleamed like a schoolboy's. "This is the real deal, boys! She's definitely bronze, which means there's gold here somewhere. We're going to take this baby back to Key West and mount it right at the fish house gate!"

Trapping in the Bahamas

Neither Bill nor I had thought of the possibility of salvaging the cannon. "But Mr. Bacle, it's almost two hundred feet to the boat, and this thing must weigh a ton."

"Don't worry about that Bill, we'll figure out something. You boys look over the cannon and see if there are any markings on it. It should have the name of the ship and we can find out for sure if it was carrying treasure."

A cursory look revealed some kind of markings. The tarnish and light coral growth would not allow us to clearly see it, so we dismissed it as unreadable. Certainly, with a wire brush we could have easily made out and recorded the markings, but it didn't seem worth the effort. Today, we cringe at our stupidity, but the markings seemed of minor importance, and we assumed the cannon would always be there for later inspection.

The markings would certainly have been the key to the history of the ship itself. Documents still exist in Spain which recorded every detail of the ship's sailings. Cargo lists were sent from Mexico on all the lost and plundered ships, and every piece of treasure was dutifully listed. Dad was surely aware of that, but like us, thought it was something we could always do later.

For the next couple of days, we did nothing but search for treasure. The entire seafloor was a mosaic of broken glass and Chinese porcelain. We identified no less than six separate wrecks, and assumed at least one of them had been carrying a cargo of bottles and dinnerware.

There were so many artifacts encrusted in coral and lying partially exposed in the sand that we didn't bother with anything unless it appeared highly unusual. Though we made mental notes of where we saw lobsters, we bypassed them, truly convinced we would not need them to make our fortune. We had eyes only for real treasure and worked feverishly for the moment when the gleam of gold would reveal itself.

After two days of continuous diving, we were completely waterlogged, and realized it was time to return to our lobster hunt. Dad had devised numerous plans for retrieving the cannon, the most likely of which was to use our empty fuel drums to float it out to the boat. While it was highly doubtful we could actually accomplish that feat, the problem of then getting it into the boat was unsolvable.

Bill and I tried to move the cannon and could not get it to even budge a little. We assumed we could have moved it using a long board as a lever, in order to try Dad's alternate plan. By tying together both three-hundred-foot anchor lines, he proposed towing it out this way and that way through the valleys between the coral formations. The last-ditch plan would have required dozens of short drags in every direction, but the reef was such a tricky maze that we could not find a way leading to open water.

We discussed lashing the cannon to the boat and towing it back to Key West, but Dad decided the possibility of either sinking our boat or having the cannon drop into three thousand feet of water was so high we could not risk it. The mood was glum, as we realized we were probably not going to find a treasure, and were not even going to be able to salvage the cannon.

The deck was littered with our finds, and we finally started sorting through them. Most of the items were unidentifiable and thrown immediately back into the water. Others, which appeared to be something of value, but were deemed in poor condition, were also pitched. A few handmade bronze spikes, some larger pieces of porcelain, and a small collection of the best-preserved artifacts were thrown in a box to take home.

"Now listen up boys. You're getting discouraged way too easily. We're going to be here ten more days and you never know what you're going to find. This is a mighty big area and we've only checked out a small part of it. Hell, I know a fellow named McKee from up the Keys who spent years looking before he finally found the treasure. So, let's don't be giving up too quickly.

"Besides that, I think I've got a plan to get that cannon. I know a couple of Navy pilots who fly helicopters. If they can borrow a helicopter for the day, I'll get a couple of those boys from the Underwater Swimmers School and we'll fly over here and snatch

Trapping in the Bahamas

that thing right out of the water. I hate to show anyone the location, but we don't have to do it anytime soon. What the hell, it's been here for centuries. I'm sure it can wait a while longer."

It was sometimes impossible to know the difference between Dad being serious, or just seriously teasing. Nevertheless, Bill and I were truly impressed with the plan, and once again Dad had fired-up his troops. "Gees Mr. Bacle, that sounds like a great idea! Can Peter and I go in the helicopter with you?"

"Well Bill, I don't know about that. After all, it is a military helicopter, and the Navy brass might not think too much of us letting a couple of civilian boys on board. But let's don't worry about that now. We'll see when the time comes."

True to Dad's prediction, by the fourth day the traps had some lobsters in them, and by alternating days of diving with trap pulling, we managed to salvage the trip. The last couple of days, we got down to serious spearfishing, and topped off the iceboxes with grouper and snapper before heading home. Bill's share for the entire summer—which he still remembers vividly forty years later—was $400, which was not very much even in the '60s.

I made several more trips the following summer without Bill, and always swam over to look at the cannon when diving the reef. The following year, Dad gave up on the Bahamas, though he did have some very successful trips. The difficulty of finding crews and being away from home and business proved to be too much.

The cannon and its treasure were left behind, though plans were made for years after to mount a real expedition. When the Bahamians gained their independence from Great Britain, dreams of treasure faded away and the Spanish galleon with its bronze cannon became just a story we told over and over. I could hardly have imagined after my last lobster trip as a twenty-year-old college boy, that it would be thirty years before I would return with friends whose only interest was to view the fabled cannon.

9

Marriage and Work

After dating for four years, Monica and I were married in the summer of 1969. She had finished two years at the University of Tampa and I still needed one more semester to graduate from Florida Atlantic University. Though our parents approved of the match, they wanted both of us to finish school first. When they realized we would not be talked out of the wedding date, they enthusiastically accepted the decision and even offered to support us through my final semester.

Our June wedding turned into a larger affair than I had imagined. Being very socially active through Donald's Beauty Shop, Monica's parents knew practically everyone in Key West. Large weddings were highly-anticipated social events, and the invitation list grew long as Donald and Ann worried over inadvertently offending someone. Slyvia Knight, a close friend of the Barbers, became the wedding coordinator and she meticulously planned every detail—but nothing was more important than the invitation list.

As their only daughter, Monica was Donald's little princess, and he spared no expense for her wedding. Much to the consternation of Sylvia, I had little interest in the gala affair and would have been just as happy with a small family wedding. The reception was held at the Key West Country Club, and Sylvia was infuriated to look out the picture window and see me playing golf only hours before the ceremony, while she was frantically setting up for the party afterwards.

The wedding was held at the First Baptist Church on Eaton Street, which is now a closed-down theater. Despite the constant crisis-mentality beforehand, the whole affair went very smoothly. The following day, Monica and I left for a two-week European honeymoon—a wedding gift from Aunt Rose and Uncle Gerry. We arrived at the Grosvenor House Hotel in London at 6:00 a.m. and had to sit in the lobby with our suitcases until our room was ready at 4:00 in the afternoon.

Monica's goal in London was to shop Carnaby Street. Beatlemania had brought glittering attention to England, and London's Carnaby Street was considered to be the fashion center of the world. Miniskirts were the latest fashion rage and Monica was going to get in on the action by purchasing two of them from the very place where they had first been introduced to a shocked world.

Peter and Monica - honeymoon 1969

Trapped in Key West

They were the most eye-catching fashion women had ever worn in public, and even in the miniskirt capital of the world, Monica received a lot of stares. While they gave her a good look in London, in Spain she was a sensation. The conservative Spanish women were no match for her. With the traditional dark-attire covering everything but their hands and faces, Monica stood out like a beam of light on a dark night. The men in their dark coats and ties were so attracted to her that we picked up a following wherever we went. When we left our hotel and boarded a bus for the Prado Museum, we remained standing, so we could have a better view of the city. We were both grinning when we saw both men on the near-empty bus holding onto the same pole she was, nuzzled up next to her as if it was standing room only.

After working in Key West for the rest of the summer, we moved to Boca Raton for my last semester of college. I had already been notified by the local draft board that I would be allowed only one more semester of deferment before induction into the Army, and not to plan on starting an immediate career. When I obtained my degree, Glynn Archer, the principal at Key West High School and my former coach, hired me as a substitute teacher to take over a senior math class that had already driven out two instructors. For several weeks I kept the class at bay, but even though teachers were draft-deferred, when he asked me to take over for the rest of the year as a permanent substitute, I declined.

I wanted to go in the family business in the worst way, but was reluctant to get started and then be called away. Without the teaching job however, I was forced to start working at the fish house. A couple of months later, as I was really getting excited about work, I received my draft notice and reported to the Army Induction Center in Coral Gables. I was met by a busload of Key West boys and we were immediately put through our physicals.

By 1970, the Vietnam War had lost its appeal to my generation. The teenage bravado of *getting in on the action before it's over* had been replaced by the cold realization that our government was no longer in it to win, but was just operating a holding war while they looked for a way to extricate America from the unpopular conflict. Though we still felt it was a moral obligation—as well as our patriotic duty—to go if called, no one was anxious to be cannon fodder for the politicians.

My childhood friend Titi Roque, had already been killed in the war the previous year. We hung out together one last time when he was home on leave, and just after he volunteered for a third year in Vietnam. "Titi! Man! Are you crazy? Why did you do that? You made it through two years, and now you're going to push your luck with a third?"

He chuckled when he replied, "Believe it or not, I like it over there. I'm good at what I do and I have the respect of the other men. What am I going to do in Key West? Dig ditches? You're right, I am crazy, but the only thing I'm good at is killing gooks . . . You and me are different now. You belong here and I belong over there. I guess the truth is, I really don't care if I get killed."

Shortly after we completed our physicals, we were all gathered in a room where a soldier with a clipboard starting reading names. "Now, everyone listen up. I'm only going to read these names once."

There were about fifty of us in the room, and when he finished reading names about half had been called. Bacle was not one of them. "All right now! All of you whose name I called stay in this room. The rest of you, get your gear and go on outside. The bus will be here to take you back home. You will be given instructions in the mail as to your future in the Army."

Over the next few months, I received a couple of form letters, and several of the guys who had been sent home to wait were eventually called up, but with Dad needing me and a baby on the way, I was hoping I had been forgotten. When Lauren was born in November of 1970, I went into a different classification, essentially exempting me from being drafted unless there was a major call-up of troops. Shortly after her birth, a draft lottery was instituted and I drew such a high number that I was effectively exempted except in the case of all-out war, and settled into a life of commercial fishing.

Trapped in Key West

Dad was somewhat disappointed I wouldn't be "putting in my time," but was elated I was entering the family business. To ensure I wouldn't quickly become discouraged, he made me a partner from the beginning. For the first couple of years, the hours were long, the work was hard, and the money was little. However, Dad was re-energized by having me in the business, and with his experience and my enthusiasm, the fish house's production volume increased dramatically.

The Conch's ban on Cubans trapping lobster had run its course by then, and we actively helped fish boats convert to lobster by supplying them with traps and hydraulic winches. With an old pickup truck and the ambition of youth, I ran back and forth between the fish house and the shrimp and charter docks, picking up thousands of pounds of extra fish each day. Within two years, fish house production increased from several hundred thousand pounds a year to several million pounds, and we were looking to expand.

In the next five years, we purchased the two adjoining properties to give the fish house its present configuration. Allied Electric Inc. built a competing fish house next to us in 1968 and turned it over to the former sheriff of Monroe County, Reese Thompson, in 1970. With no experience in operating a fish house, he failed within two years, and we purchased the property.

Between our two properties was a three hundred-foot section of the abandoned U.S. Highway 1, overgrown with mangroves and littered with forty-years-worth of accumulated junk. Maurice Jabour once offered the piece to Dad for $10,000. Jabour however, was a shrewd businessman who immediately understood how his pitiful-looking property was the key to joining our two parcels and making one contiguous property out of Stock Island Lobster Company.

Dad thought the amount was excessive, but finally agreed to contact Jabour and tell him we would buy his property. Jabour informed him the price had risen to $20,000, and an outraged Dad vowed to let the property "sit there and rot." He refused to talk to the man again, and when I contacted Jabour to tell him we would take it at $20,000, Jabour immediately raised it to $30,000. Before it was all over, he would get $60,000 for the parcel, with Dad shaking his head at my youthful stupidity, and vowing he would never again speak to the man.

The property was unusable in its existing condition, and needed to be dredged and filled to be of practical use. After three years of trying, we obtained what were reputed to be the last mangrove removing and bay bottom dredging permits issued by the Army Corps of Engineers and the state of Florida. The permits were good for five years, but we were unable to afford to have the work done. When the permits were about to expire and the government agencies had denied an extension, I contacted Edward and Frank Toppino, the owners of the company that had originally dredged and filled Dad's property.

They were surprised by the permits to take out mangroves and dredge bay bottom, and extremely concerned that they were about to expire. "Don't worry about the money. We need to get the job done before the permits expire, because you'll never again get permission to do it."

As soon as I entered the business, I started working a few lobster traps with the *Ocean Motion*. By the late '70s, I had followed Dad's lead and was working a full load of traps in the deep water outside the reef. Dad's lifetime of smoking had caught up to him, and he was no longer able to work a boat full time. Though he occasionally worked the traps, he was primarily limited to nonphysical work. The fish house was booming, but Dad was still not happy being on shore, and time would prove that his fishing days were far from over.

In 1977, I opened Pete's Fish Market on Duval Street. Ben Lowe, my good friend and mate on the *Ocean Motion*, managed the market. Besides a bustling retail business, it supplied most of the restaurants with their daily seafood. Ben soon moved on to the Monroe County Sheriff's department—eventually becoming an investigator—and Thornton Sanchez took over as manager.

Trapped in Key West

After purchasing a larger building across the street, I took on Danny Roberts as a partner.

Sponge buying at Pete's Fish Market – Florida State Archives

We soon started serving some basic take-out orders like steamed shrimp and conch salad, and then put in a couple of small tables. Within a year, we had expanded to a sit-down restaurant, and were full seven days a week. With the entire production of the fish house at our disposal, we were able to sell the freshest seafood at a price no one could match.

With a wholesaler's mentality, we worked on small profit margins, expecting to be successful with high volume. Using throwaway plates and utensils, and large portions of locally-caught seafood, we drew not only hordes of tourists, but also a huge local lunch crowd as well. The waiting lines were so large at night that the police made us station a person outside to keep a single line formed back into the parking lot, so it wouldn't block the sidewalk. The commercial smoker we added sent the sweet smoky smell of buttonwood wafting over all of Old Town and drew in even more crowds.

Marriage and Work

It was a great high to have such a successful establishment, but in no time at all, we found ourselves with over thirty employees and no family life. Monica, who was pregnant with Leah, our fifth child, was working full time with the books and at the cash register. Sixteen-year-old Lauren was a server, while thirteen-year-old Natalie and ten-year-old Jenny bussed tables, and five-year-old Lucas peeled shrimp and tailed lobster in the prep rooms.

By the mid 1980's, Pete's Fish Market had recovered from a huge loss in the scallop business, and survived the disastrous loss of a shrimp boat to drug smugglers. The intensive and often wide-open drug smuggling had not only affected us financially, but with commercial fishing boats a constant target for the illicit trade, also stressed our family life and dampened enthusiasm for our very successful restaurant. By 1986, the worst of the drug smuggling was over, but the residual effects were wearing Monica and me down.

There was rarely a day when all scheduled employees showed up for work. Many of our workers were in Key West to have a good time and were only concerned with earning enough to maintain their laid-back lifestyles. Others had assorted drug and drinking habits, or had come to the end of the road to escape from the real world.

Short order cooks seemed particularly unreliable, and I was into a routine of cooking at least two nights a week in addition to spending every available minute there during the week. After four years and an exceptionally rough week, we made the decision to sell the restaurant. That week started with me going in unexpectedly on a morning I was supposed to be out in the boat, and finding the office and back room enveloped in marijuana smoke. Several of the employees—if not most—were in the habit of starting out the day with a reefer, knowing the fish smoker would quickly overwhelm the smell. A cursory search of the premises revealed two pot stashes, of which no one claimed ownership.

A couple of days later, Monica was forced to fire our best waitress. Employee theft was a continuous problem, but when she caught our top server giving free meals to her friends, she no longer knew whom to trust. On the same day, she figured out the source of our continuous problem with defective cans of whipped cream. A young Navy man, whom we considered to be one of our most reliable workers, had been spraying the cans wrong side up into a paper bag and sniffing the gas that pressurized the contents. Then, the following day, a dumpster inspection revealed a bag of pilfered lobster tails waiting for pickup.

For at least a year, Monica and I had been coming to the realization that running a restaurant in addition to a fish house and raising five children was wrecking our family life. Pete's was open 105 hours a week, and we learned from rueful experience how it was essential for either Danny, Monica, or I, to be there at all times. Though we had fully recovered financially from the scallop and drug losses, one bad week finally pushed us into the decision we knew had to be made, and we arranged to sell our majority interest to Danny—all the while telling ourselves we would just open another restaurant when the kids were older.

Time for the family
Monica, Lauren, Natalie, Leah, Peter, with Lucas and Jenny in front.

Marriage and Work

Out from under the restaurant and fish market, our family life returned to normal. The eighteen-foot bowrider we called the 'blueboat,' was once again in use. In 1975, I purchased the brand new boat after owning several junkers which never seemed to run when we wanted to use them. Monica agreed that since our recreational life revolved around the sea, we should have a reliably safe boat to take out our two young daughters.

The girls took to the boat as if they had been born on it. Four-year-old Lauren established her permanent position on my lap with both hands on the steering wheel, while one-year-old Natalie waddled around the boat as if it were a large playpen. As Jenny, Lucas, and Leah each came into our lives, they became immediate crewmembers, and most free days were spent in the boat.

Though commercial fishing was my life and a large part of it was spent on the ocean, I still enjoyed taking the family in the blueboat on my days off. Everyone loved to fish and dive, but our favorite outings were spent on the islands with beaches. Despite the fact the Florida Keys consist of several hundred islands, the long coral reef and shallow inshore waters have only allowed a few beaches to form.

The Snipe Keys are a small string of islands running north and south on the Gulf side of the Keys. The northernmost island has a small permanent beach, but the attracting feature is the sandy beach which becomes exposed only at low tide. Typically, for a few hours when the tide goes out, a beautiful white sandbar becomes the finest beach in the Keys. Though its size changes with the periodic hurricanes, it is normally about one hundred yards wide and a half-mile long.

At high tide, the sand bar is under two to three feet of water, so it is necessary to follow the tide tables to enjoy the beach. It was the favorite spot of our family, and with our boat sitting ready at our backyard dock, a twenty-minute boat ride would put us there at any time of the day. On weekends and holidays, there might be several other Key West families enjoying the spot, but most of the time, we had the beach entirely to ourselves.

Trapped in Key West

We frequently left the house at 5:00 p.m. in the summer months with a bucket of chicken or sandwiches, and stay until there was just enough light to find our way home. The children would fan out on the beach—some with dive masks and others looking for seashells or building sand castles—and the few idyllic hours would pass very quickly. As more people obtained recreational boats and Key West expanded to a year-round tourist industry, the secret of Snipe Point got out, and our secluded beach became far too popular for our family—or maybe just for me.

Though our family trips to the islands became more infrequent, the boat continued to get use for fishing and diving. All of the girls loved the boat as children, but each one eventually grew out of her desire to take a boat trip every time they were out of school. Lucas on the other hand, seemed to have inherited the addiction to the water, and even as a baby—with the boat pounding and rolling under the roughest sea conditions—he would be lulled to sleep.

As a preschooler, he spent most of his time at the fish house. Flopping around with my boots and gloves on, he was constantly trying to help with the fish packing and any other job allowing him to get as smelly as possible. Cutting bait and handling the ground fish chum were his particular favorites, and Monica complained that he always used his shirt and shorts as rags to wipe his hands. Though Lucas and I could not detect it, she maintained the odor of fish would never come out of his clothes, and they had to be kept separate from mine in the laundry room lest one shirt smell up a whole dresser full of clean clothes.

At the restaurant and fish market, Lucas was a four-year-old bundle of energy. Shoveling ice, repacking fish, and filling trays, he accomplished as much as some of the adults through sheer persistence. Though he frequently annoyed the employees by being in the way, he could peel shrimp for two hours at a time and then immediately ask for something else to do.

Lucas loved anything and everything to do with boats and the ocean, but he was fairly obsessed with fishing. Like all the children, I bought him a kiddie rod and reel as soon as he was able to hold it.

Unlike the girls however, he never got tired of using it. He fished in the canal at home and off the dock at the fish house. He fished in the mangrove roots, under the docks, and off the back of any tied-up boat.

The girls were intimidated by the larger fish, but Lucas would put a huge bait on his little rod hoping for a monster. It was not unusual to be startled at the fish house by a leaping tarpon bigger than Lucas that he had hooked on his three-foot-long 'GI Joe' rod. Though he lost several rods when they were yanked out of his hands by the huge fish, he never stopped trying to land one of the big ones.

Lucas knew all the fishermen and they watched over him at the fish house as if he were their own. Many of them were disturbed that he was often on the dock alone, and was allowed to use a small knife. When he was led to me by a fisherman holding a three-inch-long paring blade as proof that Lucas had been using a knife, he looked at the man and was genuinely puzzled. "Well, how are you going to cut your bait if you don't have a knife?"

Almost from the time he could talk, he was learning the names of all the fish. With my boots covering his entire legs, he would slog stiff-legged through the boxes of fish asking the name of each one. The fishermen were tickled by such a little guy who knew the names of even the most obscure fish, and frequently tried to stump him with an unusual catch. Late one afternoon, Wimpy Gibson pulled up to the dock calling out, "I bet I got one today you don't know."

"What is it?"

"I'm not going to tell you. You have to guess."

"Well, where is it? Let me see it."

"Just a minute. Take it easy now. Let me get the boat tied up, and I'll show you."

Enjoying the excitement he had provoked, Wimpy dug deliberately through the ice and produced a large, shiny silver fish. "Well Lucas, have you ever seen anything like that?"

With a look of true amazement on his face, Lucas stared at the fish and said, "No! I have never seen one like that!"

211

Wimpy and his brother Charlie smiled at each other, pleased they had shown Lucas something new, but the smiles turned into laughter when the little guy followed up with the observation of a grizzled veteran, "That's the biggest shad I've ever seen!"

The fishermen didn't know Lucas was doing his homework every night. The National Marine Fisheries sent large color posters of fish to the dealers to aid in identification. One had pictures of all the reef fish, such as snappers and groupers, and the other contained all the pelagics, like mackerel and swordfish. Monica framed the posters and hung them on Lucas' bedroom wall.

He was instantly enthralled by the lifelike pictures. He had me move them to the wall next to his bed and would stare at them quietly for long periods of time. Sitting on the side of his bed, I pointed at them each night with an old pool cue, and he memorized the names of every fish in the ocean. Whereas the girls all wanted to be read to, or told a story before lights-out for sleep, Lucas only wanted to talk about fishing. The only book he was interested in was *The Old Man and the Sea* by Ernest Hemingway. The first reading took two months because of all the questions he asked, and as soon as we finished the book, he insisted I start over.

He wanted to know the facts on every species of fish and no detail was insignificant to him. "What's that one next to the mangrove snapper, Dad?'

"That's a cubera snapper, son."

"Well, it looks just like the mangrove snapper."

"Yes it does. When they are small, I don't know if even I can tell them apart."

"Well, what happens when they get big, Dad?"

"Once they are over seven or eight pounds, they have bigger teeth and the snout becomes blunt, but even then, they are a little hard to tell apart except they get much bigger."

"Well how big do they get Dad?"

"I've seen some from Mexico on the shrimp boats that were close to one hundred pounds, but the largest one I've seen caught in Key West was about fifty pounds."

"Well, if they look so much alike, how do you know it's not just a big mangrove snapper?"

"You know the little line running all the way down the middle of the fish? That's called the lateral line, and it's different on every kind of fish."

"So, even when they're little, you can tell them apart by the lateral line?"

"That's right son."

"Well then, why do you have trouble telling them apart?"

"Ahhhh . . . I guess I'm just not that familiar with lateral lines."

"Have you ever caught one, Dad?"

"I've only caught three or four in my life. They don't seem to be very common around the Keys."

"Well how big was the biggest one you ever caught Dad?"

"It was about thirty pounds. All right now, son. That's enough questions for tonight. It's about time for you to get some sleep."

"Well, wait a minute Dad. Where did you catch it?"

"Near Sand Key Light."

"Well how deep was the water?"

"About one hundred-fifty feet."

"One hundred-fifty feet! Wow! Is that where you always catch them—in the deep water?"

"It's bedtime son. We'll talk more about the fish tomorrow."

"Wait Dad! Don't turn out the light yet. Just tell me what that red one with the black spot on its fin is. It looks just like the red snapper."

"Good night son."

"Dad! Hey Dad? Aw, come on Dad. Just turn on the light for one more minute."

Vacations were no different. We traveled in a small motor home for about ten years and Lucas was drawn to the water at every stop. When he spotted fish in a small pond in central Florida, he insisted on trying to catch them though we had brought no fishing gear. With dental floss, a safety pin bent into the shape of a hook, and a hot dog for bait, Lucas pulled in several small fish as an audience of adults looked on.

213

In backwater Virginia, we walked down to the river flowing by the campground. Used to the clear blue waters of home, he was turned off by the muddy brown river, believing it was little more than a giant mud puddle containing tadpoles, but nothing else.

He spotted two elderly men sitting on folding stools by the riverbank, patiently holding fishing poles. "Hey mister! What are you fishing for?"

The men were obviously annoyed at the interruption and answered curtly, "Catfish."

"Catfish? Hey mister, there won't be any catfish in that dirty water."

Both men looked dumbfounded at the childish impertinence. "What are you talking about, kid? There's plenty of catfish in this river."

"Hey Dad! Did you hear that? They think they're going to catch catfish in this dirty water!"

"Leave the men alone, son. They know what they're doing and they don't need you bothering them."

"You mean catfish can live in that filthy water, Dad?"

"Of course there's catfish in there, and it's not filthy, son. That's just the color of river water. Now leave these men alone!"

"Wait just a minute Dad. What are you using for bait, mister?"

"Chicken livers, kid."

"Chicken livers? . . . Hey Dad! Get a load of this! They think they're going to catch catfish using chicken livers! You can't catch fish with chicken livers, can you Dad? Tell them they're just wasting their time."

"Son, I told you. Leave these men alone! You don't know anything about this kind of fishing. I'm sure they know what they're doing. Sorry fellows, he just loves to fish. I'll get him out of your hair. He won't bother you again."

"Tell your kid we caught six of them yesterday."

"You caught six catfish yesterday?"

"That's right kid."

After a long look at the brown water, then at the bait bucket, and finally staring at the stringer with no fish on it, he turned to me with the guileless questioning of a child. "You think that's true, Dad?"

"Lucas! Of course it's true! I'm really sorry guys. He's only five years old. Come on son, we're going!"

"Wait a minute Dad. Hey mister, how big were those six fish?"

"Let's go Lucas! Now!"

"Okay Dad. Hey mister? Did you catch them right here using chicken livers?"

"Yes, kid! Yes!"

Back at the motor home, my attempts at correcting Lucas went over his head. Explaining how he had not only bothered them while they were relaxing alone, but had also insulted them and hurt their feelings by questioning whether or not they were lying, brought only a minimal response. "I guess I should have whispered, huh Dad? Just like in church. So, what do you think Dad? Were they telling the truth?"

During dinner, there came a rap on the door. Looking out the window, I saw the two elderly fishermen and thought they came for a talk about Lucas' behavior. "Hey mister! Bring your kid out here a minute."

Lucas and I stepped outside to face the music, but to my surprise, both of them had big smiles on their face. The one man lifted up a stringer with four fish hanging from it, including one exceptionally large catfish. "Well kid. What do you think of this?"

"WOOW!! I guess they were telling the truth after all, huh Dad? How much does that big one weigh, mister?"

"Six pounds."

"Six pounds! Are you going to eat them?"

"Sure, kid. Catfish are delicious."

"Well can I see how you rig your line?"

For the next half-hour, Lucas and the two men sat at the picnic table discussing every aspect of catching catfish. The scene was so entertaining and the three were so absorbed in their discussion I said not a word. "What size hook did you use?"

"How long was your leader line?"

"Why do you use a bobber?"

"What pound test is your line?"

"Are the fish in the middle or near the shore?"

"Where do you buy chicken livers?"

"What else can you use for bait?"

"What time of the day is best to fish for them?"

"Hey Dad! Can we get some fishing poles and chicken livers tomorrow?"

With Lucas still pulling out last minute information, the men finally said they had to get back to their motor home. "That's a great kid you got there. So long Lucas. You can have our spot.

Lucas with catfish

We have to leave in the morning, so good luck. See you, mister."

Bright and early the next morning, we loaded up on fishing gear and chicken livers. By noontime, Lucas had caught half a dozen fish and we had our first-ever catfish dinner. Though we enjoyed the meal, we all agreed catfish was not going to become our favorite fish—except for Lucas, who thought they were deee-licious.

10

Drugs on the Ocean

From the late 1970s through the early 1980s, drug smuggling became a major industry for Key West. With hundreds of smaller-sized run boats available to offload the freighters at sea, commercial fishing found itself at the center of the maelstrom, and it was impossible to not be affected. The going rate of $25,000 for a night's work left little incentive to catch fish for $.50 a pound. Though many of the fishermen resisted the temptation, fish house production was drastically impacted by the easy money, and Dad and I both had to work full time in our boats to keep the bills paid.

After giving college a very quick try in 1976, younger brother Jimmy started working lobster traps with me on the *Ocean Motion*. Before he could go out the first time, a hurricane passed west of Tortugas, and when the seas calmed a little, we put out 165 big traps I had been saving for the windy winter months. Five days later, we went back to check them and found the biggest 'crawl' of lobster I had ever seen. In three days, we caught eleven thousand pounds from the same 165 traps, and like any self-respecting eighteen-year-old, Jimmy immediately bought a new Corvette.

Shortly after the initial bonanza, we were pulling traps near Sand Key when we spotted something in the water. We knew it was a heavy object with most of it below the surface, because of the way the water was breaking over it. We passed it off as a large piece of tree trunk floating our way on the Gulfstream Current from Central America.

As we got closer, it became apparent it was not a tree trunk, but something compact and solid. Pulling alongside, we found a bale of hay. We theorized it had either fallen or been thrown from a ship transporting horses. Because it was a hazard to navigation, we decided to put it aboard and dispose of it back at the dock.

It was completely waterlogged, and we had a struggle winching it into the boat. Once aboard, we slid it to the side and forgot about it until we needed the space to stack traps. We then threw the bale back in the ocean and forgot about it.

Several months later, I was talking with our local Florida Marine Patrol Officer Mark Walker, and told him about the bale of hay. He started questioning me about it, asking, "Was it long thin leaves? Did it have seeds? Was it wrapped in plastic?"

I had to admit I hadn't looked very closely, but it did have the shredded remains of a plastic covering. "Well, what you had was not a bale of hay, but a bale of marijuana. That's how they pack it for transporting on the ships, and someone must have panicked and thrown it in the water."

That single bale was the first hint of the deluge of smuggled drugs that would soon inundate the Keys. Within two years, freighters loaded with bales of marijuana anchored within sight of Key West and offloaded their illicit cargo onto any type of vessel brave enough to try. The going rate was $25,000 to $50,000 per load, and many boats went night after night.

At first, many people were leery about trying, but as more and more people collected the easy money—seemingly without repercussion—scores of men became 'mules' for the smugglers. Within a year, new cars and trucks were everywhere. Sunburned chests with shirts open to the navel, sported bodacious gold chains and medallions, and new fiberglass boats—built to smuggling specifications—sprang from new fiberglass boat builders.

Thousands of new traps were constructed to give some credibility to the new boats and make a superficial attempt at covering the money trail. Despite the new boats and traps, fish house production dropped dramatically as the easy money continued to flow. Fueled by the outrageous flow of cash, many fishermen decided to strike out on their own, and new fish houses sprang up everywhere, even as production dropped.

An artificial market was created as smugglers washed their money by paying ever more for the fewer fish being produced. The new fish houses were advancing money for virtually everything a fisherman could want. Even many of the fishermen who had not become involved in the illegal activities moved to the new fish houses to take advantage of the financing opportunity for new boats and more traps.

Production at Stock Island Lobster Company dropped to less than half of normal, and the fish house remained marginally profitable only because Dad and I were working traps full time. Many fishermen resisted the temptation for easy money and they helped to keep the fish house running at a reduced level. With each day that went by, the smugglers became ever bolder, and they finally approached me.

The first offer was one they thought no one could refuse. On a certain night, I was only to make sure the fish house did not open to unload a boat. For that simple complicity, I would find $50,000 in a paper bag on my boat the next day. When I said I was not going to participate in a crime and no one was going to unload drugs on my property, I received the first of many threats.

The spokesman for the drug smugglers was one of our fishermen, and he passed along his best advice; "Look, man! These people are going to unload whether you like it or not, and if I was you, I would stay away because they can play rough. Oh, and please don't think about calling the cops or you'll be in for a really big surprise."

With the little bluster I could summon, I assured him I would indeed call the authorities, and furthermore, it was time for him to pack up his boat and move to another fish house. The man had been our top-producing boat for a number of years, but by that time, was not only arrogantly flushed with cash and gold, but also hooked on the drugs he was smuggling.

Trapped in Key West

Fifteen years later he showed up at the fish house, shaking my hand and hugging me like a long-lost family member. Fidgeting and blinking uncontrollably, he was a pickled remnant of the man I had known. When our forklift backfired, he dropped into a karate stance and skittered around like a fiddler crab—desperately searching for the person who was shooting at him. When it finally entered his burned-out brain that he was not being fired at, he continued talking as if nothing had happened.

Dad and I were at a loss as to what to do. Rumors had been flying for a long time about the local police being involved, and we genuinely did not know who to trust in law enforcement. With drug smuggling so wide open for so long, it was easy to believe everyone was involved and we could be endangering our families and ourselves by reporting what we heard.

It eventually became common knowledge the cops were on the take, and even when I was a witness to the activities, I didn't know who to call. On a calm day, while running west from Cosgrove Light—about thirty miles from Key West—my mate and I were enjoying an easy day of trap pulling. We had been catching a lot of lobster and were heading toward traps we knew were full.

In the distance, I spotted something floating which I thought was a small dinghy or possibly a large piece of Styrofoam. It was bobbing in the water, and as I got closer, I spotted another and then another, and finally a dozen more. It wasn't until we were actually on top of them that I realized they were bales of marijuana. They were wrapped in plastic, and had been dropped so recently they had not absorbed any water and were bouncing around like corks.

As far as we could see there were floating bales, and I realized we were looking at hundreds. It was a major drop shipment, not a few strays or some offloaded in panic. I saw we were in a very dangerous situation, and turned back to the way we had come. I knew if I called the Coast Guard on the VHF radio, I would not only be identified, but would probably start a riot with boats coming from everywhere to harvest the 'square groupers,' and make an easy $10,000 per bale.

Drugs on the Ocean

As we headed away from the load at full speed, I saw another boat going toward them and assumed it was one of the pickup boats. When I finally recognized it as a boat I thought would not be involved, I gave chase to warn him away, but his boat was too fast for me, and I knew that soon enough he would see for himself.

He did spot the contraband, but instead of leaving, loaded his boat with seventeen bales. Unfortunately for him, he was eventually apprehended a few years later. As so often happened, he was 'ratted out' by someone who wanted to receive a lighter sentence, and it cost him four years in a federal penitentiary.

Not long after spotting the floating bales, many policemen and city officials were busted by federal drug enforcers. We hoped that would end the drug days, but after everyone laid low for a while, the smuggling got back up to speed and things were as open as before.

For several years, it seemed the ocean itself was producing the bales, and they often floated around like seaweed, always appearing when least expected. Pulling traps was something of a duck shoot, and many fishermen cashed in on the $10,000 bales they found floating.

While working near the tail end of the reef—about forty miles from Key West—I spotted a bale on an extremely rough day. My regular mate Antonio was with me, along with a man named Elio whom I had taken for the first time. Antonio said Elio was a *"loco Marielito,"* but we needed another man that day and I couldn't be too choosy. Antonio had also come over in the Mariel boatlift of 1980, but was apparently not one of the 'crazies' Castro cleaned out of his prisons and mental hospitals to send to the United States.

The bale was off the starboard bow and riding low in the water. I hoped with the heavy seas and the amount of lobster we were catching, they would be too preoccupied to spot it. I would have pointed it out to Antonio if we had been alone, since he was very appreciative to be in America and didn't want to do anything to endanger his status. Elio, however, was an unknown, and he came across as a very rough character with a couple of screws loose in his head. Both Antonio and I were wary of him and had quickly decided we wouldn't take him again.

I was relieved when we went by without it being spotted. But just as I was breathing easily, an excited shout rang out, *"Oye, Capitan! Oye! Oye! Capitan! Capitan!"*

Elio was screaming and ran forward to grab me by the arm and show me the prize. There was no question in his mind we would salvage the bale and he would be the hero for spotting it. He was so excited he didn't comprehend my response. "I see it! But we're not picking it up."

Elio continued shouting, *"Mira! Mira, Capitan! Etta ayi! Etta ayi!"*

"Elio! Yo lo veo! Yo lo veo damn it! *No lo voy a recojer! Comprende?* We're not picking it up! . . . No! No! No!"

Elio was stunned. No is a universal word, familiar in every corner of the earth, and he was trying to understand, *"Capitan, por favor. Que paso, Capitan? . . . Que paso? . . . Antonio? Que paso?"*

"Antonio, please explain to Elio why we're not taking the bale on board. Tell him they put you in jail for that in this country, and when he gets out, they will send him back to Cuba."

"No! No! No, Capitan! Por favor? Todo el mundo lo hace, nadie tiene problema!"

"I know it seems like everyone is doing it and no one is being caught, but we're not going to do it. So just shut up and get back to work! *Callate, y ves a trabajar!"*

A couple of years before, I put a rearview mirror by the steering wheel, so I could keep an eye on the mates. The original purpose was to make sure they baited and cleaned the traps properly, and to see when they were ready to drop the trap back in the water. On that day, I was especially glad I had the mirror as I watched Elio gesticulating and yelling at Tony while they pulled the next trap. I knew it was far from over with Elio.

When things are not going well, it seems everything happens to make the problem worse, and so it was then. Looking out the side window, I saw another bale float by as we pulled up to the next trap. As it passed by the stern of the boat, Elio saw it immediately and turned to Antonio with arms extended, palms up, and right in his face.

Drugs on the Ocean

I didn't have to hear the words to know the gist of what he was saying: *"Now will you listen to me? The captain is crazy! We need to make him do this!"*

I watched in the mirror as Tony stopped pulling the trap and started arguing with Elio in a highly animated confrontation. With arms and hands waving wildly, they were nose to nose, bellowing in each other's faces. As they each became screamed out, I could tell Elio was demanding that Tony talk to me.

Tony obviously did not want to do it, but with Elio adamantly pushing him, he finally came forward. "Petey, please. It's not me that wants to pick them up. But he wanted me to ask you if you will give him a life jacket, so he can swim the bales back to Marquesas. He says you don't have to do anything else and he will give you half the money when he sells them."

"That is insane! It's over twenty miles to Marquesas. If I put him in the water, I would be killing him. There is no way! Tell him this is the last time I want to hear about it! If there were one hundred bales in the water, it wouldn't make any difference to me! So just forget it!"

"Petey, this man really is crazy. I don't know what he might do, but we need to watch him very carefully."

Elio seemed to calm down after Tony broke the news to him, and I hoped he was resigned to the decision. After ten minutes of trap pulling, I thought the crisis had passed. Elio turned to me between traps and said he was sorry and wished to come shake my hand. I motioned for him to stop about five feet from me and told him to say it from there.

"Capitan, por favor? Perdoname por lo que te dije. Pero, puedo usar su radio?"

"No, Elio! You can't use the radio! I don't want to hear anything more from you! Do you understand? *No mas! Fini! Se acabo!* I don't want to hear any more about it! Now, get to the back of the boat!"

Elio became enraged and started screaming like a madman, "You *mucho* money, me *nada*! You *automobile nuevo*, me *bicycleta*! You *casa grande*, me sleepie boatie!"

Trapped in Key West

He reached out and grabbed me by the arm, and I was shocked by the strength of his grip. Without waiting to see what was coming next, I grabbed him by his shirt, pulled his face up to mine and yelled, "*Callate!* Now get to the back of the boat and stay there!" as I shoved him hard toward the stern. He fell, and his momentum and the wet deck slid him all the way to the back of the boat, where he crumpled up against a crate full of lobsters.

Expecting him to come back at me, I reached down below and grabbed a twenty-inch butcher knife we used to cut cowhides. To my surprise, he just sat motionless against the lobster crate with his head hanging down. For a moment, I thought he was hurt or even crying, and almost felt sorry I had been so rough with him.

Tony helped him up, and I put the knife under my jacket on the console as we resumed pulling traps. I thought it was finished then, but never took my eyes off the mirror. Ten minutes later, I watched as he slipped a knife under his rain jacket. It was so casual I would have missed it if the knife hadn't hung up for just a second on his jacket.

A few minutes later, when he felt certain I hadn't noticed, he started forward with his hands held out in an apologetic gesture. On his second step, I pulled out the butcher knife and pointed it at him. He knew without a word exactly what I meant, and the day continued without further incident. I refused to let him come forward for the long wet ride home, and for two hours, he cursed and threatened me like a lunatic.

Tony was very concerned about the warnings to kill us both, but I was more concerned about the threats to burn the fish house and sink the boat. We took extra care for a few days, but never saw Elio again. Some time later, Tony heard he had returned to Cuba and was put back in jail.

In the midst of that wide-open drug era, something new turned up in the waters of Key West. North of Marquesas, the shrimp boats were finding scallop beds so big their nets were becoming full in a few short minutes. The scallops fouled the shrimp nets and destroyed many of them, as they were not properly constructed for the heavy weight of the shells.

Drugs on the Ocean

Scallops were fairly common in Key West, but not in such abundance, and the calico or bay scallop, was always too small to be commercially harvested. By the 1970s however, processing equipment had been developed that would take in a small scallop shell at one end and turn out a cleaned and packaged product at the other end.

In 1979, I took in my longtime friend Danny Roberts as a partner in Pete's Fish Market. By that time, a scallop processor from the east coast of Florida had sent a couple of boats to Key West and started harvesting. In a decision we would soon come to regret, we decided to try the scallop business.

Because of the huge amounts being processed, we assumed scallops would always be prolific in Key West, and hired a man in Cape Canaveral to start building a mobile processing plant. Anxious to get started, and believing our equipment builder would have us in operation within three months, Danny and I flew to Bayou La Batre, Alabama to buy a scallop boat.

Converting any dragger to harvest scallops is relatively easy, so we purchased a seventy-eight-foot steel hull shrimp boat named the *Stanford Morse*. I previously asked the advice of several friends in shrimping, and they all advised against entering the business. I had not confided the fact that we would soon be using it for scallops, and felt confident I didn't need to know anything about shrimping. At the time, Danny and I could see nothing but success in our future, never imagining the name *Stanford Morse* would haunt us for years to come.

Since it would be a quick job to convert the boat to scalloping, we decided to let the boat make a little money shrimping while the scallop equipment was being constructed. With high hopes and an experienced captain, we sent the boat out on its first trip. Five days later, it returned with $6,000 worth of net damage and a busted trip. The profits we expected from the shrimping never materialized, as trip after trip the boat lost money—exactly as I had been warned it would.

Trapped in Key West

In 1979, the major fear of boat owners was a captain deciding to take the boat on a drug run, or drug smugglers stealing the boat and having it disappear into South or Central America. Our first captain was a local man whom we strongly believed would never be involved in drugs. We felt secure that even if the boat did not make us a lot of money, at least it would be safe until the scallop equipment was ready.

Author with Stanford Morse shrimp boat

Two months after we purchased the boat, I was at a school board meeting at Grace Lutheran Church when Danny called. "Peter, something is going down with the *Stanford Morse*. Joe Williams, the Customs agent, says the boat has been anchored at Smith Shoals Light for the last two nights. The weather is perfect, and all the other boats have been dragging each night and catching a lot of shrimp.

"He believes the boat either has engine trouble—which we would surely know about—or more likely, is about to leave on a drug run. Customs can't board the boat because they haven't done anything wrong, but he says we need to do something tonight or the boat will probably be on its way to Columbia."

Drugs on the Ocean

"Okay, meet me at the *Monica Ann* in half an hour. I think it's better to have a thirty-four-foot Crusader than to have the speed of my eighteen-foot Wellcraft. I've got the AR-15, a shotgun, and two pistols. I'll meet you at the boat in a half-hour."

"Peter, I'm sorry. But you know how sick Maria is. I can't just leave her in this condition."

Suddenly remembering that Danny's wife Maria had just been released from the hospital, I realized he was right. "I still need someone to go with me!"

"I knew you would, so I asked Joe Williams, and he said he'd go with you. He said he can't go in an official capacity, but would accompany you as a friend who was off duty."

Even in my excited state, I knew that for a U.S. Customs officer, the off-duty stuff was nonsense. Joe was a federal law enforcement officer, and I was happy to have him with me in any capacity, but I fully understood he and his agency were trying to determine whether Danny and I were conspirators in a drug deal, as virtually everyone in the fishing business was under suspicion.

It was a calm night, and from a considerable distance, I could see the boat was still anchored very close to Smith Shoals Light, about ten miles north of Key West. As we neared the boat, two men—who were obviously expecting someone—ran out on the back deck to throw us a line. Neither of the men was part of the regular crew, and I kept my spotlight shining in their faces. "Hey, man! Turn out the goddamned light! You're all tied off man! Turn it to hell off!"

As Joe secured the bowline, I ran forward with a pistol in my belt and the AR-15 in my hands. As I jumped aboard, the men's eyes cleared from the spotlight glare and saw they were looking down the barrel of what is known today as an assault rifle. "Hey? Man! What the hell is going on here! C'mon man, don't shoot! Don't shoot! We haven't done anything!"

"Where's the captain and crew?"

"I don't know man! I mean like, they left man. I mean, like I thought you were them coming back."

"Who are you, and what are you doing on my boat?"

The talker seemed visibly relieved to hear I was the owner and realized he was not going to be shot. "Oh, man. Yeah, yeah, man. We're like uh, like uh, mechanics, you know? Yeah, they brought us out here to work on the engine, and we've been waiting for them to come back. Like, we're sure glad to see you man, cause now we can get back in."

"Who else is on the boat?"

"No one. It's just like, uh me and my helper."

I made them sit on the deck, handed Joe the pistol, and asked him to keep them covered while I checked the rest of the boat. No SWAT team member ever approached a bust with more apprehension than I had about entering the wheelhouse. I allowed for only two possibilities: either I was going to be shot at, or I was going to find the captain and crew murdered.

With my back against the steel bulkhead, I reached out and let the door open. When there were no shots, I was relieved, but still entered commando style—crouched low and ready to fire. The wheelhouse was empty, and I crept toward the two small crew-quarters rooms and the head.

The bathroom door was open and it was empty, but the crew room doors were closed. The first room proved to be empty also, but the second room held the big surprise. It was stacked to the ceiling with boxes of electronic equipment. The *Stanford Morse* was already fully outfitted with all electronics, including radar, lorans, and a single sideband radio for long-range communication. The boxes contained new spares for everything.

Not only were there spares for all the electronics, but even for the compass, binoculars, fire extinguishers, and all other non-electronic essentials. Additionally, there were starters and alternators for the engine, and boxes of hoses, belts, gaskets, and other repair items for anything that might go wrong with a motor. There was no doubt the boat was leaving on a drug run.

I reported the findings to Joe, and we both agreed we might find something really awful in the ice hold. The 'mechanic' assured us we were wrong. "Man, you all are crazy! I told you, we're just mechanics, man! We're not drug smugglers, and we're sure not murderers!"

The ice hold on the *Stanford Morse* was cavernous and it had been filled for a long trip. It would be the obvious place to keep dead crewmen, and with great trepidation I removed the hatch cover. Mercifully, there were no bodies, but it did contain another surprise. Thousands of dollars worth of refrigerated goods lay buried in the ice. There were hundreds of pounds of beef, pork, and poultry, and boxes and boxes of milk, butter, eggs, and other items that needed refrigeration. The boat was fully stocked for the trip to Columbia and it was about to leave.

We then thought about the possibility we were being watched. The bright lights illuminating the back deck for night-work were spotlighting our actions to anyone within a couple of miles, and we knew we had to get the boat back to the dock. Neither Joe nor I had ever run a shrimp boat, so I had the mechanic crank the engine and drive us in.

Our mechanic became very friendly instead of confrontational, and told us the story of his life on the two-hour trip back to shore. "Yeah man, I'm sure glad you guys came. Your captain just left us out there man, and I've got like, other jobs and responsibilities, you know? Yep, I'm sure going to be glad to get back."

I quietly asked Joe what he thought would happen to the two men when I turned them in to the authorities. "Pete, I hate to tell you this, but these men are going to end up walking. They really haven't broken any laws by being on your boat. I'm afraid you're just going to cause yourself a lot of headaches and it will all be for nothing. Unless you can get the captain or crew to testify that these men broke some law, they won't even be charged. And we both know the captain is not going to do that because he would undoubtedly be implicating himself as well."

"It just doesn't seem possible these guys could be in this obvious drug smuggling situation and not be charged with something!"

"Sorry, Pete. I could probably get in trouble for giving you this advice, but the law is very particular about proof and I really don't think you have any."

"So, I'm supposed to thank them for bringing us in, and maybe ask for a bill for fixing the engine?"

"Look, you can file charges against them if you want. I'm not telling you not to. I'm just trying to keep you from going to a lot of trouble for nothing."

We took the boat into Johnny Yung's shrimp house adjoining the Coast Guard station, and told the men to get lost. The one man had never spoken except to give us a name—which was undoubtedly not his real one—but the mechanic could not believe he was being let off so easily and decided to press his good fortune.

"All right man. Sorry about your crew, but I'll contact you in a few days to see what happened to them. Listen man, I'm like, not even going to charge you for the engine work, okay? Let me just get my things and I'll be out of here."

I put my hand on the pistol in my belt. "You're getting nothing off the boat. Get out of here now or I'll call Drug Enforcement."

"Man, that's my personal stuff on there! You can't just keep my binoculars, my tape player, and my clothes! I need that stuff!"

"Well, if you want to call the police, do it now. Otherwise, get the hell out of here! . . . Now!"

We stood on the empty dock and watched the 'mechanics' disappear into the dark night. "Joe, I don't know how I'll ever be able to thank you for going with me. I could never have done it without you. If there is anything I can ever do for you, just let me know."

"Well, how about I just take that single sideband radio and we'll call it even?"

His request was such a shock that it made my blood run cold. That a law enforcement officer would want a $3,000 radio for going with me had my mind racing with wild thoughts. Was he a dirty cop? Was he setting me up? Was he testing me? Was he in on the deal?

Drugs on the Ocean

I stammered in response. "Joe, I don't know about that. I mean, I don't know what's going to happen next. They might want their stuff back and I might have to give it to them. And you might get in trouble somehow. I really think we should wait a while and see what's going to happen."

"Hey, Pete, you're absolutely right. I couldn't accept it anyway. I just wanted to see what your response would be. Sorry, but its part of my job. You have my number. Anything at all that comes up, you call me and I'll be there."

I wanted to believe him, but the damage was done. Until he asked for the radio, I had complete confidence in him, but I was already so suspicious of law enforcement that I could never bring myself to call him in the troubling days ahead.

I arrived home in a taxi at 5:00 a.m. and took a relaxing hot shower. Monica was in bed, but had been unable to sleep. "Well? What happened? Was it a drug run? Is the boat all right?"

"Yes, it was a drug run. We stopped it and the boat is safe by the Coast Guard Station. There was no trouble. I'll fill you in on the details after we get some sleep."

I was wondering how much I should tell Monica. She shared every detail of my life, and by 1980, she was helping with the fish house and our recently-opened Pete's Fish Market Restaurant. Lauren, Natalie, and Jenny were attending Grace Lutheran School, and Monica was working with everything at our busy restaurant except the kitchen.

As I dozed off, I decided she had enough to deal with. Our businesses were important to her, but like all good mothers, her children were the dominant force in her life. Between the children and the restaurant, she seemed to be on the go seven days a week. She certainly did not need a new worry.

Through all the drug problems before, I had never felt my family was threatened, but just then, I didn't really know. I had personally ruined a multimillion-dollar drug smuggling deal and was in possession of thousands of dollars worth of equipment and supplies. As my mind left thinking about what had happened, it turned to what was going to happen next. I knew there would be repercussions, but decided to hold off telling Monica of my concern until I really needed to.

Neither of us were quite asleep when the ringing phone startled us. "Hey, man. How you doing? Hey, like I hate to be the one to tell you, but I'm afraid you really messed up, man. You really messed up *biiiig* time. Yeah, like my people will be coming in this afternoon and they are, like really, really, really upset. I feel sorry for you man. These people play rough man, and they are really pissed at you. You know what I mean? Like really *pissed*— and these are not people you want to piss off! "

As I slammed the phone down, Monica was frantic. "Who was that?"

"It was nothing to worry about. I'll tell you later."

"Peter! I heard what he said. What did he mean?"

The decision over how much to tell Monica was made for me, and as I carefully explained the situation in a way that would not unduly alarm her, the phone rang again. "Hey, man. Listen man. Like don't be hanging up on me like that. I like you man, and I don't want to see you get hurt. I'm a little scared of these people myself. They don't care about nothing man. I really think you should start out by like, giving them back all their equipment, you know?"

"Listen asshole! I'm not giving back anything! You guys have cost me a lot of money with this, and I'm keeping everything to make up for some of it. Tell your *people* that they know where to find me! And don't you ever call again or I'll have a warrant out for your arrest!"

"Oh my God, Peter! Oh my God! What are we going to do? You don't think they'll hurt the children, do you? Peter, this is serious! We have to call the police!"

"Darling, please! Just take it easy. This is all a bluff. They are the ones who have done something wrong, not us. The deal is dead. They're not going to make more trouble for themselves by coming after us. There are no people coming in this afternoon—or any afternoon. This guy is just trying to get something out of it for himself. Besides, who are we going to call? The Key West Police Department?"

"Well, call the Customs man who went with you. He really did go with you, didn't he?"

"Yes, Monica. He went with me and said he would be there any time we needed him. They know a Customs man was with me, so that's another good reason they will leave us alone. Don't let this creep get us panicky over things that are not going to happen."

"Well, I sure hope you're right, but our kids are not going to school today! They are staying home with me!"

I sure hoped I was right, too. I didn't feel any of the confidence I had displayed to Monica. My experience to that point with drug smugglers indicated they were a lot of bluff, but little action. I also realized my experiences had been with the local amateurs who were useful primarily as mules, and I had never had a confrontation with the real masterminds behind the operations. Some of them were truly frightening people whose actions were completely unpredictable to me, and without a doubt, I did not wish to cross them.

Though I genuinely felt professionals would not be looking to bring more attention to their operations by harming innocent families, I was prepared to give back the equipment if they requested it in person. I was not going to give it to the mechanic, but I had no intention of battling hard-core smugglers over a few thousand dollars worth of electronics, and just wanted to put the threat to my family life behind us.

Despite my feeling they would not actually harm us, I nevertheless knew I had to make plans to ensure the safety of my family. Between the tension-filled night, the threats, and Monica's anxiety, my sleep-deprived brain concocted a number of outlandish protective schemes. In the end, I decided I would simply carry a pistol with me at all times and wait to see what was going to happen next.

I didn't really expect his people to appear, but I spent the next day at the fish house filled with apprehension over every unfamiliar car coming through the gate. The pistol was under my shirt, but I was almost as concerned about carrying an illegal concealed weapon as I was of the smugglers. The people did not show the first day, which in some ways only increased my concern.

All was quiet at home, too. The kids were happy to be home from school and Monica was feeling somewhat better. As we agreed, she had not answered the phone all day, but was concerned over it ringing so frequently.

I was home only a few minutes when I answered the ringing. "Hey man. You got lucky today. My people were like, delayed by the weather. Don't think you got too lucky, though. They'll be here tomorrow, and they said they want to see you in person. Like, good luck man. You're going to need it."

"That was him, wasn't it?"

"Yes Monica, it was him. It's the same thing. He's bluffing. You see, the people didn't come today, and they're not coming tomorrow or any day. Just don't answer the phone and this jerk will give up."

The phone rang again. "Hey man. Like, I forgot to tell you. They want their equipment. You're going to be, like responsible you know, for another busted run if they don't get it tomorrow."

Though I consistently hung up on him, the phone would always continue to ring until I unplugged it. We secured the house and spent a very restless night trying to catch up on sleep. My pistol was on the nightstand and I patrolled the house half a dozen times during the night.

Monica informed the school and was assured the children would go with no one but her. Each time we plugged in the phone, it would start ringing within minutes. I answered it the next evening after the people had once again not shown. "Come on, man. You can't like escape this by not answering the phone. My people are here man, and they want me to pick up the goods."

After four days, Monica was a wreck and I had just about decided to give up the equipment when I answered a call that made my blood run cold. "Hey, man. Where you been? We've been, like trying to get hold of you for two days. My people said to tell you that they really like children, you know man? I mean like, they have kids of their own. And it would really be a shame if something happened to those sweet little girls over at Grace Lutheran School just because their old man wouldn't give up some boxes of electronics. Come on dad. I mean, is it really like, worth it man?"

For the first time, I lost control, and he hung up as I screamed threats and profanities at him. Monica was petrified but I was furious, and frustrated I could not get my hands on him. I realized I truly would have shot him if he were there. Though we both expressed concern over the safety of the kids, nothing had ever caught me more by surprise or angered me so out of control, as the direct threat to harm my children.

I knew then, there had to be a confrontation. We could not live like that, and threatening the children had taken the bizarre game to a different level. Monica made up her mind to keep the kids at home until the situation resolved itself, and I waited for him to call again.

Playing mind games with me, he waited until the next day to call. "Hey, man. Sorry I upset you so much. But I'm just like, the messenger, you know? Like, don't take it out on me man. I warned you these people play rough."

"Okay, what do they want from me?"

"Hey man, now you're talking. All they want, is like the electronics. Give them to me and they will leave you alone. And oh yeah man, like don't forget my stuff too."

"So, what about your people? Are they going to be with you?"

"No man. They say you've already seen me, and they don't want you to be able to identify them. Hey, that's good for you too. I wish I didn't like, know them. You know what I mean, man?"

"Okay, meet me at the back door of the fish market tomorrow morning at 10:00, and I'll have everything for you."

"Smart move, man. Smart move. Like, you're going to get me off the hook with these people too. So listen, don't be like thinking of doing something crazy. These people are a lot crazier than you and me and they don't play games, man."

"Just be there at 10:00."

Though Danny had never been directly threatened, he and Maria understood they were at risk also. That evening, I called Danny to explain the new development. "Just remember Danny, he's mine first. After I beat the crap out of him, you can have your piece. Then, we'll drag his sorry ass over to the police station and have him arrested."

Danny didn't think too much of my plan. He was certain I was the one who would end up in jail, and was not as sure as I was that the man was operating completely on his own. It didn't matter to me. My anger over him threatening my children would not subside. I knew. I really, really knew, the man was not going to harm my children, but my desire to hurt him for saying it couldn't be repressed.

I didn't care about how badly I might hurt him. I didn't care that I might go to jail and I didn't care that his people might come for me. It was all irrational and I knew it, but I wanted to get him anyway.

The next morning when I arrived at the fish market, Judy told me she was really glad to see me. Danny had "gone nuts" on some guy and everyone was afraid to go in the back room.

I immediately raced into the back room. "Peter, I'm really sorry. I saw this guy hanging out in the parking lot, and I knew it was him. I had him come in and wait in the back room, but when I confronted him, he said he was only talking to you. Then, he started getting belligerent and demanded the electronics. Before I knew it, we were going at it. I thought I hurt him real bad, but when I went to the phone to call the police, he took off running and I couldn't catch him. I'm really sorry."

I was furious with Danny. I wanted to exact my revenge first, and then take him to the police station and have him booked. I knew they would let him go, but at least they would have his picture and a record of the threats on file. That, I reasoned, would be enough to make him disappear from my life forever.

Drugs on the Ocean

What was to happen next? Would the guy realize I wasn't going to cooperate and just leave me alone, or was I back to where we were before the confrontation? Would the beating make him do something crazy—or worse, make them do something crazy? The uncertainty was the worst part, but I finally reasoned if there was going to be further trouble, I would hear from him very quickly.

We took extreme care with our children and our movements, but after a few days of hearing nothing, we began to feel as if it was over. I still carried the gun everywhere, but slowly we started relaxing. It was months before our lives returned to normal and years before we could put it completely out of our minds.

Our captain was nowhere to be found and we heard some time later he was running a boat in Texas. His father came to see me a few weeks later and explained how the smugglers had come on the boat with guns, given his son $5,000, and told him to get lost. He claimed his son had done nothing wrong and didn't keep any of the dirty money, but feared for his life if I tried to get him to testify. I did not believe his story, but by then, I had become so cynical I didn't believe anyone.

We recognized after the incident, the need to be more security-conscious with the boat. It was apparently a perfect vessel for hauling tons of marijuana, and we didn't want a repeat performance of the smuggling attempt. We installed a fuel restriction device on the engine to prevent it from being stolen while we searched for a new captain. The device would allow the engine to run for a while, but when the fuel in the line was used up, the motor would shut down. Only a real mechanic would be able to find and eliminate the device, and we felt the boat was secure.

Less than a month later, on my regular morning check of the boat, I found it gone. I thought there had to a reasonable explanation, and checked every other dock to see if it had been moved. It seemed incredible, but the boat was really gone.

I called Danny to report the missing boat and he gave me more bad news. "Well, that explains the phone call I just had. Bill Jamison, the charter boat captain, called his wife on the radio and

237

told her to tell us our shrimp boat was drifting out near Western Dry Rocks. I told her it couldn't be our boat because of the fuel restrictor, but apparently it is."

By the time I arrived at the fish market, Danny had already arranged for a boat to tow it back to the dock. I called the Coast Guard and was told they had been trying to get in touch with me. They said a local fisherman had seen the boat drifting and was standing by until help arrived.

The local fisherman turned out to be a fourteen-foot skiff with a small outboard motor. He had a thin piece of trap rope tied to the seventy-eight-foot steel hull shrimp boat, and was claiming salvage rights because he had prevented the boat from drifting up on the reef and foundering. The *Stanford Morse* was so heavy that a fleet of twenty such small-sized skiffs would have been dragged up on the reef along with our boat.

Nevertheless, the preposterous claim had legal standing under the laws of the sea and had to be treated seriously. Fortunately, we knew the man, and when he found out the boat belonged to Danny and me, he agreed to not file the claim after we offered him a generous reward for saving our boat.

Between the marine mortgage, the insurance, the operating losses, and the attempts to steal it, the boat was bleeding us dry. With reasoning that cannot be explained today, we decided the boat would make us money and be safer in Texas. With a new crew, the *Stanford Morse* spent three disastrous months in Galveston and returned with more red ink and a lawsuit.

One of the crewmembers claimed a pad eye had snapped, hitting him in the eye and causing a loss of vision. In addition, the captain tried to salvage the trip back to Key West by catching a load of shrimp in strange waters and destroyed all six of the nets. Several months later, after some substantial attorneys' fees, we learned the crewman had been injured by a pool cue in a barroom fight and the lawsuit was dropped.

The fabrication of the scallop equipment was going slowly, and we considered chaining the boat to the dock until it was ready.

Drugs on the Ocean

Inexplicably, we never considered the sanest option, which was to sell the boat and buy another one when and if the scallop equipment was ever completed. Once again, we chose the dumbest alternative; put another captain on the boat and send it out shrimping again.

In a burst of brilliant decision-making that would haunt us for years after, we chose as captain a man named Leonard who had never run a boat before. He convinced us his years on the back deck qualified him, and in any case, he would never do anything illegal, so the boat was safe with him. With a newly outfitted and freshly painted *Stanford Morse*, we sent him to sea to salvage our fortunes.

The first trip, he returned with a fair load, and except for the loss of two nets, we would have broken even. After two months, we were losing a little less money than before, but the boat was still draining our working capital. In another smart move, we told Leonard his next trip would be the last unless he made us money.

By the tenth day of a seven-day trip, we knew we had problems. Every boat in Key West had an eye out for the *Stanford Morse* and no one had seen it since it left the dock. The Coast Guard searched for a few days to no avail, and the boat was officially listed as missing. There was no doubt in our minds the boat was in Columbia.

Our despondency was complete when the local FBI agent called us in and said they had proof the boat was on a drug run. Not only had we lost our boat, but as owners of the boat, we were once again under suspicion. To make matters worse, Dad was dropping a full "I told you so" on us, and declaring he was washing his hands of the entire fiasco. It didn't seem possible things could get any worse.

Several days after the FBI meeting, a call came in from the Netherlands Steamship Company. Our boat was found drifting at sea by one of their ships, and had been towed into Aruba where it was being held until all costs were assessed and paid. It was somewhat of a relief to know the boat was in private hands, but Aruba—an island in the Netherlands Antilles—was within sight of Columbia and we knew we had to act fast.

Trapped in Key West

Because of my experience, I was elected to get the boat returned. It would be a very dangerous trip, and I felt strongly I should have someone accompany me. I discussed the situation with Hugh Morgan, who was not just a good friend, but also my attorney. I knew he would be a letter of the law person in a possible lawless situation, but he also had an adventurous spirit, and when he offered to accompany me, I gladly accepted. We packed our bags, purchased airline tickets, and arrived the next day in Oranjestad, Aruba.

At the local police station, we were treated just like any other drug dealers. They were polite, but aloof, having witnessed many times the problems drug smugglers have on their clandestine trips. The amount of the claim had not yet been assessed by the steamship company, and the boat was chained to the dock at one of the huge cargo ports. We were given directions and told not to leave the island without checking back in with the police department.

The order to not leave sounded ominous, but we were determined to convince the local authorities we were not involved in the drug run. We had no reason to believe the authorities even cared whether we were involved, but assumed we would get better treatment if seen as innocent victims.

The cargo dock was a very intimidating place. Thousands of containers were stacked alongside, and the *Stanford Morse* was completely hidden by them. There was not a soul to be seen, and we realized something could happen to us without anyone seeing or hearing.

From the dock, we could see no one on the boat, and cautiously approached it, while being as quiet as possible. We were half-expecting Leonard and the crew to be waiting for us with guns drawn, or even worse, to be met by a gang of swarthy-looking Columbian hit men. Our imaginations were running wild, and we would find at every step in Aruba, we mentally prepared for the worst.

We waited for some time on the dock without seeing anyone or hearing voices, and finally stepped onto the boat. The wheelhouse door was open, and we stealthily checked out the cabins. There was no one to be seen and the electronics and other gear were all intact. Finding the crew gone, we feared the boat would be stripped of everything of value, but it didn't appear that way.

We quietly checked out the cabins, expecting to find another huge catch of spare equipment. Unlike the first smuggling attempt, the only spares were those the boat would normally carry. As we walked the deck to the other side of the wheelhouse, we both stopped abruptly, stunned at what we saw.

Lying on a towel was a woman, who at first glance appeared to be dead. A moment later, she opened her eyes and serenely looked us over. She was merely sunbathing in the nude. She was a stunning, blond-haired, blue-eyed beauty. She stood with no sense of embarrassment, and stared at us as I stammered out, "Hi. Uh, who are you?"

"Who are you to ask?"

She was not American, and from her fair looks and accent we took her to be Dutch. "I am the owner of this boat, and I would like to know who you are, and how you came to be, uh, sunbathing on my boat. And would you happen to know where I can find the captain?"

With a sudden show of modesty, she turned from us to put on her bikini. Our vision of a goddess was instantly destroyed, when Hugh and I both noticed her buttocks and upper legs covered with angry red sores. We turned our gaze from her and grimaced at each other.

"My name is Anika, and I am a guest of the captain who is my boyfriend."

"Boyfriend? Leonard is your boyfriend?"

"Yes, Leonard."

"Where is Leonard?"

"He is buying food."

"Are the mates with him?"

"There is only one other man, O'Shea."

"Do you live in Aruba?"

"I am from Switzerland. I met Leonard in Jamaica."

"Jamaica? . . . Jesus! . . . When is Leonard coming back?"

"Soon."

"Please tell Leonard we will be back in a couple of hours, and to wait for us alone. We just want to talk. We are not trying to have him arrested."

We decided it would not be a good idea to throw Leonard off the boat until we had arranged to take it back to Key West. We reasoned that as long as he thought he had a chance to continue the trip, he would not strip the boat. We would however, have to ensure the boat would be unable to leave the dock until we were ready.

When we returned, Leonard and O'Shea were both on the boat. Leonard was a little nervous, but talked to us candidly and in a friendly manner, as if he thought we might actually retain him as captain. "I hung around the Keys for two weeks waiting for the order to go. I moved almost every day, so no one would get suspicious, and came into Key West to fill up with ice before we finally left for Columbia."

Though Danny and I had talked with almost all the shrimpers in Key West, not a one had let on they had actually seen our boat during the two weeks. One or two reported they thought they had seen him shrimping, but couldn't really be sure. The mind-your-own-business mentality was so strong in Key West that no one even told us he came in to take on ice, though it was five days after we had started searching for the boat.

"By the time we were about halfway to Columbia, we realized we weren't going to have enough fuel, so we went into Jamaica to take on diesel. We got word to our people that we needed $5,000 to take on fuel and supplies. After waiting two days, we were told the deal was for us to deliver the boat to Columbia and then they would give us some money. I managed to borrow $1,000 for fuel and we continued on the trip.

"Shortly after we left Jamaica, we realized we had taken on dirty fuel, and spent the bigger part of each day changing filters. We finally ran out of filters and the engine quit for good. No matter how we cleaned the old filters, the engine would not restart. I think the injectors are fouled, and we definitely need a mechanic.

"Anyway, a freighter answered our distress call and agreed to tow us into Aruba. It was so damn rough it took us five hours to get a towline secured, and then took twenty-four hours to tow us less than one hundred miles.

"So, here we are. I'm really sorry man. I thought by now I'd have your boat back to you with a bagful of money and everyone would be happy. It's been a bitch of a trip so far, but if we can get the engine running and the fuel tanks cleaned out, I'll make it up to you. I really appreciated you giving me a shot with this boat and I'm going to see that you don't lose on it."

Hugh and I listened like an enraptured audience as Leonard revealed all the details of his 'temporarily aborted' drug run. He seemed to feel he only needed to establish his credibility in order to convince me he was capable of finishing the trip successfully. In the surreal world of drug smuggling, it was never a matter of right and wrong, but only a question of how much. How much was the risk, and how much money was to be paid?

It did not occur to Leonard that we would not cooperate. In his mind, I wouldn't even be breaking the law, since I didn't have anything to do with planning the trip. Therefore, it was the perfect situation for me. Collect free money for doing nothing, and with no risk.

He said his Columbian friends were coming in that night and we could meet the next day to see what they wanted to do. Hugh and I said little, neither agreeing nor disagreeing with his plans. An inebriated O'Shea watched us with the narrow-eyed stare of a drunk looking for a fight, and interjected surly comments from time to time. He clearly did not trust us, but Leonard took our ambivalence as a negotiating ploy and was visibly confident as we left him.

Hugh and I spent the day with the local authorities and understood they would never let the boat leave without collecting the money we owed. They seemed very knowledgeable about drug smuggling activities and the people involved. They also had no problem being the beneficiaries of the drug trade, as long as money was collected according to Aruban law.

The police chief seemed to think we might be innocent victims and gave us some friendly advice: "You must take care with these people. There are many Columbians here and they are very serious about business. Most people fear them and will be reluctant to help you. I'm sorry to say this, but we cannot always control the situation since Columbia is just a short boat ride away. Many people in circumstances similar to yours have disappeared, so be very careful in your movements."

We were relieved the boat was secure, but had a greater sense of our lives being in danger. After the advice, we worried even more about the inevitable confrontation with Leonard and the Columbians. The next day, they would have to be told emphatically that we would not cooperate, and the police chief's warning had us in dread of their reaction.

We thought the boat was not a very secure place to meet them, so we decided to get a message to Leonard saying we would meet elsewhere. When we returned to the hotel, we found a note from Leonard saying we would meet at a certain restaurant at 1:00 the next afternoon. Hugh and I thought the hotel lobby would offer us the most safety, but agreed a public place like a restaurant would have us reasonably protected. The taxi driver looked over his two American tourists and questioned our choice of eating places, but delivered us promptly.

The restaurant was a waterfront dive. Under other circumstances, it might have been a neat little native hangout where we could get some authentic Aruban food. But for us, each customer in the place appeared menacing, and we thought we had walked into the exact situation the chief had warned us to stay away from.

Before we could turn around and leave, Leonard spotted us. He was alone at a table on the open-air side. We eyed the table suspiciously, but saw near it only a very large black man whom we took to be a dockworker. Leonard was smiling and had a large paper grocery bag in the seat next to him.

"All right guys, the deal is done. I got you $200,000 and you don't have to do a thing. Just go back to Key West and we'll take care of everything. In thirty days, you'll have your boat back in perfect condition."

Hugh and I sat on one side of the table and could see the large black man facing us, directly behind Leonard. He was a fearsome-looking man, and stared straight in our eyes as Leonard revealed the plan. Hugh and I looked at each other, knowing we had to get it over with.

"Leonard, listen to me carefully. If I take money from you, I am guilty of conspiracy. I have no intention of doing anything illegal, so I can't give you the okay to finish the drug run. So far, unless I press charges against you for stealing my boat, you haven't really done anything illegal, either. What we need to do now is fix the engine and get this boat back to Key West."

"But you won't be doing anything! You're just leaving me in charge of getting the boat back to Key West. Look man, if you're worried about taking the money on the plane, I'll just bring it to you when I get there with the boat. Come on man, let's don't mess this up over some minor details."

"Leonard, you are not hearing what I'm saying. There will be no drug run with my boat. Now, you have to make a decision whether you are with me or with them."

As the reality sunk in, Leonard's eyes became wild and his voice a frantic whisper. "Decision? Man, are you really that stupid? Do you really think I can just walk away from these people? Take a good look at this guy sitting behind me. He lives to kill people! I've been scared shitless he's going to knock me off and just take the boat! If I tell them this, they're just going to kill us all and take the goddamned boat anyway! . . . Man, please? . . . You don't understand these people. They talk about killing like it's just going out to have a beer or something. I'm warning you. If you don't take this deal, you better get the hell out while you can. These people are everywhere here. If you stay, they'll get you."

"Sorry Leonard. There will be no drug run, and I'm not leaving without my boat."

We left the table and had the bartender call us a taxi while Leonard sat forlornly at the table. He looked like a man who had just had his death warrant signed, and the black man continued staring. Though we were in a public place, Hugh and I both feared for our safety. There were only two other people in the place, and both of them looked like they belonged with the black man.

Leonard finally walked to the door and gave us a pitiful, hangdog look, as he passed by. The black man followed close behind and stopped to give us a bone-chilling look. The hair stood up on the back of my neck as I held my breath, half-expecting him to pull out a gun and shoot us right at the bar.

The ten minute wait for the taxi seemed interminable, and when it finally arrived, the driver was Columbian. We felt certain we were either being taken to see the 'people' in person, or to some remote place where we would never be heard from again. Hugh and I made a hushed plan to leap out of the taxi if he deviated from the road leading back to our rooms.

As we got out of the taxi in front of our hotel, we laughed nervously, a little embarrassed that we had allowed our imaginations to get the best of us. Surviving the taxi ride however, did not change the situation, and we sat at the bar discussing our options. Until the talk with Leonard, there had been a subliminal sense of adventure we both had secretly enjoyed. But the fun was over, and it was time to get very serious.

We talked about the threat to our lives, and how real it had become. We talked about our families waiting at home. We talked about going straight to the airport, and just fighting it out with the insurance company over the loss of the boat. We talked brave. We talked scared. And in the end, we decided to stay.

If everything in Aruba had been like the dingy commercial waterfront where our boat was docked, I would probably have gone back. But Aruba's clean tourist environment and our first class hotel gave me enough confidence to believe I could avoid a confrontation with the drug people and salvage the huge investment we had made in the scallop business.

I did try to talk Hugh into going back. It was really not his problem, and I felt very guilty about him becoming endangered because of me. He would have no part of returning. He stayed only because he was a friend who was not going to leave me to face it alone. I was concerned over the fact he was staying because of me, but immensely relieved.

The next morning, we had Leonard, O'Shea, and the girl, pack up their belongings and get off the boat. They had little to gather, and even Anika had but a backpack. We laughed that T-shirts, shorty shorts, and bikinis really didn't take up much room, but were amazed how she traveled the world with so little.

O'Shea was his usual abrasive self, giving us killer looks and muttering curses while he disembarked. Leonard, true to character, asked if I could loan them airfare. He wasn't sure they were going to let him leave, but he would pay me back if he got out—and if I got out. I refused to give him a penny, and told Leonard I only hoped that he and his scumbag mate would never get back to America.

Hugh and I started the process of getting the boat seaworthy, while back in Key West, Danny tried to find someone to captain the boat back to its homeport. The trip back could take a week in the rough southern Caribbean Sea, and it would not be easy to find someone who was willing to fly into drug country and steal our boat back from under the nose of the Columbians.

The police chief recommended a mechanic in a town on the far side of Aruba. Sint Nicolaas was a scruffy industrial city holding the largest oil refinery in the Caribbean. The taxi driver was again Columbian, and Hugh and I once again went through the anxiety of being led to a firing squad.

Outside of Oranjestad, which was a beautiful tourist town, the landscape turned desolate. Not only did cacti cover the dry desert hills, but it was also the preferred material for fences and landscaping. The only green was on the exotic-looking divi divi trees. The prevailing easterly winds forced all leaves and branches to grow straight out to the west, like ancient Pharaohs with arms cocked and hands pointing straight out.

In our mood, the exotic landscape appeared forbidding. We easily imagined our bodies being dropped in the cactus on deserted hills that no one in their right mind would ever traverse. We spoke little on the hour-long trip for fear the Columbian driver could understand English.

Sint Nicolaas did little to ease our fears. It was a gray and bleak-looking town, with the huge refinery dominating everything. The driver dropped us at an unpainted steel building and we nervously entered the office. To our relief, a Dutch family owned the shop, and mother, father, and children, were all involved in the business.

Though most of their business was on oil tankers and related industrial equipment, they sympathized with our problem and agreed to get our boat running. They also turned out to be the best ones on the island to clean our tainted fuel tanks. For the first time, we felt as if we were actually making progress towards the return of the boat.

With the mechanics working on the engine, Hugh and I spent our time negotiating with the steamship company and outfitting the boat for the trip home. Danny meanwhile, was searching as far away as Texas for a captain, but ended up finding one right at home.

I knew our fortunes had changed when Danny told me Reo Hill was going to fly down with his brother-in-law David Knowles and bring the boat back for us. Reo was the perfect choice. He had owned and captained dozens of shrimp boats and had the reputation of never shying away from a fight.

As the owner of eight shrimp boats, Reo believed the federal government had illegally closed a shrimping area near Tortugas. Reo refused to obey the ban, and throughout the 1970s received over one hundred citations and ended with all of his boats seized except one. Undeterred, Reo filed suit against the National Marine

Fisheries, and was eventually vindicated by the United States Supreme Court. He was definitely the man we wanted to bring back the boat safely.

While it was a fact our Columbian paranoia was full blown, it was also true we were being watched. We had been followed more than once, and when we picked up Reo, a car trailed us from the airport to the port entry gate. We had a room for Reo at the hotel, but he insisted on staying on the boat so he could get the feel of it, and see firsthand what was needed for the rugged trip home. We didn't tell Reo about being followed, but warned him to be on his guard. "Hell, you don't have to worry about that. As soon as I see what this boat needs, I'm out of here. This is one place I don't want to hang around too long."

"Well Reo, there are a few problems we need to iron out before the boat can leave."

"Problems? What kind of problems? Danny told me the boat was ready to go!"

"Well, we thought it would be, but they had to order a part for the engine, and we still need to settle with the steamship company that towed the boat here. We should have everything taken care of in a day or two."

"A day or two? Bullshit!! I know how that goes! A day or two turns into three or four, or a week. No, no! You fly me home and I'll come back when the boat is ready to leave. I've seen guys get shot, and it don't take but a second. I may be crazy, but I ain't stupid. I said I'd bring the boat home for you and I will, but I ain't gonna get my ass shot to do it."

"Reo, I understand how you feel, and I'm really sorry we didn't have the boat ready like we planned. But the mechanic has assured me the engine will be ready by tomorrow, and as soon as Danny wires the money, we will pay off the bill and the boat can leave. Remember, Hugh and I have been here a week and no one has tried to kill us. We'll put you up at the hotel and you can stay there until the boat is ready. It's really a nice place, and you and David can play like tourists for a while."

Reo calmed down a little, and was thinking over the situation. "Let me and David talk for a minute. You know I don't care so much about myself, but if anything happens to my wife's baby brother, she'd never forgive me."

Hugh shrugged his shoulders and shook his head, but Reo returned a minute later. "All right, we'll stay for two nights and that's it. I'm not going to let someone else outfit a boat I have to captain, so we're staying on the boat. You just better make sure this is secure at night, because they wouldn't even let me bring a gun on this pisspot island. Also, I need money for taxis and groceries and to replace anything I find missing on the boat."

Hugh and I felt a little guilty about convincing them to stay. It was a dangerous situation, and we really didn't know what the Columbians would do once the engine was running. Reo was well into his fifties, with the weathered look of a man who had spent his life at sea. He was as tough a man as I had ever known, and like Dad, had no fear of either the ocean or any other man. But his instincts were accurately warning him of the danger in our situation.

Reo was often unpredictable, but we knew he would only leave if he thought David was in danger. It had been six days since the bar scene, and we'd had no direct contact with anyone since then. We were feeling pretty secure when we left Reo at the boat and Hugh and I celebrated our changing fortunes with wine and dinner in a fine restaurant.

My phone rang at 6:00 a.m. the next morning and it was Reo. "We're in the lobby. Come down."

In the lobby we found a very upset Reo. "Take us to the airport and get us on a plane for home! I didn't bargain for this kind of trouble. Danny told me it was a simple deal. Fly down, get on the boat, and run it to Key West. Oh, yea! It was going to be *soooo* easy! Now, we're caught up in some kind of a damn drug battle. No way baby! We're out of here!"

"Reo! Please! Tell me what's happened. I don't understand where you're coming from."

Drugs on the Ocean

"Well, we went to the store and got our groceries and supplies. It was after dark when we got everything put away. We sat down to eat when this guy appears in the doorway. He startled the hell out of us because he didn't say anything—just stood there staring at us. Then, he slurs out, 'What are you assholes doing on my boat?'

"I knew when he spoke he was either drunk or high on something. I asked him if he was Leonard? 'No, I ain't Leonard, but this is my goddamned boat and I want your asses off now—or I'll kick them off!'"

"Reo, was he real muscular with scraggly blond hair?"

"Yeah, that's what he looked like."

"O'Shea! That was O'Shea. He was Leonard's mate. He's a mean S.O.B. Especially when he's drunk. I thought he was long gone from Aruba."

"Yeah, well I've seen hundreds like him before. A *reeeal* tough guy. Starts giving me all this crap about getting off before I get hurt, and how he loves to 'work over old fart captains who think they're hot shit.' Now, nobody talks to me like that, especially some punk mate. So, I threw him off the boat and told him not to come back."

David had been quietly listening and spoke up for the first time. "To say he threw him off the boat is a major understatement. First, he walked over to the guy and got two inches from his face and told him, 'Boy, you just made the biggest mistake of your sorry ass life!' Then, he beat the crap out of him! I mean, he beat the living hell out of him! And the guy never once hit Reo!

"O'Shea was down on the deck trying to crawl away, and Reo kept dragging him back. 'Old fart, huh! Gonna kick my ass, eh! Let's see now, whose boat did you say it is? Come on now, is it still *yourrr* boat? *Ohhh*! I see. Now it's *myyy* boat! Well, in that case, I want your chicken shit ass off *myyy* boat. And I mean NOW!!' I thought he might kill the guy or throw him in the water and he'd drown, but he grabbed him by the foot, dragged him over the rail, and threw him on the dock like a bag of garbage."

Reo was grinning at the thought of it. "He's just a punk. They all look mean and talk tough until you call them down. Then, when it's time to back it up, you find out they're yellow inside. The problem with this guy is; that aside from being a drunk and a punk, he's completely nuts.

"He finally staggered away in the dark and hid up in those containers. Then, the crazy bastard starts howling like a goddamned wolf! I'm not kidding you—am I, David? Like a wolf! With that big moon up there and not a soul around, I got to admit it gave me the cold chills.

"Then, he starts throwing out threats between the howls, 'You're a dead man! You will never see the sun rise! The Columbians are on their way, and they're gonna slice you into little pieces! Did you ever see anyone cut up nice and slow? They're experts at it, and you know what part they start with? Hey, big man! You know what part they start with, don't you? Yeah man, you're gonna be squealing like a stuck pig! Then, we'll see how tough you are.'

"He kept that up for hours, and we never did get any sleep. I started to go look for him, but then I thought he might have help and that would be what they wanted me to do. We waited until daybreak and got a taxi to the hotel. I hated to leave the boat, but I didn't want David to get nailed because of me. I really don't think O'Shea's going to do anything—his kind never do—but I don't know about his friends. Hell, they might be on the boat right now."

"Reo, I'm really sorry that happened, but the boat should be ready today, and once you get away from the dock, you'll be home free. I don't think they'll try anything during the day, and if the boat has to stay one more night, you can sleep in the hotel and I'll try to hire a guard."

After telling his story and hearing my assurances, Reo settled down and agreed to stay. Hugh was finally forced to return to Key West for a court date, so after dropping him at the airport, we cautiously checked out the boat. It was untouched, but we still had the uneasy feeling O'Connor was somewhere among the containers watching our every move.

Drugs on the Ocean

Reo and David stayed on the boat for the next two days while the engine was repaired, the fuel tanks cleaned, and $25,000 paid to the steamship company. The boat was officially cleared to go, but the fuel truck did not show, and the trip was delayed yet another day. I was unable to find a trustworthy guard, but nothing happened during the night, and I waved goodbye to Reo and David at 10:00 the next morning.

I waited another day for a plane reservation out, and stayed in the hotel the entire time. Being completely alone in Aruba with the drug smugglers for the last five days was a very unsettling experience, but after ten nerve-wracking days, I made it home in one piece. Reo arrived five days later with the *Stanford Morse* after an uneventful trip.

Hugh had already started the paperwork for our claim with the insurance company, and we waited for the inevitable rejection. Whenever drugs were involved, the insurance companies started off with a presumption of guilt on the part of the owners. They reasoned that if the owners had any complicity, they would never be willing to go to court and risk being exposed.

Unfortunately, the reasoning was correct frequently enough to be the strategy they used in every case. The rejection came and we filed suit against the insurance company. After many months of depositions and continuances, we were one day away from the trial in Miami.

The night before the trial, I received a very surprising phone call. A man identifying himself as an insurance investigator named Paul Bailey, supplied me with information that would help in court. "Mr. Bacle, I am privy to the formal investigation of you that was done by your insurance company. It was a thorough investigation and you came out completely clean.

"I know how insurance companies operate, and I'm sure they haven't revealed the report to you as required by law or they would never be going to trial. Tell your lawyer to hold back the information until the time is right, and then tell the insurance attorneys you know they have a written investigation report and you want to see it. The judge will order them to produce it, and he will then give a directed verdict in your favor."

"Sir, I hardly know what to say. This is incredible information you're giving me and I truly appreciate it, but can you please tell me why you are doing this?"

"Mr. Bacle, I assure you there is nothing in it for me. I'm eighty years old, and I stand to lose a very large business if my name is ever revealed. I just find it unconscionable that they would drag you through a trial and try to smear your good name— especially after the excellent report they received on you. I also noticed you are a Missouri Synod Lutheran, and have been president of your congregation and chairman of your school board. I am also a Lutheran, and have held those same positions in my church."

Mr. Bailey and I spent the next half-hour talking about the problems associated with operating a Christian day school. The next morning, I related the conversation to Hugh on the plane ride to Miami. Hugh was incredulous over the insurance company not giving us the report during 'discovery', but was even more flabbergasted that the man had actually revealed the highly confidential information to me.

The court proceeding went exactly as Mr. Bailey said it would. Hugh let the insurance lawyers proceed for a while with their sleazy attempt to implicate me in the drug run, and then slammed them with the request for the report. When the two attorneys sheepishly produced the report, the judge was furious, and not only ruled immediately in my favor, but penalized the insurance company with a double attorney's fee to Hugh. Then, the judge topped off the ruling by bringing ethics charges against the insurance attorneys.

The sad saga of the *Stanford Morse* unfortunately did not end there. In what appears retrospectively as a never-ending quest for more trouble, we once again hired a new captain and sent the boat out for shrimp. The *Stanford Morse* —despite its proven history as a pariah for both owners and smugglers—proved to be an irresistible lure for lawbreaking bumblers.

Drugs on the Ocean

In seeming defiance of the laws of probability, the boat once again disappeared into the Caribbean smog. A month later, the boat turned up on the French island of Guadalupe. The smugglers, in an apparent attempt to avoid the Yucatan Passage back to America, tried the longer Eastern Route, and were seized with twenty tons of marijuana while refueling.

The French law on Guadalupe—unlike American law— proscribes that you are guilty until you prove your innocence. I was willing to take a chance with fighting smugglers, but I was over the *Stanford Morse* and not willing to risk being thrown in jail in a strange country with even stranger laws. Hugh however, did not feel the risk was that great and accompanied Danny. They were unsuccessful in obtaining the boat's release, though they did manage to escape the island themselves.

Shortly after their return, while Hugh was in the process of filing a claim, the boat became a total loss when our insurance company filed for bankruptcy. Along with the loss of the *Stanford Morse* came the depletion of the scallop beds. The carpetbagger boats from Cape Canaveral cleaned out the scallops, and then packed up their equipment and went home. With $500,000 worth of unused scallop processing equipment sitting at the fish house, and facing huge bank payments for the next eight years, we forswore any more loony, get-rich-quick ideas, and settled into making money one dollar at a time.

11

Mariel Boatlift

In April of 1980, several months after the return of the *Stanford Morse* from Aruba, but before the loss of the boat in Guadalupe, the Peruvian embassy in Havana inexplicably opened the gates and removed the guards. The word quickly spread throughout Havana, and within hours, the embassy compound was jammed with seven thousand people requesting political asylum.

The mass flight of citizens from the communist country was a huge international embarrassment for Fidel Castro, and he responded by announcing that under no circumstance would the "traitors" be allowed to stay in Cuba. According to Fidel, they were the dissidents who were trying to sabotage his dream for Cuba, and he maintained the country would be better off without them. Just how they would get out of the country was their problem and the Peruvians, but he would not allow them back out of the gate.

In America, the large exile community in Miami was in an uproar. Imagining the embassy incident was the start of a counter-revolution, many made plans to join the coming fight, while others plotted to get the refugees to America. In an amazing chain of events, Fidel Castro announced that if America wanted the people, they should come get them, and President Jimmy Carter—in an apparent show of compassion—let it be known that a Dunkirk-style rescue mission by Americans would not be interfered with by our government.

Mariel Boatlift

President Carter's tacit approval of a boatlift rescue set off a massive wave of boat buying and chartering by Cuban-Americans. Every boat owner in Miami and the Florida Keys was approached with an offer. The price of boats and the cost of charters rose by the hour, and within days, virtually every craft with a working engine was either bought or rented.

Somehow, the American families of those in the embassy knew they had relatives waiting to be rescued. There was never a list of names of the impulsive refugees cooped up in the embassy compound, but the Cuban 'telegraph' assured thousands of Miami residents they had family members waiting for rescue. With the wild rumors added in, most of the one million exiles in America thought they had relatives waiting, and Key West was jammed with people looking for boats.

The fish house was also in an uproar. The docks were swarming with people trying to buy or rent the fishing boats. It did not matter how big the boat or its condition. If it had a working motor and was floating, it could easily be sold for two or three times its actual value. Some fishermen took the opportunity to sell, but most decided to charter their boat or simply go for the sake of family or friends needing help. The just-ended lobster season had been a poor one, and many of the fishermen saw the opportunity to take a quick charter to Cuba for an exorbitant amount of money as a godsend.

Danny was among the first to be approached and was anxious to head for Cuba in the *Stanford Morse*. Because it was illegal to travel to Cuba, I would not agree to the trip, but when President Carter gave the okay, things started happening fast. The Miami Cubans came in droves with cash money, and the price of charters rose quickly.

Danny called and said he had six people who were willing to pay $5,000 each for a quick trip over to pick up their relatives. Shrimping had also been poor, and $30,000 would make our boat payments for two years. With our government's approval and the desperation of the relatives, it seemed like taking the money was actually the humanitarian thing to do. Something about the whole deal didn't seem quite right, but with no apparent reason not to go, I ended up agreeing with Danny that the opportunity was just too good to pass on.

Meanwhile, three other boats from the fish house—*Miss Kriss, My Donna*, and *Honey Pot*—were hurriedly readying for the trip, and I was approached by another group wanting to charter my fifty-three-foot lobster boat *American Dream*. I had already told many others I was not interested in chartering, but it seemed everyone was going and I wasn't going to be left behind. I recently found a journal I kept during the trip and was reminded of my reasons for going, and the progression of events over the following ten days.

April 22

I am caught up in the fever also. The money sounds so easy and the times so hard, that I cannot resist the temptation. Finally decided on a group of six who are willing to pay $10,000. So easy. Just run to Cuba in four or five hours, pick up a load of people, and come back. Think I might do it as long as Castro allows. Might pull us out of the hole, and of course, it's all perfectly legal.

The four men and two women are all from Miami. They are Juan P. Delgado, Felix F. Albiza, Maria T. Albiza, Jose R. Lorenzo, Mercedes Lorenzo, and Ricardo Lorenzo. They seem at first like very nice people. Am very rushed as I want to go with Steve Kern and Bubba. Steve has loran. We leave at 3:30 with chance to get only fuel and five-minute rush home for toothbrush, small hurricane stove, and couple of other items.

My brother Jimmy and I had recently built the *American Dream*. Shortly after we started, it became apparent he was—though eleven years younger—the far more skillful boat builder, and he essentially took over construction. It was the first of several hundred he would build in his career, and at fifty-three feet, the biggest. We had been forced to work the lobster season with the boat being unfinished. Though everything worked on the boat and we had trapped the entire season with it, the cabin and flybridge were unpainted and any bare skin touching the unfinished fiberglass would pick up the invisible slivers and itch incessantly. It would not be a fun boat to live on, but then, we intended to be back within twenty-four hours.

Though my passengers included four men, I wanted a mate I could rely on in unexpected circumstance. Jimmy refused to go, believing we would all end up in a Cuban prison. Jack Phillips, my fish house manager, agreed to go after assuring his wife we would be back by the next afternoon in plenty of time for him to leave on his annual vacation.

Dad didn't approve of the trip, but agreed we really needed the money. I realized his mild opposition stemmed only from the fact that he was not going. On my return, he had his bag packed, ready to make a second trip with the boat, despite the vehement opposition of the family. Only an announcement by the Coast Guard that they would forthwith be seizing all boats prevented him from going.

My passengers were all political refugees who had fled Cuba in the previous twenty years. All spoke some English and were firmly middle-class working people who had already adopted America as their new country. They were desperate to get their families out of Cuba, and were willing to pay, what was for them, an exorbitant amount to do it. We agreed on $5,000 up front and the other $5,000 when we returned—with or without their family members.

They also claimed to have secured papers—which I assumed to be some kind of visas—for the legal entry of seven family members into the United States. I was unsure of the legality of their papers, but really didn't care. I felt certain I was in the clear, and figured the public statements of Carter and Castro, placed any problem with entry of people on the passengers.

There was also concern about the safety of my passengers with regard to the Cuban government. Castro was very vocally contemptuous of those who had fled Cuba, believing the flight of the professional class had set back his plans for a communist utopia. Outrageous rumors were flying in the Cuban community about the boatlift being merely a ruse to lure the exiles back for punishment. While I didn't give the rumor any credence, those who might end up in prison did. Castro had already proven himself to be an irrational leader, and the exiled Cubans knew with him anything was possible. Despite their concern, all were willing to take the risk to free their relatives, and we left for Cuba with no hesitation.

Wednesday, April 23

Trip slow but uneventful. Arrive outside Mariel Bay, thirty miles west of Havana, at 2:00 a.m. Met by Cuban gunboat which takes our names and all info on boat. Tells us to wait with group of boats. At daylight, we proceed to harbor entrance where we wait with eighty to one hundred other boats for permission to enter harbor. Boats are crazy. All size, shape, and condition. Captains are pushing, shoving, and zigzagging to try and get to front of line. Small Cuban immigration police ignore boats rushing to front, and take boats randomly from group. We get in about 10:30 a.m. Surprise! Inside bay, we turn corner and find at least three hundred boats already inside, all anchored. Can now see that there will be no quick turnaround.

American Dream entering Mariel Harbor

Mariel Boatlift

At 5:00 p.m., the police-army boat came around, took names of all on boat, all info on American Dream, and gave us a number for the window—124. We are settling in for a long stay. Feeling very discouraged. They didn't even take the names of those we wish to take back. By now, it seems that every boat in Key West is in this bay. We are at one end, one hundred yards from a big gunboat. In the hills we see army troops in trees and bushes to make sure no one leaves or gets on boats. The countryside we can see is beautiful, rolling green hills. Would very much like to see Cuba someday.

We rafted up our four boats side by side, and with passengers and crew, had about twenty-five people. After assessing our supplies, we realized we had enough food for one day. No one had anticipated a protracted stay, and in our rush to leave before our government changed their mind, we hadn't even taken on board the normal amount of canned goods we always carried on a fishing trip. The American Dream was not yet set up for sleeping, so it had no pillows, pads, or covers, while the other boats had bare sleeping essentials for crew only.

Steve Kern, Bubba Faircloth, and Mike Pappas—the other boat captains—and I, discussed the situation. We had acted compulsively and irresponsibly by leaving with such haste, but consoled ourselves with the fact we were on a mercy mission where time was of the utmost importance. We had, after all, scrounged up life jackets for our passengers—but then realized we had none for any Cubans we picked up for the return trip. We recognized there was nothing to be done at that point except wait.

As we settled in for a long stay, I had the first opportunity to talk with my passengers and my first impressions were confirmed. They were ordinary working people with strong family ties. With their success in America came a sharp sense of obligation to bring the rest of their families to the land of the free. Their fears for their family and desperation to free them were so compelling, that I soon felt the first pangs of guilt for charging them.

Trapped in Key West

April 24

The people on my boat are terrific people, confirming my first impression. They are very soft-spoken, polite, and considerate. Have been trying to suppress feeling (conscience?) that I am doing something wrong in taking so much money for helping people. The more I talk to them, the harder it becomes to rationalize the whole situation. No one else has the slightest qualm. The logic and reasoning are all on our side. I am certain that there is nothing we are doing wrong. The only concern of the other boats is that they might not be getting as much as some others are getting. It's all just another business deal. Why I'm even thinking about it I don't know. Haven't slept in over forty hours.

*Miami Cubans who chartered American Dream
- Cuban gunboat in back*

The first night, everyone crashed wherever they could find a spot. We gave the ladies the cabin down below for privacy, and I was thankful I had just installed a new hand-pumped toilet. For a little privacy of my own, I chose to sleep on the flybridge under the stars. The night was cold and the air was very wet. The bare fiberglass had me itching from the start, and I was forced to sleep on the cardboard I intended to use for a blanket. There was little sleep to be had that night, and I was angry with Jack, who started snoring the moment he laid his head down.

Mariel Boatlift

April 25

Couple of hours of uncomfortable sleep last night. Generators,
spotlights, loudspeakers, drunks.

Fortunately, the next morning we had an ample supply of the
most important commodity on a commercial fishing boat—coffee.
In the morning, the customs boat came by and took the names of
the people we wished to take back. The Cuban soldiers were very
pleasant and accommodating, and my passengers—in a mood of
conciliation they would regret almost immediately—gave the names
of thirty-one other relatives who also wished to leave, rather than
just the seven who were in the Peruvian Embassy.

As soon as the customs boat left, my passengers were fearful
they had 'outed' members of their own family to the dreaded secret
police. The women were almost inconsolable, and their extreme
anxiety for the safety of their family revealed the awful fear that
life under communism engenders. The soldiers also gave us the
depressing news, that although we would be taking back people
from the embassy, they were unlikely to be the ones we came for.
As to when we would be able to load and leave, we received only
a "soon."

The general dismay over our sorry plight was somewhat
relieved when we saw a grocery boat making the rounds. At least
we wouldn't starve while waiting for our defectors. Under other
circumstances, the communists' first attempt at capitalism might
have been humorous. The 'grocery' boat had only Cuban rum and
cigars, Czechoslovakian beer, water, and Vienna sausages.

A bottle of rum and can of sausages were $1 each, while a beer
and box of cigars were each $2, and the water was $3 a gallon. We
bought some of each and discussed at length the significance of
their pricing structure. Juan Delgado, who spoke the best English
among the passengers and was their unofficial leader, supplied us
with the best explanations.

Though America was hated by Castro, the Yankee dollar was
the currency of choice in the world, and with the disastrous state

of the economy under communism, Castro desperately needed every one he could get his hands on. The grocery boats were run by the army and all money would go to the government. He also explained how the communists were not sophisticated at Western-style business, but Cubans were fast learners and the prices for everything would rise quickly.

He said the cigars were the steal of a lifetime, and recommended we buy all we could get at that price. The rum was basically moonshine, and he warned us against buying it at any price. *Aquar Diente* was distilled from the dregs of sugar cane and not fit to drink. In the countryside, it was stored in open barrels and ladled out to the sugar cane workers. The rum we had already bought was transported in old, wooden Coca-Cola cases, and every bottle was different. Reused wine and whiskey bottles predominated, but soda bottles and any other type of the rough size to fit in the case, had a cork in the top and a label plastered on the outside.

Despite the warnings from our Cuban passengers, the rum proved irresistible to the boat crews. With the expectation of a long, boring stay, everyone was feeling down and the rum seemed the only diversion. By mid-afternoon, the rum had worked its magic and the party was going strong. Loud discussions over fishing and sports gave way to arm wrestling competitions and other confrontational activities. With threats of fights causing grave concern among our passengers, it became obvious the rum was responsible for actions from the men that beer and other alcohols did not induce.

Without anyone paying attention to his actions, Mike Pappas—who had gone from belligerent to sullen—went over to his boat, the *Honey Pot*, and cranked the engine. When he started untying the lines, he got our full attention. Unable to talk him into shutting down his engine and retying the boat, Bubba got on the *Honey Pot* to do it himself. Just as he stepped onto the boat, Mike climbed up to the flybridge controls, threw the engine into gear, and gave it full throttle.

We watched in disbelief as the *Honey Pot* lurched forward and Bubba tumbled head over heels to the stern of the boat. As Mike roared toward the massed boats, Bubba scrambled on his hands and knees to reach the flybridge ladder, and then hung on for dear life as Mike zigzagged through the hundreds of anchored vessels. The Cuban gunboat took up the chase as Mike circled around and passed by us with arms waving.

Bubba started up the ladder, but was thrown from side to side as he futilely attempted to reach Mike. The boat suddenly came to a stop when an anchor line caught up in his propeller, and Bubba and Mike were abruptly thrown forward. The Cuban military police, with automatic weapons at the ready, quickly boarded the boat and prevented Bubba from beating Mike to death.

The soldiers accurately assessed the situation and threw Mike to the deck with rifles pointed at his head. From a distance, we could see the man in charge screaming at Mike with arms flailing, and then turned on Bubba. We knew Mike was going to jail, but were fearful they would take Bubba also, even though he had done his best to prevent the fiasco.

Helpless to do anything, we watched as the drama played out. People from other boats, who had near misses on a collision and were slammed around by the unexpected wake from the speeding boat, were cursing and threatening Mike. Screams of "shoot him" rang out across the water, and though we didn't expect that to happen, neither did we want him back tied up next to us.

We could see Bubba talking to the man in charge and the situation was calming down. A few minutes later, Bubba jumped in the water and untangled the anchor line from the propeller. Amazingly, the Cubans got back on their boat as Bubba sat at the controls of the *Honey Pot* and Mike helped push off their boat. Bubba idled back alongside with the gunboat following closely. After a final warning to all of us, the Cubans took up their former position, and a subdued Mike passed out after a chorus of derision from everyone aboard.

We were still amazed to see them both released, and Bubba explained the miraculous persuasion. "Man, they were mad when they got on board! I really thought for a second they were going to shoot Mike. The leader was sticking his pistol at Mike's head and screaming at him. I didn't understand the Spanish, but I could sure guess what he was saying.

"Fortunately, he spoke English, even though I couldn't understand him until he settled down. Once he understood that Mike was drunk, they all relaxed and I explained the situation. I told him Mike was never like that, but he just couldn't handle the Cuban rum. He relayed my explanation to the other two men, and they all started laughing. They were very pleased to hear their rum was too much for him, and said they would let us go if I promised to let Mike drink only *Yanqui* liquor.

"I guess the rum thing was big joke for them. Mike was sitting on the deck with his head rolling, and they were laughing and wagging their fingers at him like he was a little kid. I laughed too, but then I would have done anything to stay out of a Cuban prison."

Shortly after Mike's adventure, we learned that everyone was allowed to leave the boat and travel to Havana. Not wanting to pass up a chance to visit with long unseen family members and hoping to get more accurate information on the embassy situation, several of my passengers made the trip. As much as I wanted to see Havana, I was afraid to leave the boat untended. I talked to Danny on the CB radio and heard that of the thirty-four people on the *Stanford Morse*, twenty-five of them spent the night in Havana.

Saturday, April 26
First halfway decent sleep. Got pad off chair on Steve's boat and small blanket from man who spent the night in Havana. Everyone's hopeful that today is the day. I doubt it.

There was little to do during the day. Between all of the boats, there were a few books, but none worth reading. We quickly tired of talking about fishing and speculating over what the Cubans would do next. Food had been one of our main concerns, but the situation was somewhat alleviated when the newly christened *"cantina"* boat showed up with an expanded inventory of grocery items.

In addition to the Vienna sausages, they had beans, rice, and papayas. True to Juan's prediction, the price slowly went up on everything they carried. By the time we left Mariel, the price of a box of cigars had risen from $2 to $40.

There was also plenty of time to get better acquainted with my passengers. I was becoming very sympathetic to their situation and found myself feeling very personally involved. I felt I had to do everything I could to help them free their relatives, and wondered long and hard whether I would be able to take the $5,000 upon our return. Yet, there was little I could actively do in the face of our discouraging situation, except try to provide for the passengers' needs.

April 26

Day progressed very slowly. No contact at all with Cubans. Boats just keep pouring in. Heard it's over 1,000 now. I believe it. According to newcomers like Gene Suggs, the going rate is now $20,000 plus. Seems that every craft that can float has been chartered. There are at least fifty shrimp boats and about ten large craft in the eighty- to one hundred-foot range. Half of Cuba could go back on these boats. Helicopter just went over, and of course everyone is swearing they saw Fidel in it.

April 26

Went in <u>Miss Kriss</u> to <u>Stanford Morse</u>, and got twenty-pound swordfish that Danny had bought for four dollars per pound. Danny says he's selling ice at five dollars a basket, but I think he's putting me on. Then, went to <u>Noopy</u> and talked to Gene Suggs for a while. Got some wild rice and a cooking pot from Andy Griffith. Meal was first real food so far. Heard on radio that boat sank with two hundred people. Scary.

It was becoming apparent that the few boats leaving Mariel were being loaded far past their capacity. At first, we thought the captains were being paid by the number of people they carried, but eventually realized they had to take others as well, in order to get the family members. I explained to my passengers how I was responsible for the safety of everyone on my boat, and if the Cubans insisted on overloading the boat in order for us to get their people, we would have to go back empty. Though they listened quietly, their despair was obvious and one of the ladies started crying.

From the moment I first met them, they were tense with anxiety. The fear they might not get their relatives and the fear that they might even be arrested themselves, hung over them constantly. The most insignificant rumor or innocent comment from the Cubans was liable to bring on extreme reactions and the most desperate speculation. Merely mentioning the possibility of not getting their family members doused their hopes, and it was impossible not to be affected along with them.

Sunday, April 27
First decent night's sleep, but warm and mosquitoes. Nothing of note as far as leaving. Rumors fly. Every time a Cuban boat comes near, everyone gets excited. They are so anxious and so afraid that everything may be called off at any time. The waiting is rough. Try not to think about Monica and kids, but it's almost impossible. Miss them terribly, even worse than Aruba. I'm sure Monica is upset, and wait 'til Maria finds out Danny is planning to come right back.

That afternoon, a squall came over with winds of fifty to sixty miles per hour. Within ten minutes, the harbor was a disaster area. Anchors dragged and boats slammed into each other. Awnings, chairs, clothes, and even a few of the flimsier cabins were flying through the air. Boats piled up on the shore and several sunk. It was a scene of general chaos, and most of the passengers—used to being safely indoors during such violent weather conditions—were frightened out of their wits.

Unfortunately, Jack was at the cantina boat with Steve when the squall hit. Our own anchor was holding well, but other boats were bearing down on us. I was forced to start the engine and move the boat, in order to avoid the ones about to crash into us. With Jack gone, there was no one else I could risk putting on the bow to tend the anchor under such conditions.

Mariel Boatlift

Though there was little room for maneuvering, I was forced to run up on the anchor and have Juan gaff the rope, so we could pull it from the side. A large sailboat was about to smash into us, and as I kicked the boat ahead, Juan missed the line. The wind blew us back across the rope and it became entangled in the propeller. With no other options, I tied a line around my waist and dove under the boat to disentangle the line. Once it was cleared, we were able to pull the anchor and avoid the careening boats.

Typical of the violent squalls, the strongest wind quickly passed and we were able to tie back together with the other boats. The harbor looked like the aftermath of a hurricane. Experienced boaters are used to squalls and would have handled the situation in a calm and orderly manner. However, between the scows that had miraculously survived the ninety-mile trip from Key West, the inexperienced captains, and the crowded conditions, the harbor became a scene of pandemonium.

By the next morning, the harbor was again calm and quiet. Several boats had sunk and debris littered the shore, but we settled back into the interminable wait, and I became more familiar with my passengers.

Monday, April 28
Had long talk with Juan Delgado this morn. The more I get to know them, the more I like them. They are hardworking, honest people. He is a truck driver. The others are gardener, plumber, etc. Juan says he will take second job to pay for relatives' freedom. Felix Albiza says he has been on one vacation in twelve years. Saves all of his money to bring relatives out of Cuba . . . It becomes increasingly difficult to think about taking money for helping these people.

I was by then feeling as if I had come to rescue the people, instead of chartering for the money. What started out as a cash deal had become a personal matter and my early feelings of sympathy turned into full-blown empathy. Mother's brother Jose (Uncle Joe) and his wife Metrita were still living in Cuba. Aunt Rose had been sending money and medicine for years, but we were only vaguely familiar with the true conditions under communism. At Mariel it was coming home to me in all its totalitarian reality.

We had last seen Uncle Joe in 1956, and with me being only ten years old, he was more a dim memory than a real person. Grandfather Felipe retired from civil service at Guantanamo Navy Base in 1958 and moved to Miami to live with Rose and Gerry. Joe wanted to move to Miami also, but his wife would not leave her family. Against his father's advice, Joe anticipated that Castro would not allow him to keep working for the U.S. Navy and quit his own civil service job at Guantanamo to work as an electrician in Caimenera.

When Castro took over in Cuba, he amazingly allowed the civil service workers to keep their positions, and with a regular income of Yankee dollars, they were among the wealthier private citizens in Cuba. For the rest of his life, Joe would regret not following his father's advice. Despite working for the minimal wages under communism, Joe had a better than average lifestyle because of the money sent by his family in America.

When Metrita died in 2001, Joe expressed a desire to come to Key West. In 2002, my sister Suzanne traveled alone to Cuba and managed to get him out in two weeks—a process that generally takes a year. Suzy—by circumstance and nature—was the most independent and dauntless of the siblings. Like Dad, she was a romantic who had little fear of the unknown, and viewed the trip to rescue Uncle Joe as an adventure, rather than a dangerous journey to a totalitarian state. She has been teasingly close-mouthed about the details of the rescue, but Joe was impressed beyond words, and the rest of the family tells the improbable story with head-shaking admiration.

Mother and Rose had not seen their brother in forty-six years, and over the next two years—until his death at the age of 89— we enjoyed having a reunited family and hearing amazing stories from a master storyteller. Joe claimed he never took medication, and always traded away the aspirins Rose was sending. The year before he came to Key West, he contracted pneumonia and was on the brink of death. A nurse came to his apartment and treated him by putting a nail in the wall and hanging an IV from it. Each day, she came back to see if he was still alive and to give him a new IV. By the fourth day, it was apparent he was going to live, so she stopped coming.

Joe also refused any medication in Key West, and managed to check out of this world in grand style. Four days before Christmas, Monica and I were having a party at our home. With thirty family members present, Joe was in his glory—regaling everyone with stories of his childhood and life in Cuba. Sitting next to Mother at the dining room table, he finished a plate of lobster enchilada and had a beer in his hand, when he calmly laid his head on the table and died.

The scene that followed was a story Joe would have loved to tell. An ambulance was called, and the first responder for the emergency medical team came through the door in a Santa Claus outfit. We had interrupted their Christmas party, but it didn't stop Santa from attempting to revive Joe. It was difficult to explain to the children, but we all agreed it was a fine way to go

We were patiently waiting for some sign we could pick up our passengers and start home. Any movement by a patrol boat raised everyone's hopes, but too many false alarms left most everyone discouraged and lethargic. Then, when we had almost given up hope, one of our boats was called to the loading dock.

Tuesday, April 29
12:30 p.m. We had just finished eating our first hot meal—potatoes, black beans and rice, and Cuban hot dogs, when the boat came up and said it was My Donna's turn to load. Everyone is going crazy. They are all certain we are next.

3:30 p.m. No word yet. Really miss Monica and kids. Can't stop thinking about them. I'm sure it's been more of a strain on Monica than me. If I had known it would be this long, I don't think I would have come, although we do need the money. I hope this thing

is over by the time I get home, so I won't have to decide whether to come back.

6:30 p.m. Just picked up WGBS on radio. First American station we've been able to receive and clear as a bell. Unfortunately, song playing is Barry Manilow's "I can't smile without you"—Monica's favorite.

One of the people went to Havana and came back with all the food we had for lunch. They had to go through the bags of black beans and the packages of rice first, not just wash, but to pick out the rocks and other stuff. Just another of the things that make life so pleasant for Castro Cubans.

When *My Donna* was called to load, we felt certain we were next, and prepared the boat to travel. It soon became obvious however, that boats were not being called in the order of their arrival. More boats were arriving each day and a school of Spanish sardines could not have packed together more tightly than the boats in Mariel Bay.

We assumed we would have to be patient until all the boats that arrived before us were called. But when boats were summoned that come in two and three days after us, the strain of waiting became even worse. My passengers were quiet and a gloom settled over the boat. All I had to do was shrug my shoulders, and they immediately imagined us returning empty-handed.

Juan and the others would have waited a month, but I had to get back to my business and Jack was unrelenting in his hectoring of me to leave. Juan let me know how they all understood, and said they did not blame me for wanting to get back to my own life. As anxious as I was to be home, I dreaded our arrival because I would then have to make a decision on the other $5,000. Nerves were starting to fray among the passengers, but everyone remained civil and began to accept that one way or the other, we would have to leave.

Mariel Boatlift

Wednesday, April 30

Petty Cash got called in the middle of the night. Rest of us just waiting. Activity on boat is practically at a standstill. Everyone is worn to a frazzle mentally. Somehow, we manage to put together the next meal. But it is becoming increasingly difficult. Fortunately, there has been no friction between people. I think we are going to entertain the possibility of going home empty.

The waiting becomes worse. I'm beginning to think it's hopeless. If nothing else, having to spend a week with Jack is enough to drive anyone crazy. I've heard how he's supposed to leave on his vacation at least a thousand times, and how his wife is going to kill him at least two thousand times.

Stanford Morse went over this afternoon and told them he had to go back. It worked. Bill Moore and Bubba left at 4:00 p.m.

I had set May 1 as the day we would head home. At first, I planned to simply start the engine and leave, but after seeing other boats go straight to the loading dock and push their way in, I felt I owed it to my passengers to give it a try. The loading dock, which was not clearly visible from our anchorage, was an amazing sight. It was jammed with armed military personnel and what looked like a senior citizens' convention. There were no children and virtually every person assembled had gray hair.

We tied up at the end of the dock and watched the chaotic situation. People were herded onto boats like cattle, but the extreme emotional distress of old people leaving their homeland forever seemed to have no effect on the soldiers. They were efficient and tough, and I was not looking forward to a confrontation with them. It was clear no one was checking names, and people were simply loaded on boats until there was either no more room or the boat was in danger of sinking.

The appalling scene on the dock became surreal when the loudspeakers started blaring a blistering speech by Fidel Castro. The angry harangue was blasting from the docks, from the army and cantina boats, and from sites on the shore surrounding the bay.

Trapped in Key West

In an incredible display of stamina, the speech thundered over the bay for hours. It was not necessary to speak Spanish to understand the speech, for *Americanos* and *Yanquis* were spit out in virtually every sentence

Thursday, May 1

Decided to try what <u>Stanford Morse</u> did. At this point we have to try something.

5:00 p.m. Well, it worked. <u>Miss Kriss</u> and <u>Honey Pot</u> have already been loaded. Somehow, we ended up last.

Communism becomes a reality here. Boats piled with people trying to escape. The clincher is the loudspeaker exhorting the army and Cubans. The loudspeaker yells, "Viva los communismos," and the troops yell it in return, "Viva la revolucion," and everyone stops what they are doing to yell, "Viva la revolucion! Viva Castro! Viva Castro!" Reminds me of old films of the Nazis and Hitler. The loudspeakers have been going for almost a half-hour so far. I don't know if this is daily ritual or due to May 1 being a communist holiday.

There are about fifty boats waiting near the loading dock, including <u>Stanford Morse</u>. Hopefully, we'll get loaded by tomorrow morning. In addition to shrimp boats, yachts, fishing boats, and pleasure craft, there must be one hundred of these cigarette hulls, all run by punks riding high on drug money.

During the night, I decided to force my way to the loading dock. At first light, I stood ready, and when a boat pulled away, I nosed the *American Dream* in. The military seemed not to care who was at the dock, and I chastised myself for not trying it a week earlier. Two soldiers with rifles and an officer, immediately boarded and demanded the captain. The officer spoke English and said we would be loaded directly and then must leave Cuba immediately.

I asked about the relatives of the people I had come for and he ignored me. Juan came forward to plead for the family, but the officer refused to speak to him and ordered him back. I asked Juan for the entry papers he had for his family members and handed them to the officer. "These are the people we came for, sir. Are we going to have them on board?"

With an imperial look, the officer flipped through the papers and handed them back to me. "We load now."

Holding up the papers, I said, "Sir, I came to get these people. If they don't come, I won't be able to take anyone."

The officer looked at me out of the corner of his eyes and then gave a quick look at one of his men. The soldier took a step toward me and lightly touched the barrel of his AK-47 to my stomach. "You take."

In the next fifteen minutes, the soldiers loaded the boat until there was standing room only. When they reached ninety-nine, it was apparent the boat would hold no more. It was the sorriest-looking group of people I had ever seen. Most were sad and frightened elderly citizens, but conspicuous among them were a number of hard-looking younger men. There was a suspiciously criminal look about them, and I warned Jack and Juan that under no circumstance were any of them to be allowed in the wheelhouse on the way home.

Incredibly, none of the people had any baggage. Whether they had small packages or some things in their pockets I don't recall, but they told us they were forced to leave all their worldly possessions behind and not a single word was uttered as they were loaded. The eerie silence of so many people quietly boarding empty-handed, stunned Jack and me. The thought of people leaving their lifelong home and starting over again at their age was hard to imagine, but the fact they were going to a strange country without even a single possession to their name seemed unthinkable. Hard-nosed Jack looked them over and shook his head. "Poor bastards. Must be hell over here."

As if having the boat grossly overloaded wasn't bad enough, a weather system moved over us with extremely high winds and massive squall lines hanging to the north. As the gunboat escorted us to the harbor entrance, I thought about refusing to leave. The *American Dream* was a solid boat with a very large carrying capacity, but it was dramatically overloaded, and I had a dozen life jackets for more than a hundred people. As soon as we left the harbor and started rolling in the seas, I could feel the sluggishness of the boat. Instead of riding the waves, the heaviness of the load caused the boat to stay low and plow through the water as the waves broke over the bow.

The possibility of foundering was very real, and I thought it best to turn back. Heading north into a northeast wind with a normal load would have been a fairly good ride with a lighter load, however, when I tried to turn back, we were hit with a side sea and the refugees were drenched. Seeing what I was doing, the gunboat threatened us and forced me out to open sea. It's easy to see today they would not have shot, and may even have stood by for rescue if I had continued turning back. But at the time, I feared they had so little regard for the people who were leaving that they might actually open fire if I did not continue north.

With only the twelve life jackets for 106 people, there was no question that practically everyone would drown if we sunk. We were alone on our voyage, and I had no time to concern myself with the passengers. When only two miles out, Jack reported several people already seasick and many of the older ones unable to stand. My original passengers were terribly dejected at not getting their relatives after such an ordeal, but were doing what they could to help the refugees.

The boat was riding as well as could be expected under the conditions. As we cruised farther offshore, we started feeling the effects of the Gulf Stream Current. Flowing into the teeth of the northeast wind, it was creating jumbled sea conditions. Spume flew from the tops of the large waves and they were more erratic than expected with the wind speed, but I was still feeling more confident by the minute that we would make it safely to Key West.

About twenty miles from Cuba, the first squall hit. Like most squalls at sea, it was led by a howling wind. The wind in a squall will not always follow the prevailing wind, but under any circumstance, it is necessary to head directly into the gale and maintain complete concentration at the wheel. The strong winds usually moderate after a while, but it was a particularly impressive-looking storm, and I could see it also contained heavy rains.

The passengers were terrified. Most had never been on a boat before and were frightened even before the squall hit. When the first blast of wind struck, the crys rang out. Above the screaming wind came the shrieking wails of people who knew they were about to die. *Con yo su madres* and *Santa Madres* pierced the wind. The scary ones cursed their bad luck, and the older ones prayed for the Lord to deliver them. There was general pandemonium among all the passengers as they waited for the inevitable sinking.

I couldn't leave the wheel for even a second to try and calm the people. I was not worried about the boat sinking, but feared some of the passengers might fall over and we would never be able to rescue them. I ordered Jack and Juan to have everyone sit on deck. It didn't matter whether there was enough room, or that they would be piled on top of each other. "Just get them down!"

To add to the misery, more people started getting sick. As the boat heaved and lurched, most every person on board was vomiting. They were sliding and rolling on the deck, throwing up all over each other as the rain poured down. The people were in such a foul and wretched state that even Jack got sick. Many moaned with misery, others sobbed with disbelief, and some calmly and stoically awaited their fate. It was a pitiful group, and nothing could make them believe everything was going to be all right.

We were not the only ones in such condition. The radio crackled with calls from other boats in trouble. Frenzied appeals for assistance screamed out from the speaker as two other boats said they were sinking. The desperate pleas for help were especially frightening as our own boat pitched and heaved in the wild seas. Juan and the others were frantic with worry for the people on the sinking boats, but I was totally preoccupied with our own situation.

I was finally forced to emphatically declare that there was nothing we could do. The rain was coming down so hard we could not see one hundred feet in front of the boat, and without navigational equipment to direct us, we had no idea of sinking boats locations. Furthermore, I had to keep the bow into the storm until the winds subsided, and even if we did find them, we ran the risk of sinking our own boat if we loaded it any further.

The Coast Guard was on the radio to the boats and doing everything they could to get an idea of their location. In truth, the distressed boats could have been twenty miles in any direction, and the chances of finding them under such conditions were extremely remote. I assured Juan that the Coast Guard had a far better chance of finding them than we did, but if I did spot them, we would surely do everything we could to help.

When the squall finally passed, we found ourselves in moderately rough seas. Though everyone was wet and miserable, there was a general feeling we would all survive after having weathered such an ordeal. We ran through only one more squall, but the people were by then experienced sailors and knew we were going to make it.

Late that afternoon, we pulled into the mole at Truman Annex. U.S. Customs had set up a receiving station, and there was a crowd of Cubans waiting to see if any of their relatives were on the arriving boats. All of my passengers were very subdued as we pulled into the dock, but the majority of them got down on their knees and kissed the ground when they stepped on shore. Even Jack, who was finally going to get his vacation, was moved.

For most of the boats participating in the Mariel boatlift, the fallout lasted for years. Shortly after we left Key West, the president issued an order prohibiting boats from going to Cuba. All boats that subsequently left had huge fines levied against them and a lien put against their vessel by the government. While most never paid the fine, the title was not transferable with the lien, and many spent thousands in legal fees to clear the charges.

Later, we learned more about the boatlift. Castro had taken the opportunity to rid his country of thousands of nonproductive elderly people, whom he saw as merely a drain on the Cuban economy. While he did let the embassy refugees leave, he also forced the boats to take many undesirables from the island.

Mariel Boatlift

As we had suspected, he cleverly cleared the prisons and mental hospitals, and put several on each boat they loaded.

As we said our good-byes the following day, Juan and the others were in much better spirits. They learned that many of the Peruvian Embassy refugees had arrived, and hopes were high that their relatives might make it after all. Despite the frustrations of the ordeal, they returned home feeling the trip had been worth it and they had all done the right thing by going.

12

Bahamas and Cannons

As our family expanded and schedules became more complicated, we found there was less and less time for recreational boating. Even without Pete's Fish Market, working traps, fishing during the summer months, and running the bustling fish house was devouring my time. With schoolwork, athletics, and other extracurricular activities for five children added into the week, the blueboat sat neglected for months at a time. Even the occasional guy trips my friends and I snuck in between family days became a thing of the past, as all my friends were busy with work and raising families of their own.

Ed Swift and I knew each other as classmates in school, but became best friends after we were each married. Our children were cousins on their mother's side, and Ed and I later became brothers-in-law when he married my sister Nancy. We have remained the closest of friends throughout our lives, and rarely do anything without consulting each other.

As my friends and I reached middle age, we tried to make more time for the boat, but the years flew by while we made excuse after excuse. Each time we managed to sneak in a day for the guys, we had such a good time that we swore we would go more frequently from then on, but never did. At least we never did until Ed and I were approaching our thirty-seventh year. We spent the morning diving for fish and lobster with half a dozen of our friends, and set up a grill on an island to cook our catch.

Bahamas and Cannons

With a cooler of beer, a bottle of rum, and a bag of key limes, we were all high from the thrill of the hunt. We recounted each fish that had been shot and every lobster that was netted. By late afternoon, we talked our way through fishing, work, and women, and settled in on the subject we usually talked about when the day was ending: "Why don't we do this more often?"

Probably because of the rum, that day actually produced a promise by all of us to take a boating day once a month regardless of the circumstance. In the end, only Ed and I stuck by our vow. For ten straight years we held fast to our agreement, and from then on - regardless of weather, business problems, family objections, or the resentment of friends—we took our day in the boat each month.

In the beginning, everyone thought it was a grand idea, and it soon became a topic of conversation even outside our usual circle of boating companions. "You actually do a day every month! I don't know how you do it. I could never get away every month. But I sure would like to go with you some time." Some were even so completely smitten with the idea they wanted to sign on. "Man, I'd love to do that with you. Just let me know the day and I'll be there."

One day a month crew: John DePoo, Peter Bacle, and Ed Swift.

Trapped in Key West

So few people actually accompanied us, that after a year we stopped going out of our way to invite others and just gave everyone a date. "Meet us at the boat if you're going." Occasionally, one or more of our friends would accompany us - most frequently John DePoo - but for the most part, it was just Ed and I. At first, we missed having a bunch of guys along, but soon realized we only had two people to please.

By the end of the first year, the boat day was becoming a comfortable part of our monthly routine, but others were becoming noticeably exasperated. Our wives were particularly irritated by the frequency of our trips. "You're going again? Didn't you just go? . . . You know, the last two times they really needed to get in touch with you from the fish house and I had to worry all day about what kind of emergency they were trying to handle without you . . . So? Does this mean I get to drop everything in your lap one day a month too, or are these special days only for the men folk?"

Our intransigence in the face of guilt brought more pressure from Monica, and her initial annoyance gave way to outright resentment. "Let me get this straight now! You can take a whole day to go out in the boat with Ed—every month—but you can't spare one afternoon to look at furniture with me . . . Let me think a minute. Hmmmm! I'm trying to remember the last time you took a day off just to be with me . . . Okay now! Let's get down to the bottom of this boat-day business. I have sat quietly by like the dutiful wife for a whole year, while you dumped everything on me, so you and Ed could have your fun! Now! Exactly how much longer do you expect me to put up with this recharge-your-batteries business?"

Ed was dealing with a similar situation at home and even our most credible excuse—"But darling, it's a work day. You wouldn't see me anyway."—fell on deaf ears. It became the sorest topic for discussion, and while we did everything to avoid the subject, it always seemed to be lurking on the periphery of our conversations. One evening at dinner, Monica more or less had the final word after Linda asked, "I just don't understand why you have to go every month. Can't you go every other month? Or take Monica and me one month, and then just the guys the next month? Why do you have to be so hardheaded about it?"

Monica was ready and she vented her frustration. "Why? I'll tell you why! Because they're men! And men don't care about anyone but themselves! They're going to do exactly what they want to do and the heck with everyone else."

Partners and business associates could sometimes be as blunt as wives. "You sure are lucky. I wish I could just drop everything and leave . . . Don't you think you ought to call off that trip tomorrow, so we can get this taken care of? I mean, it seems to me that this is just a little more important than a day in the boat . . . You know, every month means twelve working days a year. That's like an extra two and a half weeks of vacation. Are we all going to do that?"

While virtually everyone thought the day in the boat was a grand idea and inevitably expressed a forlorn envy, the people closest to us remained resentful. In truth, it was a case of putting our own desires above everything else, and unless one had a conscience made of stone, overcoming the guilt was even harder than clearing the calendar. Through it all, we bolstered each other's courage, and refused to let the other off the hook regardless of the circumstance.

The guilt always dissolved as soon as we left the dock. In the pre-cell phone age, we were blessedly out of touch with the world, and the only way to contact us was to send another boat out. Our being completely out of touch apparently caused everyone else endless anxiety, but once away from the dock, Ed and I felt only the most euphoric sense of freedom.

Through it all, we always understood we were acting irresponsibly, yet refused to give it up. It sometimes appeared the more people fought us, the more determined we became. Meanwhile, our agreement seemed to take on the status of a legal contract that would mentally break us if we violated it. In the big picture of life, it was a small act of defiance, but for us, it was a vital sign we were in control of our lives and were not going to wake one day and say, "Why didn't we do that when we were young?"

Trapped in Key West

We encouraged and even threatened each other to not give in, and then praised each other for showing up each time. As soon as we cast off and raced toward the islands, the exuberance set in, and the first ten minutes were usually spent trying to outdo each other as to who exhibited the most capricious behavior by going out that day. Ed's all-time top choice was the day he skipped out on a bank closing for a loan critical to his business, and mine was leaving when the fishermen were on strike and demanding a meeting with me under the old casuarina tree in front of the fish house? Even to us it seemed like an odd thing to claim bragging rights on, but as a thoroughly annoyed Monica said, "That's little boys for you."

Though we enjoyed every single day, each time we took someone else along, we realized we were missing out on the companionship of many of our friends. In our monthly excursions, we came across a grassy clearing on one of the islands and decided it would be a great spot to gather all our friends for the day. We set aside a day several months in advance, which allowed the ten friends we invited plenty of time to clear their calendars. The day was a great success, and everyone pledged we would get the group together every year at the same place and time.

Within a couple of years, our annual day evolved into something of an informal boys' club whose sole purpose was to get together one day in the year for a diving or fishing excursion, and then retire to the island for an afternoon lunch. Through the years, we have added and subtracted from the group—one even died— but a core of about a dozen guys has remained intact. Our crew has been getting together annually for over twenty-five years, and while circumstance always seems to knock someone out each year, it is a day everyone tries not to miss.

Monica, when she is most exasperated with me, maintains that all men are the same in one respect. "They are never satisfied with what they have! Every one will either want something else or want more of what they've already got." So it was with our monthly day in the boat. We wanted more. Not just more days, but consecutive days, so we didn't have to go in because the sun was setting. Time flew by on our boat trips, and it seemed the day was always ending just as we were really starting to relax.

Once a year crew: kneeling l-r *Gerald 'Mo' Mosher, Ed Swift, Bob Bernreuter* Center – *Hugh Morgan, Fred Salinero, Chris Belland, Peter Bacle, Paul Toppino* Back row - *Bill Wickers, John dePoo, Tony Willis, Mike Wilson*

Without my realizing, the crew became fascinated by my stories of trapping and diving in the Bahamas. Mel Fisher had just discovered the *Atocha*, and when Bill Wickers and I told them about the bronze cannon we found on one of the trips, they were all enthralled by the thought of real Spanish treasure. The stories of our dive trip to the Cay Sal Bank also had them intrigued and the idea of a week long trip started to take root.

Ed was the main catalyst. He had heard me tell stories of the Bahamas for years. The clear waters, virgin beaches, and prolific sea life were luring him with increasing intensity. He never tired of hearing the tales and was determined to be a part of any future stories about the Bahamas. "Come on, guys! Let's quit talking and make this a reality! Peter has the boat and the experience. We can do this if we make the commitment. What do you say? This summer, we'll go for a full week to the Cay Sal Bank."

In June of 1988, the Bahamas trip became a reality. Ed, Hugh, and I were joined by Chris Belland—Ed's business partner—and Tony Willis—a mutual friend who came to Key West from Georgia. Like men living out a dream, we spent a full week diving the brilliant waters of the Cay Sal Bank and exploring the surrounding islands. The trip was everything we imagined it would be, but true to Monica's admonition about men, it only made us want more. The following year—and for the next twelve years after—we made two-week trips to the Out Islands of the Bahamas.

Once we had a taste of the islands, there was no stopping us. No sooner would we get home from one trip than we were planning for the next year. The fur flew on the home front, and arguing over a single day in the boat was a breeze compared to taking off for two weeks. With the start of the Bahama trips, Ed and I gave up our monthly trips and just kept the annual boat day with the guys. That did little to placate our spouses. The wives were acquiescent the first year when we went for a week, but when we announced we needed two weeks to have a really good time, the battles began.

Monica was left at home with five children, and the rest of the wives all had school-age children. Our wives were trying to be modern, understanding women, and had hoped if they tolerated one trip, we would get it out of our system. The realization that we wanted to go every year—and even longer trips—was the signal for all-out war. Though we planned the trips months in advance, because of the friction with spouses, we often had doubts about each crewmember right up until the day of departure.

The first year, all the wives and kids were at the boat to see us off. By the third year, we were hustling aboard in the predawn hours without so much as a farewell wave from the wives. Most of our 'boys club' guys caved in to the pressure, and either never went or would fly over when possible to spend a couple of days. Ed, Chris, Tony, and I, like the hard-core, uncaring chauvinists we were accused of being, never gave in to the browbeating and went on every trip.

Unlike the other wives however, Monica was not one to simply accept defeat. After our third voyage, she announced that she and two girlfriends would be doing a three-week trip through Europe. She told me the dates were set and the reservations made, so I had better start arranging my schedule to accommodate it.

Her toughest argument against my trips had always been, "What if I just up and left you to take care of the kids by yourself for two weeks?" My only possible retort had been that if she was willing to leave her children for two weeks, then she should go right ahead.

When she called my bluff with the European trip, there was little I could say except a very weak, "But I never went for *three* weeks."

European vacation l-r Monica Bacle, Monica Lester, Maria Crostley

Trapped in Key West

In truth, Monica's trip worked out for both of us. I had a great time with the children and got to experience firsthand the difficulties of being a full-time mother. Monica, not only had a fantastic vacation, but she also realized for the first time how it was good to get away from family and responsibility every now and then. After Europe, she took periodic trips without me, and peace finally reigned over our Bahama trips—at least in the Bacle household.

As we approached the island of Cay Sal on our first trip, Tony screamed out, "Back her down! Back her down!"

After crossing the three-thousand-foot deep Gulf Stream waters, we came up on the Cay Sal Bank next to its namesake island. The water was so astonishingly clear that Tony imagined we were about to hit bottom when the Fathometer revealed thirty-five feet of depth beneath the boat. The waters around Key West are known for their clarity, but the Cay Sal Bank lies between the Florida Keys and Cuba, and the Gulf Steam current—which carries the purest water in the hemisphere—washes across it year-round.

Though I had often told them of the extreme clarity of Bahama waters, none had expected it to be so crystal clear. They were to find like I did, that even after years of traversing the Bahama Banks, we would still be frequently fooled by coral heads appearing to be just below the surface, and cautiously idle across them though the Fathometer showed plenty of water depth.

I hadn't been there in twenty years, but from a distance, Cay Sal Island looked as exotic as I had remembered. However, as we got closer, it was easy to see the coconut tree population had been decimated. I thought at first a recent hurricane must have uprooted the trees, but it turned out to be the same blight that wiped out the trees in Key West. Lethal yellowing is a wind-borne disease affecting primarily the Jamaica Tall species of coconut—the predominant variety in the Caribbean. Today, they have been replaced with the Malayan varieties which are blight-resistant.

Only a handful of trees survived on Cay Sal, but never having seen the tropical grove of coconuts, the crew was delighted with the beauty of the island. Most disappointing however, was the disappearance of the small, whitewashed stilt homes which had given Cay Sal such romantic appeal. They had been bulldozed and replaced with a metal barracks building housing the Bahama Defense Force. The proliferation of drug smuggling and the running gun battles on the sixty-mile-long Cay Sal Bank prompted the Bahamian government to remove the population and install a permanent military force to protect the sovereignty of the twenty islands.

As we anchored several hundred yards from shore, the entire Defense Force of about a dozen men assembled on the beach and waved us in. We intended to check in upon arrival, but the impatient soldiers gave us no time to secure the boat properly before they started firing their weapons into the air. Ed and I hustled over to the beach and found the men with no boat and ordering us to take them out to the *Dream*—my brother Jimmy's thirty-nine-foot boat we used only on the first trip—for an inspection.

Once the men felt assured we were harmless, they were extremely relaxed and very cordial. They had however, been initially on guard with rifles at the ready after seeing our stash of weapons. The AR-15 'assault rifle' had particularly unnerved them, but once we agreed to let them hold our weapons while we were at Cay Sal, they seemed convinced that we really did have the weapons only for protection against drug pirates.

The men explained how Cay Sal was not an official entry point for the Bahamas, and technically, we were not supposed to set foot on the island without first clearing customs in Bimini some two hundred miles away. We were disappointed, but when we took them back to shore, the captain's parting words were, "Mon, if you are on the other side of the island, maybe we don't see you."

The Defense Force was a very informal group. Most were wearing only one part of a uniform, and discipline appeared to be very relaxed. But the assault weapons they carried gave them a menacing authority, and had they not actually extended us a backwards invitation, we would not have dared to step foot on the island.

Trapped in Key West

The waters on the north side of Cay Sal flowed over a grassy bottom packed with conchs. Thousands upon thousands of the shells littered the bottom, and we quickly retrieved enough to last the entire trip. The taking of conchs had been banned in the Keys, and though the thick-lipped shells of Cay Sal were not as large or as colorful as ours, they made up for it with sheer numbers.

With a substantial pile of shells in the bottom of the skiff and a large ice chest filled with beer, we headed to the back beach to clean the conchs. Getting the meat out is an extremely messy job, and we set up a cleaning station on the water's edge—after a quick look to see if any soldiers were in the area. Fifty yards from the beach, a twenty-foot-high dune blocked our view of the island, but a trip to the top showed no Bahamians in sight.

The first step in cleaning a conch is to make a hole near the tip of the shell to release the suction of the tough-muscled animal. Because of the beauty of the 'broad lip' shells at home, we were in the habit of making as small a hole as possible and then dislodging the animal with an ice pick. The plain-looking Cay Sal conchs were so thick-shelled that we simply pounded them with the sharp end of a mason's hammer—giving no thought to saving the shells.

The animal itself is one of the slimiest creatures in the ocean. The glutinous film is so sticky it must be scrubbed off the hands, and is best removed by the vigorous rubbing of beach sand. Covering the tough edible muscle, is an even tougher skin, and stripping it off with a knife is a skill few people possess. Having operated Pete's Fish Market while conchs were still legal, I had cleaned thousands of them, and Ed and Hugh were experienced skinners as well.

The beach was so beautiful, the water so alluring, and the beer so cold, that we gave no thought to hurrying through our job. We threw a couple of key limes and a bottle of Tabasco Sauce in the ice chest, and ate the first five conchs as quickly as we cleaned them. No further thought was given to the Defense Force, until we turned toward a rustling in the bushes and saw two soldiers foot-slide down from the top of the dune.

Bahamas and Cannons

We stopped in mid-action as the two came straight toward us, looking very official. Both were in uniform, and one carried an automatic rifle, while the other had a handheld radio. They nodded back to our hellos, but carefully analyzed our activity.

"What you do, mon?"

"We're just cleaning a few conchs to eat."

"You have the permit?"

"Uh, no. We didn't know you had to have a permit."

"You have to have permit."

"Well, can we get one from you?"

"No. You must take de permit in Bimini."

"I'm sorry. I thought your captain gave us permission to be here."

"Come on de island, yes. Take de conch, no!"

"I guess we misunderstood. We'll put them back in the water. Sorry."

"Who teach you to clean de conch, mon?"

"Oh . . . Well, we've been doing it all of our lives. We live in Key West."

"Key West?"

"Yes. Do you know Key West?"

"Yes, mon. In the Exumas, but you not Bahamian."

"No, we're from the other Key West. In the States . . . you know, in the United States. We're Americans . . . It's an island at the end of the Florida Keys."

"Ah, Florida. Yes, I know Florida."

"Well, we have conchs there, and that's how we learned to clean them."

I stood with a conch in one hand and a knife in the other, while he eyed me suspiciously. "Let me see de knife, mon."

We watched with astonishment as he stuck his rifle barrel into the sand, took the conch from my hand, and started skinning. He was obviously unimpressed with our Florida conch-cleaning skills, and for the next hour, taught us everything he knew about the mystical mollusk. As the beer flowed, the cleaning party got cranked up, and before long, we were all talking and laughing like old friends. When

Chris noticed the tide had risen to cover the barrel of the rifle, the man casually dismissed it. "Mon, you can't hurt dot gon."

When they confided the secret of the 'pestil' to us, we felt like privileged conspirators. The pestil is a long worm-like appendage on the conch, reputed by islanders to give extraordinary masculine power to men who consume them. Assuming no one but Bahamians could possibly know the pestil sucking ritual, they swore us to secrecy and initiated us with the time-honored ceremony. With mouths open and facing the sky, we sucked down the pestils like baby birds taking a worm from their mothers, and were declared to be honorary Bahamians.

We learned how the men were stuck on the island for a month at a time without a boat, and only a Citizens' Band radio for contact with the world. In our experience, the Bahama Defense Force has always been well trained and professional, but our new friends had just signed up and were immediately shipped off to Cay Sal for their training. With no form of entertainment—including television and alcohol—and still a week to go before they were relieved, the undisciplined men were primed for our timely diversion from their boring routine.

The following morning, we decided to move on to other islands and landed on the front beach to retrieve our weapons. Our two Bahamian brothers looked a little ragged and persistently averted their eyes when we tried to signal them. The captain, who was extremely cordial to us and mercifully returned our guns without comment, gave our new brothers a couple of hard looks, leading us to believe their dereliction of duty had been uncovered by the shrewd officer.

The sixty-mile-long Bank has only Cay Sal Island on the westerly and southerly side, but is completely rimmed by a string of rocky islands on the north side and sand-covered islands down the east side. We headed toward Anguilla, the most southerly of the eastern islands. I had dived the waters and explored the deserted island many times during Dad's Bahama days, and wanted my friends to swim on its reefs and witness its forlorn beauty.

Bahamas and Cannons

About a mile long, but only a couple of hundred yards wide, Anguilla is a classic tropical island, with beaches and coves on all sides. The middle of the island rises one hundred feet or more from the shoreline, and has a number of hardwood hammocks as well as coverings of fragrant, flowering bushes. Long before we sighted the island, we caught fleeting whiffs of the sweet-scented joewood blossom as it wafted across the bank on the easterly breeze.

On the windward side are rounded bluffs covered with low-lying vegetation, which allows extensive views of the beaches and open ocean. The rocky parts of the shoreline are riddled with underwater caves, some of which open up inside the island and create geyser-like blowholes when the wind is strong. A rusty rain-filled pond dismally dominates the southern end, completing the lonely allure which has drawn us back many times.

On our first Bahamas trip, we set up camp on the longest beach on the island—about a half-mile of white-powder sand. The beach is one hundred feet wide, rising gently to an upper dune and then straight up for fifty feet or more to the high bluffs. Chris and Hugh set up a large tarp for shade, while Ed, Tony, and I, ferried ashore all the necessities for a day on the beach in Ed's skiff *Patsy*.

The skiff was not named for a wife, girlfriend, or daughter, but for our favorite singer, Patsy Cline. By the third day of the trip, we had practically worn out Tony's Patsy Cline tape, and in a salt-lime-tequila toot, voted to honor her with the skiff name. At a time when all boats and hurricanes were reverentially feminine, no shiny new Hatteras Yacht was ever treated with more deference than our ragged little skiff named *Patsy*.

Chris and Hugh walked to the upper dune and quickly found four large poles to mount the tarp. The dune was a virtual lumber store, and there was enough wood on the one beach to construct a fair-sized house. While there was a substantial amount of true driftwood, the lumber was primarily dunnage, which are the boards used on freighters to secure the cargo.

Aside from the lumber, the upper dune was a beachcomber's dream. Flotsam from all over the world found its way to the sandy perch and presented a surprising mixture of items. It did not have the normal look of trash on a beach, but appeared more like a seashore flea market. Handblown glass balls from the fishnets of the world and deep-colored wine bottles decorated the dune like Christmas ornaments, while the boat parts, furniture pieces, and turtle shells led us to endless speculation on their origins. Except for a few plastic jugs, there was little of the beer cans, soda bottles, and plastic wrappings we often saw on the beaches of Key West.

Apart from the upper dune, the beach was pristine. There was not a piece of trash to be seen, though at times it had some of our ever-present Key West seaweed. It appeared that most trash floated by Anguilla in the Gulf Stream current to the north or in the Great Bahama Channel to the south. Looking over the sparkling clean beach, witty Chris jibed the rest of the crew, "Boys, does anyone else feel just a little guilty about sullying this virgin beach with our vulgar presence?"

After three trips to the big boat and several close calls with swamping *Patsy*, the beach was piled high with our junk. We wondered aloud at the items of civilization we brought to the deserted island. We had spent months planning and dreaming of the moment, and the beach was fairly littered with all the things we thought we couldn't do without.

Bahamas base camp

Bahamas and Cannons

Ice chests—one for food, one for beer, and one for drink ice—fold-up chairs and a table, a grill, charcoal, and dive equipment were thrown randomly on the beach. In a large pile were plastic bags full of towels, spare clothes, glasses, plates and utensils, coolie cups, hats, windbreakers, and a score of other personal items.

The last trip brought in the most carefully handled items: Bacardi Reserve rum for Ed and I, Chivas Regal scotch for Tony, Jose Cuervo tequila for Hugh, and Wild Turkey bourbon for Chris. A bag full of key limes, Cuban cigars for Chris and me, the tape player and tapes, and our guns to protect us from pirates and drug smugglers. Hugh, who was the federal magistrate in Key West, had his own cigars from Nicaragua because he said our Cuban ones were contraband.

The sun was hot, the beer was cold, and the crew was mellow as we swam in the crystalline waters and 'chilled out' in the breeze under our flimsy awning. Jimmy Buffet played on the tape deck and the excitement of setting up camp and actually being there had given way to quiet reflection. We were all close to dozing before Chris broke the mood with another of his Confucian observations. "Well boys, we all have to believe in something . . . So, I *believe* I will test that Wild Turkey."

The crew all came to life when Ed said, "Come on guys, let's get this party going! Break out the rum. I'll light the charcoal and get the lobster on the grill. Someone turn up the music!"

Anyone who has lived or sailed in the Caribbean could easily guess the identity of our favorite singer. Jimmy Buffet's music spoke to us on our first trip as if we had written the songs ourselves. By the end of the week, we knew even his most obscure songs by heart and had worn out multiple copies of each tape. We found that neither the tapes nor the tape players did too well with the fine Bahamian sand, and were thankful we had all unwittingly brought the same tapes and extra players.

Ed knew Jimmy Buffet when he was just another penniless Key West musician, looking for a place to play. He dragged me

Trapped in Key West

down to Lou's Bar one night to hear the budding star by promising, "I absolutely guarantee you are going to love this guy!" I went home at 3:00 in the morning when Jimmy had still not appeared, but Ed stayed and said he showed up at 3:05 and sang until closing time.

Ed met Jimmy through his camera store. Though Ed knew nothing about music, he decided to expand his business by selling musical instruments. Jimmy was a frequent patron, buying mostly guitar strings, but wishing he could afford an electric guitar. He finally traded in his acoustic guitar for a shiny new electric one and Ed—to his everlasting dismay—put the old one in the window and quickly sold it.

As the rum flowed and the mood accelerated, Tony had a bibulously brilliant idea. "Guys, I think we need a little practice with our weapons. I mean, what if we were attacked now and didn't even know how shoot the guns? I've never fired an AR-15 and the captain has never shot a .44 magnum. I think we should take a little target practice."

The crew was gung-ho over the idea and everyone raced to get the guns and set up targets. Only Hugh—our ever-present legal conscience and arbiter of prudent behavior—voiced any concern over a bunch of tipsy amateurs firing assault rifles and high-powered pistols. "Listen up, guys. Hey guys! Listen to me! Peter! Peter! Jesus, won't anyone give me one second to talk? Come on Captain, tell the crew to shut up for just a minute!"

"All right men! Let's settle down and let Hugh talk—even though we all know what he's going to say."

First came Hugh's appeal to our good sense. "Listen guys, I don't know if shooting these guns now is such a good idea. I think we should wait until the morning when we're all sober and clear-headed."

"Booooo!"

"Forget it, Morgan! We're shooting!"

"No way baby! It's now or never!"

Next came Hugh's legal appeal. "You know guys, this is the

Bahamas and Cannons

Bahamas. We don't know what their laws are. Just because we're allowed to have guns, doesn't necessarily mean we can bring them ashore. And don't forget, even though we checked in at Cay Sal, the Defense Force Captain said it was not official. My advice is to at least wait until we're on the boat."

"Get real, Hugh! There's not another person within a hundred miles and the dune makes a great backdrop for the target. This is the perfect place. Besides, what if the drug smugglers attack and you don't even know how to load the AR-15?"

With a deep breath and a look of supreme frustration, Hugh turned to me for his final try. "Peter, you're the captain. You really need to stop this."

"Sorry Hugh. We're on shore now, and my authority as captain is only valid on the boat."

With his most solemn expression, Hugh watched the focused crew load the clips and guns. Hugh finally broke into a slight smile of resignation when I said, "Well bubba, it looks like you're going to be the new safety officer, so you'd better get a fresh drink before they start firing."

Captain Pete on guard duty

Hugh has always been a stickler for the letter of the law, and when the letter is not clear, he will abide by the spirit of the law. Even Hugh however, knew when he was beaten, and resigned himself to the duty of assuring our target practice was conducted according to all the rules of firing safety.

The guns were something we were reluctant to bring on a pleasure trip, but even more reluctant to leave behind.

Trapped in Key West

Drug smuggling was rampant in the late '70s and '80s, and many of the smugglers were hardened criminals who played for keeps. The very island we were on had recently been the scene of a major gun battle between smugglers and law enforcement, and we had been advised by everyone to choose a different destination. Because of my familiarity with the area, and maybe because we were secretly looking for a little danger, we assured everyone we could take care of ourselves as long as we had the weapons.

It was not unheard of for boats in that area to turn up abandoned somewhere after drug smuggling pirates boarded them and disposed of the crews. Whether or not the guns afforded us protection, we all felt better having them on board. Despite having the loaded AR-15 at my side, I slept very little on that first trip. Any noise or odd wave smacking on the hull had me reaching for the gun and scanning the dark ocean.

The guns, and in particular the AR-15, would cause us to be searched intensively in the future by the Bahama Defense Force and the U.S. Coast Guard. They never truly understood why a bunch of middle-aged businessmen on a supposed pleasure trip would have need of such high-powered weapons, unless we were up to no good.

On a subsequent trip, we had an incident which almost ended in disaster, and had us debating the wisdom of carrying the AR-15. At 2:00 in the morning, I was awakened by something. It was a cloudy, moonless night, and so dark I could not even see Ed across the cabin. I scanned the blackened night for boat lights, but could see nothing. I listened, and could hear nothing. Yet, there was *something*.

With my AR-15 at the ready, I crouched to the back deck for a better look. Ed, who is also a light sleeper, awoke thinking I was walking to the stern. "Sure is a dark night."

"Shhhhh."

"What? What is it?"

"I don't know. Maybe nothing. Get your gun."

I stared into the dark off the port beam with gun pointing

and whispered to Ed, "I can't see a thing, but I'm sure I heard something."

Suddenly, a brilliant blinding spotlight beam shone directly in my face. I instinctively raised my gun to shoot out the light when a megaphone voice called out, "PUT DOWN YOUR WEAPONS!"

I hesitated as my mind raced for a decision. "Is it drug smugglers? Who else would sneak up on us at this time of the night? If it's pirates, why don't they just shoot? Maybe they don't intend to kill us unless I fire first."

"PUT DOWN YOUR WEAPONS OR WE SHOOT!"

The voice was Bahamian and I was still confused as to who it could be, but made the decision to disarm. "Put the gun down, Ed."

Chris had also grabbed his gun and questioned the decision. "Are you sure about this, Captain?"

"Yea Chris. Put it down."

The spotlight still had us blinded, and we were totally exposed and at the mercy of whomever had us covered.

"EVERYONE MOVE TO THE STERN AND KEEP YOUR HANDS HIGH!"

Chris woke Tony, who probably would have slept through an all-out gun battle, and we all moved to the back of the boat. The spotlight stayed on until four men with automatic rifles boarded and put us under guard. I never thought I could be relieved to have an AK-47 pointed at my chest, but when the spotlight was turned off, we could see it was the Bahama Defense Force and knew we were going to live.

As our eyes cleared, we saw just how close we had come to a permanent vacation. Thirty feet from the side of the *Big Crawl* was a Bahamian gunboat with its huge deck gun pointed directly at our boat. Any action on our part would have ended with us being blown to pieces, as the AR-15 had identified us as probable drug smugglers.

The Bahamian soldiers were very young and very nervous. The sweat poured off them, and their guns shook as they pointed at our chests. We tried to reassure them by explaining we were just a bunch of old men enjoying a fishing trip in their beautiful waters, but our guns had them extremely nervous. With a gun at my back, the captain of the boarding party sent me below to get our boat papers.

On that particular trip, we had cleared customs at Chub Cay before going to Cay Sal, and there was a noticeable relief to all when our papers proved to be in order and the guns were found to have been properly declared. They did, however, continue with a search of the boat—even counting our bullets. After we found it was illegal to bring guns ashore in the Bahamas, we never again fired them, and all the bullets declared at Chub Cay were still there.

Unfortunately for us, one of the men found our arbalete spear guns packed away under the v-berth in the bow. They asked us if we understood that spear guns with triggers were not permitted in the Bahamas, and I assured them we had the spears packed away and were only using the pole spears lying on deck.

That seemed to placate them until one member of the boarding party noticed the rope running out behind our boat. He pulled on it and found our skiff, which he entered and searched. With a grin as big as our dismay, he proudly held aloft an arbalete spear gun.

The chief took the gun and as he looked it over said, "Well Captain, what have we here?"

"Oh yeah, I forgot about that. We don't actually shoot fish with it, though. We keep it out for protection. You know how many sharks there are in these waters. We just keep one ready in case of a shark attack."

The chief and then all of his crew laughed heartily at the explanation. "That's very quick thinking, Captain. However, I'm afraid we will have to seize these spear guns since they are neither allowed nor declared."

The four spear guns were all very expensive wooden arbaletes, and Chris was moved to speak, "Sir, that gun was given to me by my father who is now passed away. Do you think there is any way I could possibly keep it?"

The still grinning captain replied, "Why certainly. I know the Magistrate in Nassau quite well, and he is a very compassionate

man. I shall be pleased to complete charges against you and tow
you to Nassau. When you tell the honorable judge your story, I'm
sure he will let you keep the speargun."

Chris, knowing when he'd been bested, shrugged his shoulders
and said, "Aw, what the heck. You just go ahead and keep it."

The target practice went off without a hitch. The crew, as
expected, could be as serious as the situation warranted and
everyone was a model of safety with a loaded gun in their hands.
Though all of us were familiar with guns, it was our first time with
an AR-15, and we were all impressed by the damage it wreaked
on our target.

The day passed as if we were in a dream. There was no talk
of business, health, or family problems. Life was good. Life was
fantastic. We swam. We drank rum and smoked cigars. We lay in the
warm sand. There were loud jokes and quiet stories. We smiled and
chuckled and laughed. We talked of life and love and old girlfriends.
And we were all silently thankful for the blessing of good friends.

When finally motivated to move, we climbed over a rocky
outcropping and walked a shorter beach to the north of our camp.
We saw a couple of old turtle trails on our beach, but the northern
end was fairly covered with them. The smooth symmetry of the
sand was disrupted along the entire length of beach by the labored
crawl of the nesting turtles—one flippering trail up from the water
to a depression in the sand that held the eggs, and a matching trail
returning to the water. There were more than twenty such trails in
one hundred yards of beach.

Chris noticed a small casuarina tree trying to get a foothold in
the upper dune, and we wondered why there weren't more of them.
In Key West they are prolific and commonly known as Australian
pines. Several environmental groups are in the process of removing
them because they are not native to the Florida Keys. I like the
name casuarina far better and wonder how a seed carried by the
ocean to distant shores can be considered non-indigenous. They are
exotic and romantic looking, and might have been left alone in Key
West if called casuarinas, instead of Australian pines.

Trapped in Key West

After leaving the turtle nesting area, the lazy walk continued back on our beach, and no one was in a hurry to get anywhere. Chris, Ed, and Tony walked the water's edge, and Hugh and I strolled the upper dune. We barely heard their muted voices and watched as they ambled along, wandering into the surf, picking up shells, and occasionally walking backwards to tell a story with more emphasis.

Hugh and I picked through the flotsam, finding here and there an item of interest. We talked quietly of simple and insignificant things, as we slowly made our way down the beach. The rambling chatter from a long day of diving and drinking had worked its way out of our systems, and given way to a quiet contentment as we shuffled along.

In a flash, the mood was broken! A deafening roar slammed us to the sand as if a bomb had exploded right above our heads. Stunned, we all looked up to find that a U.S. Coast Guard jet had screamed across the island and passed over the beach at an altitude of thirty feet.

I had heard the sound before. On a couple of occasions while pulling lobster traps, I was shocked in the same manner by military fighter jets. Whether the pilots were using me as a target or just having fun, I never knew for sure, but I had strongly suspected they were not precisely following regulations.

During Great Britain's Falkland Islands War in 1982, British pilots were practicing in Key West and we had been surprised by two Vertical Takeoff and Landing Harrier jets. One plane roared directly over the bow and the other over the stern not twenty feet above the water. My mate Antonio—a recently-arrived Cuban refugee—dropped to the deck and scrambled forward on his elbows and knees, fully believing they were coming back around to blow us out of the water.

I assured him we were perfectly safe, and in any case, the cabin would offer small protection. They repeatedly circled and treated us to a spectacular show of hovering and tricky maneuvers which could only be done with those special planes. As a last gesture, they flew past again, and while at eye level over the bow, gave us a friendly wave and smile. We enthusiastically waved back—Antonio with both hands.

I had never fully understood the aerodynamics of sound. The plane was traveling at less than the speed of sound, so it seems we should have heard it coming. Yet, the jet came from the other side of the island without us hearing a thing. Remembering the other times, I smiled when I stood again, but the rest of the crew was outraged at the shock to our mellowed sensibilities. Curses flew from the beach, and if the pilot had a rearview mirror, he was treated to a good cross section of some very traditional Key West salutes.

"Peter, I really don't think our Coast Guard should be doing that. That pilot is going to get himself in trouble one day."

"You're right Hugh. You are absolutely right."

Proud of his fellow crewmen for the fine parting shot, Hugh grinned in spite of himself as we watched the jet head out to sea, "Well, at least the boys gave him a nice send-off."

We watched the plane as it raced away from the island and then started turning. It was coming around for another pass. After a long loop, the plane started back toward us from the far end of the beach at the same dune-high level.

Hugh was serious once again—the federal magistrate coming out in him—and wondering if he should report the egregious violation of our fun to the proper authorities. "This guy is definitely going to get himself in trouble. Look, he's coming directly at the boys."

Being on top the dune, we were at the level of the plane and had the entire scene in our sight when Hugh noticed something odd. "Hey, what are those guys doing down on the beach?"

The three huddled together for a moment and then lined up with their backs to the plane. Seeing they had their heads turned to watch the plane come down the beach and their thumbs hooked over the waistbands of their bathing suits, the full realization of what was about to happen came over Hugh.

"Peter! What the hell are those guys doing?"

"Peter! I think those idiots are going to moon the plane!"

"Peter! Stop them! This is not funny!"

"Peter! Do something! They have cameras on those planes!"

"*Captain!* . . . Ohhh shit!"

As Hugh's life and career flashed before his eyes, the three culprits performed a gold medal moon-job. The three conspirators and I fell to the sand howling with laughter, as the shamefully-mooned pilot roared off into the sunset. The island, the rum, and the moment had obliterated the seriousness of the situation and any sense of propriety that mature businessmen would ordinarily maintain, as we collapsed in uncontrollable hilarity.

Hugh was mortified. Certain that a federal crime had been committed, he could only shake his head in disbelief as the boys whooped and hollered and high-fived each other. He was positive we had all lost our minds, and imagined us in irons as a Coast Guard cutter hauled us back to Key West.

Back at camp, there was a renewed vigor among the crew and the rum once again flowed. The sweet scene was replayed over and over, and forgotten was our promise to return to the safe anchorage on the other side of the island before dark. As evening came on, the sandflies came out. Ordinarily, the vicious little 'no-seeums' would have driven us mad, but that night, nothing could make us abandon our beach.

We started a fire to keep the bugs away and it turned into a monster. Like giant ants, we fanned out in the dark and dragged back huge pieces of wood to kindle the flames. From long four-by-fours and sheets of plywood, to chairs, tables, and boat cabins, our little campfire grew into a gigantic blaze that was probably seen all the way to Cuba.

About halfway into a bottle of tequila, Hugh could no longer resist the uncontrolled merriment and joined in the fun. Along with the rest of us, he was once again a crazy college kid, stoking the game-day bonfire far beyond all sense of reason. Like aboriginal warriors, we surrounded the mystical flames and howled at the 'mooning' far into the night. As our bodies cried for rest, we became hypnotized by the dancing flames, and one by one crashed out on the beach.

We awoke in a vast sea of darkness under a canopy of billions of brilliant stars. The fire and the crew were almost dead and the sea was calm, but for some inexplicable reason, we decided we had to get back to our anchorage on the other side of the island. In the miraculous way that God watches over children and fools, we made it back without foundering along the rocky route.

It was a sorry crew the sun awoke the next morning. Sunglasses, coffee, and quiet were the order of the morning. We each cringed inside as we reflected on our actions, trying to recall each thing we did and wondering if there would be repercussions.

An hour later, Tony staggered up from down below and headed straight for the stern of the boat. "Uh oh! Did you guys see this?"

Hugh's worst nightmare had come to life. A large black ship with a red diagonal stripe—the unmistakable colors of a Coast Guard cutter—was anchored about five hundred yards off our stern. We watched silently as an inflatable launch was lowered to the water and six well-armed sailors started toward us. A Coast Guard boarding was the last thing we needed that morning, and each of us tried to think of what crime we had actually committed.

We were all expecting recriminations and I-told-you-so's from Hugh, but he was all business. "We haven't done anything illegal. Mooning a Coast Guard plane may be crude and stupid, but it's not against the law. Even if the fire and gun shooting are a violation of Bahamian law, our Coast Guard can't do anything about that. Unless we have something out of order on the boat, we shouldn't have any problems."

"Hugh is right," I said. "We haven't done anything wrong, but I still want everyone to keep quiet and let me handle it. I've been boarded many times by the Coast Guard and they have been unfailingly polite. However, this is a different situation, and after all the trouble they've had around here, I don't expect we will be treated very gently."

"Everyone please move to the back of the boat." They were polite but firm, and I could see they were very young and very nervous. Automatic rifles were pointed at us even before the launch reached our boat, and we were under guard by two unblinking young Coasties.

"Who's the captain?"

"I am."

"Do you have any weapons?"

"Yes. We have a rifle and three pistols."

A man was directed to get the guns and he reappeared a moment later with the AR-15 and a look of triumph on his face. "Here's the *rifle*, sir."

The chief sniffed the gun and looked at me.

"We fired it a few times just to try it out."

"An armed man will escort you to get your boat papers. Please do not touch anything but the papers."

The mood had changed with the appearance of the AR-15, and we were being treated as suspects of something. Hugh decided to film the search and the chief became hostile. "Sir, put the camera down!"

"I'm breaking no law by filming this boarding."

"Sir, I want the camera turned off!"

We looked at each other and shrugged. Hugh's natural discretion took over and he turned off the camera, but his point had been made—the chief knew we weren't a gang of lawbreakers who were intimidated by their presence. The boarding party was then wary of Hugh, who was quite obviously making mental notes of their every move.

One man sat at the table and went through the boat papers, as the chief looked over his shoulder. Meticulously inspecting each passport, they gave us menacing looks, as they connected faces with names. Two other sailors were inspecting every nook and cranny on the boat, looking for contraband. Every bag was rifled through, every container opened, and even battery caps were removed for inspection.

I knew we didn't have anything on the boat to be worried about. A thorough inspection on a commercial fishing trip can be very nerve-wracking, since a captain can never be completely certain a mate doesn't have drugs in his bag. That time however, I was certain the boat was clean and even our guns were registered— though not really required by law. Nevertheless, there are so many regulations governing documented vessels, and in particular commercial boats, that it's nearly impossible to be certain every detail of every law is complied with.

A hostile boarding party can always find something to nitpick about, and the temper of the inspection was leading me to think we might have trouble. I thought our actions from the previous day may have contributed to the mood, but couldn't even be sure they knew about the mooning.

"Which one of you is Hugh Morgan?"

"I am."

The chief and his mate studied Hugh for a moment, then studied the passport. The mate whispered something to the chief, then turned and asked, "Sir, are you the federal magistrate in Key West?"

"That's right."

Seconds later, the chief turned to us with a smile and said, "Thank you very much, gentlemen. We appreciate your cooperation. Men, put down your weapons and conclude your search. Sorry for the inconvenience, fellows. We'll get out of your way now and hope you enjoy the rest of your trip."

Coast Guard returning to ship

Trapped in Key West

Our crew was amused by the sudden change, but remained quiet as the boarding party disembarked. I gave them a polite send-off, and we watched until the cutter weighed anchor and headed away. The adrenalin rush did wonders for our hangovers, and we were once again reduced to a bunch of laughing nitwits.

Several years later, Monica and I were having lunch with Captain Bob Scobie and his wife Dorothy. He was the Commandant of the Key West Coast Guard Station and she was the Principal of Grace Lutheran School. I related the story of our Bahamas adventure, and when he got a big laugh out of the mooning incident, there was something in his manner that led me to believe he finally had the full story behind a picture he had seen in a classified file.

The story of Bill and I finding the bronze cannon in the Bahamas was never far from Ed's mind. Like an excited child, he asked for the story over and over, each time trying to mine new details and adding fresh speculation to the mystery of its origin. He was determined we would someday make a trip to see the cannon. Many times, I explained how the cannon was in plain view in the middle of the shallow reef, and with the proliferation of recreational boats and the popularity of diving, someone had probably salvaged it already. Nothing I said mattered.

When Mel Fisher found the treasure of the *Atocha* near Marquesas, Ed was enthralled. Steve Condella, a former schoolmate of ours, was a renowned cannon collector who actually owned one of the *Atocha*'s cannons. He confirmed Dad's contention that usually only the treasure ships carried the bronze cannons.

Ed became consumed with planning a trip to find the cannon, and each year found us closer to making the commitment. The cannon was a full day's run beyond Cay Sal, and I knew I would have no problem returning to the exact spot, but unlike Ed, I was reluctant to make the long risky trip when I doubted we would actually find it still there. But Ed didn't really care whether the cannon was still there or not—he wanted the journey as much as the find.

Bahamas and Cannons

Chris and Tony were anxious to make the trip as well, and Bill Wickers was not about to be left out. He was the first one to spot the cannon and was determined to be the guide for everyone. However, only Bill and I fully understood the risk of the journey. The island was over three hundred miles from home and isolated in several thousand square miles of ocean between the southern Bahamas and Cuba. With a single engine boat and no generator, there were dozens of mechanical problems that could leave us stranded in the middle of nowhere. Equally of concern was the September weather. It was the peak of hurricane season and a time when powerful squalls packed hurricane-force winds and sprang up at any time with no warning.

Ignoring our better judgment, we planned the trip for September of 1992. For months, we readied ourselves and the *Big Crawl* for the trip. At the last minute, disaster struck for Bill, when his wife Linda became ill. While it wasn't life threatening, it added to her extreme anxiety over Bill being gone during the peak of hurricane season, and he dutifully decided to stay home with her.

Our first Bahama trip had been during the month of June, but all crewmen found too many family conflicts in the summer months when the children were out of school. All subsequent trips were in September, when the waters were still warm enough to swim comfortably and—unless a hurricane was close, or a squall passing over—the seas were generally calm. It was however, a simple fact that in the month of September, there was always a hurricane somewhere in the Caribbean. To the consternation of our wives, in a dozen September voyages, we never let a hurricane call off a single trip.

One year, we let a storm run us back to Dry Tortugas after the hurricane did not follow its predicted path through the Bahamas. It dogged our westward movement with a parallel course along the south coast of Cuba and finally slammed into Mexico. On another trip, we hung out by Elliot's Key near Miami, while a hurricane careened around Puerto Rico and finally sent us back to Marquesas when it headed north toward our Bahamas destination. But after six months of planning and anticipation, we were not about to let a hurricane cancel our cannon trip, unless it was actually going to hit Key West.

The cannon's isolated location required far more preparation than the average trip, since we anticipated little chance of seeing either the Coast Guard or another boat. We had mechanical necessities, like spare belts and hoses which we always carried, but on that trip, we even packed spare alternators, starters, and batteries. Additionally, we carried a large number of scuba tanks, and such fanciful items as a metal detector and sieves and paddles to sift the sand for treasure. With plenty of food and booze loaded, we could have survived for several months without making a port call.

A hurricane had already bypassed Key West, but the two others formed far out in the Atlantic didn't pose an immediate threat by the time we left. After two leisurely days on the Cay Sal Bank, we spent a long unusually rough day cruising to our tiny island destination. With seas continually breaking over the bow, it was impossible to steer from the flybridge, and everyone hunkered down in the cabin for the long trip. When a big wave hit the boat from an unexpected direction, everything not tied down flew around the cabin.

I had already warned the crew to secure themselves by telling about a freak wave that hit while I worked lobster traps on the *Monica Ann*. While walking back to the wheel on a day with similar-sized seas, a huge rogue wave slammed into the starboard side and threw me headfirst over the captain's chair into the side window. My head shattered the heavy glass, but I was miraculously only dazed with an egg-sized knot on the top of my head. I didn't tell them about Monica saying how fortunate I was to have hit the window with my head.

Though there was much jubilation at our arrival, the speck of dry land provided little protection from the wind and seas. The island was less than one hundred yards long and so low we could see over the top from the flybridge. We rode back and forth, trying to find the calmest spot, but when we finally anchored, the boat rolled and bucked worse than any place we had ever set the hook.

Bahamas and Cannons

When the constantly-running current bounced into the strong easterly winds, the seas sloshed around the island in all directions. With crazy waves swirling around from both ends of the island, the leeward side was actually rougher at anchor than the windward side. The reef, however, came right up to the island on the easterly shore, so we had no choice but to ride it out.

The relief of actually being there overcame the conditions, and the crew was not in a mood to complain. The boat was a jumble of supplies and gear from the rough ride, but Ed had somehow prepared everything for conch chowder and put it on to cook as soon as we stopped. As the aroma of the chowder filled the boat and the second bottle of red wine was uncorked, we forgot about the seas and concentrated once again on the cannon.

In the midst of our arrival celebration, I silenced the crew when I heard the faint sound of an engine running. We all scanned the stormy horizon and spotted a boat that appeared to be heading toward us. As isolated as we were, I had not expected to see any craft other than ships passing in the Bahama Channel. The boat slowly got nearer and we realized it was coming directly to our island. When we saw a ragged-looking Bahamian commercial boat rather than Coast Guard or Bahama Defense Force, we got out all the guns and put them close at hand.

The boat came directly for us and idled by thirty feet from our starboard side. What we saw chilled our blood. The *Captain Sleg* was an old wooden fishing boat with rust dripping from the head of every nail and screw holding it together. It had a large low cabin and standing on top of it were ten young Bahamians. They were shirtless and shoeless and not one smile or wave passed from them. As the boat inched by, they glared down menacingly at us, and all thoughts of the cannon were erased from our minds.

The boat made a tight circle around the *Big Crawl* as we moved close to our guns, and then anchored about two hundred feet away. We looked at each other with eyebrows high and wrinkled foreheads as we all silently pondered the situation. Moments later, the *Captain Sleg* launched a skiff and two men putted their way over to us. I immediately warned the crew, that under no circumstances were the men to be allowed on board, and they were to keep their guns ready at all times.

The two Bahamians—one black who spoke the King's English and one white who spoke the rudest island dialect—grabbed hold of our rail to steady their bouncing boat and then introduced themselves. They were lobster divers and were under the impression our commercial boat was there to steal their catch. They were much relieved and very cordial when we assured them we were just a group of guys on a dive vacation and would take no more lobster than we could eat.

We were not as easily convinced, however, that they were merely innocent commercial fishermen, and our lonely location was no place to try and be friendly little neighbors. With some trepidation, I allowed them to tie off and we carried on a long conversation over the side of the boat. They were friendly and happy, and when they asked what we were drinking, Ed gave them a glass of rum. Their captain did not allow alcohol on his boat and the two men were thrilled to get a real drink.

One drink led to another, and when it started to rain, the men were sitting under our awning on the rail of the *Big Crawl* before anyone had a chance to object. Several drinks later, they were offered a bowl of Ed's conch chowder, and one of them made a seat on the icebox while the other made himself at home, sprawled out in my captain's chair. Two bowls later, the white Bahamian pronounced it the best conch chowder he had ever eaten and instantly became Ed's new best friend.

The rum made us all big buddies and our security precautions turned out to be a joke. The man in my captain's chair stretched out and his hand dropped on Ed's .44 magnum. He jumped completely out of the chair, and stood looking at it like it was a tarantula. "Mon! Why you got de gon? I skeared dos tings! Nooo body gon huirt you, heah!"

Bahamas and Cannons

Our new Bahamian friends – center seated l-r *Tony, Chris,
author seated right*

Though Key West was as unfamiliar to them as Outer
Mongolia, they were curious about our knowledge of the sea. They
were particularly interested in how a bunch of white Americans
knew enough to clean conchs and make a chowder. When one asked
if we knew anything about turtle, we assured him we had all eaten
our share, but since they were then protected in America, it had
been a number of years since we had tasted any.

Hours after they arrived, they remembered their captain had
not only sent them over to check us out, but also to see if we could
spare some Coca-Cola. After we retrieved a case of Coke for the
captain, they flopped into their skiff and returned to the big boat.
A short while later, we heard their outboard motor crank up again.
They pulled up to our stern and threw a turtle flipper onto the back
deck—compliments of the captain.

We gathered around the prize while a thirty-second morality
play was acted out.

"Whoaaa! Look at that beautiful thing!"

"Yeah. What a huge hawksbill!"

"What a shame they killed it, huh?"

"Yeah . . . Must be five pounds of meat on it, eh bubba?"

"I guess they don't know about them being endangered."

"Well, they *are* legal over here."

"Yeah, they're legal for Bahamians. I wonder if it's okay for us to have it on the boat. I mean it was given to us. We didn't actually kill it."

"That's right. Gees, what are we supposed to do? Throw the thing overboard?"

"All right guys. That's enough crap! Everybody's done their conscience-clearing thing. So let's get this flipper steaked up and packed on ice. When we find the cannon, we feast!"

It was a nasty stormy night with little chance for sleep, but to our relief, the Bahamian boat left at daylight in the midst of a steady downpour. We had some concern over the foul weather being part of a low-pressure system developing right over the top of us, but decided our luck couldn't be bad enough to have a hurricane form with us sitting right in the middle. The sea conditions wouldn't allow us to use the skiff on the windward side of Guinchos, so we spent the day piddling around the boat and exploring the small island with our metal detector.

During one of his treasure hunting phases in the early 1970s, Dad purchased an 'Outlaw Discriminator' to hunt for gold coins that may have washed up on the beaches during hurricanes. When it arrived in the mail, we tried it in Dad's front yard and found two rings and a number of coins. The rings were a complete mystery since they were unfamiliar to everyone and the grass itself had only been in place for a couple of years, but gave us wild dreams about what might be found in a place with real treasure.

The metal detector we quickly found to be of no use on the island. It had a constant buzz, and though it was accurately pinpointing metallic objects, we quickly tired of uncovering nails, cans, and assorted pieces of scrap iron. The island was, nevertheless, a beachcomber's heaven. The shore was decorated with colorful shards of porcelain plates, cups, and pots—all of unknown origin or age. Occasionally, we found large colorful pieces we stashed for souvenirs, while still expecting to uncover far greater valuables in the water.

Bahamas and Cannons

The little speck of dry land in the middle of the ocean, which looked pristine from a distance, was actually more like an eclectic junkyard. Garbage from the four corners of the earth hung up on its tiny shore, yet it still looked more exotic than trashy. Strange-looking bottles and floats lay among huge planks of wood, and large pieces of rusty, twisted steel appeared as modern works of art. Because there was so much debris from assorted wrecks, we speculated the island might have actually formed around a ship that foundered on the small reef.

By late the next morning, the wind had subsided somewhat and it was only partly cloudy instead of completely overcast. The sea conditions were not good, but we were anxious to look, and slowly made our way around the island in the overloaded skiff. Despite the heavy winds of the last few days, the water was clear, and I knew if the cannon was still there, I would find it. With the reef being shallow, the waves were breaking in some places with crashing spumes of white water. It was necessary to anchor the skiff farther away than I wanted because of the heavy seas, but the breaking waves showed us the easiest path through the outer edge of the reef.

The ocean seemed very big and our boat very small as we entered the water. A strong current was running, and it was necessary to flipper hard just to stay by the skiff. Right behind us, the bottom dropped down to two thousand feet and appeared pitch black. In front of us, the water was brilliant blue, and the vibrant staghorn and elkhorn corals glittered golden in the refracted sunlight.

As we neared the reef, there was a surge from the breaking waves, which alternately pushed us back toward the bottomless depths for a few seconds, and then rode us forward toward the massive corals. As we maneuvered our way through the outer part of the reef, I felt a twinge of stupidity for having put my innocent friends into such a dangerous position. The seas were not of the fierce pounding breakers that may have killed us, but I was the only one to have experienced such diving conditions and I feared one of them might be severely injured if a wave broke on top and drove them into the jagged coral.

Trapped in Key West

Once past the outer coral heads, all worry left. It was relatively calm and everyone, including myself, was dazzled by the beauty. Like Bill and I had done many years before, everyone just floated while they tried to take in the spectacular scene. If there had been nothing else but the enormous staghorns rising from the bottom like gothic cathedrals, the brilliant elkhorns spreading their wings like fantastical butterflies, and the massive golden brain corals anchoring the reef, it would have been a breathtaking sight. But with thousands of tropical fish in all their radiant colors flitting over the corals, and schools of yellowtail, cardinal fish, and ballyhoo casually passing by, it became an enchanting scene.

Eventually, everyone returned to the mission at hand, and with four heads bobbing out of the water, I instructed them to search over an area about one hundred-foot square. I felt certain I would recognize the formations and go straight to the cannon, but even though I knew we were very near the spot, nothing looked familiar. The cannon had been sitting up high as if mounted to fire when Bill and I saw it, and would have been impossible to miss. After a quick search of the area, I knew the cannon was either gone or lying in a new position requiring more careful inspection.

I thought it possible but unlikely the gun had been removed. Also, sitting where it was in the middle of the hard reef, I doubted it had been buried in the sand. As I surveyed the area, I became more convinced the ancient weapon was simply grown over with coral. Like twenty-five years before, I focused on the colossal piles of broken coral lying on the seafloor and the spectacular new growth rising from the rubble.

I had been stunned years before to see the enormous coral stands lying shattered on the bottom, and attributed it to the aftermath of a hurricane. With the broader vision of age, I studied it closer, and realized I was looking at a natural cycle of death and regrowth that had been going on for thousands of years. I could see twelve-foot-wide elkhorns lying on the bottom and still living, while others under them were white and disintegrating into sand. It convinced me the cannon was overgrown with coral, and we would find it by searching for a cannon-shaped coral stand.

Bahamas and Cannons

Again we fanned out and renewed the search. When we once again found nothing, I was still not convinced. Not trusting my inexperienced buddies, I covered every square foot of the area until I was absolutely certain it was not to be found. Disappointment came slowly with the long search, and by the time we returned to the skiff, everyone was resigned to not finding the elusive cannon—but they were far from dejected.

All had pockets and hands full of hand-hewn bronze spikes, and other relics from long ago wrecks. Disappointment was tempered by the exhausted high of wondrous hours spent diving the dazzling reef. No one was ready to call it a day, but the seas on the outside of the reef were still rough, and we were all a bit intimidated by the black abyss we were straddling. It was decided to move around to the inside of the reef where the seas were calmer and spear a Nassau grouper for dinner.

As we carefully skirted the reef, we passed over a white sand spot and Chris said he saw something on the bottom that looked oddly symmetrical. We passed back over and Ed confirmed that it did look like something, though the water was a little too rough to see clearly. Cannon fever immediately returned and I was quickly dispatched to check it out. Before the bubbles had even cleared from my jump, I was able to clearly identify the matching objects.

Without taking another breath, I returned to the surface and found all three crewmen on their knees staring into my face. The skiff looked like it might capsize, but the three could think of only one thing and were alive with anticipation. "Well! What is it? Is it a cannon?"

"No," I replied as I lifted myself into the opposite side of the boat and took off my mask. "No, it's not a cannon," and all three faces fell at once. "It's two friggin cannons! They're both lying there as if someone placed them just for us!"

Three frozen faces stared at me for just a second, all trying to determine whether I was putting them on. Then, Chris' face broke out in a grin and the purest look of joy I had ever seen. The whoop he let out sent everyone into action. All three immediately started crashing around the fourteen-foot skiff looking for their dive gear. Crawling over each other, knocking over ice chests, and slipping and falling in the bouncing boat, not one of us could control his eagerness to get into the water.

"Ed! Hand me my flipper!"

"Get it yourself!"

"Hey! Get me that spear gun!"

"You don't need a damn spear gun to look at cannons!"

"Man, you got my snorkel!"

"Well, use mine!"

With flippers slipping on the slick deck and shins cracking on the pitching boat's rail, everyone made dodo-bird-like entries into the water. Ed realized in midair he was jumping right on top of me, and twisted his entire body around in a vain attempt at avoidance. Tony tried a scuba entry, but a wave bounced him over into an ungainly half back flip. And Chris' attempt at a careful jump ended when his flippers slipped and both shins cracked on the rail before he splashed into the water with an undignified belly flop.

The four of us floated above the cannons in a mild state of shock. All the years of storytelling were suddenly validated, and all the skepticism and disbelief was instantly forgotten. It mattered not that it wasn't the fabled bronze cannon. There was not just one, but two real live cannons from a treasure ship lying on the seafloor right beneath us. Tony said later that for a fleeting moment, he had been a little spooked by some ethereal feeling he was bobbing alone in the middle of the Atlantic Ocean, peering at apparitions.

The cannons were covered in light coral and small sponge and sea fan growth, but were otherwise lying in perfect condition in fifteen feet of water. They had obviously been recently exposed by a storm, but there was still something slightly eerie about the way they lay together in the open bottom, as if they had just been placed there for us to see. We all mentioned afterwards how we had felt immobile because the whole scene had a touch of weirdness to it, but Ed finally broke the trance by diving down and inspecting them closely.

Bahamas and Cannons

Peter, Ed, and Chris with cannon

Fortunately for us, when Ed surfaced, he said he was getting his camera out of the skiff. In our haste to see the cannons, we had neglected to anchor the skiff, and Ed took off after the distant *Patsy*. As happened many times over the years, someone was looking out for our reckless actions, and with the wind going against the tide, the skiff had not drifted as far as it should have under the windy conditions. In any event, we would not have been stranded in the middle of the ocean since the *Big Crawl* was about a mile away on the other side of the island, but it would surely have ruined our celebration.

For an hour, we swam around the cannons. Everyone touched them and rubbed them, looking for any marks identifying them as part of a treasure ship. Ed used all his film as we repeatedly posed with the double-barreled find. Though completely exhausted from the excitement and the long day, we were reluctant to leave the cannons. We sensed we would never see them again and tried to absorb every thrilling aspect of our find. One by one however, we pulled ourselves into the bouncing skiff and returned to the *Big Crawl*.

Trapped in Key West

Back at the big boat, we celebrated our good fortune far into the night. The turtle steak came out of the ice, and numerous bottles of red wine were uncorked as the evening progressed. We discussed over and over the inconceivable probability of not finding the bronze cannon, and then unexpectedly—and by pure chance—finding two others.

We were even more convinced than Dad that we were on the site of a Spanish treasure ship. The odds seemed too great to find a bronze cannon, and then years later stumble across two iron ones in the same place. We speculated endlessly on what we would find if we had a search pattern and actually knew what we were doing, yet recognized we might never return.

To end the perfect day, Ed presented us all with a piece of treasure to remember the trip. So certain was he that we would find something, he purchased four silver coins recovered from a Spanish treasure ship—ready to present them as soon as we made our find. When we returned to Key West, we had dinner at Bill's house to fill him in on the trip and show him the coins we claimed had been found at the treasure site.

Bill was incredulous, but with the proof right in his hand, he said he had been certain all along we would find some treasure near the cannon. Just picturing us finding coins on the ship he had seen first was a little more than Bill could take, and he ended up in a spat with Linda about why she had kept him from going. We finally confessed our duplicity after the argument got a little too heated and Linda blurted out, "Bill! What's the matter with you? Can't you see they're lying about the coins?"

13
Smoking and Gambling

L ike most Navy men of his generation, Dad was a heavy smoker. He started as a boy in the backwoods of Louisiana, and after joining the Navy at the age of fifteen, it became a habit for life. Like all branches of the military, the Navy accommodated smokers in every way—even supplying them in wartime rations—and it was a sign of manhood to have a smoke hanging from the lips. There were no filters on cigarettes, and each smoke gave a full shot of tar and nicotine directly into the lungs.

Dad was a little larger than the average men of his time, and a lifetime of hard physical work made him muscular and powerful. Into his early sixties, he could still sling traps and stack boxes of fish like a man half his age. Because he was aging and still doing such physical work, little notice was given to his increasing breathlessness. The connection between lung disease and cigarettes was not as clear-cut as it is today, and Dad's persistent hacking was simply dismissed as 'smoker's cough.'

He was never one to complain about his health, so he hid his problems as best he could. To his family, it almost seemed he was healthy one day and the next day could not walk to the truck and back without being out of breath. Mother was fearful he had pneumonia, but Dad assured her it was just a "little chest cold" and would soon pass.

Trapped in Key West

The chest cold did not pass, and Dad was soon so incapacitated he had to lean across the hood of his truck to catch his breath after walking from the office. Physical labor became impossible, and he spent each day sitting in the office, reading and dealing with fish house problems. He had always detested the office, but claimed it gave him a chance to catch up on his reading. In truth, he was a man of the sea confined to a desk, and he was miserable.

Despite our constant urging, he refused to seek help. The only thing I had ever known Dad to be frightened of was hospitals. He had last been to one during the time he was working in the Bahamas and nearly died from a bleeding ulcer. Almost unconscious from blood loss by the time Mother was aware, only emergency surgery saved his life. He was forced to remain in the hospital for two weeks to fully recover, and the doctors practically needed a straight jacket to keep him confined.

Now, some ten years later and unbeknownst to me at the time, Dad had another reason for not going to the doctor. He was deathly afraid he had lung cancer. He watched several of his Navy buddies waste away to a grisly, slow death, and while he was not afraid of dying, he had always planned to go suddenly. Lung cancer was a death sentence that would be lingering and known to everyone. More than anything, he feared everyone knowing about his problem and viewing him as an object of pity.

After a couple of years of becoming increasingly incapacitated, he finally agreed to seek medical help. As a retired veteran, Dad was entitled to free medical care, but the naval hospital in Key West had recently closed, so we encouraged him to see a local doctor. He was leery of all doctors, believing their goal was to get a person into the hospital where they could have complete control over him.

He agreed at last to make an appointment with Dr. John Calleja. Dr. Calleja was a contemporary of mine, having graduated from Key West High School a couple of years before me. After medical school, he returned to Key West and was the youngest doctor practicing on the island. Dad reasoned that if he had to see a doctor, he wanted a young one who knew all the "latest stuff."

322

Smoking and Gambling

Over the years, it proved to be a very fortuitous choice. Not only did Dr. Calleja become Dad's trusted medical advisor, but also a friend who truly cared about his well-being. He faithfully provided Dad with the latest medication for his condition, and it was common for Mother to receive a phone call in the evening inquiring of Dad's reaction to a new treatment. A reserved Christian man, Dr. Calleja was the ideal doctor, and Dad respected him—as a doctor and a man—like he did few others.

On Dad's first visit, he got the chest x-ray he had been dreading. A few days later when the results were in, Dad returned from his office visit the happiest man in Key West. He didn't yet know what his problem was, but it wasn't lung cancer. It would be several weeks before his problem was diagnosed, but whatever it was would be preferable to the dreaded scourge of cigarette smokers everywhere.

After a battery of tests over the next few weeks, Dr. Calleja diagnosed his problem. I was in the back office when Dad returned and dropped into the chair. When he had sufficiently caught his breath I asked, "Well, what did the doctor say?"

Still breathing heavily, he replied, "He says I've got emphysema. I've only got about 10 percent of my lungs working. The rest of it has turned into charcoal or something."

"What's he going to do for you?"

"He gave me some spray to breathe in, but he says there is really nothing that can be done. He says I did it to myself with fifty years of smoking, and now it's too late to save the lungs. He said when it really gets bad, he'll start me on oxygen . . . He told me I might as well get used to watching a lot of TV."

Not knowing what to say, I sat silent for a while, and then asked, "What are you going to do?"

He looked me straight in the eyes with his characteristic squinting stare and said, "Well, I'll be damned if I'm going to die in front of a TV set! I'm going to get myself in shape and get back out in the boat where I belong—or kill myself trying!"

His fire and determination caught me off guard. Even from Dad, I expected doom and gloom like any normal person would have felt at such a grim sentence, but there was not a hint of defeat or self-pity in him. Throughout his life, he had always been a fighter, and I don't know why I expected anything different. He detested the thought of pity, and was not about to feel sorry for himself or allow anyone else to feel it towards him.

"Did the doctor tell you some exercises to start on?"

"No. He just basically said I should sit around and take it easy."

"If you're not able to exercise, how will you get in shape?"

"I'm going to start jogging."

"Jogging! . . . Dad? . . . Jogging? . . . I mean, you can barely walk, how are you possibly going to be able to run?"

"Well son, I've been thinking about that and I believe I've got it figured out. I'm going to start slow by running in place and then increase it a little each day until I get my wind back. I know it's going to take a while, but what the hell have I got to lose?"

To drive home his point, he stood up and said, "And I'm going to start right now!"

With a mighty effort, he jogged about ten steps and collapsed into the chair. When he could speak again, he coughed out, "There! That's enough for today."

Overwhelmed by the piteousness of his attempt, I could only stammer out, "That's good, Dad. That's real good. If you can stick with it, you'll be back in the boat in no time at all."

I left the office far more depressed than he was, and when I went back later, he was sitting comfortably reading a book and made no further mention of his condition. I was still learning to understand a man like my father. His rules for living seemed very simplistic, but the self-discipline that motivated him to live by them made him a very complex man because he never spoke of the rules or how to live by them.

His rules were essentially: work hard—be a man—put women and children on a pedestal, and never cuss around them—don't complain—take care of your friends—never take a handout from anyone—especially the government, and never bring up a distasteful subject at the dinner table.

Smoking and Gambling

After one discussion, the time for talking about his condition was over. Once the actual problem was identified and clearly in front of him, it was time for action. He often infuriated others and me at his refusal to be delayed on a job by waiting on an easier way to do it. If an engine needed to be moved, he would round up three men and a come-along and move it one foot at a time, rather than wait until the next day for a forklift. If four men could load a boat with traps in two hours, he would spend all day loading it himself, rather than wait until help was available. He was a do-it-now type of man, and his method was very simple: start at the beginning, and when you get to the end—stop.

So it was with his personal plan for rehabilitation from emphysema. Unknown to me or anyone else, Dad was faithfully following his self-imposed regimen. He was not interested in "yakking" about his condition, but we first noticed he didn't seem to be getting any worse. Too proud to show his weakness, he was doing his 'jogging' in private, but within six months, it was clear to us he was actually improving. He was by then walking with ease to his truck, and even around the fish house yard.

So unobtrusively we hardly noticed, he started walking for his exercise. In the beginning, he walked halfway up the block and back. We didn't know he was methodically keeping track of both the distance and the time it took to cover it. He would walk a certain distance for a week, and try to beat his time each day. Then, he would increase his distance by one more house length and go for a new record each day. By the end of a year, he was walking up and down the street three times a day, and there was no denying he achieved a remarkable improvement in his health.

His biggest concession to his condition had been to give up smoking. He smoked unfiltered Lucky Strike Cigarettes for forty-five years, and then when tobacco smoke was linked to cancer, he thought he was saving his health by switching to a filtered cigarette. Dr. Calleja convinced him that with only 10 percent of his lungs functioning, continued smoking of any kind was a fast track to the cemetery.

Trapped in Key West

When Dad made a decision to do something, there was no turning back or quitting. With smoking, he simply stopped when he walked out of the doctor's office. There were no patches, pills, or therapy, and he never backslid or cheated. Again refusing to show weakness, no one would ever know how strong his craving must have been, since cigarettes just mysteriously disappeared from his life.

Almost as hard to believe was his change toward alcohol consumption. Again, the Navy had introduced him to beer drinking, and as far back as I can recall, he had some amount of beer every day. Though I never saw him drunk, he had a "couple of brews" when he got home in the evening, but never touched one before 5:00 p.m. Dr. Calleja told him alcohol robbed the blood of oxygen, and advised him to give up his beer along with the cigarettes.

Dad readily accepted how cigarettes were hurting him, but was unsure the beer could have anything to do with his breathing. At first, he dismissed it saying, "Let's try one thing at a time."

Several months after he quit smoking, he brought up the subject again. "What do you think about this business of beer robbing the blood of oxygen?"

"I don't know Dad. Offhand, I can't think of a logical reason why it should, but I'm sure Dr. Calleja isn't telling you that just to take away all your pleasures."

"Yeah, I've been thinking that too. I guess he's been right about everything else so far . . . What the hell, I just might give it a try."

Again without any further discussion, he quit drinking beer. It must have been much harder than giving up cigarettes, but no one would have ever known. He went on with his life as if he had never smoked or drank, but his family could easily see the difference in both his health and his increasing optimism about working again. He made it seem so simple that we thought little of the agonies of withdrawal he refused to acknowledge.

Some time in his second year of rehab, he started walking South Roosevelt Boulevard. The street runs alongside the beaches and the ocean, and whether he was proud of his restored physical ability or just liked seeing the ocean, he had chosen one of Key

Smoking and Gambling

West's most public places to walk. Each day—after lunch, and an hour of reading—he drove his truck to 'houseboat row' and began his walk promptly at 3:00 p.m.

Dad walking South Roosevelt Boulevard - age 80

He marked off the mileage with his truck's odometer, and meticulously kept a record of his time and distance. He was by then more willing to talk about his exercising, and each day he set a new time or distance record was a good day. Mid-afternoon was the hottest part of the day, but no degree of persuasion could get him to change the time. "Good grief, son! If you're not suffering, it's not doing you any good!"

By the end of his second year of rehab, he was fast walking four miles a day in the stifling heat of the afternoon. Monica frequently walked with him, but eventually had to quit because he walked too fast. "The man is incredible! My legs are just too short to keep up with him. I have to take two steps for his every one and he doesn't like to slow down for anyone."

Out of curiosity, I walked with him one day, just to see for myself how he handled it. By the end of the walk, I was completely whipped. Though thirty-five years younger, the heat of the broiling sun and the exertion of the fast walk, wrecked me for the rest of the day.

It seemed every drop of fluid had been drained from my body, but Dad didn't believe in drinking any liquids until he was cooled off completely after the walk. He maintained that if you drank the water while you were hot, you just immediately sweated it back out.

Despite the seeming lunacy of a seventy-year-old man subjecting himself to such self-torture, my walk with him was an eye-opening experience. Dad had become something of a celebrity along the south beach walk. Whether because of his age or his health condition, each person he passed recognized him and offered encouragement. Unwilling to ruin his time by slowing to talk, Dad would give a slight nod of acknowledgment and continue on his way.

The most distracting part of the walk however, came from the passing cars. Like being in a Parisian roundabout, horns were honking almost continuously and cries of "Hey, Pete!" and "Looking good!" were shouted from open windows. I was constantly trying to see who was calling and give them a look of recognition, but like a star tolerating his adoring fans, Dad just gave a little wrist wave to let them know he heard their call.

During Dad's walking years, I would come to understand just how many people drove the long way around on South Roosevelt Boulevard. Into the 1970s, many of the old Conchs still took an evening drive around the island, and between his walking exposure and the fish house, Dad was a familiar figure to far more people than I had ever realized.

With the advent of mass-produced fiberglass boats in the 1960s, most families either had a boat or knew someone who did. Today, it is necessary to have a license to sell fish and to meet strict income qualifications to obtain the permit. But at the time, anyone could and did sell fish. It was a source of pride to catch enough fish to eat and then to be able to pay for the gas and other expenses with the excess. Weekends and holidays were a constant stream of recreational boaters bringing their catch to be weighed in at the fish house.

Hundreds of local people sold their fish, and the accumulation of so many small amounts was a significant source of income for the fish house. Selling the fish was frequently a family affair, and it was not unusual to have children, parents, and grandparents all hanging around the scales as the fish were sorted and graded. Through the fish selling, a large part of the population of Key West visited the fish house, and though not an old Conch himself, Dad became well known to most of the local population.

Dad was not good with names, but almost everyone remembered his. Many letters made their way to the fish house with minimal addressing, such as *Pete's Dock*, and *Stock Island Fish House*. When the Cubans started coming, the Postal Service delivered a letter to *Pete Bacle–Stock Island*, though it was addressed only in the idiomatic, Spanish-accented English:

Pebeco

Tocaile.

As Dad started feeling reinvigorated, he cautiously returned to some of his old habits. When the reward of a Saturday night beer didn't seem to make a noticeable difference in his breathing, he started having one each day after his walk. Though it made Mother unhappy, no one else—not even Dr. Calleja—thought it was very harmful, and it made him feel as if he was really making progress.

Late one day, I returned from the fish house and saw Dad sitting on his front porch. The late evening light clearly showed smoke coming from his mouth, and I rushed over fearing he had started smoking cigarettes again. To my surprise, he held a long cigar between the tips of his thumb and four fingers. "What are you doing with that cigar? You know what the doctor said about smoking!"

Leaning on his knees when I approached, he casually sat up straight in the chair. Dad was not about to be chastised by anyone, let alone one of his children. With a look of disdain, he took a puff from the cigar and blew the smoke toward me. After taking a slow second draw, he answered like a father explaining something a son should already know. "Son. You don't inhale cigars. You just puff on them," he said, as the smoke rolled out of his nose. Much to the consternation of his wife and daughters, Dad smoked several cigars a day for the rest of his life.

Trapped in Key West

Our family was extremely pleased with Dad's recovery, but Dr. Calleja was incredulous. He had treated many cases of emphysema and gave Dad little chance of any significant improvement. He expected a steady deterioration in Dad's condition and was unprepared for an actual turnaround. Neither he nor the other doctors in his office had ever seen anyone improve with such an advanced stage of emphysema.

Once he understood Dad's stubborn determination to recover, he offered constant encouragement and provided him with every new treatment as soon as it became available. He maintained nothing could have been done for the 90 percent of his lung capacity that was destroyed, and attributed his recovery to strengthening of the remaining 10 percent. Even years later, Dr. Calleja maintains Dad's case gave him a new perspective on emphysema treatment, and offered hope to many other victims of the disease.

Dad announced one day he was ready to "get back in the boat." He'd been out a few times on calm days with me, but getting back in the boat meant he was ready to Captain again, and fish for profit—not pleasure. From Rigoberto Perez—a Cuban refugee—I had recently learned to use hand-pulled long lines. The line was about a mile long, with one hundred hooks evenly spaced and a large lead to hold down each end. Over the course of a couple of summer months, I refined the method, and was having amazing success catching mutton snapper and grouper.

Dad was fascinated with the new fishing method and was anxious to try it himself. Typically, he thought if I could do so well with the trot-line method, he would be able to catch twice as much. When the rest of the family opposed the idea of Dad getting back in the boat, it only made him more determined. Between the fish house, restaurant, and boat, I had little free time in my life, and readily agreed to alternate fishing days with Dad. Once back to sea, Dad felt his recovery was complete.

Nothing fired his enthusiasm like doing something new, and the trot lining was the perfect therapy. He added his own improvements to the system, and with his knowledge of the

330

fishing areas, increased both of our catches significantly. He was physically whipped at the end of the day, but as he puffed his cigar and watched them weigh-in his large catches, there was never a happier man.

He was not yet ready for the rigors of everyday trap pulling, but through the lobster season, he fished on the days I wasn't working traps. Each day he wasn't in the boat, he walked the beach, and even started using hand weights to increase his arm strength. By the following summer, he was fishing the boat more than I was, and even made several very successful weeklong trips to his old fishing grounds at Dry Tortugas.

He was so enthused with the fishing, that at first he thought little of working lobster traps. After watching my success with lobster however, the old competitiveness came out and he wanted to put traps out again. I was having some big catches in the deep water to the west, even matching Dad's single day high of forty-four hundred pounds. That was more than he could "take lying down," so we purchased Willy Wicker's old boat, the *Sandy Bill*, and Dad completed his full recovery by once again working lobster traps.

After one season with the *Sandy Bill*, Dad wanted a bigger boat, and my brother Jimmy started building the forty-three-foot fiberglass boat *Big Crawl*. The name was a euphemism for the migrating pattern of the lobster. It was something of a joke in our family that all good things would come with the "big crawl," and Dad liked the name for the boat.

Despite his love for wood, he took to the modern "plastic" boat as if he had worked one all his life. The original mold for the hull was built by Claude Torres, a master boat builder, and Jimmy bought out Claude's entire operation when he retired. It's a sturdy craft with beautiful lines, and can take a sea as well as any fiberglass boat that's ever been built. Dad loved the boat, and after his first day of working from the flybridge, never steered from down below again.

When out in the boat, Dad always thought of himself as invincible. Though he often said "Everyone's got to go sometime," and "Hell son, even I can't live forever," he went about his life as if he could. Overcoming his emphysema and "returning to active duty" aboard his lobster boat only reinforced his feeling he could do anything he put his mind to.

My sisters and brother felt at the age of eighty-five, he had no business being out every day in a lobster boat, and asked me to speak with him. I disagreed with them, but had to admit the boat was not a very safe place for Dad and he would be hard pressed to deal with a real emergency in bad weather. The safety of his crew and his reliance on the loran because of his poor vision convinced me to talk to him. But on the other hand, it was great to see his enthusiasm, and I knew exactly what his reaction was going to be.

Dad at helm of Big Crawl - age 85

"What do you mean they don't want me to go out in the boat?" he roared, "Who asked them anyway? Hell! The worst thing that can happen is I'll die at sea, and I'd damn sure rather drop dead out there than in a hospital bed!"

That season he came very close to getting his wish. With two new mates on the boat, he was having all the problems that come with inexperienced men trying to pull lobster traps. Adding to the problems was the fact they had recently arrived from Cuba and neither one spoke a word of English, while Dad didn't speak Spanish.

Despite only a sixth-grade education, Dad was a very intelligent and resourceful man. Because of his lifelong reading habit, he was so self-educated he could carry on conversations about Mukluk Indians, black holes in space, or American politics with equal ease. In a very real sense, most every task he set his mind to he could accomplish. However, when it came to speaking Spanish, he was at a total loss, and it always seemed a source of wonder to me.

I would have thought while spending so much time in the Philippines, Mexico, and Cuba with the Navy, he would have picked up a few words. Or surely, having been married for over fifty years to a woman whose first language was Spanish, he would have learned a few proper phrases for different occasions. And most certainly, having worked side by side with Cuban fishermen for over forty years, he would have picked up a rudimentary working use of words that are common in everyday commercial fishing usage.

Despite all the opportunities to learn, Spanish remained a mystery to Dad. Words like *llelo* (ice) pronounced yea'lo, became "yellow," and *escaramollo* (barnacle) became "scarimoo." Other English words with a Spanish twist, known as Spanglish, such as "trucky" and "boatay," he picked up quickly and sprinkled liberally throughout his conversation with Cubans—always believing he was speaking Spanish.

The Cuban fishermen were endlessly amused with Dad's butchering of their native language. Having been through the same process learning English, they could identify with his difficulties. Some of his mispronunciations so captivated them, that the words—jokingly at first—were adopted into common use. One of the Cubans' favorites was *palangre* (trotline) pronounced puh-lan-gray, which Dad transcribed into "palonga." Even today, the word can be heard in conversations as if it's proper Spanish, and one Hispanic fisherman told me he thought "palonga" was the English word for trotline. The Spanish names also baffled Dad, and a fisherman nicknamed *Huadapo* (sugar cane) is still known as "white apple" years after Dad mispronounced it only once.

Through all of his years communicating with Cubans, one method remained consistent, and that was to raise his voice. By repeating the words over louder each time, he was sure understanding would come. A poor, uncomprehending fisherman would find himself with the owner of the fish house inexplicably yelling at him. "Yellow! Yellow! Yellow! Get me some damn yellow!" And then, without a trace of humor, "What's the matter, can't you understand Spanish? Good grief, man! Have I got to get the ice myself?"

As often as not, when the man heard the word ice in English, his eyes would light up and he would suddenly understand. "Ahh, isa! Okay, okay." Dad would just sit there shaking his head over the fact that he always had to raise his voice to be understood.

For his two new mates who had recently come from Cuba, learning to work lobster traps from a man like Dad was a confusing and frustrating job. Dad always had a booming voice and the mates heard it often, but with those two mates, Dad would have to repeatedly climb down the flybridge ladder and actually show them what to do. Frequently, in frustration he would jump from his seat and lean over the rail on the back of the flybridge, yelling orders while pointing and gesticulating at what needed to be done. Somehow, they managed to get the traps pulled even on the roughest days.

On a cold and windy January day, they struggled halfway through a line of forty traps when Dad went to the rail of the flybridge to yell some instructions. While the men were trying to understand him, a huge wave hit the boat and sent Dad flying headfirst over the rail. The men watched in horror as he fell twelve feet, slammed into the boat rail chest first, and bounced into the ocean.

They quickly ran to the side and saw he was conscious, but barely able to stay afloat. Between the rough seas, his injury, his emphysema, and the heavy jacket he was wearing, there was not much time to save him. They tried to reach out to him with a gaff, but the strong winds were quickly pushing the boat away. They threw a rope, but he was unable to swim even a few feet to reach it. One of them finally threw the life ring with a one hundred-foot rope tied to it, but was unable to get it near Dad because of the wind.

Panic-stricken, the men tried to think of what to do next as they watched Dad floundering farther and farther from the boat. Neither of them knew how to run a boat and neither of them knew how to swim.

Realizing that in a moment he would either drown or be too far from the boat to be rescued, one of the men impulsively grabbed the life ring and jumped into the water. Holding onto the ring with one arm and paddling with the other, he reached Dad just as the rope was stretched to its full length. The other mate then pulled them back to the boat, and miraculously, they were able to lift him back into the forty-three-foot lobster boat despite the heaving seas and no help at all from Dad.

As he lay out on the deck, gasping for breath and shivering uncontrollably, the men thought Dad was surely going to die. Each gasp for air also brought excruciating pain as he had an unknown number of broken ribs.

Finally able to understand some of his gasping directions, they got his wet coat off and wrapped him in a blanket. Fearful of trying to move him, they tried to get instructions on how to use the radio to call for help. The word 'radio' is the same in both languages, so Dad knew what they wanted, but would have no part of it.

Within a half hour, he was breathing a little better and managed to get on a dry jacket. In another fifteen minutes and despite their protests, Dad had them help him to his feet, and then, one agonizing step at a time, up the ladder to his seat on the flybridge. He then called for a cigar and had them block the wind as he lit it.

After a few good puffs, he said, "Okay, let's go." The men started putting things away preparing for the trip in when Dad wheezed out a painful, "What the hell do you think you're doing!" As he started pointing wildly, they realized he intended to finish pulling the line of traps they had been working. Unable to convince him otherwise, they pulled traps for another hour before finally going in.

In spite of the broken ribs, Dad didn't say a word about the incident to anyone. To all inquiries about his sudden difficulty with standing straight and breathing, he simply said he had exercised too much and needed to take a little break from the boat.

Two days later, the mates came in the office to get paid and told Mother the whole story. Their detailed account sounded bizarre, but she knew every word of it was true. The men both agreed Dad was "*loco*," and they would never go out again with such a madman.

Dad, for his part, just shrugged it off as another small thing being blown out of proportion. "Hell, I've been through a lot worse than that many times in my life," he said, and steadfastly refused to go to the doctor despite the badgering of Mother and my sister Nancy.

We had been taking Dad's recovery for granted when he startled me with a request. "Listen, son. I don't have much longer in this world, and there's something I want to do before I die."

Dad's words caught me off guard and had me holding my breath in anticipation of what he would say next. Moments before, he took me aside after our Sunday family lunch and asked if I had a few minutes to talk. After a quick look around the room, he nodded toward the front door and mouthed the words, "Let's go out on the front porch."

After his ominous words about one last request before he died, he left me hanging while making preparations for the talk. On the porch, he got his chair perfectly positioned and then had me move mine: "Right over here, son. Move that table over this way a little,

336

will you? Watch out for that ashtray. Damn! Son, would you do one more thing for me? In my top dresser drawer there's a cigar under the socks. Would you get it for me? . . . Oh, and don't let your mother see you."

Once he had the cigar, it was necessary to go through the lighting ceremony. I had recently watched unnoticed from the side yard as my four-year-old son Lucas performed the ritual. Sitting in his little chair next to his Grandpa, he proceeded to 'smoke' his long, cigar-shaped pretzel.

After sliding it back and forth under his nose, Lucas took a few deep sniffs, and then held it out and stared appreciatively while giving it a nod of approval. Then, slowly twirling it, he drew it along his lips while lightly licking the length of the 'cigar.' Once the pretzel was properly moistened, Lucas put the tip between his teeth, nipped off the end, and spit it off to his left just like Grandpa.

With the pretzel sticking out of his puckered lips, he then lit it. Striking his imaginary match, he cupped it in his little hands so the evening breeze wouldn't blow it out. After sixty years of lighting cigarettes and cigars in the face of stinging sea winds, Dad always held his match as if small craft warnings were posted, and Lucas imitated him perfectly.

With many small puffs, Lucas made sure his cigar was evenly lit by slowly turning it over the flame in his protective hands. After discarding the match with a flick of his thumb and middle finger, he settled back in his chair for the first real puff. After a long draw, he removed the pretzel, holding it between his thumb and four fingers while inspecting his light. After a very slight nod of approval, he tilted his head up, and through pursed lips blew the imaginary smoke skyward.

On the porch, Dad was meticulously going through the same routine and would not be rushed. Every detail was important, and I was often craving one myself by the time he finished. Trying to hurry him was futile and would usually bring forth a mildly spoken, but stinging rebuke such as, "Look son, if you're too busy to talk now, we'll do it when you can spare the time."

Finally, Dad blew the first puff heavenward and started back in as if there had been no pause. "Like I was saying, I'm not going to be around much longer, and I was thinking that maybe you and Nancy could arrange something for me." While imagining he was talking about some grim subject like funeral arrangements, I was forced to wait while he took another puff, another long look at the cigar, and another blow of smoke. "I want to go gambling."

"Gambling?! . . . What do you mean by gambling? Greyhound races or the horses at Hialeah? Or get up a little poker game?"

"No, son! I mean real gambling. Craps! I want to roll the dice one more time."

Very few things he could have said would have surprised me more. Except for on the boat, he had not spent a night out of Key West in twenty years. Two of his very close friends, Herb Tanis and Troy Baker, had died while on trips off the island. For years after, he told us he had warned them not to go, but they wouldn't listen. Dad laughed about superstitions, but we were never quite sure if he really believed he would die if he left Key West or if it just suited his purpose of not wanting to be pestered about going somewhere.

When Nancy graduated from Florida International University in Miami, he went up with us for the ceremony and we were to spend the night at Rose and Gerry's house in South Miami. After the graduation, we all went out to dinner and settled in for a nice quiet night at their home. At 10:00 that evening, Dad was sitting in a chair reading when he suddenly jumped up and said, "I'm going home!" No amount of talking could get him to stay and Mother drove him back to Key West that night.

"Well Dad, the nearest place I know of with a craps table is Nassau. If we go to the Bahamas, it will mean staying overnight."

"Of course we'll have to spend the night, but one night doesn't leave much time for gambling does it?"

Nancy was very skeptical at first, but Dad assured her he meant it, so she made the arrangements. A three-day weekend was planned, and she booked rooms for her and husband Steve, Monica and I, and Dad, at the Crystal Palace Hotel and Casino in Nassau.

Smoking and Gambling

Although we remained doubtful as to whether he would actually get on the plane, Dad seemed unconcerned about leaving Key West and was truly excited about making the trip. His major concern was gathering all the supplies he would need. He imagined Nassau to be like the backwater Pacific island towns he had visited during his Navy days, where everything was in short supply. We assured him Nassau was a modern city, and he could get peanuts, spam, and cigars without carrying them over in his suitcase.

Despite our assurances, Dad put together a bag full of necessities, which included half a dozen cans of mixed nuts, vanilla wafers, and a couple of boxes of his favorite cigars. He also had a case of Michelob, which we finally convinced him to leave behind.

There were very few things more important to Dad than his beer. At 5:00 p.m. each day, when Dad considered it officially beer time, he would pop open a bottle of Michelob. After drinking Schlitz for most of his life, he switched to Michelob when Dr. Calleja okayed his daily brews, and would go without rather than drink another brand.

The beer drinking followed a ritual similar to the cigar lighting, and all of the fishermen were as familiar with it as Dad's family. At 4:00 p.m., after his walk, the beer would be put in his small cooler and covered with ice. At 5:00 p.m., he would put either three or four cubes of ice in a Styrofoam cup and open the first Michelob. After filling the cup with a big head of foam, he would set it down.

While the foam was settling, he'd take out a cigar and go through the preliminaries of unwrapping, sniffing, licking, and biting off the tip. Once the foam settled, he would set down the unlit cigar, and take a long and noisy drink of the beer. The sounds emitted after the first drink were worthy of an oasis scene in the Sahara Desert. "Ahhhhhh! . . . Whewwwww! . . . Hooooo!" and a final sighing, whistling exhalation, "Whewwwwwww."

Unquestionably, Dad would rather not go to the Bahamas than be there without Michelob, but I assured him they would have all he wanted in Nassau. "Dad, I've been to the Bahamas a dozen times and I guarantee you they have Michelob. They have every kind of beer in the world and I have drunk dozens of brands you have never even heard of."

"Sure, son. Sure. But have you ever actually bought a Michelob in the Bahamas?"

"Dad, you're worrying about nothing. They will have it! I guarantee it."

Dad's last flight was twenty-five years before when he flew to Texas for his brother's funeral. The plane hit an air pocket and dropped several hundred feet straight down, injuring a couple of passengers and scaring the wits out of the rest. Dad was therefore, apprehensive about the flight, but by the time we got in the taxi at Nassau Airport, he was in great spirits and insisted we stop at a liquor store before checking in.

"Just get me two six-packs for now," was all Dad said when we pulled up in front of the taxi driver's favorite liquor store.

Steve looked at him for a few seconds, and then said, "Two six-packs? Okay Grandpa, but what kind do you want?"

"What kind! What do you mean what kind? Michelob of course!"

"Michelob? . . . Sorry Grandpa, I don't think they have that in the Bahamas. What's your second choice?"

Dad's mouth dropped open and he immediately stared at me with a narrow-eyed "You lied to me" look. Then, he coldly spit out, "If they don't have Michelob, I don't want anything."

Steve, who lived in Miami and was relatively new to the family, sensed the gravity of the situation and we both bypassed the rum and vodka and made straight for the beer cooler. Budweiser, Coors Lite, Millers, Busch, Paul Revere, twenty-six different beers made in America, but no Michelob! The trip appeared ruined before it even got started, but the proprietor gave us a ray of hope when he said the government liquor store would probably have it.

Dad was ready to fight when we came out, but when I told him we would have to go to another store to get it, he seemed skeptical, but willing to give it a chance. The government liquor store was a considerable distance past the hotel, which left the taxi driver the only one smiling.

The store was impressive-looking with plate glass windows all around, and had the look of an establishment that would have our elusive Michelob. The place had even more beer than the first, but once again, no Michelob. To make the situation slightly worse, the clerk assured us, "No, mon. They don't have Michelob in Nassau."

There was nothing to do, but break the bad news to Dad and hope he would get over it. With a look of perfectly distilled disgust, Dad rode all the way back to the hotel without uttering a word. By the time we checked in and got back to the lobby, it was 5:00 p.m. and we all sat at a table and ordered beers—including one for Dad. He let his sit for a while in protest, but when he finally took a sip, his spirits improved, and after finishing the first cold Budweiser, the conversation turned to gambling.

No doctor of philosophy understood the art of savoring any better than Dad. The same requirements he accorded to his cigar lighting and beer drinking, he also attached to the gambling. Nancy and Steve, who knew how to play craps, were anxious to attack the table, but Dad would have no part of it. "Good grief Nancy, it's not even dark yet, and there's only a couple of people at the tables. You've got to come back a little later when the action heats up and see which table gets hot. You guys go get something to eat while I check out the players and pit crews. By the time you get back, I'll have a hot table lined up for us."

We were divided over whether to leave the hotel. Monica had no interest in gambling and voted for eating in town. I had never played anything but poker with buddies, and agreed we should go out. Nancy and Steve wanted a quick bite at the hotel in order to leave plenty of time for gambling, but finally decided the night was young and agreed to go into town.

Nancy loves gambling, but is disciplined enough to set a daily limit and actually stick to it. She is a very conservative bettor, but is extremely animated and can liven up a crowd very quickly. Steve, on the other hand, also loved gambling, but could not control his betting, and needed Nancy to dole out his cash slowly or his gambling would be over the first day. While we were still discussing what to do for dinner, Steve told Dad, "You know Grandpa, there are not many people in here now, but a little while ago, there was a nice crowd at the tables."

As soon as Nancy heard that Steve had "just walked through the casino," she demanded to see his wallet. After a spirited verbal battle of accusations and denials, Steve finally confessed he had lost his day's allowance in ten minutes. In rebuttal to Nancy's outrage, he informed us in a confidential tone—after first looking around to make sure no one else was listening—"This is a terrible casino. I hate to tell you this, but none of us will win anything here. Nan, you better keep a close eye on Grandpa because this place will fleece him out of every dime he's got."

"Oh sure! You go wild and lose your money in ten minutes and now you're an instant expert on the whole casino. Well, you've been fleeced in every casino we've ever been in, so what makes this one any different? You're just trying to weasel more money out of me, but it's not going to work. You can just watch us gamble for the rest of the night."

Dad, who had been quietly taking in the whole scene, immediately labeled Steve a "black cat" and let us know that at all cost, we were to keep him away from the table while he was rolling. Steve laughed it off, but as he was to find for the next three days, Dad was dead serious.

Dad was insisting we leave, so we went into town and found a restaurant with fresh conch. We arrived back at 9:00 p.m. to a raucous casino. The yelling and shouting were unmistakably the sound of a hot table with a lot of winning going on. Dad was nowhere to be seen, but we saw all the action centered on a single craps table with people four-deep all around it. Each throw of the dice brought a roar from the crowd and threw Nancy into a fit of anxiety. "Oh my God! Someone is having a fantastic roll and we're missing it! Hurry! We need to get in on that roll."

Smoking and Gambling

Just as Nancy was saying, "But what in the world has happened to Dad," an arm at the end of the table stuck up above the crowd, and a familiar-looking cupped hand started shaking the dice. She turned to me with a wide-eyed look of shock, "That can't be him, can it?"

She then started elbowing her way through the crowd. People were not inclined to give up their spot at the table even when she implored them with, "I think that's my father rolling! Please let me through."

Dad heard her and asked the people to let his daughter through, but no one was willing to give up a spot at the table. The pit boss noticed the commotion, and Dad explained he was trying to get his daughter and son to the table. The head man immediately ordered everyone to move aside, and the people quickly parted.

There standing like the consummate *bon vivant* was Captain Pete. He was on center stage and looked as if it was exactly where he belonged. In front of him were over $25,000 in chips and he was puffing on a $20 Cuban cigar. "Come on over here next to me, darling," he told Nancy as he reached down and took a sip from a bottle of . . . Michelob beer.

Nancy's eyed darted from one thing to another as she tried to make sense of what she was seeing. All eyes were on her and the table was quiet as they anxiously waited for the pit boss to start the action. Nancy turned to me and exhaled a weak, "Oh my God! What's going on here?"

Turning back to Dad, she sputtered out, "Oh my God! Are all those chips yours? How much did you start with? . . . Oh my God! Is that your $1,000 on the pass line? . . . Oh my God! Are all those black chips above the line yours?"

Dad just grinned and said, "We can talk about that later. Right now, we've got to keep this hot table going."

The croupier looked at Dad and said, "Whenever you're ready, Pete."

Nancy turned to me again with a disbelieving grin on her face, and mouthed out, "Pete?"

Trapped in Key West

As Dad got the dice, the table again became uproarious. We knew enough about craps to understand the roller's hand must keep the dice over the table at all times, but Dad took his dice and shook them behind his ear and then over his head before rolling. Exhorting his dice with "Come on, baby!" and "Mama needs a new pair of shoes," he made his point on the first throw. Nancy instantly became his loudest cheerleader and the new good luck charm for the entire table.

Dad's rack was overflowing and Nancy was stuffing $100 and $500 chips in her purse while urging Dad to pull or reduce some of his bets. He ignored all her advice and kept rolling and rolling. When he made his point for the third time, Nancy turned to me grinning incredulously and shrugging, "He's out of control."

Sister Nancy,
Dad's good luck charm.

When he finally crapped out, there was a boisterous round of applause for the great roll. As the noise died, a voice behind Dad said, "Nice roll, Grandpa."

Dad's head spun around and he recoiled in shock when he saw Steve standing next to me. "Steve! . . . Damn! . . . How long have you been there?"

When Steve said he had just come over, the reason for Dad crapping out became apparent. "Good grief, man! Didn't I tell you not to get around me when I was rolling? You just cost me a hell of a roll! Go play blackjack or something. I just hope you haven't turned the whole table cold."

"But Grandpa, I don't have any money left."

Dad quickly handed him a couple of $100 chips and sent him on his way. Steve's black cat status was good for a lot of laughs, especially because we all thought Dad was serious about it.

Smoking and Gambling

On the other hand, Dad cared little about mistaken impressions and would often let tongue-in-cheek comments go on until he was the only one left who knew he was just playing. At times, I queried him as to how he could say a certain thing, and he would chastise me with an exasperated, "Good grief, son! Don't you think I know that?"

We were anxious to get Dad away from the table and hear the whole story—particularly where the Michelob had come from—but Dad wasn't about to leave a hot table. Soon enough, he determined it had officially turned cold, and after he obtained a fresh cigar and another Michelob, we moved to a table for some talk.

Nancy got straight to the point, "All right Dad, I want every detail from beginning to end. When did they start calling you Pete? Who got you the Michelob and the Cuban cigar? And why are they treating you like royalty?"

"Nancy, I don't really know what the hell is going on. It seems like the more of their money I win, the more they want to give me."

As if to confirm his statement, a casino host came up to the table and handed Dad a room key. "Pete, we've changed your room to a corner suite in the Casino Tower overlooking the ocean. I think you will find it far more comfortable than the room you're in, and it will be compliments of the Casino Manager."

"Changed my room? Hell, I didn't ask anyone to change my room! Look, mister, tell your boss thanks a lot, but I'm happy right where I am. I've got my son and daughter in rooms right next to me and that's the way I want to keep it."

"Sorry, Pete, we're just trying to make your stay here as nice as possible. Whatever you want we try our best to accommodate. Let me get you next to your children again. I'll be right back."

Nancy was stunned, "Dad! Are you out of your mind? Do you have any idea what a suite is like in the Casino Tower? They were going to give you a $1000-a-night room for free and you just turned it down! My God! This whole night is getting more bizarre by the minute!"

"Now wait a second, Nan. I didn't come here for the rooms. I came to do a little gambling and be with you kids. I just hope these people will leave us alone now, so we can get down to enjoying it . . . Besides, I didn't hear the guy say anything about it being for free."

"What are you talking about? The man said it was compliments of the Casino Manager. That means they're going to 'comp' the room. Sometimes, for the high rollers, they comp rooms, meals, liquor—basically everything on your stay."

"Well honey, I don't know anything about this comping business. I just came here to gamble and I can pay my own way."

Before Nancy could sputter out another word, the casino host walked up. "Okay Pete. We've got you back next to your children. The porters are moving their bags right now to the rooms next to your suite. Mr. Virgilio sends his compliments and says if there is anything else you need to please let him know."

Nancy for once was speechless. All she could do was look from person to person shaking her head and grinning. Dad was still annoyed at having been interrupted once again. "I don't know, kids. Is this move all right with you guys? They could have at least asked us first, or let us check the rooms."

"Dad . . . Please . . . Don't say another word about it. The rooms will be fantastic. I know you just want to be left alone, but this is good. This is real good. Now let's get back to the story. The last thing you told us before we left for dinner was that you were going to check out the tables and wait for us to return. What happened?"

"Well, things were kind of slow, so I was just going from table to table watching for some action when this real pretty girl and her boyfriend went up to that table. Heck, they were right in front of me, so I couldn't help but overhear. He wanted to play, but she didn't know the first thing about it. He was explaining the game to her and then gave her some chips and said he wanted her to roll when the dice came around.

"She was really excited and I knew a pretty girl like that

rolling for the first time was a sure winner. I had to be in for her roll, so I told the stick man I wanted some chips. Well hell, he just gave me a dirty look and said, 'Don't lean on the table, sir! Put your money on the table and we'll get your chips as soon as the lady rolls.'

"The guy was so nasty, I started to leave, but I figured she was going to have a long roll and I wanted to be in on it. So what the hell? I took out my money and dropped it on the table like the man said, and then everything stopped. The nasty guy in the middle bangs on the table with his stick and this other fellow comes over to me and wants to know my name."

"Wait a minute, Dad!" said Nancy with hands fanning rapidly. "Wait just a minute! Exactly how much money did you drop on the table?"

"Well, I wanted to start out easy until you guys got back, so I dropped down $5,000. Hell, I thought I was in trouble or something, so I asked the guy what business it was of his to know my name. When I used to play back in my Navy days, the only ones who asked for your name were the Shore Patrol or someone looking for trouble. But the guy turned out to be the pit boss, and from then on I couldn't get rid of him.

"He said he was there to take care of whatever I needed to make my stay more enjoyable. I told him the only thing I wanted was some chips, so I could get in on the girl's roll. Well, he held up the whole table while they got my chips and let me put a bet down. I put $1,000 on the pass line and the stick man said there was a $700 bet limit. I wasn't complaining, but when he started to change my bet, the pit boss said to 'let it play'.

"I thought we might have ruined her roll by delaying for so long, but by the way she was smiling when I put my bet down, I knew she was going to be hot. She was so excited, she threw one of the dice right off the table, but then darned if she didn't come right back with an eleven. I told the stickman I wanted to let that $2,000 ride on the pass line. He looked at the pit boss and he just nodded, 'Okay.'"

Dad was now into his story and there was no way to rush him. He reached over and took a sip of his beer, caught his breath for a minute, and took another drink. Then, he picked up his cigar, which had gone out in the ashtray, and scraped the ashes off with a wooden match. We watched impatiently as he finally got it relit and took two or three long, slow puffs.

"So, then that pretty gal rolls those dice like she had been doing it all her life, and comes up with the sweetest little seven you ever saw. She was clapping and cheering by then and the betting was picking up. For some stupid reason, I scaled my bets back to the house limits after that, and she went on to make six passes. I made a little pocket change off her roll, but if I hadn't gotten so conservative, I would have made some serious money.

"When she crapped out, I was going to leave the table until you kids got back. While I was gathering up my chips, I threw $100 on the line for the next roller and darned if he didn't hit two sevens in a row. I stayed in while he made his point three times, and I knew the table was too hot to leave. I like to start out slow and get warmed up good before I start betting heavy, but the table wasn't leaving me any time for warm-ups.

"This whole time, the pit boss, Ray, was keeping his eye on me and making me uncomfortable. He asked me if there was anything I needed, and I told him I just wanted to play some craps. He kept insisting, if there was anything at all I wanted, just to let him know. He seemed so anxious to get me something, I finally told him I had been trying to get a Michelob since I got to the Bahamas, but everyone said there wasn't one on the whole island. 'No problem, Pete.' He stuck his up his hand, wiggled his finger, and this drink girl comes right over."

"'Pete, this is Julia. She's going to get your Michelob and anything else you need. Don't hesitate to ask, no matter what it is.'

"Well, that beer sure put me in the mood, so I asked if it was all right to smoke a cigar. The next thing I know, this girl brings me a Cuban Montecristo. By the time the roll got to me, I knew I couldn't lose.

Smoking and Gambling

"I put $500 on the pass line, and from then on, I couldn't do anything wrong. People started coming from everywhere, and the longer I rolled, the wilder it got. I was getting so many chips in front of me, they were spilling over to the people next to me, so I figured I better stick some in my pocket. Then, Ray pops up and says, 'Don't worry Pete, no one will touch your chips.' He has a way of saying things that makes you believe him.

"There was so much money on the table, that it was taking forever between rolls. I thought sure the table was going to go cold, but when it's hot like that, nothing can stop it. Hell, if Steve hadn't sneaked up on us, I'd probably still be rolling."

We never did find out exactly how much money he won—he was still too secretive about some things—but we guessed it was between $30,000 and $50,000. Certainly there were other players in the casino for whom it was a modest amount, but for Dad, it was probably the largest amount of cash he had ever had at one time; yet, he remained as calm and cool as if it was just another routine day at the fish house.

I learned to play craps and for the first time found a gambling game I really enjoyed. Nancy, Dad, and I would take over the end of a table and play for hours. We all won money, but Dad insisted I was making loser's bets and it was just beginner's luck that let me win. "Besides," he chided. "You can't win any real money with $10 chips."

Epilogue

Dad died on January 2, 1998, at the age of eighty-seven. The next day, his ninety-year-old brother Jim—with whom he left home to join the Navy at the age of fifteen—passed away.

I think of Dad often, especially when I walk the property in the early morning or at the end of the day. All the fishermen liked Dad, and hardly a day goes by that one of them doesn't mention him and smile. Inside the office door, there's a picture of him sitting on a lobster trap—the same one on the cover of this book - and they all take a quick look when entering the office. I like the picture because I can see the little boy who stayed in him his whole life.

Jenny runs the office now—and the entire fish house a good deal of the time. She started working in the office at the age of fifteen, and Dad was thrilled to have his granddaughter helping with the bookkeeping. Mother is fully retired from decision making now, but at the age of ninety one, still drives herself to work every morning. Despite Mother's high profile in the business, Dad always thought of commercial fishing as a man's world, and would no doubt be confounded to see Mother still working and Jenny dealing with a fish house full of tough fishermen.

Mother and Jenny

Epilogue

It's late in the evening and late in September when I walk out the office door. The fish house is almost deserted and instead of getting in my truck, I turn to walk. Even though the temperature is eighty degrees, the northeast wind brings the first hint of fall. People from the north laugh, and say September is indistinguishable from July or August. I've heard it enough to know they really can't detect a Key West autumn in the air, but the change of weather is as clear to me today as if a first snow had fallen.

The road across the front of the property is the last section of old U.S. Highway 1, and I think of the hundreds of times Dad and I walked the path together. Circumnavigating the entire property entails a trek of almost a mile, and when all the lobster and crab traps are stacked on shore, it's necessary to walk every inch of it to see what's really going on.

We made frequent inspection tours to make sure the fishermen were keeping their places 'shipshape.' He would not tolerate trash anywhere on the property and insisted all fishermen keep their own spot orderly and clean. Most kept their workplace in order, but Dad was constantly irritated over the miscellaneous junk fishermen were trying to save, or bring from their homes to store at the fish house.

He particularly wanted the docks left clear, and chewed out fishermen for leaving used oil next to their boats and not disposing of it properly—though I never heard one admit to leaving the oil. "No no, Pete! That's not my oil. I always put mine in the tank! You know that. Some jerk just left it next to my boat, so he wouldn't have to go to the trouble of dumping it."

"So, it's not your oil, huh? I suppose that junk refrigerator's not yours, either? Who's supposed to pay to get rid of that?"

"No, Pete! That's not a junker. I just brought it out here to put a new motor in it. I was taking it home with me tonight."

He often chuckled when we walked away from the little confrontations. The old Navy chief loved to catch someone red-handed, and then amuse himself by watching the man try to "wiggle out" of the jam. In truth, he had little interest in the inspections, and spent most of the time stopping to "shoot the breeze" with each fisherman he saw.

Because he never really cared for the business, he turned it over to me to run at a very early age, so he could work his boat without diversion. My imprint is undoubtedly here, but the place is his legacy. For him, the fish house was his real home and the fishermen were his real friends. The buying and selling of their catch held little interest for him, and he ran a business only so he could keep the fish house—not to become wealthy. Having a place for his boat, and his fellow fishermen around, was really what attracted him to the fish house.

He particularly loved trap building, and got a special amusement out of putting people to work. When he set up to build traps, he would prepare a couple of open places at the work bench with wood, nails, and a hammer—ready for anyone who happened to stop for a minute. "Hey, if you're just killing time, you might as well drive a few nails for me. There's a hammer right there waiting for you. What the hell, we can talk and hammer at the same time, can't we?"

When I switched to an air-powered staple gun like all the rest of the fishermen, he did everything he could to talk me out of it. Dad was unimpressed by speed. Trap building was not a chore for him, but one of life's intangible pleasures. "Hell! You can't even think, much less talk with all that racket going on!" The modern time-saving tools took all the fun out of it for him, and he never built a single trap with a staple gun.

I'm walking the property alone now. With seventy-five thousand lobster and stone crab traps stacked on shore, the entire place is a maze of narrow roads and alleyways. But at this time of the year, the traps are all in the water and the size of the fish house property surprises even me. From the office, the boat at the far end is usually not visible, but with the traps gone, there is a very expansive view of the entire property and I can see it clearly.

352

Epilogue

If I let it, each thing I look at gives me some reminder of Dad. Francisco's boat, the *Alice Mary*, was the first lobster boat made of the new fiberglass material. Dad tried to talk him out of it. "You get one of those plastic boats out there in a heavy sea, and it'll crack like an eggshell." Francisco started working on his father's fishing boat at the age of three in Cuba. Fifty years of caulking and repairing leaky wooden boats was enough. He didn't care what anyone thought—he bought the 'plastic' boat.

Now, after seventy years at sea, he is selling his boat to Luis 'Tanga' Delgado, one of the few men who will produce as much lobster as Francisco. Luis was drafted into the Cuban army, and sent by Castro to fight in Tanganyika, Africa, whence he picked up the nickname Tanga.

Across the narrow channel sits the *Miss Shawna* and the *Miss Delaina*. Glenwood (Wimpy) Gibson and his brother Charley are inseparable. They both fish their forty-foot boats without mates, and they leave together and come home together. There are less than five of their generation still fishing, and this was probably their last year. Their older brother, William (Big Dilly) Gibson, passed away twelve years ago and was an icon among the Conch fishermen. Dad had long before sworn off funerals, vowing, "The next funeral I go to, I'm going to be the star," . . . but he went to Big Dilly's.

Greg Rodriguez' boat, the *Trinity*, sits clean and ready. Dad noticed Greg forty years ago when he was still a boy helping his father. "That kid knows how to work. If he becomes a fisherman, he's going to be a good one." Greg did become a fisherman, and not only has he been a top producer every season, but is frequently a spokesman for all the fishermen.

When Greg's boat unloads after a five-day trip, his mates do not get paid right away. The following morning, he pulls his boat around to the front of the unloading dock and the mates must clean it from stem to stern. His rigorous cleaning process is so thorough it has worn the Gelco finish off the hull. Dad would watch in admiration as he puffed his cigar. "By George, there's at least one man here who knows how to clean a boat!"

Trapped in Key West

Luis Avila's boat, *Luis y Mary*, sits quiet and ready. He worked with Dad when he came from Cuba in the 1960s. His opportunity to own his own boat came at another fish house, and for twenty years Dad always said, "That's one man you want to get back over here with us." Shortly after Dad passed away, he did come back. He has survived cancer twice, but at the age of seventy-four, still has no thoughts of retirement.

Mike Gonzalez works the smallest boat at the fish house. He's an old school fisherman. Dad's kind of fisherman. He minds his own business, finds his own fishing spots, and likes to work alone. Lately I've noticed him taking a mate, but I wouldn't want to ask if it's a concession to age.

This late in the afternoon, the fish house looks like a ghost town. Signs of life are everywhere, but I don't see a person until I spot a movement behind one of the sheds. A string of freshly-painted trap floats is bobbing, and as I get closer, I see Pancho at the back of the shed dabbing at them with his brush.

He doesn't see me and I stop for a moment to watch. Dad would have stopped too. He would have watched Pancho's halfhearted, slow-motion painting for a moment, and then turned away, shaking his head. Dad never thought much of Pancho's slow but steady work method, and rarely allowed him to do any work for the fish house.

Unlike Dad, I'm not observing his work ethic, but Pancho himself. With a cigarette dangling from the corner of his mouth and the ever-present beer sitting on a turned-up fish box, Pancho works until the sun dies like the generations of fishermen before him.

The solitary man in the fading light could be from the nineteenth century. There is nothing in sight to indicate the electronic age, and he works contentedly with the tools of a hundred years ago. Since he came from Cuba over forty years ago, the fish house has been Pancho's home. He has quietly vanished many times in the past, but always shows up again. Now that he's older, he lives here full time, I suppose.

Epilogue

Pancho is not really a fisherman today, though he once was. Occasionally, he's coaxed into filling in for a missing mate, but his primary occupation for the last twenty years has been cutting cowhides for bait in the traps. We bring in thousands of salted bull hides each season, and they must be cut into five-inch squares and have a hole punched in them for hanging in the traps. The mates are supposed to cut the hides, but they all pay Pancho out of their own shares to avoid the grungy job. Over the years, Pancho has raised his rates from $5 to $25 per hide. It's still a deal.

Unbeknown to me, Pancho once turned an eight-by-ten-foot shed into a *casita* and took up residence. Some time after, a contingent of fishermen's wives came to me indignantly insisting I run "Pancho and his whore" out of the fish house. Claiming he had a notorious Stock Island streetwalker living with him, they were apparently fearful their husbands would be enticed by her shameless charms, and demanded to accompany me for a showdown with the brazen couple.

Knowing Pancho and the size of the shed, I found the whole story unlikely, and would have believed it a joke had the tale come from a fisherman, instead of the distressed wives. In order to prevent an assault and a torched shed, I refused to allow the wives to accompany me, but assured them I would take care of the problem at once.

Approaching the shed, I immediately recognized the source of the problem. The woman saw me coming and stood defiantly— staring at me through vacant eyes. I didn't know if the wives' assessment of her profession was accurate, but I recognized her as a familiar Stock Island street person. With a beer in one hand and a cigarette in the other, she stood stone still in a skimpy tank top with short shorts unbuttoned and half unzipped. Even in her floozed condition, it was easy to see she was a handsome woman, and if cleaned and properly dressed, would seem threatening to the fishermen's wives.

Pancho rushed toward me, not so much because of the woman, but to head me off before I reached the open shed door. The small garage-type door was fully up however, revealing the contents of the shed. To my astonishment, most of the shed was taken up with a queen-size bed, complete with headboard and footboard. Reading lights were on either side, and stuffed into the opposite corner was a two-burner stove atop an old end table. An air conditioner large enough for a ranch house dominated the far wall, but was cleverly hidden from the outside by old traps stacked around it. The bed was neatly made with a fine-looking comforter, and when lying on the frilly pillows, one would have a view of a flowery painting set among the ropes and tools hanging from the wall.

I was taken aback by what I saw. Pancho and his street lady did not belong in such a domestic scene. I looked at them, and then back at the pretty little room, and once again at the unlikely lovebirds. Like a stone statue, she had not moved an inch, but Pancho was desperately trying to bum a light for his cigarette from several bystanders as he tried to think of something to say.

Before I could speak, Pancho got his cigarette lit and his wits about him, and explained the entire situation: It was not what it appeared. He was merely storing the bed for a friend, and by chance, he was coming that very day to pick it up. He didn't know how the air conditioner got there, but had never used it and didn't think it even worked. The woman was just an old friend who was visiting, and the fisherman's wife who screamed *puta* at her, must have mistaken his lady for someone else.

I had yet to say a word. I looked over the other people standing around and each nodded a hesitant greeting. They were not fishermen, but were vaguely familiar—more of Pancho's street friends. "Okay, Pancho. I'll check with you tomorrow." I gave one more look at the lady, who had yet to even blink, and walked back to the office. The woman was gone the next day. I don't know about the bed.

I can't see Pancho without thinking of Nino and Pepito. The fish house is their home too, I suppose. The brothers are on-again, off-again fishermen, who mostly serve as day labor for the boats. Dad first took Nino on the boat when he arrived from Cuba as a boy, and may have been responsible for the nickname. He fired him a dozen times and took him back a dozen times. Every time he disappeared, Dad gave a sigh of relief, and then reluctantly allowed the prodigal boy back when he inevitably showed up again months or years later.

Wherever Nino went, Pepito wasn't far behind. More of a boat person than Nino, he has worked for dozens of captains, but despite Dad's constant encouragement, would not fish anywhere except Stock Island Lobster Company. Tired at last of living on different boats, he bought a van in order to have his own home. I have told him a dozen times he can't live in his van at the fish house, but I see it now parked down on the point behind some old wire traps. I know if I walked down there, I would find him sitting alone in a lawn chair and fishing off the dock with the open waters in front of him.

The Blue Jillion rests easy at the dock, but Steve Kern has a reputation for not listening to weather reports and working in the foulest weather. He started out as a mate on Troy Baker's boat and has had more highs and lows than any fisherman here. Dad liked him because he has a passion for venturing into unknown territory. Like Dad, Steve hates fishing around other people and has gone to extreme lengths to chase the giant lobsters far out into the Gulf of Mexico, or the once unknown golden crab into a thousand feet of water.

Steve even became interested in seashells after finding so many in his traps. Uncle Gerry, with his world-class shell collection, encouraged him to be on the look for rare specimens. Always a man of extremes, Steve rigged up a dredge and went to his favorite hunting grounds in one thousand feet of water. He recovered dozens of extremely rare and new shells, and even has one named after him.

Jesus Diaz got the *Blanca Rosa* the hard way—his father Diego died of a heart attack at the age of forty-eight. Diego was a blonde-haired, blue-eyed Cuban. Everyone said it was true Spanish blood, but I don't know. Like most of the Cubans, he came to this country penniless, but then ended up as the sole owner of an old boat when his partner hung himself over a woman. Soft-spoken and unflappable, he worked his way up, but always seemed like the last person who would suddenly die young.

Dad watched as the shattered son transferred licenses and trap certificates to his name. "It's a damn shame, but I don't think that boy's ever going to make it. Hell, he's just a kid! I don't think he even knows how to run the boat."

Dad was wrong. Jesus did make it. Maturity can come very quickly in such circumstances, and he became as good a producer as his father. In his thirties now with a wife and daughter, he is a survivor in his shrinking generation of Key West commercial fishermen.

I walk by the *Thunderbird*, tied up in its favored corner dock. I can never look at it without thinking of Roberto and our long-ago Bahama trips. We still laugh together about those strange days, and talk of how crazy it seems that Dad decided to carry traps hundreds of miles from home with no electronics and two old single engine boats. We laugh, but both have in the back of our minds the narrow escapes from the Cubans, Dad being lost, and the busted trips with no paychecks.

His son Robert is his lifelong fishing partner. He was only five years old when his father brought the family to America in a leaky old fishing boat. With the love of the ocean in his blood, he shows up every day at 4:00 a.m. to work on traps or do maintenance on the boat. The *Thunderbird* is the cleanest commercial boat in America, and the other fishermen tease Robert about keeping his engine as clean as his evening dinner plate.

Billy Gibson inherited the *Gloria Jean* from his father Big Dilly. The *Gloria Jean* was one of the first net boats with a power roller, and Billy became the spotter pilot for his father, and eventually the entire Key West fleet. The state of Florida banned nets in 1990, and the fishermen were relegated to working federal waters fifty to seventy-five miles from Key West. At the time of the ban, we had a permanent fleet of nine boats catching upwards of two million pounds of Spanish mackerel, kingfish, and pompano. When only a small allotment of king mackerel was made available for commercial take, the net fleet disbanded, and the dozen remaining part-time netters typically catch the year's tiny federal quota in three days. Billy is now the last of our net boats.

"Shorty" Quesada was the kingpin of the net fleet. He didn't have the biggest boat, but was always the first man out and took the biggest chances. He sank three times with an overloaded boat in heavy seas, putting him at the top of Dad's "hell of a man" list. The last time, the slick fish were piled so high, they started undulating like a giant mound of Jello, and the boat flipped over in one smooth motion. Half conscious and disoriented, Shorty managed to swim out through a cabin window and be rescued by a following boat.

Shorty was also the social director of the fish house. There was always something going on at his compound of shacks and sheds, and Dad constantly complained that no work ever got done around the fish house when Shorty was at the dock. Each day he wasn't in the boat, the smell of fish chowder, conch fritters, and lobster enchilado drew fishermen from all over the yard to his one-burner kitchen. Slamming dominoes down on an old trap table, Shorty's banty rooster of a father 'Tampa' had no favorites, and heartily cursed everyone who showed up for a free meal.

When Shorty decided to roast a pig for New Years, the idea caught on with everyone. After the party expanded to include the entire fish house, one of the Cuban fishermen brought in eight live pigs from Homestead. The truck door was barely open when the pigs bolted out and took off in every direction, with screaming kids and fishermen chasing them helter-skelter across the fish house yard. Eight pig roasting boxes were set up around Shorty's sheds, and drawn by the aroma of a thousand pounds of sizzling pork, people poured in from the trailer parks and boats. Massive amounts of black beans and rice, yucca, plantains, beer, rum, cigars, and Cuban music, kept the huge party rocking far into the night.

Trapped in Key West

Shorty worked lobster traps and did a little snapper fishing in the summer, but he lived for the net season. When the net ban was passed, he gave up a lifetime of fishing and moved his entire family to Texas. Only Tampa refused to go, and the former bantamweight boxer passed away soon after all his family left the island.

Glancing up and down the path at the rows of work sheds, they all seem out of place in modern-day Key West. Every one is different and there is little order to the way they are laid out. Forward and backward, sideways and angled, each is set up according to the individual fisherman's taste. Dad complained it looked like a shantytown, but Ed said commercial fishing is the last real thing left in Key West and coming through the fish house gate is like stepping into the past.

Walking back to the fish house, I look again at the long row of sheds comprising Dad's "shantytown." He was right. They are shanties. I see now why the inspector said they looked a little dumpy, and the property appraiser apologized for having to tax me for them.

Over a period of fifty years, we have never told fishermen how to build the sheds, only where. Greg's is a small metal shed from Sears with a large wooden awning coming off the front. It is no bigger than he needs, and is orderly and neat like Greg. Roberto has always been next to Greg, but his shed is a square box made of plywood. It is functional and devoid of any trim, but each time a hurricane passes, it's still there afterwards.

Victor is a small man with a small boat and a small number of traps. His shed however, is voluminous. Awnings stick out in every direction and satellite sheds are stuck on the end of those. One of the awnings is the cabin from his first boat, but it's necessary to be his size to work under it. On another, the canvas sags in the middle from rain collecting and slowly dripping through. It's been that way for many years, and a simple matter of running a two-by-four across the middle of the awning would solve the problem, but Victor can walk under it and has apparently never noticed the sag.

Epilogue

'Eagle' Roche's shed backs up to Victor's. It was retrieved from a construction site and has a large plywood awning. Eagle is the oldest active fisherman in Key West. He is of Cuban heritage, but was born on the island and never attended school. Key West was the poorest city in the state when Eagle was a boy, and he had to start working on the boat with his father when he was six years old.

Eagle Roche's fish market

He lost a leg to "sugar diabetes" a few years ago, but still runs the boat. Working alone for most of his life, he had to swim home twice. Both times, he was knocked out of his boat by big waves while the engine was still in gear. Once, his boat ended up in Marathon and the other time it kept circling, almost running him over several times before he could swim out of the way. He and Dad fished the deep water together. Eagle remembers in vivid detail those glorious days, and sorely misses my "Daddy" and all of the other "boys" he used to fish with.

Each year we think is his last, but Eagle just keeps on working. "Pete, I've worked every day of my life. I don't know anything else. I can't sit home. There's nothing there for me. I just hope I die out in the boat one day, so I won't be any trouble for anyone." His nickname has always been Eagle, but the younger ones—who think he's nuts to continue working so hard at his age—call him 'Cappy' out of respect.

Sixto Rioseco's boat sits across from Eagle's shed. The *S&C*, along with two smaller boats, make up his little fleet and take up the length of the dock. He is a member of the Arencibia-Rioseco family—the largest Hispanic fishing family in Key West. Each of them has fished for us at one time or another. Many of them have left the fish house and then come back, often multiple times and usually for reasons that completely befuddled Dad.

No sooner would one of them leave because his cousin needed him at another fish house, than the man would appear again like Dad's long lost friend and ask if he could get some of our bait because he liked it better. Dad may have taken it personally when one left, but they believed leaving for family reasons should give no offense and felt comfortable with moving their boats back at any time. As Dad's own family started growing and then branching out in unexpected directions, he came to better understand the blurry and often irritating line between business and family.

Sixto is on his third—or maybe fourth—time around at our fish house. He is the renegade of the family. He has had two boats confiscated and can still see them on patrol as part of the National Marine Sanctuary fleet. Law enforcement people call him a criminal, but no one else does. He is an outspoken individualist who rails against abuse of authority and sincerely believes the American fishing bureaucracy is little different than what he left in Cuba.

Epilogue

None of his 'criminal' acts have been against another person, but have been fishery violations in which he was positive the government was wrong. He is convinced that if he had the money to fight in court, he would be exonerated and have his boats returned. Meanwhile, he enjoys his fishing life, and talks of his past with a humor that would surprise his detractors.

Rick Barber's boat sits in the corner of the T-basin. He is Monica's cousin and a part-time fisherman. Several years ago, the state of Florida and the National Marine Fisheries Service instituted regulations requiring a percentage of total income to be derived from commercial fishing in order for a fisherman to maintain his license. Rick is a fireman and must work hard on his days off to catch enough lobster and stone crab to meet the income level for license holders. The pressure to produce and the strain on his family life is too much. This is his last season.

I walk along the waterline now on new docks. The old wooden ones I built in 1974 were always repairable after the roaring winds of a dozen or so storms, but were totally destroyed with the rising water in Hurricane Wilma. The dock insurance excluded wind and flood damage and the flood and windstorm insurance excluded docks, but we borrowed the money and rebuilt them anyway. It's a pleasure just to walk on them—especially with my own grandchildren. Dad would have been very pleased.

In the corner in front of the fish house, sit two new fiberglass boats being finished out by Bacle Boat Company. Jimmy worked traps for a couple of years and then tried the fish house, but decided three chiefs were too many and started building boats. His father-in-law, Jack Ming, who owned a competing fish house, also had a boat building business and Jimmy bought bare fifty-three-foot hulls from him and finished them out.

Jimmy eventually bought out Torres Boat Builders, and acquired the molds for a forty-three-foot boat. He has built a hundred or more commercial boats and yachts, and has a perfectionist's reputation for fabricating high quality custom boats. Ed and I bought one of his boats secondhand and renamed it

Last Mango. We recently sold it, but Jimmy is building me a new one to my exact specifications—and I am vowing once again that this is positively my last boat.

There were once half a dozen companies building commercial boats in Key West, but now Jimmy is the last. The shrinking of the fishing industry, combined with the fact that fiberglass boats last virtually forever, has reduced the need for new commercial fishing boats. Today, he builds primarily recreational yachts and specialty boats like island taxis for the Bahamas. His sons—James Jr. and Rhett—work with him, but he is considering moving out of Key West because of the high cost of doing business and the shortage of experienced labor.

Bacle Boat Company; Rhett, Jimmy, and James Jr. (JP).

Shorty's compound of sheds and awnings sit next to Jimmy's boats. They are unused for anything now except general storage, though Lorenzo has started building traps on one end. In the farthest corner, Billy Atwell built a shed that looks more like a new house, and the other men joked about his shed being better built than their homes. Billy hung old signs on the walls advertising Cuban mix sandwiches, fritters, and bollos, causing a neighbor to complain to county inspectors that we were opening a restaurant without permits.

Epilogue

Jeffery Arnold sits between Lorenzo and Billy. His traps were completely wiped out in a recent hurricane, but he scratched his way back and once again ranks with the top boats. His father Willie fished for Dad in the 1950s, and then opened his own fish house. He died in his forties of a heart attack after giving up fishing for politics.

Yordy Martinez and Juan Soca are the new generation of Cuban-American fishermen. Yordy's father Alberto (*Carajuelo*) defied the odds, and became the top producer of lobster by working near Key West with a small boat. Like his father, Yordy has aggressively expanded their operation and has the same ambition to be number one.

Juan's father sunk last year in heavy seas with a load of traps on the boat. This year, the same thing happened to Juan. His father's boat was salvageable, but Juan's was beaten to pieces in the crashing seas. Undeterred, he has purchased a new boat and with the confidence of youth, fully intends to be among the top boats this year.

Danny Trevor's shed guards the front gate. He works more traps than anyone, and has that competitive desire to be top boat that all fish house owners like to see. Trap building and repair goes on at his shed year-round, and he protects his corner of the yard with motion detectors and video surveillance. He talks of retirement like most in our generation, but I suspect he might hang in like Dad and Eagle—and me.

From the corner of the lot, the fish house looks peaceful and safe, but I remember the wife of a part-time fisherman who came to collect for her husband's catch. The man was in the Navy, and out on sea duty when she entered the office. "Oh God! My husband would kill me if he knew I was here."

My guard went up as I recalled other instances of couples fighting over the fish money. "Miss, is there some reason your husband would object to you collecting this money? I don't want to get caught in the middle of anything here."

"What? No! Why would you ask a question like that? I mean,

I've got his ticket and his card to collect with. Isn't that all I need?"

"Well, yes. But why did you say your husband would kill you if he knew you were here?"

"Oh. You know, being on Stock Island—at a fish house—alone."

"So, he doesn't like you being out alone?"

"No. You know, with all these fishermen around and everything."

"Ohhhh. You mean he would be worried for your safety around a fish house?"

"Yeah. I mean you can't really blame him, can you?"

"No, I suppose not."

To that point in my life, it had never occurred to me that anyone would think of the fish house as dangerous. I had always been as comfortable there as I had at home, and never once worried about the safety of my wife or children. Fishermen's wives, girlfriends, and children had been out there by the hundreds, and I have never heard of a single instance of one being bothered.

Jeri Goldner, is currently our only woman fisherman. With her husband Dave, they have been our top yellowtail boat for twenty five years, and she maintains she has never felt uncomfortable in the man's world of commercial fishing. When the National Marine Fisheries Service decided the name 'fisherman' was sexist, I asked her if she felt better being called a 'fisher.' Her reply was typical for any fisherman. "What? That's stupid! Who cares?"

Dave slipped, and fell overboard one afternoon while fishing alone. The strong current carried him swiftly away from the boat. Desperately swimming against the tide, and with the last ounce of strength in his 6'7" frame, he hooked one finger in the mesh of the chum bag, and saved his own life.

Cliff Sawyer is Dave and Jeri's friend, and they fish the same areas. Dave and Jeri work the new way with rod and reel, but Cliff sticks to the old way and fishes only with a handline. Cliff is a well known local musician, and plays the piano and sings at the Little Palm Island Resort. Despite the demands of his musical career, his love of the ocean won't allow him to give up yellowtail fishing. When Cliff—a dedicated Christian—named his boat *Fisher of Men*, one of the other fishermen did not recognize the biblical connection, and was genuinely puzzled. "What gives with that name? Is he gay or something?"

I'm standing on the dock where John dePoo kept first his sailboat and then his houseboat. Though twenty years older, John is one of my closest friends, and the only person who's been allowed to keep a recreational boat at the fish house.

His mother was a circus performer who married Key West's most prominent doctor, Julio dePoo, and then became the island's most famous artist. John's father wanted him to follow in his footsteps, but when he proved squeamish around blood, the annoyed doctor sent him off to a military finishing school in Cuba. In the merchant marine during WWII, he survived numerous submarine attacks, and then served in the army before rejoining the merchant marine again after the war. Back in Key West, he worked as a machinist and deputy sheriff before being elected to the Key West City Commission..

Though he had never sailed before, in 1980 he bought a sailboat in the Bahamas and headed for Key West. He foundered in a storm near Key West, and saved himself by swimming to a tiny island on the reef known as Pelican Shoals. Though I had known him casually before, after the boat was raised, he took up residence at the fish house and we became fast friends.

Looking at the back dock of the fish house, I picture the unloading nights of the past. When a strong northwester was approaching, the boats would pile in ahead of it and unloading the lobsters would go on far into the night. Wives, children, grandchildren, and friends poured into the fish house by the carload. All brought food, beer, and rum for the extended unloading party.

Women who hadn't seen their husbands in a week came dressed to kill. Fully made up with their sexiest outfits, and perfumed to override the smell of a fish house, they greeted their husbands like conquering heroes. As the kids yelled and laughed, the drinks flowed and the music played, I always ended up humming the old Hank Williams song, "Shrimp boats are a coming, there's dancing tonight!"

Standing on the unloading dock, I stare at the *Big Crawl*. Dad's imprint is all over the boat. When we were children and asked Dad when we were going to get a television set, or car, or anything else, his answer was always, "When we get that big crawl of lobster."

If he didn't exactly like the fiberglass boat because it didn't feel or smell right like a wooden one, he at least loved the name. He also liked the flybridge. Reluctant at first to run the boat from up top, he rarely came down once he got used to it.

Lucas runs the *Big Crawl* now. His grandpa thought it was fine for everyone to go to college, but would have been far prouder to see Lucas at the helm of a lobster boat. Lucas and his grandpa were inseparable. When Monica and I told Dad we were going to name our son Lucas Peter, Dad was not happy. "Since my great-grandfather Pierre came to New Orleans from France in 1840, there's always been a Peter Bacle."... We changed the name to Peter Lucas.

Lucas fished practically every day of his childhood. Dad would often sit for hours while Lucas fished off the dock, and no matter how long he watched, it was always, "Just one more fish, okay Grandpa?"

At the age of six while casting his line, Lucas buried the hook in the back of his leg, and Dad told him to get a pair of wire cutters from the toolbox. He watched with curiosity as his grandpa took hold of the shank of the hook, imagining he would learn some new method of easily de-hooking a fish. When Dad gave a sudden twist and pushed the hook through the other side of the skin, Lucas let out a shocked yelp. Without a tear, his curiosity returned, and he watched his grandpa cut the barb off the hook and easily pull it back through his leg.

After a quick, "Thanks, Grandpa," Lucas returned to his fishing. With the hook still in his hand and blood on his fingers,

Epilogue

Dad stood perplexed for a minute, then shook his head and smiled with pride as he watched Lucas tie a new hook on his line.

Monica's family roots go back to 1827 when Richard Roberts immigrated to Key West from the Bahamas, making her a sixth-generation Conch and our children seventh. Like most Conchs, they think it's no big deal, even as others make a fuss about the dwindling number of genuine natives in an island of imported residents.

Monica, it seems, must be related to a thousand or more people. Weech, Saunders, Albury, and Roberts—they all throw out names when they meet until a common relative is found. Dad was amused by the fuss over extended families, and indifferently accepted that his grandchild's cousin's father might somehow have a common blood connection with him.

It happened slowly at first, but as Dad's children's children started marrying and having babies, the extended family grew so rapidly that he didn't even try to sort out the familial connections. Dad and Mother just built a forty-foot long family room on the back of their house to accommodate the crowd. The reserved and once unsocial couple became the hosts for huge and frequent family gatherings. They kept adding chairs until they could seat thirty-five adults for dinner and scores of children at smaller tables set around the room.

Christmas, Easter, Thanksgiving, birthdays, anniversaries, out-of-town visitors, or the start of a lobster or stone crab season were all good excuses for having a party at Mother and Dad's. They really never knew who all might be there, and Mother only asked for a head count while Dad would just say, "Of course, you can invite them. What difference do three or four more people make when you've got a mob like we have?"

Even at someone else's birthday party, Dad was somehow the central figure, and his indifference to the role of family patriarch only commanded him more attention. When Dad told a story, the raucous table went silent and remained quiet even through the long pauses, while he took another bite or two of food.

In his last years, Dad wanted nothing more than to have his family around him. Standing in the kitchen as another party wound down, he looked with wonder at the boisterous family he had sired, and then turned to me and said simply, "Son, a man couldn't ask for much more than this out of life."